Advance Praise for re*Wealth!*

"This is the book the Presidential candidates should be talking about! In re*Wealth!* they will find the path to revitalizing our economy, restoring our environment, and renewing the quality of our lives. For all the talk of change in this Presidential cycle, the candidates have all missed the economic sea change that Storm Cunningham has found and revealed in re*Wealth!*"

—**Bill Leary**, former Director of Natural Resources, White House Council on Environmental Quality

"Storm Cunningham's new book, re*Wealth!*, is sure to be well purchased and widely read . . . especially here in Ontario, where he has gained such a solid reputation."

—**Wayne A. Dawson**, Vice President, Ontario Region, Cement Association of Canada

"Cutting-edge academic programs in business, engineering, planning, environment, and public policy must put re*Wealth!* on their required reading lists! Rewealth is our future, and a surprisingly large part of our present. This book is a powerful revelation and an action strategy for students, faculty, and working professionals alike."

—**William Humber**, Director, Centre for the Built Environment, Seneca College, Toronto, Ontario

"Compelling, urgent, and full of opportunity . . . anybody who has an interest in business and/or the environment will want this book. It would take a complete fool to put it back on the bookstore shelf."

—**Todd Latham**, publisher, *ReNew Canada* magazine

"Thought-provoking, insightful, and hopeful. In an age of climate change, destructive development, and species extinction, re*Wealth!* points to us to a new paradigm of restoration and replenishment. Re*Wealth!* is a fundamental rethinking of our economic models and the way we grow our cities. Sustainability is but a step along the path towards restoration; Cunningham does a fantastic job of illuminating this new path to global renewal."

—**Barry Patterson**, Biomimicry Guild

"Storm's vision is extremely important for us and for the next generations. Everyone who cares about our globe has to listen to him. This can make a difference!"

—**Amos Brandeis**, (www.RestorationPlanning.com) Architect and Urban & Regional Planner, Vice Chairman of the Israel Planners' Association.

"A visionary in restoring communities and natural resources."

—**Grant Davis**, Executive Director, Bay Institute, San Francisco, California

"I was most impressed by Storm's original book, but his new message appears even more powerful and well-crafted. He's talking about a simple, practical approach to reversing some of our most intractable economic, environmental, and social problems."

—**Dr. Mohan K. Wali** of the Ohio State University (OSU), Professor of Ecology and Environmental Science; Director, Environmental Science Graduate Program, School of Natural Resources; Professor at OSU's John Glenn School of Public Affairs.

"Revitalization guru Storm Cunningham's new book contains your future. Re*Wealth!* offers construction industry practitioners an edge as the world economy moves into uncertain times. I was hooked by the time I'd finished the introduction."

—**Will (Korky) Koroluk**, Construction Columnist, *Daily Commercial News*.

reWealth!

Stake Your Claim in the $2 Trillion *re*Development Trend That's Renewing the World

storm cunningham

New York   Chicago   San Francisco   Lisbon   London
Madrid   Mexico City   Milan   New Delhi   San Juan
Seoul   Singapore   Sydney   Toronto

1 2 3 4 5 6 7 8 9 0   DOC/DOC   0 1 4 3 2 1 0 9 8

ISBN   978-0-07-148982-9

MHID   0-07-148982-7

McGraw-Hill books are available at special quantity discounts to use as premiums and sales promotions, or for use in corporate training programs. To contact a representative please visit the Contact Us pages at www.mhprofessional.com.

This book is printed on acid-free paper.

To Scott Cunningham (1960–2003).
The world is immensely poorer without you.

Contents

Foreword

The Impact of *The Restoration Economy* on the World

Much has changed in the six years since publication of the first book to document the global renewal trend.

As the first book on the fast-growing global trend toward redevelopment and renewal, *The Restoration Economy* introduced the world to the huge, multifaceted restorative industries, and was the first book to encompass restoration of both our built and natural environments.

The Restoration Economy documented the various crises, disciplines, and industries underlying the vast global trend toward renewal. It focused on the bits and pieces, in other words: restoration of ecosystems, historic buildings, brownfields, and so on. The present book is about comprehensive solutions . . . how do you put all those forms of asset renewal together to create that magical, emergent thing we call "revitalization"?

The Restoration Economy made two significant contributions to helping community builders better perceive, organize, and harness the emerging power of restorative development. The first was in the area of terminology: it documented, for the first time, the rise of a trillion-dollar global industry that restores our natural and built assets, and provided it with some much-needed vocabulary, such as "restorative development," "integrated restoration," "restoration economy," and more. Additional new terminology, such as "restorable asset" and "renewal engine" is introduced here in this book.

The second contribution was in the area of taxonomy. A taxonomy is simply a system for classifying or organizing things, such as the species-genus-family-order taxonomy used by evolutionary biologists. *The Restoration Economy* made the first attempt to organize and categorize this enormously economic, technical, and scientific sector. It identified the following:

- Three global crises—contamination, corrosion, and constraint—were identified as the catalysts of the trend toward restorative development.
- Eight sectors of restorative activities—ecosystem, watershed, fishery, agricultural, brownfield, infrastructure, heritage, and catastrophe damage—were

shown to have been born (or had grown dramatically) in response to those three crises.

■ Three modes of economic development were documented. This "trimodal development perspective" helped readers realize that all of this renewal, redevelopment, restoration, and renovation is not just a new growth market; it is a basic mode of development, largely invisible to our economic reporting systems. The book suggested that we need to adopt the trimodal perspective into our planning, budgeting, and policymaking if we wish to retard destructive development and accelerate restorative development. Those three modes are:

a. New development (aka: "destructive development," "pioneer mode," or "sprawl") is the beginning of the development lifecycle.

b. Maintenance/conservation is the middle of the lifecycle ("maintenance" is conservation of the built environment, whereas "conservation" is maintenance of the natural environment.)

c. Restorative development is the end and new beginning of the lifecycle.

What Has Changed Since *The Restoration Economy* Was Published

Over six years have passed since *The Restoration Economy*'s manuscript was finalized. The basic premise of the book, along with its contributions to terminology and taxonomy, has been accepted without significant challenge in the worlds of business, nonprofits, government, and even academia.

Prior to publication of *The Restoration Economy*, city councils or government bodies of any kind could not sit around the table making simple statements like "For the next 20 years, let's put 20% of our money into new development (sprawl), 40% into maintenance of our built environment and conservation of our natural environment, and 40% into restorative development." They could not make such statements because "restorative development" was missing from their vocabulary. The closest they could come was "capital improvement."

The Restoration Economy helped catalyze a move toward greater integration of projects, people, and programs. We tend to define and separate ourselves by geography or by what we work on (farms, computers, highways) rather than by the net effect of our work (destructive, neutral, or restorative). *The Restoration Economy* linked all the restorers, no matter where they were or what they worked on.

The Restoration Economy documented in a single place virtually all types of restorative projects. Customarily, practitioners and researchers operate in specialized "silos," largely unaware of the efforts of their counterparts. Heritage architects care about restoring historic buildings, biodiversity-related scientists care about restoring ecosystems, infrastructure engineers care about restoring roads, bridges, sewers, or power grids, but few of them care much about the others' agendas. The same applies to those restoring agricultural lands, watersheds, fisheries, brownfields, and catastrophe damage. *The Restoration Economy* helped all of these restorative professionals to "look up and see each other" . . . to realize that they were all part of a vast, fast-growing, new global economic sector known as restorative development.

Cunningham's initial foray into the field of restorative development gave these many disciplines a shared vocabulary, a common taxonomy, and a theoretical basis for working together, which has helped accelerate a move toward more collaborative, multidisciplinary approaches. Many of them had long acknowledged a need for more integration, but lacked an effective context for advancing it. Community revitalization has become that context, because it only emerges when quality of life has been enhanced by restoring the natural, built, *and* socioeconomic environments.

Most communities do not track their restorable assets—brownfields, abandoned buildings, vacant lots, eroded/polluted streams, derelict infrastructure—much less have a program for coordinating their renewal. In fact, most communities still refer to them by their twentieth century name: "problems." As a result, many revitalization opportunities are lost.

Some communities *do* track their restorable assets, but renew them in a disjointed, project-by-project manner. The renewal momentum of each successful project is lost in this stop-start approach, as are many potential efficiencies and synergies. Each renewal project is designed and launched in relative isolation, lowering both its funding potential and the likelihood of its contributing maximally to a community's rebirth.

The Restoration Economy assisted communities, counties, states/provinces, and entire countries to realize that restoration, redevelopment, and revitalization comprise the majority of their economic future. They began to see the sprawl model of economic growth as a vestige of an earlier age. What was once necessary had morphed into a self-destructive behavior that created multiple new problems for each one it solved. As a result, restorative development is entering the lexicon and conversation at all levels of planning, budgeting, and reporting.

Another change catalyzed or accelerated by *The Restoration Economy* has been the emergence of curricula and degrees—at universities, colleges, and trade/technical schools—that arm technicians and professionals with the skills and knowledge needed to restore our natural resources and revitalize our communities (and to get hired by the companies and government agencies that are doing this work). But most higher education and technical training is still stuck in what this new Cunningham book refers to as "dewealth" mode: wealth creation that depletes and degrades our resource base.

For instance: civil engineering curricula related to waterways still focuses primarily on draining swamps, straightening rivers, and building dams, rather than on restoration, which requires a very different set of skills, hard to find in today's academic curricula. The time has come to start distinguishing restorative engineers (and other disciplines) from those who are still stuck in the mode of conquering nature. Just as budgets need to distinguish development from redevelopment, so too do our degrees. But where can a student go to get a Ph.D. in Watershed Restoration? Such courses and degrees are now being created.

Of course, *The Restoration Economy* was not responsible for the rapid, recent evolution of the "rewealth" sector—it simply was the first report on the subject—but the resulting public recognition probably accelerated the trend. The book helped industry, government, and society recognize what was happening, and facilitated talking about it across disciplines.

*re*Wealth!

This book is primarily about programs and strategies for revitalizing our communities and our planet. *The Restoration Economy* was primarily about the many varied types of projects and tactics such programs would involve. Consider:

- *The Restoration Economy* did not reveal exactly *how* communities brought themselves back from death's door via restorative development;
- *The Restoration Economy* did not address the revolutionizing effect the growth of restorative development is having on our economic systems;
- *The Restoration Economy* briefly mentioned—but did not offer many examples of—the renewal trend's impact on personal issues such as education, careers, investments, retirement, and lifestyles;
- *The Restoration Economy* did not deal much with social and cultural renewal, key goals of many revitalization programs;
- *The Restoration Economy* claimed that we need to integrate the renewal of our natural, built, and socioeconomic environments, but did not say how.

In other words, what *The Restoration Economy* did not cover could fill a book. And now it has. You're holding it. *re*Wealth! addresses all of those crucially important subjects, and much more. Enjoy . . . and learn!

William H. Hudnut III
Former four-term mayor of Indianapolis
Senior Resident Fellow, Urban Land Institute

Preface

The Impact of *The Restoration Economy* on My Life
Restoring the world for a living feels really *good.*

⎯⎯⎯⎯⎯⎯⎯⎯⎯⎯⎯⎯⎯⎯⎯⎯⎯⎯⎯⎯⎯⎯⎯⎯⎯⎯⎯⎯⎯⎯⎯⎯

The November 2002 publication of *The Restoration Economy* changed many things, including my profession.

In 1996, I set out to write a book on sustainable development. During the research, I noticed that the most exciting examples of sustainable development were actually restorative ... they went beyond simply not damaging the Earth or its people, to repairing previous damage. I started looking for more forms of this "restorative development."

I was surprised to find it everywhere I looked, in a quantity and diversity that was astonishing. By the time I finished the manuscript, restorative development had usurped the book; the larger-but-fuzzier concept of sustainable development had been relegated to half of one chapter, by that name, anyway. In truth, restorative development is the epitome of sustainable development. It's the "sweet spot," where "doing no damage" and "undoing earlier damage" meet.

The only nomenclature alteration I've made since 2002 was changing the "disaster/war" sector to "catastrophe." In 2006, I expanded the eight sectors of natural and built restorable assets into the 12 sectors referenced in this book by adding a socioeconomic category of assets: education, commerce, social services/security, and culture. With that addition, all of the basic ingredients of community renewal were in place. What was still needed, however, was a reliable recipe for turning those ingredients into revitalization. That's offered in *re*Wealth*!*. I call it the *re*solution.

On page 16 of *The Restoration Economy* (first hardcover edition), I stated "This book offers only brief flashes of the trend toward integration; this trend deserves its own book, and will get it." *re*Wealth*!* is that book, but integration has become far more vital than that neophyte author envisioned. Then, I was only talking about integration of the eight project sectors, plus integration of metropolitan and rural renewal agendas. While I had perceived a trend toward increasing restorative development and decreasing destructive development, I hadn't yet perceived the underlying dewealth/rewealth socioeconomic shift. This historic transition affects virtually every aspect of our life today.

How *The Restoration Economy* Changed My Life, and Led to This Book

During the six years I spent writing *The Restoration Economy*, I was an outsider to the world of restoration, redevelopment, and revitalization. I accidentally stumbled upon a trillion-dollar economic sector that had never before been reported on, and I wrote about it from the perspective of "Wow, look what I found!"

During that six-year period, I was director of strategic initiatives at the Construction Specifications Institute (CSI), a professional society of some 17,000 architects, engineers, specifiers, and construction industry product manufacturing representatives. In May of 2002, I left CSI and began designing my new career, using the upcoming (November 2002) publication of *The Restoration Economy* as a springboard.

Professional public speaking was the first step. Consulting gigs—ranging from entrepreneurs to Fortune 500 firms to federal agencies—started coming in shortly after that. But the major change came with the founding of the nonprofit Revitalization Institute. You'll read more about it in Chapter 14. The institute has just entered a major new growth phase as of the publication of this book, with me stepping down as Executive Director, and the institute moving from Washington, DC, to Toronto.

As a result of these activities, I've spent the past six years deeply immersed in restoration projects and revitalization programs all over the globe. In fact, I might be the only person on earth whose life for the past half-dozen years has been entirely focused on "re" activities in all their many flavors, and in all types of locations.

My professional life has been spent exclusively at conferences, classes, project meetings, and strategy sessions related to restoring fisheries, farms, watershed, and ecosystems ... restoring brownfields, infrastructure, historic structures, and catastrophes ... restoring educational systems, social services, cultural assets, and commercial activity. These activities have been in both rural communities and huge metropolises ... in both industrialized and lesser-developed countries.

Give a man a fish, and you'll feed him for a day.
Teach a man to fish, and he'll buy a funny hat.
Talk to a hungry man about fish, and you're a consultant.
—Scott Adams

I haven't actually been "doing" any of it, of course. I've only been advising, analyzing, and connecting the people, projects, and organizations that really restore the world for a living. Their stories fill the pages of this book. The perspective I've gained from helping them revitalize their communities and regions spawned the insights in this book. I hope their stories inspire you to follow their lead, if you're not already restoring our world for a living.

You'll read stories of investors, educators, nonprofits, and businesses that are reinventing their strategies and their organizations. Each is a story of *rewealth*; wealth creation based on *re*plenishing natural resources, *re*storing structures, *re*developing neighborhoods, and *re*vitalizing cities. This is as opposed to the *dewealth* model that humanity has relied on for 5,000 years: wealth creation based on *de*pleting, *de*veloping, *de*grading, and *de*stroying.

The goal of this book is to help you, your organization, or your community make that shift from dewealth to rewealth, too. Whether through your profession or through your investments, you can start enjoying some of the $2 trillion worth of rewealth generated annually worldwide. Two trillion dollars might sound like a lot of money, but the dewealth/rewealth shift has only just begun.

Storm Cunningham
Washington, D.C.

Acknowledgments

Alist of the people who contributed to this book would likely take up an entire chapter's worth of space, so I'll have to focus on those whose influence was the greatest. Dr. Maria MacKnight, my lovely and loving wife, must come first. She supported me in every way possible, which included her restorative, classical Chinese medicine and her equally restorative classical feng shui (not to be confused with the commercialized, hyper-simplified "feng shui" usually practiced in the United States). Alma Cunningham, my lovely and loving mother, was the first to read and proof these words, and also supported me in more ways than can be told here. Andrew Cunningham, my not-quite-so-lovely but equally loving brother provided almost daily moral support. Dave Marcmann, my second-oldest friend, helped me through many of the inevitable crises of launching a new career. Bob Barton, my oldest friend, did likewise. The dynamic William Humber of Seneca College supported my work in many critically important ways. Jean Bilideau, former Director General of Environment Canada, helped me figure out how to present the renewal engine model, as did Aleks Janicijevic, who created the two excellent graphics you'll find in these pages.

Big thanks go to two additional reviewers of the original manuscript, who operated under a very tight deadline: David Rouse of the design and planning firm WRT Design, and Barry Patterson of the Biomimicry Guild.

Herb Schaffner of McGraw-Hill spotted the potential of the rewealth concept, and kept me focused on it whenever I started digressing. Herb is actually the publisher of McGraw-Hill Business, but he personally took on *re*Wealth! as editor, due to his belief in its importance. I greatly appreciate the efforts of the McGraw-Hill team: Janice Race, Ed Chupak, Lauren Lynch, Seth Morris, Kenya Henderson, Anthony Landi, Heather Cooper, and Malvina D'Alterio. My sincere thanks also to Richard Rothschild of Print Matters, Inc. for making sure the project met its deadlines.

I'd like to pay tribute to the brilliant reef restoration research of German researcher Wolf Hilbertz, who died in 2007. An idyllic couple of weeks working with him under the waters of Negril, Jamaica in the early 1990s can be credited in part as a catalyst of my "re" orientation.

At that same time, I was working with a truly multidisciplinary "renaissance scientist," Dr. Walter Adey. He was then Director of the Smithsonian Institution's Marine Research Labs, and is now associate editor of Restoration Ecology magazine. He, too, was innovating coral reef restoration technologies back before most folks considered such a thing even remotely possible. These two pioneers were my earliest link to the wonders of restoring the world for a living.

Finally, my thanks go to Bill Hudnut for graciously consenting to write the Foreword. Bill is one of the most universally admired authorities on the subject of community renewal, so I'm enormously fortunate to have his name associated with this work.

List of Acronyms

ACBA, American College of Building Arts
AdT, Aguas del Tunari
AEC, architectural, engineering, construction
AFP, alternative finance and procurement
AIA, American Institute of Architects
APA, American Planning Association
ApT, Agua para Todos (Water for All)
ART, artificial reproductive technologies
ASLA, American Institute of Landscape Architects
ASSET, Africa's Search for Sound Economic Development
B2B, business-to-business
BBO, buy-build-operate
BDO, build/develop/operate
BOO, build-own-operate
BOT, build/operate/transfer
BRAC, Base Realignment and Closure
BTO, build/transfer/operate
Cal-Am, California American Water
CALFED Bay-Delta Program
Caltrans, California Department of Transportation
CCPPP, Canadian Council for Public-Private Partnerships
CDC, City Development Company
CDC, community development corporation
CDP, Chattanooga Downtown Partnership
CNRS, Centre National de la Recherche Scientifique
CPO, compulsory purchase order
CRA, Community Reinvestment Act
CSG, Cherokee Sanford Group
CSI, Construction Specifications Institute
DB, design-build
DBM, design-build-maintain

DBO, design-build-operate

EMS, Environmental Management System

EP, English Partnerships

EPA, Environmental Protection Agency

EPIC, European Property Italian Conference

EU, European Union

EUL, enhanced use leasing

FLOW , Friends of Locally Owned Water

GIPC, Greater Indianapolis Progress Committee

HUD Department of Housing and Urban Development

ICSID, International Centre for Settlement of Investment Disputes

IMF, International Monetary Fund

IRB, Infrastructure Renewal Bond

IUCN, International Union for the Conservation of Nature

IVF, in vitro fertilization

LAEGC, Lewiston-Auburn Economic Growth Council

LDO, lease/develop/operate

LEED, Leadership in Energy and Environmental Design

LISC, Local Initiatives Support Corporation

MBG, Missouri Botanical Garden

MBTF, Moccasin Bend Task Force

MMP, Misicuni Multipurpose Project

NAR, neighborhood annihilation roads

NAWCA, North American Wetlands Conservation Act of 1989

NCPPP, National Council on Public-Private Partnerships

NGO, nongovernmental organization

NOAA, National Oceanic and Atmospheric Administration

NoMa, North of Massachusetts Avenue

NRDC, National Development and Reform Commission (of China)

OAA, Ontario Association of Architects

OIP, Ontario Infrastructure Projects Corporation

OSIFA, Ontario Strategic Infrastructure Financing Authority

P3, public-private partnerships

PES, payments for ecosystem services

PFI, private finance initiative

PG&E, Pacific Gas & Electric Company

PIR, (Ontario Ministry of) Public Infrastructure Renewal
PPP, public-private partnerships (older version)
QMM, QIT Madagascar Minerals
QoL, quality of life
R3, rapid, resilient renewal
RFP, request for proposal
RFQs, request for qualifications
RNC, Restoring Natural Capital (Alliance)
ROI, return on investment
SEED, Supporting Entrepreneurs in Environment and Development
SEMAPA, Servicio Municipal de Agua Potable y Alcantarillado
SPV, special purpose vehicle
SWOT, strengths, weaknesses, opportunities, and threats (analysis)
TIF, tax increment financing
TPL, Trust for Public Land
TVA, Tennessee Valley Authority
UN, United Nations
UNC, University of North Carolina
UNCC, United Nations Compensation Commission
UNDP, United Nations Development Program
UNEP, United Nations Environment Programme
URC, Urban Regeneration Company
USAID, U.S. Agency for International Development
UST, underground gasoline storage tanks
UVM, University of Vermont
WBCSD, World Business Council for Sustainable Development
WCDC, Winooski Community Development Corporation
WfW , Working-for-Water
WIH, waterfront isolation highway
WIHNAR, waterfront isolation highway/neighborhood annihilation road
WMATA, Washington Metropolitan Area Transit Authority

Introduction

Leaving Everything Better than We Found It

Making our old economic model greener and more sustainable is like inventing a healthier form of cancer, rather than eliminating it.

The 21ˢᵗ century will be the century of restoration.
—**Historian Stephen Ambrose (2001)**

The twentieth century was the last and worst of the "de" centuries. The "de" age was based on *de*velopment; *de*pletion (fisheries, topsoil); *de*gradation, *de*spoilment, and *de*filement (pollution, destruction of heritage); *de*vitalization (of communities and ecosystem services); *de*crease (of biodiversity); *de*cline (in the planet's inventory of fossil fuels, fossil waters, old-growth forests, and other irreplaceable assets); and *de*stabilization (of our global economy and our global climate).

"De" typified earlier centuries as well, of course, especially since the Industrial Revolution. But the twentieth is when it all came to a head, and when the global "de/re shift" began to emerge in that century's final decade. What a difference a prefix can make. *De*velopment is losing out to *re*development. *De*pletion is yielding to *re*plenishment. *De*gradation is being *re*placed by *re*mediation. *De*struction is giving way to *re*storation. *De*generation is morphing into *re*generation, and so forth.

The term "rewealth" might be crassly construed as meaning "restoring the world for money." But income isn't the only reason people renew things and places. Nor is it the only reward enjoyed by those who *do* restore for money. Leaving the world better than we found it can have a profoundly restorative effect on the soul (however one might define soul) . . . whether or not personal renewal is an objective.

We all probably agree with Woody Allen that "money is better than poverty, if only for financial reasons," but most of us also know that real wealth is measured by more factors than just income and property. It's the pursuit of those other factors that has driven hundreds of thousands of people and companies to base their careers and strategies on rewealth. Restoring the world *for a living* (as opposed to *for money*) might thus be a better definition of rewealth. A more philosophical definition is "living in a way that leaves both us and the world healthier and wealthier with each passing day."

That latter definition leaves room for folks like Todd Parmington and Wendy Valint. They get great joy from restoring classic wooden canoes. Sounds like a hobby, right? But they purchase nasty, ugly old boats for between $300 and $500 and sell them for $5,000, $10,000, even $15,000. The profit adds significantly to the joy of restoration. Their company in Buffalo, New York—Vintage Canoe Works—was featured in the August 14, 2007 issue of the *New York Times*, so we won't tell any more of their story in this book. They started restoring canoes for the joy and satisfaction; the money is almost accidental. Many people have stumbled into rewealth careers in this fashion.

But serious money can be involved. In these pages, you'll discover a former cultural anthropology student who didn't know what he wanted to be when he grew up. Wall Street now gives him a billion dollars at a time to restore the world.

You'll read the story of a couple of young surfers, one from California and the other from Argentina. They started a $10 million beverage business that restores thousands of acres of endangered rain forest in three countries. The land had been destroyed by unsustainable agriculture. They restore the ecology in a way that actually *increases* its agricultural value. In the process David and Alex discovered how to restore nature and revitalize rural communities for a living. They've invented a "market-based restoration" model that could be adopted by corporations worldwide.

You'll be thrilled by the story of a tiny town—with no money and a mayor who earns $1,000 a year—that unleashed a $240,000,000 revitalization of their historic-but-blighted riverfront. The renewal sprang from a young man who as a child had fished the river's edge with his grandfather. He had long dreamed of reconnecting the community to its waterfalls. In the process of fulfilling that dream, he used a powerful new approach that's driving literally hundreds of billions of dollars in community revitalization annually, worldwide.

A similar approach is being adapted in places like South Africa. A government-lead initiative is using it to create a global climate change solution that produces biofuels in a way that restores ecosystems, farmlands, water, and forests . . . all while revitalizing tribes, towns, and cities. Addressing climate change promises to be a phenomenal economic driver of renewal via the renovation of our energy infrastructure, the reforestation of damaged lands, and the switch to restorative agriculture. You'll discover all of these stories, and many more, in the pages to come.

The shift into such integrated modes of renewal—whereby the restoration of one asset helps restore others—is helping us avoid old behaviors that create two new problems for each one they solve. An typical example of the old approach is the recent scheme to dump rust into our oceans to take up carbon dioxide and thus fight global warming; as if the oceans don't have enough problems already.

We need to be looking for multifaceted solutions to global warming that serve many restorative agendas, not just climate-related ones. We need solutions that don't make us dependent upon a single technology or company. And these solutions shouldn't have deleterious side effects that will burden future generations.

A good start would be to acknowledge that dewealth (along with population growth, of course) is the fundamental cause of global warming. As long as our economy and our very existence is based on dewealth, any solutions we devise will be like learning basket weaving at a hospice; fun, creative, and even worthwhile … but not likely to delay our demise. The de/re shift is going to be the root of any systemic solutions. And public-private partnering will be the key to financing most of it.

The people, organizations, and places you'll read about here have put themselves in the forefront of the rewealth wave. They are being carried into a prosperous future on the 21st century's largest and most exciting trend. Whether your goal is to feed the hungry, save endangered species, reduce conflict, house the homeless, increase quality of life, renew culture, redevelop workforces, or recover from disaster, rewealth is the answer.

But shifting from dewealth to rewealth isn't the whole answer: rewealth must be combined with two other powerful factors to reliably create spectacular results. Together, they form the three universal "renewal rules." Applied simultaneously, they yield magic, and you'll learn all about them in Chapter 2.

Raising the bar from doing less damage to the world to actually healing it changes everything: education, business, environmentalism, land use, construction, agriculture, energy policy, water policy, and government, just to name a few affected areas. In fact, the shift to renewal reverses the very basis of wealth creation. Our current depletion-development paradigm has been accepted without significant questioning (until recently) for some five millennia.

Every community on earth seems to have the same basic goal: rapid, resilient renewal. Despite that, champions of restoration and regeneration are encountering more political obstacles and funding problems than they should. It's not active resistance in most cases, just passive obstacles formed by outdated, sprawl-based policies, laws, and codes. There's now a quick, efficient solution to turning such "dewealth cultures" into "rewealth cultures."

> *The nation behaves well if it treats the natural resources as assets which it must turn*
> *over to the next generation INCREASED . . . in value. (emphasis added)*
> —Theodore Roosevelt, from "The New Nationalism" (1910),
> NWTR, XVII, p. 52 [National Edition of the Works of
> Theodore Roosevelt (New York, 1926, 20 vols.)
> (cited as NWTR.)]

Until you get to the word "increased," Teddy Roosevelt's words (above) sound like a standard call for conservation, stewardship, and responsible resource usage. But that single word "increased" changes everything. Leaving the world *better* than we found it is a very, very different proposition from merely slowing the rate of depletion and pollution. Conservation is essential, but it doesn't address the needs of wildlife whose habitat has already been destroyed.

All around the world, people are working to revitalize ecosystems, watersheds, rivers, coastal areas, and agricultural regions. Restorative development has tremendous popular appeal of a nonpartisan nature. Terms such as "green," "smart," and "sustainable"—pertinent though they are—often divide (or simply bore) people. The recent emergence of dialogs that label some forms of growth as "smart," "green," and "sustainable" is a definite step in the right direction, but they usually don't get to the heart of the matter. Destroying things in a greener manner is an improvement: if you're going to put that shopping center on top of the last natural wetland in the region, you might as well put solar panels on the roof. Sustainability is certainly a worthy goal, but what about the vast majority of the planet that's already badly damaged? Is sustaining—protecting it from further damage—good enough? Why not restore it?

Rewealth activities are usually nonpartisan, whereas smart growth and sustainable development in the U.S. are often supported by Democrats and opposed by Republicans. Virtually everyone gets excited about bringing places—natural or human—back to life. It doesn't matter whether they are tree huggers or bunny kickers: they love the drama and rewards of returning dead places to vibrancy. Even those who are averse to the sustainable development trend find themselves enthusiastically involved in restorative development. Those who don't think twice about destroying our cultural or natural heritage find themselves oddly attracted to restoring it.

As one wag put it: if you ask me how my marriage is, and I say, "It's sustainable," are you going to feel happy or sorry for me? But if I answer, "It's revitalizing . . . it restores me on a daily basis," you'll probably be thrilled for me. If you can look around our planet and honestly say this is a situation you'd like to sustain, you're just not paying attention. I'm for restoring this mess.

> *Ecological restoration is the re-framed environmental movement. We can restore faith in a better tomorrow.*
> —**Keith Bowers, former chairperson, Society for Ecological Restoration International, and CEO, Biohabitats, Inc.**

Another problem is that so many rewealth advocates work in isolation . . . an ecosystem here, a historic building there. Economies and communities are living systems, and need to be treated as such. Instead, we treat them like automobile motors, yanking out an alternator or piston and slapping in a new one.

The best way to restore an asset is often to restore *more* than that particular asset, because all things exist in context. Everything is connected, although temporal lags often mask the relationship between cause and effect.

The most successful regeneration initiatives renew the natural, built, and socioeconomic environments *together*. These grand projects often have significant fringe benefits. They tap efficiencies and synergies to achieve greater profitability. They often have the horsepower to revamp public policy, making the path easier for subsequent renewal projects.

How to Power Rapid, Resilient Renewal

Few communities have the knowledge or financial resources to tackle projects of great scope or complexity, but there's a solution to that: a new-but-proven tool described in these pages as a "renewal engine." Renewal engines enable communities to reliably envision, fund, implement, and maintain an upward trajectory.

With a renewal engine, communities revitalize their economy, their buildings and infrastructure, their culture, and their natural resources *together*. A renewal engine even generates the money that drives all this activity, becoming a magnet for restorative investment. Sounds too good to be true, but you're about to read stories of those who pioneered renewal engines and those who are using them now.

Real solutions to global crises tend to have four characteristics. The renewal engine model has all four:

1. It requires little money to initiate. It can be launched anywhere, at any time, by anyone: non-governmental organization (NGO), entrepreneur, elected representative, government agency, corporation, private developer, foundation, or citizen.

2. It can be used by any community, region, or nation, regardless of its current condition, and regardless of its style of government: free-market democracy, socialist democracy, kingdom, or military dictatorship.

3. It resolves economic, environmental, and social problems together, rather than maintaining the artificial separation that is a root cause of many problems.

4. It is self-sustaining and scalable in any direction: it can be launched at a national scale and then applied to the tiniest communities, or it can start in a neighborhood and be ramped up to revitalize an entire country.

This book brings to light the industries, sciences, nonprofits, and people who thrive on revitalizing our communities and restoring our natural resources. It reveals how this historic, inevitable shift away from sprawl and extraction—toward redevelopment and replenishment—is transforming entrepreneurship, research and development, law, economics, investment, technology, government, international relations, and countless industries.

Until recently, we primarily addressed the environmental problems of the world—contaminated land, air, and water; crashing fisheries; dwindling biodiversity; exhausted or destroyed (by sprawl) farmland —by trying to slow down the rate of destruction and pollution, and by trying to save a few examples of pristine ecosystems for future generations. All well and good. But despite its good intentions, this rearguard approach only delays inevitable economic and environmental disaster; it hardly lives up to the goal of leaving things better than we found them.

This is bad news for those whose living is based on putting "green" bandages on our bleeding, dying, dewealth economic model. That model equates economic growth with the conquering of new lands and the extraction of virgin resources. Not only is that model obsolete, it has also become highly toxic.

This pioneer-style dewealth model keeps lumbering along like a zombie, the economic equivalent of the living dead, eating the assets we treasure. It's maintained by an artificial life support system of archaic industries, policies, laws, codes, and regulations based on dewealth. For the past few decades, we've been trying to make that system more environmentally and socially responsible. But that's like leaving organized crime in charge of a city after establishing a new code of ethics.

The rise of rewealth is drastically raising our expectations. We now want to reverse, not just slow, our slide into economic decline and reverse—not just slow—the decay of our quality of life. We're now seeing cities and ecosystems come back to life on a monumental scale. We're seeing a future based on rewealth, and we want it now.

We now know it's possible for a place to become healthier, wealthier, and more beautiful with each passing year, and we want to put all places on that path. Not all communities can step onto the path of renewal simultaneously, of course. But the more that are renewed, the easier it is for others to renew. Revitalization begets revitalization.

As a result of these contagious success stories, a huge new "restoration economy" (what I now call a "reconomy," as opposed to a "deconomy") has arisen. It already accounts for about $2 trillion of activity annually, worldwide. There's as much money to be made restoring our world as there was to be made from plundering it; *more* in fact, since global resources have been so severely diminished. Perversely, restoring damage has proved to be easier politically (though far more expensive) than preventing damage in the first place.

But, surprisingly, the reconomy also drives conservation. Thanks to these restorative industries, we can now put hard numbers on the cost of destroying our world. This gives us to ability to file lawsuits demanding reparation for quantifiable damages, rather than imposing arbitrary fines. We've documented that each acre of remediated and redeveloped urban brownfields saves 4.5 acres of greenfields, so brownfield reuse is both an economic growth strategy and a conservation strategy.

Before the rise of the reconomy, we never really knew how much it would cost to fully restore a gold mine (tens or hundreds of millions), or to clean up a nuclear processing facility (billions). Now we have that knowledge, and it gives us the ability to collect accurate restoration deposits from extractive industries before they begin operations. This, of course, will discourage many from starting. Such restoration cost data thus does more to prevent future damage than all the "good stewardship" philosophies in the world.

People change what they do less because they are given analysis that shifts their think-
ing than because they are shown a truth that influences their feelings. This is especially
so in large-scale organizational change . . .
　　　　—John P. Kotter and Dan S. Cohen, *The Heart of Change:*
　　　　Real-Life Stories of How People Change Their Organizations
　　　　(Harvard Business School Press, 2002)

The innocuous-sounding homily—"leave things better than you found them"—
that we sometimes heard from our grandparents is often regarded as little more than
a piece of homespun philosophy. It's an axiom, something agree with without question. But how often does it make the leap to business strategy or public policy? Now,
this same impulse that motivates a person to pick up a piece of litter, or to clean off
a toilet seat after using it, is now driving a global economic revolution. What's maybe
more amazing is that the reconomy emerged on its own; no one said "this is what
we should do" and made it happen.

Most of this reconomy is driven by the profit motive, as is the deconomy. The
difference is that turning problems into valuable assets is like turning lead into gold:
you're a magician and a hero when you do so. Turning an old-growth Douglas fir
into toilet paper or newspaper was marvelous new technology in the early deconomy.
Today it's just nasty: few will admire you—and most will hate you—for doing so,
especially when recycled paper stock is plentiful. The de/re shift thus redefines good
guys and bad guys. We now tend to hate developers and love (most) redevelopers.

Closer examination of that folksy maxim, "leave things better than you found
them," reveals it to be a revolutionary call of the first magnitude. In fact, it's already
undermining vast, well-established industries and replacing them with new industries
that are revitalizing our global economy and restoring our natural resources. What
alters the economy alters government, education, science, and society . . . and us.

Aldo Leopold said, "The oldest task in human history: to live on a piece of land
without spoiling it." Thanks to centuries of *failing* to live on our land without spoiling
it, the newest task for the human future is to restore the planet we have spoiled.

The shift to rewealth has been surprisingly fast for two key reasons. First, it
doesn't require any change in human nature. We can continue to be aggressive, selfish, wasteful, and short-sighted if we want, and we'll still be leaving things better
than we found them.

Second, it taps an entirely different wealth-creation process from the one that
we have relied on for millennia, and this one knows no limits. Unlike dewealth,

rewealth can be exploited to our heart's content. I've never heard people complain, "Our river has too many fish!" or, "We've removed too much contamination from our land!" or, "Our historic buildings are too beautiful!" or, "We don't want any more enhancement of our quality of life!"

The shift from dewealth to rewealth is upon us. Here's one sure sign that rewealth is going mainstream: it's developing its own humor. I recently came across this pun: "Wetland restoration = a repairian zone." (For nonecologist readers: the land bordering a river or stream is a riparian zone.) You didn't split a gut laughing? So sue me.

Part of the appeal of rewealth is the deep joy and satisfaction experienced by a person who takes something that's dying, useless, or ugly and returns it to health, value, and beauty. Gazing upon the results and saying "I did that!" is one of life's great thrills. Doing it for a living elevates it from momentary thrill to ecstasy. OK, that's a bit over-the-top, but it's closer to the truth than you might imagine.

It's time to ensure that the next generation is the regeneration. It's time to stop being debased, and become rebased. It's time to revitalize the world together!

Part I
Trends

Redefining How We Create Wealth Can Stop Armageddon, Not Just Delay It

Rewealth turns our 5,000-year legacy of development, depletion, and despoilment into a rich global inventory of restorable assets.

I was born for reviving and rehabilitating our nation.
—theme appearing in South Korean elementary
school textbooks for decades

What kind of world will we have when our economy is based on increasing the capacity and efficiency of our *existing* communities . . . on *increasing* (not just slowing the rate of depletion) the capacity and health of our farmlands, watersheds, and fisheries? What happens when each year leaves us with a healthier, wealthier world? That sounds to me like a recipe for increasing happiness. It sounds like a recipe for decreasing conflicts over resources. It sounds like a recipe for more beautiful cities, where crime and homelessness are in decline.

In other words, it sounds suspiciously like a comprehensive solution to the world's ills. In fact, this comprehensive solution is based on three ubiquitous trends . . . not just rewealth. These are trends you'll see at work in virtually every community, profession, and discipline on Earth. There are champions for each of those trends, but never before have the breathtaking results of their *combined* power been recognized and promoted. When decisions are based on rules derived from these three trends, renewal magic is often the result.

Chapter 1

The Rewealth of Nations

The first fundamental economic revolution since 1776: Adam Smith cured the major economic problem of his day but ignored a fatal flaw, creating many of the economic, environmental, and social problems of our day.

For some 5,000 years, our wealth has been based—directly or indirectly—on development, defilement, and depletion. Every gallon of ocean water is now polluted to some degree, all humans have some Chernobyl in their bodies, and all ecosystems in the planet are in decline or collapse. This sets the stage for the twenty-first century, the Century of Revitalization. The Age of Rewealth is already well underway to the tune of some $2 trillion worth of annual activity worldwide.

Most attempts to come up with a one-size-fits-all solution to the world's plethora of crises and injustices have all had the same fundamental flaw: they tried to improve an economy based on *de*velopment, *de*pletion, and *de*gradation; *de*wealth activities that together comprise what we're calling a *de*conomy. This was just a matter of default, of accepting the 5,000-year-old mode of wealth-creation that was already in place. After all, how else do you create a civilization than by constructing new buildings and infrastructure, and by extracting food, water, oil, metals, from raw land and pristine seas?

But hanging on to civilization's birth mode too long is now undoing both our present and our future. It's obvious to any child that a growing population on a planet of finite size cannot remain in that pioneering mode forever. Sooner or later, if we wish to keep growing economically, the basis of wealth must shift to renewing what we've already built, and on repairing the damage we've done to our natural resources. Such wealth-creating activities—*re*development, *re*plenishment, and *re*storation—comprise *re*wealth. We're shifting from a *de*conomy to a *re*conomy.

Many of the problems we now take for granted as the "price of progress" simply disappear when our existence—as individuals, companies, and communities—no longer relies on the extraction of virgin resources and the conquering of raw land. Our most fundamental assumptions about our future are altered beyond recognition when our present is based on renewing the capacity of the communities we've already developed, and on repairing the damage we did to our natural resources while developing those communities. The de/re shift turns our planet-wide catalog of woes into a vast global inventory of *restorable assets*.

This isn't just semantics or positive thinking: some $2 trillion worth of restorative business is conducted annually, worldwide. It's the fastest-growing major sector of the world economy, tapping an equally fast-growing inventory of restorable assets currently valued at some $100 trillion (more on that later). For instance: the remediation and redevelopment of contaminated sites (brownfields) didn't even exist as an industry in 1990. Today, it accounts for some $7 billion annually in the United States alone, but only a few thousand of the approximately 1,000,000 U.S. brownfield sites have been dealt with. California alone has at least 100,000 brownfields.

Likewise, ecosystem restoration barely existed as an industry 20 years ago: now multibillion-dollar environmental restoration projects are appearing, some in the tens of billions of dollars. A billion here and a billion there, and pretty soon we're talking real money. Not only is rewealth not a niche or a peripheral curiosity, it already accounts for the majority of economic growth in many—possibly most—older cities.

A note regarding semantics: this book refers to ecosystems, human culture, and other sources of often-sublime beauty by the cold accounting terms "assets" and "resources." My intention isn't to infer that they only have value if monetized. Nor is it to infer that all of them are inherently "ours." The goal is to simply fit everything that contributes to our quality of life within the rewealth paradigm. This systematic approach should make it easier for more people to earn a living restoring those things that bring us health, wealth, and happiness.

Three Types of Wealth Creation

Before we go further, let's briefly posit three categories of wealth creation:

1. Destructive wealth or dewealth: Wealth derived from depleting the planet's "savings" . . . that is its store of endowed assets that are either nonreplaceable or very slowly replaceable (not relevant to human timescales).

Dewealth destroys perpetual assets (ecosystem services that produce such things as clean water, clean air, and fish), replacing them with transitory assets (office complexes, shopping malls). This style of wealth builds new civilizations, but will undermine those same civilizations if they remain in birth mode after they should have shifted to renewal mode. This failure to transition from dewealth to rewealth briefly benefits a few people in the present, but impoverishes and poisons the majority both now and for many generations to come.

2. Preservative wealth or "prewealth": Wealth derived from preserving assets and maintaining systems. This kind of wealth is neutral, neither depleting nor *actively* replenishing the overall health or wealth of the world. Prewealth activities maintain our built environment and conserve our natural environment. Besides conserving natural systems not damaged by dewealth, prewealth preserves assets (infrastructure and buildings) created by dewealth, and maintains built and natural assets already renewed by rewealth.

3. Regenerative wealth or rewealth: Wealth derived from replenishing depleted natural and cultural resources; from remediating contaminated properties; and by restoring, renovating, reusing, or otherwise increasing the capacity and efficiency of an aging built environment. When the renewal of one asset requires the destruction of another (such as removing a dam to restore a river) preference should usually be shown to the longer-lived or irreplaceable asset. For example, a river can provide benefits to humans and wildlife for hundreds of thousands of years. Dams have a useful life measured in decades.

Let's use farming to illustrate the three types of wealth creation: sustainable agriculture (prewealth) replaces the soil nutrients removed by each crop. An example is the old Aztec beans/squash/corn system still in use on many small farms throughout Mexico. This is as opposed to extractive agriculture (dewealth), such as practiced on the Great Plains of the United States. There, the topsoil depth has decreased from 10 to 20 feet to only an inch or two on most factory farms. Contrast both with restorative agriculture (rewealth), which leaves topsoil thicker and healthier with each passing year.

Rewealth restores value without destroying existing value. The exception to the non-destructive rule is when the continued existence of an asset conflicts with an area's renewal program, such as a highway that isolates a community from its waterfront.

Within the context of community revitalization, that highway is a liability, even though it might be carried on the accounting books as a multimillion-dollar asset.

Being in a reconomy doesn't mean that all sprawl or extraction of nonrenewable resources has come to a screeching halt. A reconomy relies *primarily* on rewealth, not exclusively, just as our current deconomy already has trillions of dollars of rewealth activities within it. Many cities already base over 80% of their growth on rewealth, so almost all national deconomies have thriving local reconomies within them. Our global economy is still primarily dependent on dewealth, but not for long.

The three primary components of a dewealth economy are (1) depleting natural resources, (2) expanding the built environment, and (3) adding value to them via information and labor. The three primary components of a reconomy are (1) replenishing natural assets (and reusing/recycling the products they create), (2) renewing decrepit or obsolete built assets, and (3) adding value via information and labor.

This is not an economics book, nor is it an environmental or social sciences book. But natural resources—and the value that society adds to them through information and labor—form the basis of all economies. So, let's quickly review the natural history of the global economy.

How We Got to Where We Are

At the economy level, capacities can be endowed (e.g., natural resources, land, labor), acquired (e.g., human capital, knowledge, ideas), or built (e.g., institutional design, physical, organizational, or social capital).
—Jean-François Ruhashyankiko, "Why Do Some Countries Manage to Extract Growth from Foreign Aid?" *International Monetary Fund (IMF) Working Paper*, March 2005 (emphasis ours)

Organized agriculture was invented 5,000 years ago, in the Fertile Crescent, which was formed from sediment deposited by the Euphrates, Nile, Jordan, and Tigris Rivers when they flooded. Agriculture resulted in societies becoming sedentary. This in turn required permanent buildings, infrastructure, food storage, heating and processing technologies, more efficient trade and transportation, security forces, and everything else we now consider marks of civilization.

When organized agriculture first appeared on the scene, the human population was measured in the millions, and the planet was a vast expanse of mostly virgin resources: immaculate streams and lakes; inexhaustible aquifers; rich, deep topsoil;

unbelievably prolific fisheries; endless expanses of huge old-growth trees; almost no human-made infrastructure; and few historic buildings. What's more, there was almost no persistent, nonorganic, anthropogenic pollution.

Under such conditions, the most natural thing in the world was to form an economy based on converting unused land into farmland; on digging wells and diverting flow from rivers to water those lands; on pulling as many fish as possible from the rivers and seas; on hunting whatever wildlife was left from the nomadic days; on trading with other cultures for spices and other wild-harvested products; on turning mined ore into metal farm implements and weapons; on turning trees and rocks into buildings, roads, and bridges; and so on. Under such conditions of infinite land and resources, combined with a small population, any of us would behave likewise. This was the birth of the deconomy. Now, 5,000 years and 6,000,000,000 people later, we're still at it.

Another view of deconomies sees them based on only two things:

1. Extracting virgin raw materials. This includes mining irreplaceable assets such as ores and petroleum, as well as fishing and farming in ways that decrease global stocks of fish or topsoil, as well as using fresh water in a way that leaves remaining surface water and fossil aquifers lower in quantity and/or quality; and even using our air in a way that decreases its quality.
2. Converting long-lasting land functions into relatively short-lived uses, such as unsustainable agriculture; infrastructure; and commercial, industrial, and residential buildings. Perpetual ecosystem services that produce clean air, clean water, and wildlife are destroyed in this process. Vital natural flows—such as of wildlife migration and fresh water—are disrupted to create highways, farms, recreational lakes, power generation, and drinking water reservoirs.

As deconomies—and their resulting civilizations—mature, a plethora of neutral "prewealth" services arise whose connection to those initial extractive activities is less obvious. These include such things as babysitting, entertainment, and health care. But their dewealth-based provenance isn't hard to trace, with just a few moments thought. Dewealth activities produced most of the food these maintenance service providers consume, most of the energy used to transport them, and most of the materials in the products they use in performing their jobs.

As a result, virtually everything that people in a dewealth-based society do directly or indirectly decreases the long-term health—and intrinsic wealth—of the world, even while it might be increasing their immediate and local health and wealth. If their activity serves the public good, that helps justify its dewealth provenance. If they are doing something that damages the public good, then the project's dewealth basis only intensifies the inappropriateness of their actions.

Whether we are taking a vacation, providing community services, or simply struggling for survival, members of a dewealth-based society are making it harder for future generations to do likewise. The deleterious effects of dewealth economies are subtle—maybe even effectively nonexistent on a global scale—when human populations are low. This is thanks to the regenerative powers of nature, such as nature's ability to break down harmful compounds and sequester harmful elements.

But, thanks to explosive population growth in recent centuries, our deconomy outstripped the planet's natural regenerative capabilities some time ago.

Now, let's move from the general to the specific. Understanding how we got here makes it far easier to determine how to make a formal, policy-based shift into a reconomy.

The Industrial Revolution and the Invention of Capitalism

The Industrial Revolution enabled the past three centuries of explosive population growth. That larger population, combined with the so-called Green Revolution (dewealth agriculture) of the mid-twentieth century, created most of our current environmental damage.

The Industrial Revolution was initiated by three forces: (1) technology, starting with James Watt's steam engine regulator; (2) public education, specifically the advent of a factory-style school system designed primarily by industrialists (in both the United States and Britain) to churn out large numbers of adults conditioned to follow orders, memorize instructions, ask few questions, and show up on time; and (3) procapitalism legislation—again instigated by industrialists who needed employees—that forced self-sufficient people off the land and into factories.

Contrary to popular perception, capitalism didn't evolve naturally. People didn't just wake up one day and say, "Hey, let's let those who own land and companies tell the rest of us what to do." Those who resisted the eighteenth and nineteenth century's externally imposed, violently enforced shift to a capitalist model were jailed. Many of them ended up in Australia, a now-lovely country founded as the world's largest low-security penitentiary for anticapitalists and other criminals of the day.

To make sure people accepted wage labor, the classical political economists actively advo-cated measures to deprive people of their traditional means of support. [They] justified their position in terms of the efficiency of the division of labor. They called for meas-ures that would actively promote the separation of agriculture and industry . . . [They] were unwilling to trust market forces to determine the social division of labor, [calling] for state interventions . . . to hobble these people's ability to produce for their own needs. . . . Although their standard of living might not have been particularly lav-ish, the people of precapitalistic Northern Europe enjoyed a lot of free time. . . . [via] the suppression of religious holidays . . . employers could enjoy approximately forty additional working days per year.

—Michael Perelman, *The Invention of Capitalism*,
(Duke University Press, May 2000)

The sudden, inhumane, mandated transformation of poor-but-independent multi-skilled country folk into slave-like urban factory workers was immortalized by the likes of Charles Dickens and Sinclair Lewis. More recently, it was skillfully docu-mented by Michael Perelman, cited in the above excerpt. The cruelty and suffering of this shift spawned many utopian visions in the nineteenth century. It eventually led to widespread acceptance of reactionary, impractical ideologies such as that of Engels and Marx.

Reconomics: From the Dismal Science to the Dream Economy

Modern economic theory started with Adam Smith's 1776 book *An Inquiry into the Nature and Causes of the Wealth of Nations* (usually simplified to *The Wealth of Nations*). According to economist D. Gordon, "economics has never had a major revolution" since then. The deconomy/reconomy shift is bringing that period of relative stasis in economic theory to an end.

Again, dewealth is not bad per se, but failing to make the inevitable de/re shift when necessary *is* bad. As Thomas Payne said of Britain's rule of the American colonies, "There was a time when it was proper, and there is a proper time for it to cease." The same can now be said for the dewealth model. Payne also said "a long habit of not thinking a thing wrong, gives it a superficial appearance of being right." 5,000 years of dewealth momentum won't stop on a dime. It's deeply embedded in the most basic assumptions of government, business, academia, NGOs, and citizens.

Adam Smith lived in a world where government and nobles dominated the economy, making it almost impossible for free market efficiencies to manifest. The Church of England and the government of England were effectively one and the same, and the king had divine rights. These rights were often used in economically disruptive ways. Smith's book fixed that problem very effectively.

The Wealth of Nations is based on four core principles. The first principle was that labor is the sole creator of wealth, and that specialized division of labor is more efficient than work done by people responsible for the entire process. In factory situations this is often true, but it's not as universally true as Smith might have imagined.

The second principle was that the overriding driver of human behavior is self-interest. Smith offered no real substantiation for this, other than his personal observations. I won't dispute it, except to point out that there's increasing evidence that cooperation and even self-sacrifice play a larger role in both genetic evolution and socioeconomics than we think.

Smith's third principle was that the natural order of the universe transforms the sum total of these selfish individual strivings into public good. This principle was his central marketing tactic. Only by couching it as a quasi-religious article of faith, or natural law, could he hope to compete for mindshare with the church-state that was smothering the economy. He referred to this third principle as the "Invisible Hand" of the market, and that terminology is still in common use.

The fourth principle derived from the second and third. Assuming that self-interest drives the free market, and that a free market automatically works to the benefit of society, then the best course of action is for government to leave the economic process alone. That way, business can compete and trade in total freedom, and humankind will be the better for it. This last principle came to be known variously as economic liberalism, noninterventionism, or *laissez-faire*.

We're not going to deal with the third and fourth principles in this book. They get into the area of corporate governance, which will be discussed in the sequel to this book. For now, let's focus on his first two principles. We'll start by examining the concept of labor as the sole source of wealth (as opposed to natural resources). We'll then take a look at a distinction Smith never thought to make: how the public good that derives from pursuing self-interest based on dewealth differs from the public good produced by self-interest based on rewealth.

Labor Versus Resources: Why Take Either for Granted?
During Adam Smith's time, both human labor and natural resources were taken for granted, and both were horribly abused as a result. Smith attempted to rectify one of these abuses by asserting that labor was the sole source of value in commodities. This exaggeration was probably necessary to get factory owners (whom he largely

despised) to treat their employees (with whom he greatly sympathized) more as assets and less as slaves.

With this principle, Smith turned humans into economic agents, the engine of the economy. He failed to address the issue of our taking natural resources for granted. The study of economics has become both arcane and highly sophisticated since Smith, but all that impressive brainpower has missed the elephant on the dinner table . . . the de/re shift.

Smith's elevation of labor over everything—including raw materials—had the unfortunate side effect of theoretically decoupling the economy from natural resources. His thinking inspired the leadership of the Soviet Union. This was a pure deconomy that worshipped labor and that held the natural environment in contempt, seeing it as nothing more than a source of raw materials and a dumping ground for waste. The Soviets didn't value human heritage much higher. The concept of a restorable asset was mostly lost on them, so many gorgeous historic buildings gave way to some of the world's ugliest architecture.

[Note: The Reagan administration claimed that the arms race brought about the Soviet downfall. That was a misleading oversimplification, as any examination of post-Soviet farms, fisheries, and forests makes clear. Arms expenditures broke the bank via excessive cash outflow and infrastructure neglect, but the decline of the natural environment broke the bank via reduced cash inflow. The collapse was accelerated by the political discontent of rural populations who suffered most directly from the deteriorated resources.]

When he put labor on a pedestal, Smith made no distinction between labor that depletes resources and labor that replenishes them. There should be a *chasm* between the two, in terms of net value to society and the economy. That fatal flaw—combined with his taking natural resources for granted—continued until the final decade of the twentieth century, when the three global crises—contamination, corrosion, and constraint—forced economic thinkers to start acknowledging both oversights.

A century after *The Wealth of Nations* was published, Abraham Lincoln echoed Smith's sentiments: "Labor is prior to, and independent of, capital. Capital is only the fruit of labor, and could never have existed if labor had not first existed. Labor is the superior of capital, and deserves much the higher recognition." ("Labor" here of course, doesn't refer only to hourly workers in the factories, or farmers in the fields: the labor of entrepreneurs, managers, teachers, researchers, and other professionals counts every bit as much.) Lincoln's point was to distinguish labor from shareholder capital, whereby ownership (of land, slaves, or businesses) was the sole determinant of the right to vote, and of rights in general.

The concept of "natural capital" hadn't been invented at that time, so Lincoln was solely referring to investor capital. I'd like to suggest that Lincoln's observations (which were made to advance his antislavery agenda) could have just as accurately been made regarding natural resources. I ask readers to contemplate how a shift from dewealth to rewealth might affect shareholder capital in today's crisis-ridden world, and how increasing shareholder capital via rewealth might affect the communities in which employees, vendors, and customers live.

Laboring to Be Natural

Let's see how Lincoln's thoughts read when the phrase "natural resources" is substituted for "labor": "Natural resources are prior to, and independent of, capital. Capital is only the fruit of natural resources, and could never have existed if natural resources had not first existed. Natural resources are the superior of capital, and deserve much the higher recognition." Could anyone argue with that, especially these days, with our natural world in the emergency room?

Karl Marx took Adam Smith's thinking on labor to the extreme. He said "only human sweat and skill is the true source of all value." This later came to be known as the "labor theory of value," and was discredited when it was proved that labor was much more efficient when combined with capital; that is, the technologies, research, and facilities that capital can provide. But modern economists didn't go far enough when they corrected Marx. They overlooked the same thing Smith and Marx missed: the role of natural resources.

Actually addressing the problem was largely left to the market, which started developing "green" technologies, and which saw the sudden emergence of literally trillions of dollars of rewealth activities. Economic theory lagged behind the market, with advances largely instigated by talented amateurs like Paul Hawken, Donella Meadows, Jane Jacobs, and Hazel Henderson, with support from a few professional economists like E. F. Schumacher and Herman Daly.

In 2006, the World Bank published an important study called *Where is the Wealth of Nations?: Measuring Capital for the 21st Century*. They started by defining natural capital as total nonrenewable resources (oil, natural gas, coal, and minerals), cropland, pastureland, forested areas, and protected green space.

They then surveyed produced (or built) capital, which comprises total machinery, equipment, and structures (including infrastructure), and other urban development.

When these two totals were summed for any particular nation, they often found large discrepancies between that number and the size of the economy. In many cases, the natural and built capital didn't even account for half the economy.

The missing balance is made up of the intangibles that enable people to add value to natural and built capital. They referred to it as "human capital." It included such factors as effective law enforcement, legal, and judicial systems, effective governance, and an effective property rights system. When this socioeconomic environment is supportive, entrepreneurial activity and property investment thrives. Without that support, people tend to spend more time surviving by extracting value, and less time thriving by enhancing value.

Just as we are finally beginning to monetize ecosystem services (natural capital), this brilliant report added the other major missing piece to the revitalization puzzle: monetizing human capital. They quantified the value of intangibles such as social services and education.

According to the World Bank report, rule of law accounts for about 57% of the human capital of developed nations. Education accounts for another 36%. So, when you see references in this book to the importance of renewing the socioeconomic environment, remember that real numbers can be attached to such investments.

I couldn't help but notice, though, that this otherwise excellent World Bank report didn't have a single reference to restoration, redevelopment, or revitalization. This is a classic case of what I refer to as "reblindness" in my workshops: seeing neither opportunities for renewal, nor current renewal activities.

By contrast, the 2007 Global Environment Outlook of the United Nations Environment Programme (UNEP) contains exactly 100 occurrences of "restore" or "restoration." Here's a sample sentence from the report: "These are vast amounts of money, which could be used to revitalize agriculture through measures such as the provision of agricultural inputs and the rehabilitation of degraded land." UNEP, it seems, no longer suffers from the global affliction of reblindness. This should enable them to evolve truly leading-edge programs this century.

A Perfect Economic Storm

One of many assumptions economists make is that, because the economy is larger than it was in the past, that the world has grown richer over time. But has it? We've become phenomenally good at adding value to raw materials, and at developing services around those products. But that growth in value-added activities has been accompanied by an equally dramatic reduction in the resources on which those activities are based.

We are at the confluence of two fundamental trends in economics, one of which economists are well aware, and another of which they are still largely unaware. The first is the shift from artificially simple, static, mechanical models to more realistically complex, dynamic, "living" economic models. This shift has been about 30 years in the making, and was recently documented in economist Eric Beinhocker's wonderful *The Origin of Wealth* (Harvard Business School Press, 2006).

The second trend is not a shift in the thinking of economists. It's a shift in the actual world economy, from what might be called "de" dynamics to "re" dynamics: from depleting natural resources and developing virgin land to replenishing natural resources and redeveloping used land. In this book, we'll refer to this shift in wealth creation as being from dewealth to rewealth, and the overall economic shift as being from a deconomy to a reconomy . . . from deconomics to reconomics, one might say. Once these two trends are synthesized, we'll have a whole new science of economics that reflects both current reality and future needs.

> *The most startling empirical fact in economics is that there is an economy at all.
> . . . The economy is a marvel of complexity. Yet no one designed it and no one runs it.*
> —Eric D. Beinhocker, *The Origin of Wealth*
> (Harvard Business School Press, 2006)

Economies, both local and global, have always been self-organizing complex adaptive systems (though never as complex as today's, by a long shot). Thus, the shift in economists' thinking from simple, mechanical, and predictable to complex, living, and surprising is simply a matter of having the courage to acknowledge the messiness of reality. The shift has been greatly facilitated by economists finally having access to computing tools that can (begin to) model reality. The new field is called Complexity Economics, a term coined by the brilliant economist Brian Arthur.

Economists can be somewhat forgiven for missing the other trend, the economic shift from depletion to restoration. This oversight wasn't a matter of failed courage, but lack of data: despite its vast size, this economic activity isn't properly tagged, so the hard numbers go largely undocumented and unreported. Bureaucracies seldom turn on a dime, and the global reconomic trend has only emerged in the past two decades.

Many local reconomies go much further back, of course, such as old-but-healthy cities. But economists are primarily interested in universalities, not local phenomena, so they missed the transition from community trend to global trend.

What's more, the only previous documentation of this shift, in 2002, was a non-technical, non-numbers-oriented, nonfootnoted book by a noneconomist and nonacademic; *The Restoration Economy*. For respectable economists, its publication was a nonevent.

The confluence of this internal trend in economics—Complexity Economics—and this external trend in the economy—reconomics—should produce a "perfect storm" of creative destruction in the field. Why? Because building a new world economy based on redeveloping our built environment, on restoring our damaged and depleted natural environment, and on healing and revitalizing our degraded socioeconomic environment—is a hugely complex task. It requires effectively integrating the renewal of a huge diversity of restorable assets; natural, built, and socioeconomic. It also requires effective engagement of the multitudinous stakeholders encompassed by that scope.

In other words, it requires a system of economics that acknowledges the dynamic interdependence of all organic systems, inorganic materials, and intelligent networks on earth. This is exactly what Complexity Economics is designed to do. The primary missing ingredient is recognition of this profound and permanent shift from dewealth (sprawl) to rewealth (revitalization).

When I say permanent, I'm referring to this planet. Once interplanetary development gets underway, we might see a return to dewealth. By then, we will have (hopefully) thoroughly integrated rewealth and dewealth—restoration and exploitation—into a full-lifecycle economic model. Is that possible? A mining company called QMM is giving it a try in Madagascar. You'll read about them in Chapter 12.

Beinhocker unintentionally set the stage for this synthesis of complexity and rewealth in his *Origin of Wealth* when he acknowledged that evolutionary theory was inspired by economics. Ever since Charles Darwin read Thomas Malthus in 1838, evolutionary and economic theories have been increasingly intertwined.

Beinhocker points out that the economy is based on the same formula that drives evolution: differentiate-select-amplify. He shows that wealth creation is the product of evolutionary-style processes that constantly select for greater efficiency and value creation. But we must never forget that all of this activity is based on the physical home that earth provides us . . . on the ecosystems producing the food, water, air, fuel, and construction materials that keep us alive from moment to moment.

In this discussion of renewal, "amplify" is the key word in the above algorithm. But "differentiate" is also important, because it's the failure to formally differentiate dewealth from prewealth from rewealth. Without that differentiation, we can't "select" rewealth for our policies, projects, and plans.

Until now, we have based wealth creation primarily on amplifying the utility of materials we've extracted (usually in an unsustainable manner) from the planet. Our future—if we are to have one—will be based on amplifying the sources of those assets, not just the extracted assets themselves. In other words, amplifying the planet's capacity for renewal. In many cases, this simply means that we have to stop blocking nature's renewal power, such as when we remove a dam and allow fish to migrate and spawn.

Wealth creation will increasingly rely on collecting and amplifying (via recycling and reuse) the value of nonrenewable—and often toxic—materials we've already extracted, such as minerals and metals. It will be based on amplifying (restoring) the renewable resources of the planet, such as water, topsoil, and fisheries. And it will be based on amplifying (recycling or revitalizing) developed properties and communities. All told, we're talking about planetary renewal; one property, community, and landscape at a time.

> *We really do not know how [the economy] works. . .*
> *The old models just are not working.*
> **—Alan Greenspan, former chairperson of the U.S.**
> **Federal Reserve, November 1999**

Economic history over the past quarter of a millennium has been a search for certainty. Adam Smith (1723–1790) sought to free the market from the stifling and parasitic interference of royalty. Smith established that wealth is created by turning natural resources into useful products (via technology), and that specialization (via division of labor) increased efficiency, which boosted the wealth-generating capacity of a society.

More recently, evolutionary economist Richard R. Nelson of Columbia University divided the technologies that boost our wealth-generating power into two categories. Physical technologies are the tools that work directly with natural resources, such as turning ore into hammers. Social technologies are the ways in which we organize our societies to extract those materials more efficiently, distribute the products more efficiently, innovate more efficiently, and finance all of that activity more efficiently.

But specialized producers require trade: until we devise a delicious recipe for hammers, hammer-makers will starve without trade. The prices derived while trading hammers for ham thus become the universal factor. Pricing provided a unifying dynamic in an economic system that dealt with all kinds of products and services. Adam Smith posited that a perfectly free market would produce not just the perfect valuation of goods and services (efficiency), but the maximum value for society as a whole (quality of life).

After all, trading was voluntary, and each individual was the best judge of what goods and services would make him or her happiest. Thus, the more we pursue our own happiness, the happier everyone will be. He made this happy assumption not out of ignorance, innocence, or overweening optimism, but—as noted earlier—as part of his sales pitch to free business from government interference. Although this invisible hand superstition has long been thoroughly discredited, it's still invoked whenever an industry wishes to avoid regulations that would make it more environmentally or socially responsible.

But that's now, this is then. After *The Wealth of Nations* was published, economists spent the next two and a half centuries trying to make Smith's charming assumption—that the individual's pursuit of profit would automatically make a perfect world—measurable and predictable. Doing so required a series of assumptions that stripped away the messiness of human decision making.

In their models, humans became perfectly rational agents whose tastes and behaviors were mechanically reliable, and whose greatest happiness came from consuming the most for the least. The economists' promise went like this: once we really understand the economy properly and apply those insights, everyone at every moment will obtain exactly what they want at the perfect price, and we'll all live happily ever after.

Léon Walras (1834–1910) started this process of simplifying economics into its modern-but-irrelevant form. It's a form that keeps academics, government policy wonks, and corporate apologists employed, but accomplishes little else of value. Walras borrowed the concept of equilibrium from the newly hatched science of physics and implanted it into economic theory. Economists have been pursuing the impossible dream of static, balanced economies ever since, hoping to make them behave like gravity. Any messy behavior by individuals or society that impaired the reliability of their models was eliminated.

People won't keep consuming a particular commodity *ad infinitum*, in part because of the law of diminishing returns; the more we indulge in something, the less benefit we tend to get from each additional indulgence. Rewealth in general, and social capital in particular, seem to be the only economic factors not subject to diminishing returns. The problem of finite resources was worrisome, but it was an abstraction: few people in those days had actually seen a resource run out, and certainly not on a global level. Walras said that trade, with its variations in price based on supply and demand, fixed the finite resource problem by funding the development of alternatives. This made more sense than the invisible hand, but proved only marginally more valid.

Around the same time, William Stanley Jevons (1835–1882) was trying to figure out how that eminently rational pricing mechanism—when combined with resource limitations—could produce Smith's deliriously happy society. He came up with the concept of "constrained optimization." All of these perfectly aware agents (us) would automatically calculate exactly which goods, and what quantities of goods, would make us happiest. (The overweight, unhealthy, often-miserable clients of the fast-food industry's "supersizing" campaign might argue with Jevons . . .)

Of course, the fickleness and folly of folks' financial decisions in the real world weren't the only flies in the economic ointment. Government policies, union demands, and monopolistic industries were all messy realities that had to be ignored to make these models work. But people paid attention to the economists anyway: we, too, desired certainty and predictability. We'd even accept an illusion of it, if that were all that was available.

Well-informed patients today often suspect that their doctor is guessing at both the underlying cause of their problem and its treatment. They also suspect that the drugs or surgery being prescribed to eliminate their symptoms are likely to do more harm than good in the long run. But the doctor's impressive vocabulary and education inspire faith. So it is with economists.

Until the twentieth century, the focus of economists was almost exclusively on optimizing the allocation of wealth. They merrily assumed they had a good handle on the creation of wealth. Their problem was that the amount of wealth in the global system had been expanding exponentially since the Industrial Revolution. Growth creates change. Change of any kind was anathema to their equilibrium-based models, but a few brave economic souls decided to acknowledge the disconnect.

Economics is extremely useful as a form of employment for economists.
—John Kenneth Galbraith (1908–2006)
economist; author, *The Affluent Society*

Joseph Schumpeter (1883–1950) saw that the failure to address the conflict between equilibrium and growth was a fatal flaw. He posited that the missing element was innovation, in the form of the entrepreneur. Economic growth came to be seen as deriving from the combination of population growth and innovation. The latter increased the efficiency of turning natural resources into value.

Schumpeter saw a constant rain of innovation as building economic pressure, like water behind a dam. He saw entrepreneurs as the factor that turned this pressure into opportunity by linking technology and business creation. This broke the dam, releasing a flood of creative destruction that swept aside old technologies and businesses.

But innovation and entrepreneurialism weren't quantifiable, so Schumpeter's work remained in the realm of dialog and seldom made its way into economic models. Robert Solow and Paul Samuelson at MIT—and the Chicago school of economists that followed them—finally managed to wed growth and equilibrium in their idea of balanced growth. This approach basically ignored growth in the size of the overall economy—and any changes growth might catalyze—and focused on the net increase in individual wealth. The key driver of increasing *per capita* wealth, in this view, is technology. But the goal was—and still is for many of the old school—equilibrium.

The stage was set for a wholesale shift toward a more complex approach when Stanford University economist Paul Romer published a paper in 1990. It documented the very different dynamics of technology-based—and especially *information* technology-based—economies. Economies based primarily on natural resource extraction and value-added processing displayed largely linear dynamics. Silicon Valley-style, networked technologies tend to create *increasing returns* situations. The more wealth they created, the more wealth they create. This idea was at the heart of the mindset that created the Internet Bubble: companies sacrificed revenue generation for mindshare, but that moment of madness in no way discredits the increasing returns concept.

Once the classical economists (who were calling themselves *neoclassical* by this time) reluctantly accepted the reality of increasing returns (which they had previously dismissed as impossible), the wedge was in place. Other nonlinear dynamics were also native to complex adaptive systems, and they poured through the crevice opened by Romer's wedge.

Complexity Economics is finally addressing these fundamental economic fallacies. It's curing economics of its foolhardy search for equilibrium and its obsession with simplistic cause-and-effect relationships. Complexity is curing economics of the need to sacrifice realism on the altar of predictable models. Some day, it might even cure economics of irrelevance. If that same evolution were to hit the world of policy analysis, the terms "economic expert" and "successful national policies" might cease to be quite so oxymoronic.

Complexity Economics could enhance our ability to make the shift from dewealth to rewealth, from a deconomy to a reconomy. But, its practitioners haven't yet—with one exception—recognized that polarity shift, so they are afflicted with their own form of irrelevance. Sometimes the biggest changes are the hardest to perceive, especially when no one is measuring it. No data, no reality. Reconomic data do exist, of course, but are not being aggregated in a way that allows the extent of the rewealth trend to be perceived.

> *If we become rich or poor as a nation, it's because of water.*
> **—Sunita Narain, director of the Center for Science and Environment in New Delhi, India**

No matter how great the increasing returns, natural resources are at the heart of what's being increased. The one exceptional group that *is* beginning to apply Complexity Economics to the dewealth/rewealth shift is the nascent Restoring Natural Capital Network. You'll read about them in Chapter 8.

So, with all this economic change and research over the centuries, how many different economic systems has the world seen over the past 5,000 years? When you focus on the most fundamental factor—the underlying resources—the surprising answer is "one": the deconomy. But, we're finally tiring of dewealth's one-step-forward, three-steps-back dynamics, and rewealth is rapidly on the rise. This emerging economic model isn't just new, it's the *reverse* of the old one. That's essential, because the old model left us a legacy of distressed communities and degraded landscapes that we just can't live with.

The deconomic model has underpinned capitalism, socialism, and communism and all our other "isms" for the past five millennia. Now, we usually think of communism and socialism as political systems, more akin to democracy or monarchy than to capitalism. But the essential difference among capitalism, socialism, and communism is their determination of who owns property, and who owns the wealth created by labor. The governing style of all three is fundamentally uniform: a group of (usually) men periodically gather to accumulate more power and enrich their friends.

While capitalism, socialism, and communism differ significantly on how wealth is *distributed*, and how labor is managed, they all agree on how wealth is *created*. Each is a variation on a single theme, permutations of a single model: dewealth. It bears repeating. Ever since humans started the shift from nomadic life to permanent settlements with agriculture, we've primarily relied on "de"-based activities: *dev*elopment (of raw land), *dep*letion (of virgin natural resources), *deg*radation (via pollution, invasive species, or unsustainable agriculture), and *des*truction (of irreplaceable natural and cultural assets). It's a pioneering, sprawl-based model, based on there always being fresh green fields over the horizon.

You can build a de-based economy around capitalism, communism, federalism, monarchies, dictatorships, or socialism. Those economies can be run by elected politicians, kings, queens, hegemonies, dictators, mafias, cartels, clans, militaries, patriarchs, matriarchs, juntas, or plutocrats. But if their wealth creation is mostly based on those "de" words, they are all deconomies, no matter what terminologies, ideologies, players, or governmental models are at work. An economy based on "re" words is now poised to take over, and has already done so in many revitalized places.

The Power of a Prefix

Cleansing winds sing sweetly,
Through young tree stands,
New clothing to revitalized land.
—**Brother Lawrence**

Dewealth's inappropriateness as a path forward isn't based only on the fact that it depletes resources via extraction, or because it doesn't recognize lifecycle dynamics (lack of full-cost accounting): it also tends to add value to those resources in a way that degrades the world and harms people.

For instance, vast amounts of labor, cyanide, water, and petroleum add value to gold ore by concentrating the trace gold into usable (kinetic) form. The intrinsic (potential) value of gold was there in the ground all along, but the leaching process converted it to a higher value. Along the way, such gold operations poison the ground and the waterways, wiping out fisheries, and leaving behind tens (possibly hundreds) of thousands of physically and mentally disabled children and adults annually. That's not to mention the sheer hideousness of the mine site.

Rewealth, on the other hand, is based on *enhancing* not just the production of resources, but on adding value to them in a manner that further enhances nature and communities (such as turning that poisonous old gold mine back into usable agricultural or residential property, or wildlife habitat).

But gold mining isn't the worst example of dewealth, because most uses of gold don't destroy it. At least gold has the potential to remain in circulation forever. Even more damaging are the dewealth activities that deplete the earth for consumables such as food and energy. Not only do they deplete fossil aquifers, fossil fuels, and fossil topsoil . . . they further degrade the world as waste and pollution, rather than being reused and recycled.

Both dewealth and rewealth add value and provide employment. But the former depletes publicly owned natural resources, poisons human and wildlife communities, and decreases property value when pursued to the point that quality of life declines. Rewealth restores natural functions to the land, removes contamination, and increases property value. Dewealth operations provide tax revenues and employment only until the ore or redwoods are exhausted, and then both employment and tax revenues disappear.

Restoration generally creates far more jobs for a given amount of revenue than extraction operations. For instance, restoring a forest—clearing invasive species and planting natives—is work that requires much human labor. Clear-cutting a forest these days is primarily done by heavy equipment, with few operators. Likewise, it has been well documented that restoring a building creates more jobs per dollar of budget than constructing a new building.

A fringe benefit is that tax revenues from the redeveloped mine site can theoretically continue forever, as opposed to the disruptive burst of revenue created by mining, which often leaves ghost towns in its wake. In fact, a ghost town is a prototypical dewealth phenomenon: virtually all were created by extraction industries. Taken to its logical conclusion, we get a ghost planet.

Sources Versus Resources

The word "resource" captures the spirit of the new reconomic model. It derives from obsolete and Old French, specifically the feminine past participle of the verb *resourdre*, literally "to rise again." This in turn came from the Latin *resurgere* (from which we get "surge"), meaning "to rise."

In other words, that popular environmental phrase—"nonrenewable resources"—is an oxymoron. If something is renewable, then it's a resource, in which case it doesn't need "renewable" in front of it. If it's nonrenewable, it is not—by definition—a resource. It's only a source. The missing gold in an abandoned mining site is never going to surge or rise again, although the property itself certainly can.

Relying on regenerative processes is a far more stable basis for an economy than dependence on degenerative processes. It's not just running out of a commodity that's disruptive: even the discovery of major new sources has historically thrown economies for a loop.

The discovery of the New World's vast silver and gold mines in the sixteenth century abruptly reduced the price of those metals in Europe by two-thirds. Since currencies of that time were mostly based on precious metals, this meant that—*sans* stabilizing action by banks or government—the apparent price of everything money purchased, such as labor and food, suddenly rose by two-thirds. Discovering new *re*sources (such as fishing grounds or fertile land) is seldom disruptive in this manner.

Granted, we can overexploit a resource . . . fishing faster than they can repopulate, for instance. But that's different from relying on something that *can't* regenerate, such as gold. Some resources regenerate on a timescale that's irrelevant to human needs; examples are fossil aquifers and old-growth forests. Consequently, those should generally be treated as if they were static sources.

Sustainability is simply about not fishing faster than the fish naturally regenerate. Rewealth is about recognizing that most of our resources are seriously impaired. It's about actively helping them accelerate that regeneration, to replace not just what we're taking today, but also the excessive amounts we and our grandparents took yesterday. Rewealth is about restoring the actual ability for fisheries to regenerate, such as by restoring breeding grounds like riparian ecosystems and mangrove forests.

Apply those fishing examples to all kinds of resources, and we have the difference between sustainable development and restorative development, the difference between a preconomy (based primarily on prewealth; maintenance and conservation) and a reconomy. Both are vastly better than a deconomy, but only the latter can make a better tomorrow. A preconomy can only keep things from getting worse.

Sustainability efforts have focused primarily on three objectives: (1) using less of our nonregenerating sources (ores, coal, petroleum, well water from fossil aquifers); (2) taking excessive pressure off our resources (fish and other edible wildlife, wood from secondary forests, fresh surface water); and (3) reducing waste and pollution. All are essential, but it's not enough.

If We're All Driven by Self-Interest, and Our Economy Is Dependent on Disappearing Natural Resources, What Hope Is There for Our World?

> *BHP Billiton Ltd. and Rio Tinto PLC and other megaminers collectively have projects valued at tens of billions of dollars in the works . . . shareholders are pressuring mining companies to . . . sustain growth over the next decade. At the same time, banks and other providers of capital are becoming more comfortable financing mining ventures, including higher-risk projects . . . "It almost seems at the moment, if you have a piece of paper that has an outline for a project, you can [get money]", said Mark Tyler . . . at Nedbank Group Ltd. . . . some speculators . . . fear the global commodity boom may have peaked. "The industry's ability to turn intentions into physical production remains constrained by access to new large ore bodies," Paul Skinner, Rio Tinto's chairman, said . . . Those constraints "will continue."*
>
> —Patrick Barta, "Even Now, Big Miners Dig Away,"
> *Wall Street Journal*, February 22, 2007

Adam Smith could be excused for not questioning the apparent infinity of resources. He lived at the tail end of an era that had lasted for as long as humans had roamed the Earth; the period when natural resources were apparently inexhaustible. Resources were a given, barely mentioned in most economic theory. That illusion is now dead, but its artifacts live on in public policy, planning, and budgeting, as well as in business strategy.

So, is all wealth really based on natural resources? Not directly, no, but much wealth *is* based on it directly. All remaining types of wealth—including intangibles like happiness—are indirectly based on natural resources. We're unlikely to spend much time contemplating our happiness when we're starving, suffocating, or dying of thirst.

Close your eyes for a moment. Picture yourself in an ideal place of beauty, comfort, safety, and inspiration. Stop reading for a moment and try it . . . please. OK, open your eyes, and I'll tell you where you were. You were outdoors, right? E.O. Wilson refers to this as biophilia (he also told me this will be a century of restoration). Never doubt for a moment that your happiness is rooted in nature, no matter how much of a computer-caffeine-car–addicted consumer you might be.

Another "bio" word you'll see a lot more of as the shift to rewealth accelerates is "biomimicry," the creation of technologies based on nature's designs.

Why? Because nature's technologies are inherently restorative. Read Janine Benyus' 1997 classic, *Biomimcry*, for more insight. I predict that one of the next steps in biomimicry research will be to look to nature for insights into revitalizing communities. Nature is constantly reusing, renewing, and replacing things at both the organism and the ecosystem levels. That's what cities need to do, but we don't seem to be quite as adept at it; our redevelopment efforts have often done more harm than good.

Maybe it *will* someday be possible to decouple our economy from natural sources and resources. Maybe we'll eventually create all the food, water, air, and building materials we need from subatomic particles via Jetson's-style quantum manufacturing units. But until then, the U.S. oil industry's $800 billion in profits over the past five years makes it clear we've barely begun the journey away from dewealth, much less away from natural sources in general. With all the recent information economy techno-hype, you'd think we'll all be eating data cakes in a few years. Here's a lesser-known fact: some experts estimate that the founder of IKEA, Ingvar Kamprad, is richer than Bill Gates, Jr. On what is Ingvar's fortune based? Trees. Sure, he makes wonderful use of software to make IKEA's operation a model of efficiency, but: no trees, no furniture, no fortune.

Why Would We Restore What We Don't Value?

> *Neoclassical economists assume there is no absolute resource scarcity—as any resource becomes scarce, its price increases, providing incentives to develop substitutes. For example, two hundred years ago, biomass was the major source of fuel for societies everywhere, but as forests grew scarce, prices rose, and we developed substitutes. Coal, petroleum, natural gas, and uranium have since emerged as important resources so that, due to technology, we have more resources available to us than we did 200 years ago. As these resources grow scarce, their prices will increase, and . . . the market will again develop substitutes. The problem is that humans, like all other species, rely for their survival and economic welfare on intangible, non-marketed ecosystem services such as climate stabilization, water regulation, waste absorption and so on. Though increasingly scarce, the majority of these ecosystem services have no price, and therefore no feedback from markets signaling their scarcity and no market incentive to produce them.*

> —Joshua Farley and Herman Daly, commentary in
> *Ecological Engineering*, November 2006

Farley and Daly's brilliant analysis (above) refers to "ecosystem services." The Millennium Ecosystem Assessment identified four types of ecosystem services enjoyed by humanity:

- Provisioning services: Food, water, timber, firewood, fiber, genetic material.
- Regulating services: Climate, floods, dust storms, disease, atmosphere.
- Supporting services: Geochemical and biological processes such as soil formation, nutrient and water cycling, primary production, pollination.
- Cultural services: The raw materials of human societies, such as ideas, images, and recreation. They inform our science, our myths, and our spiritual outlook.

The ecosystem service concept has quickly gone mainstream. For instance, the Asian Development Bank (in their 2001 *Asian Environment Outlook*) says: "At risk are people's health and livelihoods, the survival of species, and ecosystems services that are the basis for long-term economic development." That same report said that Asian countries' environmental problems are "pervasive, accelerating, and unabated."

Adam Smith pointed out the distinction between an object's value in use versus its value in exchange. Things with great *utility* value (such as water) often have little exchange value, whereas things with great *exchange* value (such as paper currency) usually have little utility value.

Natural resource restoration will mushroom when "green infrastructure"—also known as ecosystem services—is monetized, creating an exchange medium for its utility. Carbon credits, water credits, garbage credits, biodiversity credits, and other such mechanisms all help heal this utility-exchange "value rift."

We've explored a lot of concepts and theories in this chapter. The stories you'll encounter throughout the rest of this book, especially in Part III, will demonstrate what happens in the real world when communities, companies, schools, nonprofits, and individuals make the dewealth/rewealth shift.

Let me reiterate: none of this is to say that development of raw land and depletion of fossil resources is *never* appropriate. Dewealth got our civilization to where it is, both the good and the bad. In moderation, and combined with subsequent restoration, dewealth will continue to be an important economic component while we transition to a full-fledged global reconomy. The simplest and most effective policy change a community or nation can do to accelerate their own de/re shift is to make rewealth the default, and dewealth the exception. More on that in the next chapter.

Is a wholesale shift to rewealth possible? It's not only possible, it's already happening. You'll see the evidence in Part III, in the inspiring stories of individuals, communities, organizations, government agencies, schools, and companies that are restoring the world for a living. But, between now and Part III, we're going to raise the bar. A lot.

What if all that rewealth activity were performed in an integrated manner that restored natural, built, and socioeconomic environments together? What if it were performed in a way that engaged all stakeholders in the renewal of their community or region? If that happened, each year might see not just economic growth, but a corresponding decrease in crime, poverty, conflict, and disease. This is where some basic rules come into play, which is the subject of the next chapter.

Patricia Ireland of the National Organization of Women has said (speaking of our newfound ability to identify and address sexual harassment in the workplace), "If you don't have the words to describe something, it's really hard to conceptualize it." This can be equally applied to recognizing dewealth and rewealth in our national and local economies. I believe it's the role of our educational system to start reforming the way we talk about economic growth.

Need a formal definition of dewealth and rewealth? Try this:

- Dewealth activities derive profit from depleting, degrading, or destroying natural, built, and/or socioeconomic assets of long-lasting or irreplaceable value, usually to create new assets of more ephemeral value, and often in ways that impair public health and/or quality of life.
- Rewealth activities derive profit from renewing the health, beauty, quantity, value, and/or functionality of—or reusing—natural, built, and/or socioeconomic assets, without depleting, degrading, or destroying other assets of long-lasting or irreplaceable value.

The Impact of Rewealth on Corporations

No discussion of the future of wealth creation would be complete without addressing the role of corporations. The days when nations were the sole (or even the primary) economic entities are long since over.

I've never met a businessperson who had a problem with the idea of restoring the world for a living. Most of the approximately $2 trillion being spent annually on rewealth is being channeled through businesses large and small. If there's profit to be made in restoration, redevelopment, remediation, renovation, and reuse, both entrepreneurs and large corporations will go after it.

But some say there are fundamental flaws in the very nature of the modern public corporation; flaws that almost force them into social and environmental irresponsibility. Some say the worst of those flaws can be traced to our kindly old friend, Adam Smith. This is too complex a subject to address here, so we'll dive into it in this book's sequel, tentatively scheduled for 2010.

For now, here's some food for thought. Imagine that corporate governance is never "fixed" . . . companies are never required to be environmentally and socially responsible. If the default basis of corporate wealth creation were rooted in replenishing our natural resources, renewing our built assets, and enhancing our socioeconomic assets, wouldn't that alleviate many of the complaints?

Could it be that our current efforts to make corporations more environmentally and socially responsible are merely Band-Aids on an outmoded economic model?

Of course, even after a wholesale shift to rewealth, some people will still be looking to play the system and get something for nothing. Damaged psyches will still commit atrocities. Politicians will still be swayed by money. But, if they are all operating within an economic system that grows via restoration and renewal, wouldn't that be a satisfying improvement? Personally, I'd rather receive a neck massage from a dishonest therapist than be shot by an honest soldier. Imperfect restoration or perfect destruction? Most folks won't have any problem choosing.

If the basis of wealth creation switches from dewealth to rewealth, our planetary trajectory takes a U-turn. Then, the world can't help but get healthier, wealthier, and happier . . . despite our human frailties. When profit and panacea go hand in hand, can paradise be far behind?

Chapter 2

Renewal Rules

Three global trends are based on universal principles that, when combined, enable nondestructive, unlimited economic growth that **heals** *nature and society.*

This chapter is a quest for the Holy Grail. The Holy Grail was an idea Christianity borrowed from the pagans. To the pagans, the grail was a gateway to paradise that possessed unlimited healing powers.

That's the meaning I have in mind when I use the term: the gateway to a dream economy that possesses unlimited power to heal human communities, and the planet. With that in mind, let's go on a quest for the economic holy grail. Or, if religion's not your thing, it's a pursuit of the impossible dream.

Any real remedy for the world's ills will need to be principles-based, so it can be applied to any situation. This chapter reveals the three core principles—rules for decisions—behind strategies that produce rapid, resilient renewal; anywhere, and under almost any conditions. Chapter 4 will move from theory to practice, revealing a complete formula for successfully applying those rules in your community, even if you have no money for renewal.

I call them the "renewal rules." Base your community's decisions on any one of them, and things will get better. Use two of them, and dramatic improvement is likely. Base your decisions on all three, and my research indicates that a miraculous transformation is almost assured. The three rules are (1) rewealth (renewal of your assets), (2) integration (of your natural, built, and socioeconomic environments), and (3) engagement (of your stakeholders).

The Power of the Renewal Rules Comes from Their Basis in Global Trends

Rules change behavior. Power over rules is real power. That's why lobbyists congregate when Congress writes laws, and why the Supreme Court, which interprets and delineates the Constitution—the rules for writing the rules—has even more power than Congress. If you want to understand the deepest malfunctions of systems, pay attention to the rules, and to who has power over them.

—Donella (Dana) Meadows (1941–2001) "Places to Intervene in a System," *Whole Earth*, Winter 1997

Is there a city that has consciously and effectively embedded all three of these rules in their policies, plans, and projects? Not that I know of. Until now, use of these rules has been mostly based on uncommon sense and good intuition. But they've been spreading like wildfire, despite their never having been documented.

Why? Because these "rules" are also global *trends*. The global trend toward *renewal* was first documented in *The Restoration Economy* (2002). The global trend toward *integrating* our natural, built, and socioeconomic environments can be readily perceived in any discipline that works with one or more of those environments. Ask almost any civil engineer, land use planner, ecologist, sociologist, or economist "what is the primary trend/challenge within your discipline," and they'll likely say something like "finding ways to better-integrate the health of nature and cities."

The global trend toward effectively *engaging* stakeholders in decisions that affect the future of a community is similarly widespread. Planners, economic development professionals, politicians, environmental groups, and academic institutions, and other institutions are all finding that the path to progress involves better engaging the people whose lives they affect.

Despite their ubiquity, these three trends have never been formally recognized as the drivers behind the most positive changes in how we design and manage our world. As a result, they've been addressed in a symptomatic, piecemeal manner.

If you want to bring your growth initiatives in line with these three global trends, you'll need to change how you make economic (and other) decisions. Thus, the three renewal rules: (1) base your economic growth primarily on *renewing* your existing assets (rewealth, in other words)—rather than on finding or creating more assets—to maximize both economic growth and quality of life; (2) integrate those renewal activities to maximize efficiencies and to tap synergies; (3) engage all stakeholders to maximize support, resources, and knowledge for these activities. So, the power of applying the rules comes in part from aligning your community with these three megatrends.

How would the world be different if economic growth not only avoided worsening our environmental and social problems, but actually reduced them with each passing year . . . threw them into reverse? What if environmental restoration, social revitalization, and renewal of our buildings and infrastructure were not just occasional activities within our economic system, but the very pillars on which it rested. . . its basis of operation? What if this restorative economic model were universal applicable and completely inclusive, benefiting all countries and people, rich or poor? Sounds insanely idealistic, no?

We spent the entire first chapter on the global trend from dewealth to rewealth, but we'll revisit the subject here from some different perspectives, because rewealth is the most important of these three renewal rules.

Not all forms of economic growth are the same, but you'd never know that from our public dialog. "Economic growth" itself is often intoned as the grail, without any modifiers to indicate whether it's destructive or restorative growth. The most vigorous growth in a human body is often malignant . . . cancerous. Other forms of excessive bodily growth lead to life-threatening obesity and crippling gigantism. We're usually careful to distinguish between healthy and unhealthy growth when discussing our personal bodies. When it comes to our community "bodies," though, we tend to treat all growth as good.

In the human body, as in any natural system, there are three basic modes of activity: new growth (expansion), maintenance/conservation, and renewal (death is part of the renewal process). The labels change according to the particular discipline that's studying the system, but they generally boil down to those three dynamics.

All three of those modes are rigorously measurable, and clearly distinguishable from the others. None is based in philosophy, politics, or opinion. None is good or bad, smart or dumb, green or brown, sustainable or unsustainable: they are cyclical modes of the mystery we call life. They create new stuff, maintain existing stuff, or restore/replace old stuff—end of story. It's that kind of clarity we now need in public policy, economic theory, and business strategy. This is the trimodal development perspective first documented in *The Restoration Economy*, so I won't belabor it here.

Once that trimodal perspective is adopted, it immediately becomes clear (to objective observers, anyway) that *restorative* economic activity is by far the most desirable in any already developed community. It has the same—if not greater—profit potential for business and public revenue potential for government as new development. But, unlike new (or destructive) development, it's not a one step forward, three steps back situation: you're not replacing long-lasting assets like watersheds or historic buildings with relatively short-lived assets like a big-box store. In fact, you're enhancing your long-lived—often irreplaceable—assets while earning a profit.

Just as creating a new building is a very different process from restoring an old building, so too is the process of creating a new community very different from revitalizing an old community. We have plenty of codified knowledge and off-the-shelf tools regarding the former, but precious little of either regarding the latter. There's no shortage of case studies and inspiring stories of revitalization, of course. But there are few rigorous systems for revitalization, complete with underlying theory, organizational taxonomies, precise vocabulary, metrics, and the like. Let's see if we can't remedy that situation to some degree.

The Quest

For most of the past few decades, environmentalists, social activists, innovative economists, and enlightened policymakers have been striving toward a seemingly unreachable goal. They've been trying to figure out how to achieve economic growth that doesn't cause environmental damage, traffic congestion, cultural destruction, or social dislocation. They want a nondestructive economy, in other words.

But that's not good enough for some people. More recently, the *most* forward thinking among those economic idealists have added another, even more ambitious agenda to that goal. They not only want a development mode that avoids damage, they want economic growth that will undo damage *already* inflicted on nature, cultural heritage, and communities. They want a "restoration economy," or, to put it in a single word, a reconomy.

But renewal is often driven by the public sector, and the public sector is often driven by politicians—politicians who want to be reelected. Getting reelected means producing visible or measurable outcomes in time for the next election. That means the renewal program has to produce *rapid* results. Nothing wrong with that: most of us prefer gratification sooner rather than later, especially if we also get the later gratification.

But even rapid renewal isn't good enough for a few of the more unreasonable folks (like myself). These whackos want rapid, *resilient* renewal. They're not satisfied with a short-lived burst of economic growth derived from a single "magic bullet" project. They want a restoration economy that continuously renews their natural, built, and socioeconomic assets in an efficient, holistic manner . . . treating them as interconnected elements of the same complex system. They are tired of seeing projects (restorative and destructive alike) "stovepiped" . . . carried out in silos as if they were irrelevant to each other.

Resilience doesn't just come from integrating the renewal of your natural, built, and socioeconomic environments, though. It also comes from effectively tapping the vision and knowledge of local stakeholders, and giving them an active voice in their future. This rectifies all manner of social ills. Resilient renewal truly serves the public good . . . *all* of the public; children and elders, recent immigrants and landed gentry, poor and middle class, regardless of ethnicity or religion.

Rules won't suffice, though. Achieving rapid, resilient renewal requires a way to effectively envision, fund, and implement actual projects based on those rules. The good news is that there's actually a reliable recipe for rapid, resilient renewal . . . really. I call it "the *re*solution," and it's revealed in Chapter 4.

The three renewal rules should guide policies and decision making at all levels of a community or region. They should also be used by businesses and investors who wish to earn a reliving, revitalizing the world.

A Closer Look at the Renewal Rules

Saying there are laws of economics does not imply that we will ever be able to make perfect predictions about the economy, but it does imply that we might someday have a far deeper understanding of economic phenomena than we do today. It also means that economics in the future may be able to make prescriptive recommendations about business and public policy with a level of scientific authority that it has not had before.
—Eric D. Beinhocker, *The Origin of Wealth*
(Harvard Business School Press, 2006)

Take the Beinhocker excerpt above, replace the word "economics" with "community renewal," and it helps explain why renewal rules are needed.

I see revitalization visions, regeneration mission statements, and renewal goals by the hundreds, due to the nature of my work. Whether European, African, Asian, or American, they start sounding the same after a while. They all tend to paint grand vistas of enhanced functionality, wealth, status, beauty, health, quality of life, and community spirit.

They share the same good intentions, but most also share the same problems. When it comes to achieving those dreams, they lack simple principles to guide day-to-day decisions in those directions. Without a significant change in the nature of their decision making at *all* levels, their big projects and programs tend to die the death of a thousand cuts.

So, my holy grail quest was to come up with the smallest number of principles that would cover all of the important decisions, and to express them in the fewest possible words. Thus, three renewal rules of one word each: rewealth, integration, and engagement.

Gail Bingham, CEO of the conflict resolution firm RESOLVE says, "Principles are a category of tools." She also points out that natural resources management is more about governance than resources, and governance is principles-based.

Each of the rules is based in common sense, and most revitalization efforts are already strong in at least one of them. But the spectacular revitalization successes, almost without exception, are strong in all three. Each rule will improve a situation if implemented individually, but surprising, near-magical turnarounds usually derive from implementing all three together. Here they are again in a bit more detail:

■ Rule number 1: *Rewealth* (asset renewal) for a better present and future. We must stop destroying our quality of life by compulsively building more and more of what no one wants more of. We must base our economy primarily on renewing what we've developed, and on restoring what we've damaged.

■ Rule number 2: *Integrate* for efficiency and synergy. We must shift away from renewing our natural, built, and socioeconomic assets in isolation. Renewing them in an integrated manner produces synergies that make projects vastly more efficient. Integration also stimulates opportunities by enhancing the natural ripple effect, whereby each renewal project makes adjacent properties more valuable.

■ Rule number 3: *Engage* for relevance and support. We must shift away from nontransparent, command and control, "decree" styles of community redevelopment. We must reengage all stakeholders in their revitalized future. This will result in higher quality visions, strategies, and plans. It will generate greater public—and thus political—support for your plans. This helps eliminate last-minute project delays caused by stakeholders who learn of projects too late in the process. Stakeholders should be engaged up front in the community vision, and each project partnership should help achieve that vision.

Since each of those three rules is also a trend, implementing them is getting easier with each passing year. People are feeling a pull in these directions already. Examples of integrative and engaged approaches in government are more common than one might expect. Once one starts looking for it, it's not that hard to find. For instance, in April of 2006, the U.S. Department of Transportation published a report—inspired by the White House Council on Environmental Quality, sponsored by the Federal Highway Administration, and primarily written by Janice W. Brown—called "Eco-logical: An Ecosystem Approach to Developing Infrastructure Projects."

Here are a few excerpts: "Eco-Logical is a guide to making infrastructure more sensitive to wildlife and ecosystems through greater interagency cooperative conservation. . . . it is possible to significantly contribute to the restoration and recovery of declining ecosystems and the species that depend on them, while cost-effectively developing the facilities, services, forest products, and recreation opportunities needed for safety, social well-being, and economic development. . . . integrative planning can start immediately. Arrange the pieces while moving forward. . . . forming partnerships between Federal, State, and local governments, tribes, landowners, foreign governments, international organizations, and other stakeholders."

Integration is the natural state of our world, but centuries of efforts by specialized disciplines to carve out a defensible professional niche—along with centuries of bureaucratic and scientific efforts to make the world measurable by isolating its parts—have fragmented and detached assets that can only work properly when connected as a whole. That's why I usually say "reconnect," rather than just "connect": we're restoring the natural connectivity that we only recently lost to the artificially isolated environments of modern planning and engineering.

Likewise, engagement is the natural state of *healthy* communities (I emphasize "healthy" to avoid confusion with "normal"). When you look at the management style of many tribes, you might say engagement is part of our human heritage, even though many have never experienced it in their lifetime. Most people are leery of change. It's thus better to talk of restoring some desirable behavior from their heritage, rather than imposing a brand new behavior on them. Dysfunctional, devitalized communities can often find a point in their history where citizens were more engaged in their mutual future, and where the economy's dependence on natural resources was more obvious.

Centuries of power-mongering by royalty, elected officials, experts, dictators, and (most recently) major corporations have significantly lowered citizens' expectations regarding involvement in their futures. This is why many community leaders get away with paying lip service to engagement: any increase in engagement feels good, even if superficial. An example would be holding a yes/no referendum on a huge community redevelopment initiative that has been reduced to those two options without stakeholder engagement.

> Engineering and the social sciences have always been elements intended to improve society. However, there is little interaction between engineers and social scientists in the western world.
>
> **—Dr. Patricia D. Galloway, professional engineer (PE), CEO of the Nielsen-Wurster Group, Director of National Science Board, and Chair of the Society for Social Management Systems, from her March 14, 2007, blog on www.ENR.com**
> *(Engineering News-Record)*

Catastrophe restoration is one place where the lack of proper integration and engagement has produced catastrophically bad responses to disasters. Too often, the urgency of the situation is used as an excuse for purely top-down decision-making. This is justified during the initial response, which benefits from military-style expediency. But disaster recovery efforts frequently fail to get out of that mode. As a result, they tend to create simplistic strategies (if they have a strategy at all), such as focusing almost exclusively on physical (usually urban) infrastructure.

While infrastructure is—in fact—usually the most critical need, they fail to achieve the overall goal of restoring security and prosperity. The needs of the rural populace are often ignored, which eventually destabilizes the urban areas. Cultural and environmental needs are also ignored, creating a destabilizing force that works against the effort for as long as they remain unaddressed.

Such excessively urban rebuilding efforts are probably the single biggest cause of the difficulties being experienced in rebuilding Afghanistan. The Taliban's strength has always been in the rural areas: by not better integrating natural area restoration and agricultural renewal—and rural communities—into the recovery plan, rebuilding efforts have been stymied by a Taliban that keeps reemerging.

In their 2007 book on effective communication, *Made to Stick* authors Chip and Dan Heath made this comment about the checklist they use for the creation of ideas that stick in peoples' minds: "The SUCCESs checklist is intended to be a deeply practical tool. It's no accident that it's a checklist and not an equation. It's not hard, and it's not rocket science. But neither is it natural or instinctive. It requires diligence and it requires awareness. This book is filled with normal people facing normal problems who did amazing things simply by applying these principles (even if they weren't aware that they were doing it)." Replace "SUCCESs checklist" with "renewal rules" and everything they said applies perfectly to the subject at hand.

Let's now examine how each rule relates to the others.

- Rewealth: Most communities make some effort at revitalizing themselves, but few achieve—or even shoot for—the ideal of rapid, resilient (and preferably regional) renewal. Sometimes that failure is because their rewealth policies or programs have "de" components that taint the entire enterprise. This was demonstrated in Northern Virginia when an ambitious transportation infrastructure renovation bill was voted down a few years back because it contained a sprawl-inducing highway or two. They got all the attention.

- Integration: Other times, renewal doesn't occur due to a lack of efficiencies and synergies among the projects. This is usually the result of renewing individual assets in isolation from each other. Much money is spent on individual rewealth projects, each of which is worthwhile, but the lack of proper sequencing and connectivity among them undermines the overall goal of revitalization.

  Rather than just integrating your assets, it's helpful to think in terms of integrating your solutions. For instance, in Africa, many advocate relegalizing big game hunting as a way to monetize endangered species, thus giving local people a reason to conserve or restore their populations. Assuming that this is a legitimate strategy, it's unlikely to work in isolation: it's far too simplistic. Add ecological, watershed, and agricultural renewal to the agenda though, and the chances of success are far better, thanks to increased funding and public support. Integrated solutions needn't be large scale or complicated, though: a single family home can be restored in a way that also helps restore the heritage, the watershed, and the ecology of the area.

- Engagement: In still other situations, the failure to revitalize derives from programs or policies that don't match citizens' goals, that aren't communicated well, or that feel imposed. A paucity of engagement undercuts the power of rewealth in part by diminishing knowledge-based action. Taking action without sufficient public support results in costly delays from protests and lawsuits. Some such projects divide and traumatize communities for years.

Developers are often concerned that broad stakeholder inclusion may lead to a loss of project control and demands for unfeasible design solutions. . . Developers who work in regions that are politically difficult gain support through charrettes. They often succeed in becoming "the good guy" in the eye of the community, making it easier to get their project built. These developers may eventually become well known and sought after by places seeking quality development.

—promotional copy from the website of the National Charrette Institute (www.charretteinstitute.org)

Let's look at the engagement principle a little closer, since it's probably the most vague of the three . . . the most difficult to define and measure. The above quote from the National Charrette Institute (one of many organizations focused on the engagement trend) promotes the use of charrettes. The charrette is a design and planning tool based on stakeholder engagement. It's being increasingly used, especially in the United States, by architects, developers, planning agencies, and private planning firms.

But charrettes often turn into charades. Like most stakeholder engagement tools, they are often abused, so they have a mixed reputation. Many charrettes are just a way of going through the motions of stakeholder engagement . . . a way to compartmentalize the engagement, giving it a clear beginning and end, and thus claiming that the citizens signed off on the design. Conducted properly and applied to appropriate situations at the right time, though, they can be effective.

The sponsor's sincerity isn't the only thing that determines "good" or "bad" engagement. The project itself can determine that: if it's a destructive sprawl project, then using a charrette or other public engagement tool is like offering a condemned prisoner a choice of noose, gas, electricity, bullet, or wild dogs. Engaging the public in unnecessary sprawl projects is better than not engaging them, but their community still ends up damaged.

Redevelopers have a big leg up on developers in that respect, since well-designed rewealth projects don't damage valuable assets, and they restore previously damaged assets. Who could object to that? Combining stakeholder engagement with redevelopment thus creates a "sweet spot" that's worth aiming at. Integrating the renewal of a community's natural, built, and socioeconomic environments greatly expands that sweet spot. Partnering to fund and implement the project turns that planned sweet spot into a funded one that can enhance your quality of life, as well as the quality of life of your human and wildlife neighbors.

When applying the integration rule, communities will often find that the majority of their work consists of undoing the work of previous planners. It's not just the built and natural environments that were artificially separated, but neighborhoods and income classes. As Urban Institute researcher Tom Kingsley says, "Nothing in American social policy has failed more than putting all the low-income people in one place."

> *Our research findings suggest that the practice of river restoration in the United States is motivated by good intentions, but suffers from disconnected approaches and very little evaluation and feedback.*
> **—Emily S. Bernhardt, Ph.D., Assistant Professor in the Department of Biology at Duke University (concerning a study published in the September 2007 issue of Restoration Ecology)**

One of the many advantages of integrative approaches is that they provide paths to regionalism. For instance, heritage restoration programs are often difficult to scale from community to region, but if they are part of a renewal strategy that includes transportation or watershed renewal, those agendas will often provide the logical connections. Transportation and water are probably the two most effective regional integrators. Regionalism is an ultimate goal that will be assumed throughout the book, even when only the word "community" is used.

Effective stakeholder engagement helps resolve conflicts between restoration needs and cultural/religious beliefs. An example of such a conflict is in India, where the revered 12th century ruler Parakrama Bahu said "Let not one drop of water reach the sea without first serving man." This well-meaning philosophy surfaced in a day of much lower human population density. It is still greatly honored in the crowded India of today, resulting in dried-up rivers and disappearing wetlands.

Some Rules Are More Equal Than Others

As stated earlier, one of the renewal rules is more crucial than the others. Of overriding importance is the economic shift from dewealth to rewealth. That one shift by itself could save our world.

The other two rules—asset integration and stakeholder engagement—are how we supercharge that renewal. We're now in the realm of the Holy Grail . . . we're galloping Rocinante toward the impossible dream. This allusion to Don Quixote's wryly named horse, Rocinante, is apt: *rocinante* means "a reversal." We're galloping toward a reversal in the way we earn our wealth. It's the only solution to what ails us.

We're way beyond being able to fix problems like global hunger, global poverty, and global warming by doing less damage: only *reversing* existing damage could possibly put the brakes on such crises.

> *An object seen in isolation from the whole is not the real thing.*
> —Masanobu Fukuoka, *The One-Straw Revolution*
> (Rodale Press, 1978)

Integrating the management of our natural, built, and socioeconomic environments would yield many benefits, but—without renewal—it's not a world saver. Engaging stakeholders in the future of their communities is undeniably laudable, but without renewal there won't be sustainable economic growth. Without the economic refocus on rewealth, integration and engagement simply produce more efficient management and more just governance. Only renewing the community's assets will harness those two excellent principles for the creation of rapid, resilient renewal.

Rewealth puts the water back in the swamps so that frogs and fish can breed. Rewealth restores functionality to historic buildings, returns flow to dammed rivers so fish can spawn, reinstalls efficiency to decrepit infrastructure, reintegrates productivity on family farms, and replenishes the quantity and quality of drinking water.

This "re" focus is popping up in some surprising places. Howard Gardner, psychologist and professor of cognition and education at the Harvard Graduate School of Education, created the theory that people have more than one kind of intelligence (such as "emotional intelligence"). In his new book, *Changing Minds: The Art and Science of Changing Our Own and Other People's Minds*, he posits that there are seven "levers" you can pull to dislodge set ways of thinking. All seven begin with the prefix "re."

Hyperconservative pollster Frank Luntz, in his 2006 how-to book on spin-doctoring, *Words That Work: It's Not What You Say, It's What People Hear*, lists "21 words for the 21st century." One is actually a category of words; those beginning with "re," such as "restoration," "renovation," "rejuvenation," and "renewal." It's basically the same twenty-first-century word list published in *The Restoration Economy* four years earlier, when I called this the "re" century.

Here's a passage from *An Inconvenient Truth* by Al Gore: "Now it is up to us to . . . make moral choices that would change the policies and behaviors that would, if continued, leave a degraded, diminished, and hostile planet for our children and grandchildren—and humankind. We must choose instead to make the 21st century a time of renewal . . . [in order to] have a future as a civilization."

I believe [the anti-immigration] movement endangers the single most important reason for American greatness, namely, the renewal, reformation and reawakening that's provided by the continuous flow of immigrants.

—**Rudy Giuliani, October 10, 1996 speech at Harvard's Kennedy School of Government. (He switched to an anti-immigration stance while seeking the Republican Presidential nomination, but these "re" words remain valid)**

Any time you find Frank Luntz, Al Gore, and Rudy Giuliani singing the same tune, you've got an engaging principle at work. "Re" might thus be the key to making crucially important issues nonpartisan. Bringing the discussion down to day-to-day business, here are some "re-word" excerpts from a press release from Caterpillar, Inc. regarding an agreement they signed with China's National Development and Reform Commission (NRDC) to promote China's remanufacturing industry. The first three are from Caterpillar officials:

- "We are proud to be a pioneer in this industry and look forward to supporting China's 4R initiative: reduce, reuse, recycle and remanufacture."
- "Remanufacturing is a highly sophisticated form of recycling that takes end-of-life components and turns them into like-new products for a fraction of the cost."
- "Our remanufacturing business is one of the fastest growing parts of our company."
- Madame Zhao Jia Rong (of China's NRDC) said, "It is beneficial for China to learn . . . to promote the development of the recycling economy."

"Recycling" sounds like old news, but one could view that three-decade-old trend as the first wedge of the reconomy. It's now growing from recycling beer cans to recycling cities to recycling the planet. Let's simplify the lesson here: if it doesn't start with "re," it probably shouldn't be a major portion of our economic model.

We desperately need to be able to separate destructive development from restorative development in our daily conversation, as well as in our budgeting, planning, and policymaking. The dewealth/rewealth terminology helps clarify how human civilization will earn its living on this planet in the coming centuries. As the old Danish proverb says: "Life is not being dealt a good hand, it's playing a bad hand well." Today's children have been dealt a mess of crises. Playing this hand well requires a "re" strategy that turns this mess into a wealth of restorable assets.

I'm not decrying all "de" words, of course, nor denying that some are positive. Let's avoid a fundamentalist mindset that wants rules to be both simple and absolute.

Dedicated devotees of restorative development in Denver, Delhi, Devon, and Detroit would decisively deck me—and declaim me as a deviant—if I deliberately defamed, denigrated, and defiled them by defining "de" in a devilish and deriding manner. In defense of "de"—and in deference to Democratic delegates and demographers—there are many delightfully delicious "de" words we have derived to describe the decent things we hold dear.

Not all "de" words depress the economy, denude the environment, or demoralize society. *De*nsification is a core component of renewal strategies in cities worldwide. *De*construction of buildings (as opposed to demolition) enables components to be reused or recycled, rather than destroyed and delivered as detritus. Even *de*molition is essential to regeneration: sometimes a structures is not worth saving, and removing them is key to restoring the value of the underlying property. All of nature is based on a constant interplay of destruction, death, degeneration, denitrification, defecation, and decomposition to achieve replacement, renewal, reuse, regeneration, and regrowth. The Hindu deity Kali represents this cycle, and most other religions depict it in one form or another.

A Declaration of Rapid, Resilient Renewal

Let's enshrine the three renewal rules in a declarative statement. With it, you can formulate public policy, guide related legislation, create teams or organizations, and write supportive goals/mission statements. "We resolve: (a) To increase our reliance on rewealth and decrease our dependence on dewealth. (b) To integrate the renewal of our natural, built, and socioeconomic environments. (c) To effectively engage all stakeholders in the vision and strategy of our renewal."

Why do I keep harping in "rapid" and "resilient"? Why don't I just say "renewal" and be done with it? Because so many tragic mistakes have been made in the name of renewal. I'll touch on it here, but we'll return to it in Chapter 4—because rapid, resilient renewal should be your performance specification, not just your goal.

Your renewal needs to be *rapid* because redevelopers are working on borrowed money, politicians needs results in time for reelection, and citizens need to see results in order to maintain enthusiasm for whatever they're being asked to support. Even foundations want speed: most of them expect measurable impact from their donations within three years.

Your renewal needs to be *resilient* for the same reason that you want your personal good health to last. Revitalization is essential not just to increasing your quality of life, but to inspiring confidence. Investors, redevelopers, employers, and new residents all need to feel confident not only that your quality of life and economic health are good, but that they will last, and even improve. Decisions today are all about the future, so don't expect to inspire lasting confidence from a renewal that's too simplistically based.

Buying banners and benches for you main street, an aquarium for your waterfront, or a stadium for your team can all be important elements in a renewal, but too often, a community's future is pegged to an single asset—such as an employer that's been stolen from another community via tax breaks—rather than to a process. That kind of "consumer" approach—"let's buy this and we'll be all right"—seldom lasts.

The same goes for making your revitalization initiative overly dependent on a single local person, especially one who might not survive the next election. With resilience, a key political or private champion can become mired in personal scandal, and the renewal initiative will survive.

A resilient initiative has vigor and integrity of its own; it's not borrowed from a sponsoring agency. Resilient community renewal means it will continue on its own trajectory even in the region goes into a tailspin. But, if you add the "regional" element to the strategy's goals—rapid, resilient, regional renewal—your community's renewal will likely gain additional resilience. It will have the added support of a healthier regional economy. A resilient economy for your region means that it will be more likely to continue on its renewal trajectory, even if the state, province, or nation goes into recession.

Lastly, "resilient" describes an initiative that not just survives revision and evolution, but that thrives on it. The initiative won't die no matter how many necessary changes are made in its goals, strategy, leadership, or members.

It's even possible that your renewal initiative could go into hiatus at some point, owing to circumstances beyond your control (like civil war). But with sufficient resilience, it will rise again when the time is right. On the other hand, "resilient" doesn't mean "invulnerable." If someone of sufficient power wants something dead, it will die. Fortunately, revitalization has few enemies.

All great changes begin in conversation.
—Juanita Brown

Those who have studied the sad legacy of planning and the engineering-to-death of our natural environment in the twentieth century will recognize the relevance of the renewal rules. The widespread asset destruction and massive social suffering caused by bad planning and inappropriate applications of engineering would likely have been avoided had those three rules been applied to any reasonable degree.

What was then called "urban renewal" (the "destroy it and they will come" philosophy of revitalization) demolished rather than restored, separated rather than integrated, and was imposed by imperious planners and designers (epitomized by Robert Moses) rather than created via engagement of those affected. In other words, it was the exact opposite of the urban renewal practices that actually work . . . the ones documented in these pages. (Of course, planners and engineers weren't entirely to blame: their tragic practices were often policy driven. They were just following orders.) Again, we'll return to the goal of rapid, resilient renewal, and how to achieve it, in Chapter 4.

A Solution to Everything?

> When markets don't work properly, when capital and expertise are scarce, governments weak, and the democratic voice limited, societies don't deal well with serious and complex challenges like a declining environment. So poor countries often find that they're squeezed in a vise. On one side they have large and still-growing populations with rapidly rising economic expectations that depend heavily on an ever more degraded environment. On the other side they have persistent economic and political weaknesses that keep them from coping effectively with environmental problems. Eventually . . . some of these countries can crack under the pressure.
> —**Thomas Homer-Dixon**, *The Upside of Down: Catastrophe, Creativity, and the Renewal of Civilization* (**Island Press, 2006**)

In his wonderful book (quoted above) Dixon reported "Haiti is now locked in a downward, self-reinforcing spiral of ecological, economic, and social breakdown." This actually describes Haiti's condition for at least the past half century, and it started with excessive dewealth activities that went unchecked because of the weak governance left in place by their French colonial rulers. Homer-Dixon also observed of the world economic trends (responding to those who say humanity can survive on an information, technology, and service economy), "There's little evidence of a general decoupling of economic production from resource consumption."

In this book, you'll read stories of what happens when the three rules come together. Haiti is what happens when all three are missing. Despite its long history of inept and corrupt governments, the tailspin really started with the wholesale destruction of Haiti's natural environment. Of course, the two issues really can't be separated: a degraded environment is a sure sign of inept or corrupt governance.

Why are all-encompassing solutions so seldom offered, other than those of a spiritual or metaphysical nature? One reason might be that problem solvers tend to suffer from the same silo mentality that spawned the problems. This relates to the oft-repeated Einstein quote: "We can't solve problems with the kind of thinking that created them."

Another discourager of holistic, universal solutions is the giggle factor. No one likes to be laughed at, and what endeavor is more likely to evoke giggles than attempting to solve all of the world's problems in three words? Hopefully, this author will be somewhat insulated from the giggle factor by the fact that I didn't invent the three rules: I merely detected and aggregated them. They were conceived, tested, and evolved in innovative communities all around the world.

The three rules, of course, do not constitute a solution, per se: solutions only come from action. But decisions drive actions. The renewal rules give policymakers, planners, designers, academics, and redevelopers a decision-making framework for research, education/training, and practice. For instance: there's a great gap between the demand for "re" professionals and the amount of "re" curricula in our schools. This could be partly addressed by properly engaging the academic sector in most restoration and revitalization, so that the projects become field extensions of the classroom, and the professionals doing the projects become mentors. The renewal rules are thus more of a path to the all-encompassing solution, rather than the solution itself. They should drive your vision and strategy, but you'll still need professional planners and redevelopment partners to make things happen.

In the past, attempts at healing communities were similar to what's referred to as "Western," "modern," or "allopathic" medicine, which is less than a century old and still mostly experimental. As a former military medic, I can attest that Western medicine is great at helping a patient through a crisis, such as a gunshot or a pedestrian-truck encounter. But it fails miserably at doing no harm.

Almost everything in the modern Western medical arsenal is poisonous or traumatic. When the body "goes bad," we punish it by ripping out organs, severing connections, irradiating it, suppressing its immune system, and introducing antibiotics (their literal definition is "antilife"). This is in contrast with the 6,000-year-old Indian and Chinese medical systems, which are based on strengthening the body's ability to heal itself, and on not doing any harm whatsoever.

Likewise, strengthening a community's capacity for self-renewal is a far better investment than simply focusing on remedying a particular community problem. Just as herbs or acupuncture are far cheaper than surgery, so too is building a community's capacity for renewal far cheaper than an endless series of imposed, uncoordinated renewal projects.

As mentioned earlier, the urban renewal "cure" for metropolitan maladies that rampaged through our cities in the 1950s, 60s, and 70s took the surgical approach, ripping out old buildings, severing old neighborhoods, and suppressing diversity with single-use zoning. Urban renewal did more physical damage to U.S. cities than all the foreign armies/terrorists ever did in the history of the nation, and the disease we created here in the late 1940s spread worldwide.

Rural areas suffered their own version of the disease, replacing diverse economies with high-input monoculture farms dependent on government subsidies. As with single-use zoning, such a paucity of diversity leaves an area highly vulnerable to being fatally damaged by a single factor, such as a change in subsidy levels, a natural disaster, or foreign flight of industry. The socioeconomic immune system is too weakened to fight back.

When all three rules are properly addressed, they can be the foundation of a resolution to most of our economic, environmental, and social problems. If such a "grail of growth" were universally applied, it could solve many intractable global problems. The good news is that there are already real-world examples of communities that have come close to this Holy Grail. My goal here is to document some of those successes, identify their best practices, and perfect their formula so we can follow their lead globally.

These three rules need to be accepted as normative on a global scale. Social scientists use the term "normative" to describe the cultural belief structures that regulate social activity. These generally accepted norms (such as love for one's family), which balance the occasional anomalies (such as crime), have a constant normative effect, which guides society toward a certain level of desired homogeneity, which in turn enhances stability. Religion, art, and philosophy have been the traditional manufacturers (or codifiers) of norms. Rewealth, integration, and engagement are the proven factors that augment both economic growth and quality of life.

This puts promotion of the normative factors of the Age of Rewealth directly in the hands of community leaders; business, academic, political, citizen, and nonprofit. While I won't usually include the news media in my listings of stakeholders—and they shouldn't be engaged in all aspects of a revitalization initiative—it can be disastrous to forget them when they *should* be engaged.

Why is it so important to engage the business sector? Because profit is the nutrient of sustained action. Farmers work their land expecting to get more nutrients (energy) out of it than they put into it. Fishermen build boats and go to sea expecting to return with nutrients in excess of their expenditure. Aboriginal hunters and gatherers expect the same. That's profit.

Profit is what makes an activity both sustainable and expandable. Expandability is what allows individuals and society to move from bare survival to comfort and security. Comfort and security—having more than one needs at the moment—increases one's ability to help others. If that profit-making activity is restorative, then people and planet profit as one.

> *"Courts in many states are taking increasingly close looks at local land-use decisions.*
> *. . . in challenges to local decisions, courts today often ask, 'How did they reach that*
> *decision?'"*
> **—Eric Damian Kelly, "Making Motions and Creating a Record,"**
> *Commissioner* **(American Planning Association)**
> **Winter 2008**

The renewal rules can be used as a basis for more detailed rules. They can also be used—by courts or citizens' groups—as a high-level evaluation of decisions that affect the community. For instance, many communities have assembled "tool boxes" of useful practices. These are used for broad issues like economic development and land use, as well as for specific issues such as heritage, brownfields, greenspace, education, etc. But when these toolboxes lack structure or don't have a basis in principles, they are basically just grab-bags of ideas.

I refer to this as the "shake-and-bake" approach to planning. Decisions are thrown into these grab-bags in the hope that they will come out coated in social, economic, or environmental responsibility. My suggestion is that the three renewal rules provide a structure—some underlying principles—that enable communities to organize such tools, and to eliminate those that don't pass the rewealth-integration-engagement test.

Drug-Induced Economic Growth

Here in the United States, our government likes simple mechanisms. Natural ebbs and flows are frowned upon. When the economy heads in a direction that's bad for the image of those in office, hands reach for either the tax-reduction lever or the interest-rate-reduction lever. Our government thinks those are the only two levers it has, so it pretends that high taxes or high interest rates are what caused the "problem." Governments have more levers available, of course, but they aren't as simplistic.

Since national economies are primarily aggregates of local economies, and since my research indicates that local economies grow faster and better when they obey the three renewal rules, my suggestion is that national governments embed the renewal rules in policy and legislation, offering communities incentives for applying them. That strikes me as being better for the economy in the long term. And it gets us away from our current "pharmaceutical" approach to economic management, whereby taxes and interest rates are administered like economic uppers and downers that eventually wear down our national immune system.

Cities and nations are complex adaptive systems, just as are beehives, ant colonies, and coral reefs. They have tremendous powers of self-organization, and miraculous powers of healing.

External factors like war, industrial exodus, and natural catastrophe get most of the credit for decline, as do physical factors like failed infrastructure or resource collapse. But internal factors are often at work. No one measures or reports on them, so these declines remain a mystery (not that economists will have any shortage of forensic explanations). Complex adaptive systems tend to be driven by a few simple rules. I posit that the renewal rules should be the rules on which we base our communities from now on.

Chapter 3

Reversing Our Relationship with Earth
The delayed-but-inevitable transition: from depleting developers to restorative residents.

Once there was a time,
We took whatever we wanted,
To survive now, put it back.
—**Brother Lawrence**

Norilsk, Russia is considered one of the ten most polluted places on the planet. Its population of 210,000 people sees nothing but dead trees, when they can see anything at all through the filthy air and highly acidic rain. This has been the situation for half a century in this former Siberian gulag. While officials are working to reduce the pollution being emitted by their metal industries, a new industry is emerging that will clean up the meter-thick layer of heavy metals lying on the city, and in the bottom of its waterways.

A new breed of miners, working for a contracting firm called Poligon, are harvesting this nickel- and palladium-rich sludge, so that it can be reprocessed. They call the sludge a "technogenic" source of ore. With nickel currently fetching over $36,000 per ton, the city finds itself covered in a "restorable asset" that had previously been seen as nothing more than a tragic, expensive problem. Norilsk could be considered emblematic of our planet's future.

. . .There are situations where [one] needs great imaginative power, combined with
disrespect for the traditional current of thought, to discover the obvious.
—Arthur Koestler, *The Sleepwalker: A History of Man's*
Changing Vision of the Universe
(Hutchinson & Co., 1959)

German philosopher Georg Wilhelm Friedrich Hegel (1770–1831) said that civilizations collapse "from a morbid intensification of their first principles." Dewealth has been the first economic principle of human civilization for some five millennia. It follows, then, that we're in trouble: the rate of "de" activities has intensified exponentially over the past two or three centuries.

Rewealth only works when you have something to renew, so it's how new civilizations are built on old. Mother Nature uses dewealth at times: some ants build colonies that eradicate almost all life and organic material from the surrounding area. Beavers build dams that flood meadows full of beautiful flowers (and flood those ant colonies). Thus, the dewealth model is not inherently "bad." It becomes self-destructive when done in excess, or when pursued too long. When a civilization has enough "stuff" (built environment), it needs to switch from physical expansion to economic expansion, from sprawl to renewal, from quantity of life to quality of life.

When the transition from sustainable to nonsustainable is made by a species in nature, it's usually because (1) the population performing the dewealth activity has become too large, (2) the species has switched from nomadic or migratory to sedentary, thus eliminating the land's rest period, when it recovers from their presence, or (3) the species has been transported to—or connected to—a new environment that has not evolved controls for that species' activities.

We see the second dynamic here in Washington, DC, where huge flocks of Canada Geese have decided that migration is too much work. They've taken up year-round residence, damaging local ecosystems that used to have extended rest periods to recover from their twice-yearly visits. Like these sedentary geese, humanity is in long-term residence on this planet, but we're still depleting and dumping as if we were just passing through. Since we're not likely to be giving this planet a rest anytime soon, we need to build recovery into our mode of existence here . . . into our economic system.

Dewealth/rewealth transitions are not a new phenomenon. Long-lived cities with growing populations have always made the switch from sprawl to restorative mode; that's why they were long-lived. What's new is that the de/re shift is now happening on a planetary scale for the first time in human history.

Three Global Crises, Two Possible Responses

In *The Restoration Economy*, three global crises—contamination, corrosion, and constraint—were identified as the catalysts behind the rapid trend toward restorative development (rewealth, for short). The first—contamination—needs no explanation;

it affects all of our natural and built environments. The second—corrosion—applies only to the built environment; it refers to the world's immense inventory of decrepit/obsolete buildings and infrastructure.

The last—constraint—refers to the limits of sprawl; we're often destroying critically important, irreplaceable assets like watersheds and cultural treasures when we could and should be enhancing the capacity of our urban areas. This sprawl is driven by three things: (1) our growing population, (2) our increasing per capita land use, and (3) public policies that fail to encourage renewal and reuse of the places we've already developed, or that make this "greenfield" development artificially profitable.

These three crises have afflicted human civilizations to some degree for thousands of years. It would be profound enough for any of these three local crises to strike on a global level. But, as the last millennium pulled to a close, all three crises went global simultaneously.

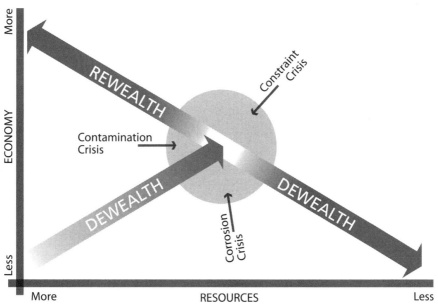

Figure 1 This "turning point" graphic illustrates how we have built our global economy on resource depletion, and how three global crises are forcing us into wealth creation that renews our resource base. If we turn "right" instead of "left," both our resources and economy decline. (See color plate.)

Traditionally, when the three crises hit a village or city, they had three options: recede, relocate, or restore. If a town chopped down all their forests and their topsoil washed away as a result, they might get hit with drought, famine, and economic decline. At that point, they can enter a phase of revitalization by restoring their forests and farmlands. Or, they can continue without restoration, in which case their economy and quality of life will continue to deteriorate, leading to collapse. This collapse can be delayed if they try to make their dewealth model less destructive (greening it), but collapse they will. Their third option is to simply pack up and move to a place with virgin forests and farmlands (or conquer neighboring tribes/countries and take theirs).

> But there is a more fundamental problem, too: there is just not enough land to grow all we need for food and fuel. Market theory suggests that high prices should lead to increased supply, with more yield per hectare and more hectares planted. Trouble is, there are few unused hectares. ". . . it will be hard to even maintain current yields," says [Snow] Barlow, head of agriculture at the University of Melbourne, Australia.
>
> —Deborah MacKenzie, "World's Poor Are Up in Arms as Pressure on Crops Grows," *New Scientist*, January 26, 2008

Now that the three crises are global, the relocation option has disappeared. That leaves us with the other two options. Maintain a deconomy and go into prolonged recession, or switch to a reconomy. By adopting regenerative practices ourselves, the latter option would complement the planet's own regenerative abilities. Human civilization and Mother Nature (or Gaia, if you prefer) would be working together for the first time, making us *truly* part of the solution. (There is a fourth option: undergo a drastic reduction in the human population. This would allow the planet to naturally regenerate, saving us from doing a lot of active restoration. Any volunteers?)

I say "truly" above because corporate and nonprofit PR campaigns have been telling us for decades that we can be part of "the solution" if we buy their greener products, or support their efforts to pressure government into reducing pollution. These are undoubtedly all good things: but not the solution. As pointed out earlier, there's a world of difference between doing less new damage and undoing previous damage . . . between being "green" and being restorative.

The Over $100-Trillion Market

While it didn't use the terms "dewealth" or "rewealth," *The Restoration Economy* documented that motivation for the shift to restorative development always came in the form of those three crises: contamination, corrosion, and constraint. Let's take an updated look at them.

Contamination is huge. In February of 2007, the U.S. Government Accountability Office reported that $12 billion will be needed to clean up contamination from 117,000 leaking underground gasoline storage tanks (UST). The EPA has already spent about $10 billion on UST remediation in the past two decades. This new $12 billion covers only 54,000 tanks that have been abandoned, and for which no party can be made accountable. Another 63,000 UST cleanups would be funded by property owners and their insurance companies. But that's not all: at least 43 of the 50 states are expected to discover an additional 16,700 leaking tanks over the next five years or so.

That puts the total cleanup bill around $50 billion. Consider: that's just for a single, fairly modern country's gasoline tanks, a very small part of the world's inventory. What's more, underground tank cleanup is just one of *thousands* of different types of large-scale contamination issues. Many contamination issues—such as combined sewer overflows—are linked to the corrosion crisis: our crumbling, outdated infrastructure. The EPA estimates that renovating U.S. wastewater systems will cost $390 billion.

The corrosion crisis is what happens when the majority of your built environment—infrastructure and buildings—is in need of renovation, redesign, adaptive reuse, or replacement. In 2007, the U.S. Army Corps of Engineers listed 120 aging levees that are subject to catastrophic failure. An article entitled "*Lights! Water! Motion!*" by Viren Doshi, Gary Schulman, and Daniel Gabaldon appeared in the Spring 2007 issue of Booz Allen Hamilton's *Strategy + Business* magazine. It estimated the global infrastructure renovation/replacement backlog at almost $41 trillion.

> *Aging water and wastewater infrastructure in many parts of the world and concern over ever-shrinking supplies of water and other resources are driving a sizzling global environmental market. Industry insiders say that projects are plentiful as developing nations continue to update and upgrade deteriorating or inadequate water infrastructure ... According to Dick Fox, chairman and CEO of Lexington, Mass.-based Camp Dresser & McKee Inc., drought and competition for water in many parts of the world are leading cities and nations to move toward a total water management approach. "It will be imperative with all of the changes that many of us anticipate with*

climate change to think of the urban water environment holistically," he says. "Over the years, people have separated the parts of the water cycle. We've separated storm water from wastewater from drinking water." Cities and nations increasingly will need to look at "closing the water cycle," he said.

—**Pam Hunter, "Environmental Market Strong as Developing Nations Update Facilities,"** *Engineering News Record,*
December 24, 2007

But it isn't just about restoration or replacement: we should be building infrastructure that's worth restoring in the future, not disposable 50-year bridges. The cost of over-building infrastructure is merely the extra initial investment. The cost of under-building infrastructure is community decline, higher maintenance bills, and even human tragedy, as recent bridge collapses worldwide attest.

This is probably a good place to introduce the definition of infrastructure that I've been using since I started lecturing on revitalization in 2001. Given the importance of flows to the vibrancy of a community—and given the inability of the general public (and many design professionals) to concisely define infrastructure—I came up with this: "Infrastructure is everything that connects our built environment and allows for flows: flows of power, people, goods, food, water, sewage, solid waste, and information."

It should be noted that Europeans have a more comprehensive view of infrastructure. They divide it into two categories, economic and social. These two categories are further divided into hard and soft. Hard economic infrastructure includes such things as roads, ports, telecommunications, and power. Soft economic infrastructure includes workforce development, trade incentives, encouragement of research and development, and technology transfer. Hard social infrastructure includes such things as schools, hospitals, water and wastewater, and prisons. Soft social infrastructure would be social services, environmental protection agencies, and social security.

Booz Allen Hamilton's $41 trillion infrastructure renewal figure doesn't even include buildings or "soft" infrastructure: it's just the narrow American definition. The United States has two billion square feet of abandoned industrial space and six billion square feet of vacant retail space, and there's plenty of old office, residential, and public buildings in poor shape to boot. Add in the cost of building renovation, restoration, and reuse globally, and we're well on our way to $100 trillion. Add to this the remediation of contaminated sites. Toss in the restoration of agricultural lands, fisheries, watersheds, ecosystems, and catastrophe damage. At that point, we've likely blown *way* past $100 trillion.

When was the last time you heard of a "new" $100 trillion market? It's not new because these problems (called "restorable assets" when in the reconomy) only just appeared. After all, many of these assets have been in need of restoration for decades, or even centuries (over a millennium, in some cases, such as the Roman Coliseum).

What makes it a new market is that these restorable assets have suddenly become viable business opportunities. This is the result of two things: (1) "re"-oriented policy changes, government projects and incentives, and technologies, and (2) pressure and urgency produced by the three crises. As most businesspeople know, urgent needs are the most profitable. Just ask the healthcare industry, or Halliburton.

The constraint crisis has been the primary driver of many rewealth-oriented policy changes. In the United States, these policies often go by the name "smart growth." Such policies don't have much rigor or underlying theory, and are more about land use planning than the economy as a whole. Smart growth is basically an intelligent dialog, not a system: it's a collection of good design principles and redevelopment tactics. Nonetheless, it's been a wonderful first step into the reconomy for many cities.

The toxic combination of population growth plus dewealth is forcing us to destroy many "permanent" or irreplaceable natural and cultural assets on which we depend. This constraint crisis has spawned many environmental groups and historic preservation groups, forcing them to get deeply involved in economic policy and planning.

Everything has its time and place. These three crises (climate change is an aspect of the contamination crisis), especially when combined with our continuing population growth, make it obvious that rewealth's time is here and now.

All effective responses to the three global crises—contamination, corrosion, and constraint—have the same core dynamic at work: they are all "re"-oriented. They are redesigning and replacing infrastructure and manufacturing technologies that pollute. They are remediating and redeveloping contaminated land. They are restoring and reusing old buildings. They are revitalizing both human communities and wildlife habitat. When environmental groups speak of humankind's "exceeding the carrying capacity of the Earth," what they are really talking about is exceeding the ability of the planet to sustain our *de*conomy. Our *re*conomy is a completely different story.

Dewealth Sinkholes, AKA "Economic Subsidence Events": How to Undermine Your Economy

On February 23, 2007, a 330-foot-deep sinkhole swallowed several homes, people, and vehicles in Guatemala City. The primary cause? A leaking sewer main.

A few years earlier, the good folks in Kentucky were wondering why their lovely state was falling out from under them. They were plagued by an attack of subsidence events (popularly known as sinkholes). Commuters would come out to their cars in the morning, only to find them at the bottom of 10- or 20-foot holes. Various geological and hydrological explanations were posited, most of them blaming Mother Nature. Then, someone had the bright idea of overlaying a map of these subsidence events with a map of previous coal-mining activity. Whoops! It was an almost perfect match.

Knowing the cause doesn't solve the problem, but at least now they can better predict where sinkholes will occur. Here's a question for you: is the cost of the damage done by these coalmine-induced sinkholes included in the price we pay for coal-fired electricity? I think not. This is just one of the many ways in which fossil fuel (and nuclear) power is made to look artificially cheap: many of the long-term costs are born by society, rather than by the energy and mining companies.

But, let's get back to sinkholes, because your future is standing on a big one. In 2005, it was announced that half the town of Kiruna, Sweden would have to be moved. In early 2007, they announced that a new site, $2^1/_2$ miles away, had been chosen. Some buildings will be demolished, and some historic ones will be deconstructed and reconstructed at the new location.

Why would they move half a town? Two reasons: (1) Iron mining at the world's largest subsurface mine had eroded and destabilized the ground under the town, and (2) the mining company wants access to an additional 800 million tons of ore, and the town is in the way. It's estimated that the move will cost about $4.28 billion, but it hasn't yet been decided who's going to pay the bill. The mayor also wants the federal government to give them the equivalent of another half a billion dollars for a tunnel to connect the two halves of the town.

The move is expected to take place over 40 to 50 years. Before you feel too sorry for them, know this: "The people in Kiruna have known since 100 years ago they were living on iron ore," said Vice Mayor Hans Swedell in a 2007 Reuters article. "They knew that sometime they would have to move." Now, you might be saying "How could they possibly not know who's going to pay for it? The mining company should pay, of course, with additional help from the feds." But the mining company is owned by the federal government. Whoops.

Such are the long-term, hugely expensive responsibilities that come with building a society primarily on dewealth activities: eventually, the foundation falls out from under your creation, sometimes literally. Dewealth economies inevitably get hit with two crippling blows: their sources become scarcer and more expensive to extract (or, like fisheries, collapse completely), and the bills come due for cleaning up the mess. In other words, revenues go down while costs go up. If that were happening to a business, investors (and employees) would be scrambling for the exits.

When these two highly predictable gut punches hit a society that's at the end of its dewealth phase—or even overdue for its de/re shift—the results could be referred to as "economic subsidence events." Since we've been mostly in dewealth mode worldwide for five millennia, we're sitting on an insipient economic sinkhole of planetary proportions. But there's a way to refill that void (*devoid?*) before it collapses: rewealth.

Having the planet fall out from under our feet strikes me as a pretty good indication that we've reached a turning point. Guatemala, Kentucky, and Kiruna aren't isolated, unusual phenomena, either. Subsidence events due to mining, groundwater depletion, oil extraction, plus leaking sewer and water mains are proliferating worldwide. The latter are common here in Washington, DC. But mining areas are lucky, in a way: if only all of dewealth's costs to society were as are obvious as theirs.

Many of the worst dewealth-derived crises are delayed, emergent, and/or incremental effects, such as global climate change, or the buildup of contaminants in an estuary to the point where a fishery suddenly disappears. Who pays then, when the offending industries are long since merged into oblivion or are out of business?

In Kiruna's case, the bills will likely be born by a partnership of the mining company, the federal government, and the town. You'll be hearing a lot about public-private partnerships in this book, because that's the future; that's how the really big revitalization projects are happening, and how the majority will happen this century.

How do the Kiruna townspeople—who like to call themselves "the no-problem people"—feel about the iron mine now? They see it as an opportunity to remake their town from a blank slate, in the best way possible. "The mine must go on, I think. But it doesn't matter to me so much," said Stig Loskog, a local automobile dealer, in that same Reuters article. "You can't have everything for all time."

You can't deplete everything for all time, Stig, but you can restore everything for all time. However, you can only switch to rewealth if your dewealth activities haven't irretrievably undermined the community you want to restore, as they have in half of Kiruna.

Population Growth and Urbanization Accelerate the De/Re Shift

> *The late 20th Century was the age of economic globalisation. The first part of the 21st Century will be the age of the city, the "Urban" Age. With investment in urban real estate, infrastructure and renovation becoming the driving force behind economic growth, the physical and social landscapes of the city are being powerfully altered. Urban policymakers are struggling to balance this massive growth in public and private investment with more sustainable forms of urban development. . . . The design of the built environment, the distribution of urban density, and their impacts on social inclusion and quality of life, are at the forefront of political discussions in towns and cities across the globe. Politicians, investors, planners and architects are, in effect, becoming "inebriated" with cities. . . . We need to come to grips with the social hangover' that will result from this sustained investment in the physical restructuring of cities worldwide to avoid the disastrous human consequences of so much "planning" of the last 50 years.*
>
> —Anuradha Bhattacharjee, March 2, 2007, Development
> Gateway Foundation website promotion
> for Urban Age conference

The year 2008 is the first in human history in which the global human population will be primarily urban. Contrary to popular belief, most of the population growth in the world's largest metropolises is coming from within the city, not from rural in-migration. That's not to say that the abandonment of marginal agricultural lands isn't a major global trend; it is. But it's not always a bad thing. In many cases, the lands that are being abandoned never should have been farmed in the first place. People were literally forced by their government to attempt a farming lifestyle there, as in China during Mao's Cultural Revolution. Other times, population growth forces people out into ever-poorer land.

The upshot is a positive new trend, in which ecological restoration is taking place on ever-grander scales as these damaged former farms become available. This allows regions to restore their wildlife, restore their watersheds, hold back desertification, and create new parks (desperately needed in many countries that weren't wise enough in the past to set aside public green space).

Growing inequality is analogous to global warming. Its effects are diffuse and long term, and there's always something more pressing to deal with. The question is how much more unequal world income distribution can become before the resulting political instabilities and flows of migrants reach the point of directly harming the well-being of the citizens of the rich world and the stability of their states.

—Robert Wade, British economist, "Winners and Losers,"
The Economist, April 26, 2001

In 1948, J.M. Juran (a founder of Total Quality Management) observed: "To be in a state of self-control, a person must know: what he is supposed to do, what he is actually doing, what choices he has to improve results wherever necessary. If any of these three conditions are not met, a person cannot be held responsible." Most public managers—while perfectly familiar with redevelopment and restoration in general, don't realize they have a choice in the basis of their wealth. They don't view their world through all three lifecycle modes of wealth creation (dewealth, prewealth, and rewealth), so they don't see the sensible, essential alternative to economic growth at the end of the asset lifecycle: rewealth.

Thus, they violate all three of Juran's requirements for self-control: (1) they don't know they are supposed to be renewing, not sprawling; (2) they don't understand the full consequences of what they are actually doing; and (3) they're not familiar with their full range of choices. The trimodal development perspective (see glossary) helps remedy the first problem. Full-cost accounting (in trimodal format) would solve the second problem to a large degree.

Familiarity with rewealth policies and tools would resolve part of the third problem. The other part of the third problem's solution comes from understanding relevant trends. Two of the most relevant trends to this discussion are population growth and urbanization.

You've probably heard the reports of lower rates of birth around the world. It's important to understand the numbers, however. Sure, India's population is now "only" growing at about $1^1/_2\%$ annually, but that still adds 16 million *per year* to their population. China's rate is about half of India's and even that amounts to a growth of almost 11 million annually, which is almost equivalent to the yearly creation of a new Beijing. Most lesser-developed countries' growth rates are closer to India's than to China's. The few developed nations whose populations are shrinking slightly have relatively small populations, but those countries have grabbed the headlines.

By 2050, it's expected that developed countries will have roughly the populations they have today, but that the populations of lesser-developed countries will grow by $2^1/_2$ billion people. Another bit of demographic dynamic that's important to keep in mind is the confluence of this population growth with the global urbanization trend: while a given country's overall population might "only" go up by 1% annually, the populations of their major cities are likely to grow at two to four times that rate.

In Jared Diamond's *Collapse: How Societies Choose to Fail or Succeed* (2004) he analyzes five historical societies that imploded, and offers insights of value to our modern world. He identified five factors leading to these collapses. In every case, overexploitation of their environmental resources was involved, as was the society's failure to respond appropriately to early symptoms of collapse. These two base factors were sometimes exacerbated by a changing climate, loss of a critical trading partner, and/or the hostility of neighbors.

> . . .*We can't escape the conflict between our growth, resource, and environmental imperatives. At best, by improving efficiency, conserving resources, and cleaning up pollution, we can diminish this conflict a bit. But we can't come close to eliminating it. That's a real problem, because there's no sign we're about to give up our commitment to growth.*
>
> —**Thomas Homer-Dixon**, *The Upside of Down: Catastrophe, Creativity, and the Renewal of Civilization* (Island Press, 2006)

Homer-Dixon's comment above is correct, as long as that improved efficiency, that conservation, and even that contamination cleanup is happening within a deconomy. But those conflicts largely disappear in a reconomy, where the basis of economic growth is the renewal of our natural, built, and socioeconomic assets.

In the past, most pollution was organic (with the exception of metals contamination from operations such as lead and silver smelters), so local contamination crises (such as that afflicting Angkor Wat in what is now Cambodia) quickly reversed themselves after the civilization receded. Sending civilization into decline isn't a politically viable solution to our present day environmental problems, though, so we're unlikely to see it proposed (although some administrations seem to be pursuing that objective without asking our permission).

Besides, we now have thousands of persistent, human-made toxic compounds—plus huge amounts of heavy metals—that won't quickly disappear, even if we do.

Only human efforts can clean them up in time to avert an acceleration of the catastrophe that is already upon us, upon wildlife, and upon future generations.

Diamond would likely include the contamination crisis under his "unsustainable resource use." The corrosion crisis could likely be traced back to an inability to pay for infrastructure renewal, which could be linked to Diamond's "loss of a critical trading partner" factor. The constraint crisis is often directly related to Diamond's "hostile neighbors" factor. Competition for natural resources—land in general—has traditionally been the leading cause of war, no matter what noble cause the political or religious spin doctors offered their publics as an excuse. War has been human civilization's traditional cure for a local constraint crisis, and it's no different today, except that the crisis is now global.

We can't relocate our global civilization, but many of us haven't quite come to grips with that reality, so we're still in "pioneer mode"; still searching for deliverance via discovery of new land and resources. Hundreds of cities around the world have already switched to reconomies, while many are still reflexively sprawling. The sprawlers are compulsively creating more and more of what few of their citizens want more of. They just don't know what else to do.

Most of those city-scale reconomies are emergent and spontaneous, largely the result of the free market's responding to local manifestations of the three crises. Few of them are adequately supported by public policy, even though many of these initiatives were catalyzed by the public sector. In fact, many of these reconomies emerged *in spite of* deconomic policies, dewealth-based building codes, and massive sprawl subsidies. Imagine what could happen when the power of the free market is nurtured and magnified by public policy that's driven by the renewal rules.

Sprawl has "worked" in China for over 5,000 years. But now that they are destroying their best farmlands, choking on vehicle and factory fumes, running out of water, and suffocating in dust storms, they have to overcome five millennia of de-based cultural tradition in order to solve these crises. Younger civilizations have the same obstacles, but they aren't as deeply entrenched.

After such a long history, Chinese policymakers will likely find many restorative principles and examples on which to base new policies that draw on their rich culture. They just need to look for them in a systematic manner. Beijing was founded around 1122 BC, so you can bet that a whole lot of restoration has taken place over the past 3,000 years. And it continues today: The restoration of the massively-polluted Beijing-Hangzhou Grand Canal—the largest human-made waterway on earth—was recently begun, and the photo on the cover of this book depicts the expanding deserts of western China that they have been trying to hold back by planting over 50 billion trees by hand during the past 27 years.

So, there's nothing new about restoring the world. What's new is making it the basis of our economy, rather than an alternate mode that's called upon after one or more of the three crises hit.

Much as we might like to see a global reconomy that is based *entirely* on rewealth, the fact remains that the global urbanization trend is forcing many cities to sprawl, often in an unplanned, squatter-based manner. What's more, the growing global population is forcing some countries to build entirely new cities, most famously in China and the United Arab Emirates, some in a "green" manner.

Dewealth thinking is rapidly being revealed as a failed model, a "dead end," as is illustrated by the story of Shenzhen, China. Shenzhen was recently a bucolic little fishing village. It sits in the Pearl River delta, close to Hong Kong. In 1980, the Chinese government declared it a "special economic zone." Fueled by a pure dewealth growth formula of cheap land, unenforced environmental rules, and desperately poor laborers who would put up with abuse, the city grew at an average rate of 28% annually until 2005, when it slowed to 15%.

Here's an excerpt from Howard French's article on Shenzhen in the December 19, 2006, *New York Times*: "Shenzhen became the literal and symbolic heart of the Chinese economic miracle. Now, to other cities in China, Shenzhen has begun to look less like a model than an ominous warning of the limitations of a growth-above-all approach. 'This path is now a dead end,' said Zhao Xiao, an economist and former adviser to the Chinese State Council, or cabinet. After cataloging the city's problems, he said, 'Governments can't count on the beauty of investment covering up 100 other kinds of ugliness.' . . . Shenzhen's boom has spread little wealth. Gunfights, kidnappings and gang warfare are rife, and crime rates are skyrocketing. 'Shenzhen may seem prosperous,' a worker said . . ., 'but it's a desperate place.'"

Let's move now from Shenzhen to Donglu. The farmers of Donglu village can't sell their wheat, because the kernels are hollow, twisted, bitter tasting, and caked with soot. The cabbage is black, and all the pollinating insects are gone, so the fruit trees no longer produce. The farmers are surrounded by a hellish scene of smokestacks, slag piles, and a haze that often limits visibility to 300 feet (cars leave their headlights on during the day). Half the drinking water wells are badly contaminated, everyone coughs all of the time, and what comes up is also black.

In fact, out of China's 560,000,000 urban residents, only about 5,000,000 (fewer than 1%) breathe safe air, according to European Union standards. The national water situation is even worse, with over a third of the rivers (and most of the urban rivers) so polluted that the water can't be used for industry or agriculture, much less drinking. This isn't surprising, since 278 of their cities (accounting for half the national population) lack sewage treatment systems.

When thinking of urbanization, one normally envisions desperate farmers arriving in the city from remote locations. But sometimes, the city comes to them. Formerly bucolic Donglu was overrun by the sprawl of Linfen (population 4.3 million). The World Bank has called Linfen the most polluted city in the world, yet this industrialization has been extremely sudden. It was referred to as the "Modern Flower and Fruit Town" in the 1980s. What does one do in a situation like Linfen? Does rewealth have any role when people are still blinded (literally, in this case) by the jobs and increased incomes generated by this explosion of dewealth? The obvious answer is probably not.

As the latest arrival on the industrial scene, China is the first major country to have had the choice of industrializing without the usual environmental damage. The government consciously rejected learning from others' mistakes, and chose to do it the old-fashioned way. The situation will get far worse before it gets better. The question is whether the resulting national near-death experience—likely to hit within the next 15 years—will stimulate China to reverse direction. China has an unusual ability to do things in a grand manner; will the world's rewealth technology leader emerge from this crisis?

Timing is everything. Restoration is part of the natural lifecycle of every living organism on earth, and of every complex system created by those organisms. Change is usually stimulated by discomfort, deprivation, fear, or pain. That's what motivated Linfen's former farmers to switch to an industrial dewealth model, and the same four motivations will shift them to a rewealth model . . . in time. When far-sighted leadership is lacking, those four catalysts are all we can rely on to stimulate a economy. The good news is that they are very reliable catalysts.

There are at least three silver linings to the urbanization trend: (1) dense cities have far greater capacity to implement efficient waste disposal systems than do low-density areas, (2) the depopulation of the countryside creates opportunities for environmental renewal as farms are abandoned, and (3) the rising populations are forcing cities to focus on enhancing the capacity of the built environment they already have.

What did the Easter Islander who cut down the last palm tree say while he was doing it? Like modern loggers, did he shout "Jobs, not trees!"? Or: "Technology will solve our problems, never fear, we'll find a substitute for wood"? Or: 'We don't have proof that there aren't palm somewhere else on Easter, we need more research, your proposed ban on logging is premature and driven by fear-mongering"?

—Jared Diamond, *Collapse: How Societies Choose to Fail or Succeed*
(Viking Adult, 2004)

In the end, Jared Diamond's *Collapse* showed that a single dynamic is the primary destroyer of all civilizations: they reach a point where declining natural resource productivity—the result of centuries of unsustainable resource use—combines with increased demand. That increased demand is the result of two factors: population growth, combined with the increasing per capita resource usage that comes from rising incomes.

In other words, there's an overlap period, during which the more sophisticated technologies (arising from decades or centuries of dewealth activities) bring about an increase in a society's standard of living, just when the natural resource base is declining in its ability to support that standard of living. We entered that period on a planetary basis several decades ago.

Communities Are Key

All development is not created equal. Communities that set low standards or no standards will compete to the bottom. If you are afraid to say no to anything you will get the worst of everything. On the other hand communities that set high standards will compete to the top.

—Ed McMahon, Senior Resident Fellow, Urban Land Institute

At the national level, there has been precious little progress in shifting from dewealth to rewealth policies, primarily because of powerful lobbying efforts by huge dewealth industries (mining, lumber, fossil fuels), combined with the fact that most federal watchdog agencies are effectively run by the industries they are supposed to be regulating (such as the Departments of Energy and Agriculture in the United States).

But, look at cities like Barcelona, London, San Francisco, New York City, and Chicago, and you get a very different view of the world: the shift from dewealth to rewealth has been rapid and extensive. None that I know of has consciously used the three renewal rules as a decision-support tool for public policy, but all have intuitively moved toward rewealth in place of dewealth. Their renewal programs aren't as integrated or as engaged as they would be if the three renewal rules were formally recognized, but all are producing excellent outcomes, if only because of the sheer volume of rewealth activities.

This is why I've long maintained that nations would be far better off recruiting their presidential and prime ministerial candidates from the ranks of mayors than from governors and (especially) senators. Mayors (good ones, anyway) grasp the process of revitalization on a visceral level, and have to deal with it daily. Senators usually deal with it only when a revitalization-related bill comes to the floor, at which time their concerns are usually limited to "who sponsored it?" and "what do I owe them?" There are exceptions, of course. In the Fall of 2007, Senators Hillary Clinton and Chuck Schumer—along with Congressman Brian Higgins—introduced the Neighborhood Reclamation and Revitalization Program Act of 2007 (HR 3498 and S. 2054). This act seeks to provide federal funding for demolishing vacant housing stock, thus setting the stage for redesigning and renewing post-industrial cities in transition.

Many metropolitan areas are already experiencing economic growth that doesn't destroy valuable assets, and that actually *enhances* quality of life for all, while *increasing* the natural resource base. Many of these pioneering reconomies are also (to varying degrees) now reaching the next step.

They are realizing that simply increasing the quantity of rewealth activities isn't enough: they must increase the efficiency of those investments and the quality of their results. Good management and high quality standards on each project will help, but the major increases in the return on your revitalization investments will come from applying the other two renewal rules: *integrating* for more efficiency and synergy, and *engaging* for more information and support.

The "environmental justice" movement, for instance, melds environmental issues with issues related to low-income and minority populations. There's a movement within the brownfields remediation/redevelopment industry to ensure that cleaned-up sites aren't recontaminated. There's a movement within the economic revitalization "industry" to better engage stakeholders, such as the National Trust for Historic Preservation's Main Streets program in particular, and the public-private partnership trend in general.

Another valuable confluence occurs when the "green" trend and the restorative development trend meet. There's already a well-established movement within the historic restoration industry to use greener materials and technologies. Reusing an existing building is obviously greener than building a new one. Even the greenest of new buildings will usually require decades, if not a century or more, to recoup the embodied energy lost when an older building is demolished. When you total up the energy it took to build it along with the energy it took to mine, manufacture, and transport the building materials, it's usually immense.

So, a "sweet spot" is found when an older building is renovated or restored using the latest in green techniques and materials. This convergence is picking up speed, as witnessed by the addition of a "Green Remodeling" track (not just a session, but a whole track of sessions) to the 2007 National Association of Home Builders' National Green Building Conference.

The Decline of Dewealth, and the Rise of Rewealth

> *Urban centers are hubs simultaneously of breathtaking artistic innovation and some of the world's most abject and disgraceful poverty. They are the dynamos of the world economy but also the breeding grounds for alienation, religious extremism, and other sources of local and global insecurity. The task of saving the world's modern cities might seem hopeless—except that it is already happening.*
> —**Worldwatch president Christopher Flavin,**
> *State of the World 2007*

In Pasadena, CA, 85% of new housing permits are for their old central district. Nearby Los Angeles, that poster child of sprawl, has gone into reverse: for the past few years, their formerly dead downtown has been attracting residents at a faster rate than the suburbs, and this reversal was accomplished purely via rewealth activities. They are now entering a new phase in this renewal that harnesses all three renewal rules, as epitomized by their master plan for their $2 billion revitalization of the Los Angeles River corridor. If Los Angeles can do it, your community can do it.

Why is dewealth in decline? Consider three facts: (1) As mentioned earlier, we've been gradually depleting, degrading, and developing our world for 5,000 years, and we shifted to a frantic pace 300 years ago; (2) The human population has grown rapidly for 5,000 years, and shifted to explosive growth 300 years ago; (3) Our planet is the same size it was 300 years ago, and (prepare to be amazed) is even the same size it was 5,000 years ago. You do the math.

This same-sized planet is now covered with aging infrastructure, dilapidated buildings, contaminated land, exhausted farms, expanding deserts, denuded watersheds, and dying ecosystems (terrestrial, aquatic, and marine). Is it any wonder that a shift from plundering and sprawling to replenishing and revitalizing is both inevitable and overdue? Is there any sane person who thinks the model of the past 5,000 years will work for the next 5,000 years? Or even for the next 50 years?

The global de/re shift is thus inevitable, and it's well underway where all global socioeconomic shifts begin: in communities.

Won't Preservation and Conservation Save Us?

During the past three decades of the green movement—conservation, pollution reduction, and the like—terrestrial animal species have declined by 31%, according to World Wildlife Fund's 2006 Living Planet Report. I could spend the rest of this chapter listing other alarming global environmental indicators—such as fish stocks, freshwater stocks, climate change, and agricultural productivity—but it shouldn't be necessary. Unless you've just returned from an extended tour of Uranus, you already know that things have become worse—far worse—since we woke up to our current model's lack of sustainability, and started "doing something about it."

Now, the time has come to wake up again. We have to realize that greening a destructive economic system won't lead to a sustainable world any more than improving the quality of warfare will lead to peace. People are catching on fast. In 2004, while all other U.S. states were bemoaning their failed "no net loss of wetlands" policies, North Carolina had a net *increase* in wetlands. This was thanks in large part to better-integrating their infrastructure renewal strategy with their wetland restoration/mitigation strategy.

We're finally starting to measure some of the right things, like tracking habitat loss, species endangerment, and pollution of many kinds. But measuring our decline at this point is like cleaning the windshield of a powerless airplane as it plunges toward the ground: we'll be able to better monitor the crash, but that won't make it less painful. We can extend the flaps and delay the impact a little bit, but that's about it. The world is now perilously close to a crash-and-burn scenario. What we need to do is to *gain* altitude, not just slow the rate of decent.

What's especially tragic is that so much energy by so many good people has been focused on decreasing the rate of our descent. The sense of false security this created ("someone's doing something about it") along with the focus on the impending crash has deflected attention from restoring power and regaining altitude.

Meanwhile, our rate of descent has actually been accelerating. Clearly, this period of putting green lipstick on the pig of dewealth must come to an end. It's time to abandon, rather than improve, our decrepit deconomy.

> *The object in life is not to be on the side of the majority, but to escape finding oneself in the ranks of the insane.*
> —**Marcus Aurelius (121–180 AD),**
> **Roman emperor and Stoic philosopher**

Want to hear something insane? Catastrophic contamination is good. Overcrowding and traffic congestion are wonderful. Resource depletion crises—freshwater, fisheries, topsoil—are lovely. Species endangerment is great. Our plague of corroding, abandoned, obsolete buildings and infrastructure is just peachy.

Why? Because without these crises, we wouldn't be making a critical shift that we "should" have made last century; the shift from dewealth to rewealth . . . the shift from being exploitive pioneers to being restorative residents. Now, thanks to those painful crises, the dewealth/rewealth (or just de/re) shift is well under way, and is accelerating impressively. Every one of those dollars, pounds, or pesos is making our world a better place: cleaner, prettier, more efficient, more biologically diverse, more prosperous, and more culturally rich.

> *We may be great problem solvers, but unfortunately we're increasingly creating problems that we aren't effectively solving. The sunny presumption that we can fix our problems once they get bad enough is undercut by the stark fact that some are already really bad, and they're not getting fixed. . . . Unalloyed and simplistic optimism about the future is really just denial in another guise.*
> —**Thomas Homer-Dixon,** *The Upside of Down: Catastrophe,*
> *Creativity, and the Renewal of Civilization* **(Island Press, 2006)**

The negative psychological and sociological effects of being surrounded by ugliness and dysfunction, and being deprived of exposure to nature—have been well documented in recent years. It's also becoming better understood that an increasing percentage of wars and civil conflicts are being fought over land or other dwindling natural resources (see books such as *Resource Wars, The Future in Plain Sight,* and *The Coming Anarchy*). Many of these resource wars are wrapped in religious, ethnic, or political "smokescreen causes," but, as police investigators like to say, "follow the money."

The result of this shift from a deconomy to a reconomy should thus set society on a course toward reduced warfare and other resource-based violence. This seemingly utopian vision is neither speculation nor prediction. Nor is it a fevered extrapolation of the renewal trend: real-world examples of the peace-generating effects of restorative projects are rife. Look at the story of how restoring the ancient Mostar Bridge helped restore relations between warring Muslims and Christians in Bosnia. Look at the way Israeli and Palestinian communities worked together (maybe a slight exaggeration) for a decade to restore the Alexander River they shared.

For an example of "restoring for peace" that's still in the making, look at why India is planning to restore mangroves along the coast of the state of Gujarat, which borders Pakistan. India's deconomy chopped down most of their mangroves, so their coastal fisheries collapsed. Desperate Gujarati fishermen risk being shot or jailed when they sneak along the Pakistani coast, where the fishing is still good. Why? Because Pakistan wisely conserved many of their mangroves, despite pressure from local industries to chop them down. In 2005, India began studying the feasibility of restoring mangroves along their Kori Creek and Gulf of Kutch. They are doing this partly to restore traditional fishing incomes that have declined because of their dewealth practices, and partly to keep tensions from escalating into bloodshed.

Given the current pervasiveness of war, famine, disease, and species extinction, it must be emphasized that it's the *trend* toward rewealth that's the current reality. We're still in a primarily dewealth-based deconomy, thus the continuing intensification of those three global crises (contamination, corrosion, and constraint).

> *Restoring agriculture is usually the first step in creating economic growth and laying the foundations for durable peace.*
> —Ian Johnson, Chairman, Consultative Group on International Agricultural Research (CGIAR), *New Scientist,* January 22, 2005, "Return to Eden" by Fred Pearce

It will come as no surprise to anyone who's paying attention that we do not yet have a global reconomy; one based primarily on rewealth. One only need look to China to see that there are places where the obsolete, self-destructive dewealth economic model still has a powerful wind in its sails. In most cases, these de-based economies are those that lagged behind those of Europe and the United States. They now believe the only way to catch up is to ape our path, complete with our mistakes, and without benefit of our lessons.

This is a symptom of our systemic reblindness: since we don't track or report on our own fast-growing, highly profitable rewealth sector, other nations are just as in the dark as we are about why so many of our major cities are coming back to life after decades of decadence and decay. We've reached a turning point.

One might wonder why such a simple, obvious distinction as dewealth versus rewealth has eluded us for so long. One reason is that, while all civilizations are born in dewealth, few survive long enough to enjoy rebirth, at least, not under their original culture or government. As a result, most of the history we study is the history of dewealth.

> *It is difficult to get a man to understand something when his salary depends upon his not understanding it.*
>
> —Upton Sinclair, *I, Candidate for Governor: And How I Got Licked* (1935)

Modern-day environmentalists and social activists who decry the overwhelming influence of extraction industries (mining, lumber, petroleum, extractive agriculture) in government need to realize that this is a completely normal situation. It's not a global conspiracy that's somehow unique in the annals of human history.

Who doesn't want renewal? Who doesn't want that renewal to be efficient and comprehensive? Who doesn't want all stakeholders to be involved—or at least consulted—in the renewal of their community? Answer: only those whose income is based on dewealth, whose expertise is narrow, and whose leadership style is dictatorial. In other words, the primary losers in the Age of Rewealth will be those who are not working in our best interests. The renewal rules can be used to identify them.

By the time the three dewealth crises—contamination, corrosion, and constraint—hit, the institutions whose fortunes are based on dewealth have little motivation to switch to rewealth. The rewealth perspective would reveal the price society paid for their success. They can be forgiven (well, understood anyway) for wanting to keep their proud legacies unsullied. The specter of mass torts is no small motivator for resisting the de/re shift.

After a 5,000-year global deconomy (interspersed with local reconomies), it should be no surprise that the old dewealth paradigm has more than a few well-entrenched and well-funded champions. Almost all private economists directly or indirectly work for dewealth industries, or do dewealth industry-funded research in universities. Almost all public economists work for government agencies that promote dewealth as their economic growth default. Both private and public economists find that their primary responsibility is often to justify whatever course their employer (or research sponsor) has already decided to pursue.

As a result, you get folks like the Massachusetts Institute of Technology's economics professor emeritus Morris Adelman. In his *The Economics of Petroleum Supply* (MIT Press, 1993) he basically denies that a concept like dewealth could even exist when he says, "Minerals are inexhaustible and will never be depleted." (Petroleum is usually counted as a mineral, despite its organic provenance.)

Dewealth industry-funded political groups are quick to turn assertions like Adelman's into dogma. Stephen Moore is a former president of the Club for Growth, a powerful neoconservative lobbying organization in the U.S. capital. Here's what he said in an April 18, 2002 *New York Times* article entitled *As 2 Sides Push, Arctic Oil Plan Seems Doomed*: "There is a belief on the environmentalist side that we are running out of oil, that we have to conserve energy. I'm adamantly opposed to energy conservation. We are not running out. All we have to do is go out and find it and produce it."

Let's make the unlikely assumption that Adelman and Moore's wishful dewealth thinking is correct. What then happens when we continue to transfer all those toxic heavy metals and carbon from underground storage into our air, water, and soil? We're already experiencing the answer to that question. It's not just a matter of supply, it's also about where those extracted source materials go, and in what form.

Our pathological disconnect between wealth creation and its effect on the world gets worse. Some of it is more based in human self-worship and a lack of empathy for other forms of life than it is in mercenary motivations, as the following quote from Peter Huber's *Hard Green: Saving the Environment From the Environmentalists, a Conservative Manifesto* (Basic Books, 2000) illustrates:

"We can go it alone. We need energy, nothing more, and know how to get it from many more places than the plants do. We don't need the forest for medicine; as often as not we need medicine to protect us from what emerges by blind chance from the forest. We don't need other forms of life to maintain a breathable balance of gas in the atmosphere or a temperate climate. We don't need redwoods and whales at all, not for ordinary life at least, no more than we need Plato, Beethoven, or the stars in the firmament of heaven. Cut down the last redwood for chopsticks, harpoon the last blue whale for sushi, and the additional mouths fed will nourish additional human brains, which will soon invent ways to replace blubber with olestra and pine with plastic. Humanity can survive just fine in a planet-covering crypt of concrete and computers."

Most educated, intelligent nature lovers with any concern for their children would hope Huber was trying to be funny. It's not likely, considering the rest of the book's contents, which author and reviewer James H. Kunstler characterized as "remarkably snotty."

Last Desperate Gasps: Some Dewealth Industries Are on Their Death Beds

Vast areas of northern Alberta, Canada sit on what's known as tar sands, where cold, solid underground tar is mixed with (you guessed it) sand. The government of Alberta sees this nasty stuff as their strategy for economic growth in a world of oil at over $100 per barrel, because that tar can be converted to liquid fuels. I say a lot of nice things about Canada in this book. This story isn't going to be one of them.

> Federal and provincial health officials in Alberta are trying to cover up "the most destructive project on Earth," aboriginal leaders said yesterday during the release of a report on the oilsands sector. The report, called Canada's Toxic Tarsands: The Most Destructive Project on Earth, and released by the leading green group Environmental Defence, accused the federal government of being "missing in action" by failing to enforce federal laws to clean up oil extraction from tarsands in Alberta. It said excavation of the oilsands in Alberta—home to the richest petroleum deposits outside the Middle East—is producing vast amounts of greenhouse gases and poisoning local water supplies. The process to strip the tar-like bitumen out of the sands and turn it into synthetic crude oil is highly energy intensive.
>
> —Mike de Souza, *The Gazette* (Montreal),
> February 16, 2008

To bring the tar above ground so that it can be refined into those fuels requires pumping steam and hot water into the earth, thus cooking the fragile, endangered boreal forest ecosystem. Natural gas is used to raise the temperature of the ground to the point where the tar can be sucked up, and more natural gas is used to boil the tar in water until the sand separates from it. It's a filthy process, and most of the toxic wastewater is simply dumped into surface ponds in the hope that someone will figure out what to do with it someday. The provincial government is reportedly turning a blind eye to this catastrophe in the making. They are apparently so overjoyed to have some kind of economic activity happening, that its impact on the First Nations people, and the wildlife of Alberta, and the planet's climate isn't of much concern to them.

If the process were efficient and the payoff huge, one might forgive the downsides. But this industry is burning one unit of the world's cleanest fossil fuel (natural gas) in order to create three units of the world's filthiest fossil fuel (tar is even dirtier than coal). Note: industry publicists have started calling them "oil sands" rather than the traditional (and correct) "tar sands." Apparently, "tar" sounds as dirty as it is, so now they're calling it "oil." It's pretty bad when your business is so environmentally unsound that you have to pretend to be in the oil business to make yourself seem clean . . .

In our oil-addicted world, with its rapidly-diminishing supplies, the tar sands development is the same sort of desperate insanity that drives a normally-law-abiding drug addict to kill an old lady and for one fix's worth of money. It's akin to a man who takes bites out of his own arm to keep from starving. This kind of self-destructive behavior is probably inevitable in the dying days of dewealth, as the momentum of 5,000-year-old deconomy delays the transition to a reconomy. In the absence of rewealth tools, people fall back on doing even more of what they've always done. To switch metaphors, it's like finding out you're digging for diamonds in the wrong place, and responding by digging faster, rather than by moving to where the diamonds are.

But *not* producing fuels isn't an option. Given the number of fossil fuel producing nations in the world, maybe one will try implementing rewealth strategies with petroleum revenue. Maybe the remaining flow of fossil fuels can be used to create a reconomy. Most Middle Eastern oil comes from countries that are deserts due to ancient deforestation, so there's no shortage of restoration to fund, and no limit to the natural resources that could be created in the process.

Before leaving Alberta, mention should be made of an excellent policy they've implemented that is worthy is being emulated worldwide. Alberta has many regular oil-drilling sites, in addition to the tar sands. The province requires petroleum companies to continue paying the lease on those properties after the oil runs dry, until the land is fully restored. (Of course, the key to the value of such policies rests in the definition of "restored.")

A vast remediation industry has arisen in Alberta as a result of this policy. The rewealth companies, rewealth workforce, rewealth research, and rewealth technologies emerging there are positioning the province as a potential reconomic leader.

This helps give Alberta a bright future beyond oil. If similar rewealth policies were applied worldwide—not just to oil, but to mining, forestry, fishing, and other extractive industries—many countries would find themselves with a future beyond dewealth.

Our economic shift from *de* to *re* is long overdue. One might say we're *re*tarded. Ending our economic *re*tardation might be the most wonderful thing humankind has ever accomplished.

The global dewealth crises are a decision point that every civilization must reach: history indicates that most previous civilizations have had as much trouble making the transition as we are having, as exemplified by the disappearance of the Khmer empire after 629 years, and the Mayan empire after a millennium. Individual cities within those empires—such as Angkor Wat—likely went through successful dewealth/rewealth transitions of their own, and might have fallen to conquest rather than to an unsustainable economic model.

Cities tend to be longer lived than nations or civilizations, so that's where we will primarily look for insights and models in Part II.

De-Re Schizophrenia

During this transition period from a global deconomy to a global reconomy, many communities and nations suffer from a malady I call de-re schizophrenia. (I'm using the popular "split personality" definition here: in clinical psychiatry, "schizophrenia" is the doctor's way of saying "I don't know what's wrong with you.")

De-re schizophrenia can strike individuals. For instance, most people have no trouble defining redevelopment: it's when you renew a property that was previously developed ... obviously. But apply it to people, and suddenly confusion sets in. People (and companies) who only do redevelopment are often called "developers," rather than "redevelopers." How's the reconomy supposed to grow when its own professionals don't know what to call themselves? Let's make this simple: developers sprawl, redevelopers renew. It's (almost) as simple as black hats and white hats.

> *If you are going to use a tree, you must do so with consciousness and respect for the environment. If you cut down a tree you should plant 10 more.*
> —Hugo Chavez, at the June 2006 inaugural ceremony for the
> Misión Árbol campaign, from "Venezuelan Reforestation
> Effort Takes Root," *EcoAméricas*, May, 2007

More frequently, de-re schizophrenia strikes places, rather than people. It manifests as a place that is destroying and restoring itself simultaneously. I can find examples in almost any sprawling nation, but I'm going to pick on Venezuela. I just want to get more of Latin America (which I dearly love) into the book for balance.

President Hugo Chavez's Misión Árbol reforestation project had a $23 million first-year budget. The goal is to reforest 370,000 acres (150,000 hectares). The program organizes peasant farmers, schoolchildren, and others citizens into conservation committees that design reforestation strategies for their land, and then pays them minimum wage (about $10/day) to do the work.

The program is making good progress, and environmentalists are quite happy with it. Many nations' "reforestation" projects (such as many U.S. Forest Service programs) are almost completely barren of wildlife, essentially commercial monoculture tree farms. They comprise only fast-growing, often nonnative species, designed to be periodically clear-cut by politically connected lumber and paper companies.

In Venezuela, the Misión Árbol program is paying peasants to gather the seeds of native trees such as cedar (*Cedrela odorata*), mahogany (*Swietenia macrophylla*), and apamate (*Tabebuia rosea*). Many communities have created tree nurseries, and four million of the five-year goal of 100 million saplings are already growing. These include critically endangered endemic trees like the walnut of Caracas (*Juglans venezuelensis*). "The idea is to use dozens of tree species, including threatened ones, that can serve as protective cover in upper river basins, provide shade for agro-forestry plantations of cacao and coffee, and provide timber at medium and lower elevations," said Miguel Rodríguez, deputy minister for environmental conservation in that same *EcoAméricas* article quoted above.

Sure, the program could be improved, such as expanding it to include damaged protected areas and river basins, but it otherwise sounds great, right? So where does the de-re schizophrenia come in? Every year, Venezuela loses twice the amount of forest that will be restored over five years. At 1.2% per year, Venezuela's rate of deforestation is twice that of Brazil. The country needs to get the illegal (but allowed by corrupt or inept officials) mining, lumbering, agricultural sprawl, and squatters under control. Otherwise, their excellent Misión Árbol program will likely be seen by the world as little more than window dressing. Restorative agriculture techniques could reduce or eliminate Venezuela's need to cut down forests for food. Large-scale reforestation could likewise reduce the need to fell high-biodiversity old forests.

A more blatant example of de-re schizophrenia is President Chavez' new national sprawl policy. Unlike most sprawl campaigns that attempt to reign in destructive development, this one accelerates it. Chavez plans to build a series of new "socialist cities." They will supposedly be sustainable, but few green architects or planners—if any—have been consulted, and forests are already being felled to make room. Forcing a healthy new city into existence is like forcing a child to grow up kind, smart, gentle, and generous. It's risky business at best, and would require huge amounts of uncommon expertise to have even a chance of success.

Again, de-re schizophrenia is rampant worldwide. It would be difficult to find a community anywhere that isn't proud of some major downtown restoration or redevelopment project, that isn't simultaneously undermining their quality of life via dewealth activities elsewhere in the community. Most of this is due not to lack of intelligence, but to the normal, lingering effects of a dying paradigm as its replacement takes hold. The quickest cure for the malady is to analyze your policies according to the rules of renewal, and make the appropriate additions and deletions.

Burning Boats and Greenbelts

The de/re shift comes much easier to cities like New York and San Francisco for whom the sprawl option expired some time ago. For them, redevelopment is the only path to growing the economy. Thanks to that constraint, their economic growth almost always enhances their quality of life, whereas economic growth and quality of life usually have an inverse relationship in sprawling, dewealth-based communities. The great challenge is to move a community into rewealth mode before it's forced on them by geographic constraints or natural resource crises.

Communities that are serious about adopting a rewealth-based strategy might thus want to go further than simply making rewealth their decision-making default, with dewealth the fallback option. When people have a familiar and thus comfortable fallback, it sometimes undermines their commitment to move in a new direction.

When conquistador Hernán Cortéz arrived in what is now Mexico, he burned his ships in order to eliminate the option of returning to Spain. As a result, his small band of soldiers conquered one of the world's great civilizations (greatly aided by epidemics introduced earlier by Columbus, and by Cortez's own troops, which wiped out 80–90% of human populations in the Americas). Almost two millennia earlier, Chinese general Xiang Yu used the same tactic when he crossed the Yangtze River, and it worked just as well for him.

The lesson? Unless there is a pressing, convincing reason to keep sprawl and other dewealth modes as an option, you might want to consider effectively outlawing them. One "burning boats" equivalent would be creating a tight greenbelt that's rigorously enforced, as Portland, Oregon and London, England did. This might be the simplest and quickest way to help a community make the de/re shift before they've destroyed all their surrounding wildlands, farmlands, and watershed.

> It's just too tough to change behavior of local governments. Why? They instinctively chase commercial jobs for their rich revenue base, and drag their heels on less-tax-lucrative housing opportunities. So housing gets pushed out, with sprawl clogging the roads. . . [Business leaders] approached Virginia Gov. Tim Kaine, Maryland Gov. Martin O'Malley, and D.C. Mayor Adrian Fenty to argue that their total jurisdictions. . .need to coalesce for global competitiveness. . . .Chesapeake Crescent. . .could be a national example of collaboration across city and state lines. . .[for] a sustainable environment.
> —Neal Peirce, "Crossing Borders, Making Progress:
> The Chesapeake Crescent Breakthrough,"
> *The Washington Post*, February 17, 2008

As the above quote attests, regional renewal should be the ultimate goal, even though it's usually necessary to start at the community level. Greenbelts are best established via regional renewal partnerships, so as to make the greenbelt "thick" enough to be effective. That way, developers don't have the option of simply skipping over the greenbelt and sprawling even further away from the city than they would have had the greenbelt not existed. That's the exact opposite of what a greenbelt is intended to accomplish. This happened around Ottawa, Ontario, where massive destructive development has afflicted the Orleans and Kanata suburbs beyond Ottawa's greenbelt.

Recalibrating Our Standards

> You can give a man a fish, you can teach him to fish, but nothing will help if there are simply no fish to be caught.
> —Alex Gesheva, "Artificial Reefs: Balancing Out Human Havoc,"
> *Guadalajara Reporter*, August 18, 2007 (describing use of concrete structures to replace coral destroyed by shrimp nets)

Alex Gesheva's observation (above) illustrates how—at this inevitable de/re turning point—many of our conventional wisdoms are rendered obsolete. For millennia, our most basic assumptions are that the basic materials of life and wealth are there to be had; our job as an innovative civilization was simply to find better ways of extracting, processing, and distributing them. That assumption is no longer valid.

To paraphrase Oscar Wilde, rewealth causes happiness wherever it goes; dewealth causes happiness whenever it goes . . .

> *Progress begins with the belief that what is necessary is possible.*
> —journalist and author Norman Cousins (1915–1990)

From here on, "creating" those raw materials—rather than finding them—will be one of the major changes in our wealth-generating processes. Biomimetic technologies will probably play a major roles in this. Of course, it will still be Mother Nature doing the heavy lifting: our role is simply shifting from depleting her stored and current output to helping her replenish her inventory and boost current production. We're evolving from from parasite to symbiont, one might say. Teaching a man to fish no longer makes sense. We must now teach him (and her, and their children) how to restore fisheries.

Humans have an amazing ability to accept the conditions of the world in which they grew up as normal and natural. Our vanishingly short life spans cause each generation to lower its expectations. We're constantly accepting reduced levels of biodiversity, social harmony, green space, cultural diversity, and economic justice as "normal." We're constantly accepting higher levels of terrorism, lawsuits, crime, pollution, climate change, and overcrowding as inevitable.

When I was a young child in the 1950s, I remember playing in local streams in Bergen County, New Jersey. They were full of crayfish, salamanders, dragonfly larvae, fish, leeches, frogs and the like. Children playing in the same creek today (assuming any of it is still exposed to daylight) would be lucky to find any animal life at all. I'll bet my idea of what a "normal" creek looks like is very different from theirs.

It's probably impossible to reconnect humanity with appropriately high standards: the biodiversity of 5,000 years ago, the natural resource productivity of 500 years ago, the community connectivity and individual freedoms of just 50 years ago. It's also probably impossible to effect the changes in human nature that would result in wiser resource usage and more just treatment of each other.

> *"For 50 years," said Wang Wu, a professor at Shanghai Fisheries University, "we've blindly emphasized economic growth. The only pursuit has been G.D.P., and now we can see that the water turns dirty and the seafood gets dangerous. Every year, there are food safety and environmental pollution accidents." . . . "You can't find many places as beautiful as this, covered by trees and bamboo," said Lin Sunbao, who moved from Fuqing to Sanming. "We use water from mountain streams. And because our water is better, it's harder to get disease." This is one of the solutions to the water crisis in China: to seek out virgin territory and essentially start the cycle all over*

again. And that worries scientists, who say aquaculture in China is not just a
victim of water pollution but a culprit with a severe environmental legacy.
—David Barboza, "In China, Farming Fish in Toxic Waters,"
New York Times, December 15, 2007

Given those two "impossibilities," is there anything that *could* break humanity out of this downward spiral of expectations? Is there anything that could defeat the corrosive effect of our fruit fly-like life spans, with their constant downshifting of standards? Collective spiritual evolution—such as greater love, awareness, and/or empathy—might do the trick, but I'd rather not stake our future on seeing that happen in the near future.

Don't let anyone convince you that things can't be turned around under trying circumstances; that restoration is a rich person's pastime. Cuba, for instance, has been suffering under the U.S. trade embargo for decades. Yet they've made great strides in reforesting their island. They had about 14% forest cover in 1959, while today it's about 22%. This supports the long-term economy (including tourism), enhances quality of life, and restores their water and ecology. The people of Cuba have also been busy restoring waterways such as their largest urban river, Havana's badly abused Río Almendares.

Look at the three million hectares of near-barren land that have been reforested— and the 25 million hectares that are being refarmed—in Niger, one of the world's poorest nations. The land was nearly desertified in 1970s and early 1980s through unsustainable farming, ranching, and firewood collection. With no financial or technical help from national or international bodies, the local villages took it upon themselves to restore their soil and their trees at the edge of the Sahel desert. "The results have been staggering" says Chris Reij of the Free University in Amsterdam (Netherlands).

Restoring our world for a living is really the only practical path. We need to change our trajectory. On a trajectory of renewal, our short life spans become an asset, at least in terms of quickly resetting our expectations. If every generation is born into a world with more natural resources, more widespread wealth, more community beauty, more social harmony than the generation before, our collective standards and expectations will constantly rise. It has nothing to do with humans becoming more optimistic by nature, it's just a matter of automatic recalibration . . . doing what we've always done: accepting the world we grew up in as "normal."

There is no security on this earth, there is only opportunity.
—General Douglas MacArthur

A sustained trajectory of increased environmental, economic, and social health *has* to affect us in profound ways. How will the widespread expectation of a healthier, wealthier, more beautiful future affect our personalities, our investments, and/or the way we govern? How will we change as a society when a better world is logically predictable from our current actions? Will we be less fearful . . . less aggressive? Will we be more focused on the long term? If so, that would set up a positive feedback loop, since those three societal changes would lead to an *even better* world.

Will we be as likely to go to war over water or fuel or productive land if we expect to have more of each with each passing year? If we do continue to go to war under such circumstances, it will likely be instigated by those whose fortunes are made in wartime. Citizens are less likely to fight with their neighbors when everyone has, and expects, more. A *re*storm is blowing through the global economy: will it blow you opportunities, or blow you away?

An appropriate symbol of this global shift is the five-year, $1.876 billion renovation of the 55-year-old United Nations complex in New York City, due to start the same time this book is published (also in New York City). This author was born around the same time and place as the UN building, so I can only hope that a thorough renovation is also in the cards for my deteriorating bodily structure, which has similarly suffered from deferred maintenance . . .

Making this global shift will require implementation of all three renewal rules, not just rewealth. The three rules could be seen as a "restorative chord." The right three notes played simultaneously yield the magic of a chord. One or two notes just won't do the job, no matter how well chosen or how well played they are.

So too can these three rules—when combined and imbedded in our decision making—yield a near-magical transformation . . . from destruction to restoration, from separating our natural, built, and socioeconomic worlds to harmonizing them, from imposing the illusion of a fixed future on citizens to engaging them in its constant creation. In my workshops, I see first-hand the reaction of public and private leaders to the concepts you're reading in this book. Based on that reaction, my guess is that parents have every reason to believe their children and grandchildren will live in a healthier, wealthier, more beautiful world than we have now.

Not all will be better, of course: the dewealth-derived juggernaut of global warming will be the major mitigating factor. But if we are earning our living in a way that leaves all things better, our trajectory can't help but be a positive one.

Part II
Practice

Restoring Our Planet by Renewing Our Communities

Insights for citizens, planners, redevelopers, investors, policymakers, mayors, and presidents.

> *What we need is more people who specialize in the impossible.*
> —**Theodore Roethke, American poet (1908–1963)**

While physicists have been searching for their "theory of everything," economists, environmentalists, and policy leaders have been searching for their own Holy Grail: a comprehensive solution to the world's economic, social, and environmental problems. That search became especially urgent in the past two decades, as many local and regional problems became crises, spawning emergent global crises in the process.

This quest for an economic and environmental Holy Grail is a respectable enterprise for academics, policymakers, and businesspeople alike. But, throw in the additional social goals of reducing poverty, crime, starvation, disease, and war, and you will be quickly escorted from respectable society by the men in white suits. You've now joined the ranks of perpetual motion inventors, utopian philosophers, overreaching optimists, and snake oil vendors. That said, this section documents what seems to be a universal formula for rapid, resilient renewal (which seems to be the universal goal), where renewal rules become renewal reality.

In this section, we'll dive into the details of bringing communities and regions back to life. If you're not a mayor, not a planner, not involved in public works or public policy, not a city council member, not involved in county or state government, not involved in natural resource management, and you're not a redeveloper, you could skip Part II. But I don't recommend it.

If you're an investor, an entrepreneur, a farmer or rancher, an academic, a nonprofit leader, or a private citizen looking for a restorative lifestyle, you *could* go straight to Part III. There, you'll read stories that illustrate how to tap the opportunities presented by our global shift from a deconomy to a reconomy. But reading Part II will help you better understand the challenges, tools, and strategies of the communities that house the opportunities you'll be pursuing.

Helping communities and regions make the transition from dewealth to rewealth is an excellent way to insert yourself or your company into the revitalization "deal flow" early on, and to make your competitors largely irrelevant. Whether you're buying and renovating a single building or a whole neighborhood . . . whether you're launching a restorative business in your kitchen or hiring a thousand employees for your startup . . . whether you're bringing a family farm back to life or restoring a million-acre watershed . . . you need to know where, when, and how to insert yourself into the area's renewal process. Understanding the strategies you'll find in this section, and helping a community apply them effectively, can make you or your firm indispensable. "Indispensable" is another way of saying "highly profitable" in the business world.

Chapter 4

The *Resolution*: A Reliable Recipe for Rapid, Resilient Renewal
How to build a renewal engine that enhances your community's regenerative capacity.

***

If you want to build a ship, don't drum up people together to collect wood and don't assign them tasks and work, but rather teach them to long for the endless immensity of the sea.

—Antoine de Saint-Exupéry

Five of the most common factors inhibiting the ability of communities to revitalize themselves are: (1) Lack of a shared vision of their future; (2) Public policy that ignores rewealth (and/or that encourages dewealth); (3) Inadequate budgets—local, state, and federal—for asset renewal (4) Insufficient ability to respond quickly and wisely to opportunities; (5) Inability to form effective, appropriate project partnerships.

You're probably thinking "so tell me something I *don't* know." OK, here's something you don't know: there's a single solution to all of those problems, and it will cost you almost nothing to create it. It's a permanent, nonprofit, public-private organization I call a renewal engine. A number of communities around the world have achieved astonishing revitalization using renewal engines they created without the benefit of design guidelines. In this chapter, I consolidate the best features of each into an ideal template that you can use to build a state-of-the-art renewal engine of your own.

The Goose and the Grail

You've read about my search and discovery of the holy grail of economic policy: a few simple rules for economic growth that leave nature and communities in better condition with each passing year.

As you saw in Chapter 2, three rules emerged in virtually every case I studied. Failed attempts at revitalization tended to ignore one or more of them. The spectacular revitalization successes almost invariably applied all three rules together: rewealth, integration, and engagement. This was exciting enough in itself, but I kept up the search.

Having only rules is like being a contractor who has only blueprints: without people, property, tools, money, and materials, nothing will be built. Economic growth is based on activity, so I now had to find the universal methods that reliably turned these rules into renewal . . . methods that worked in any kind of community or region, in any part of the world.

My search sought answers to two questions: (1) Are there any universal *processes* for effectively applying the renewal rules . . . turning them into real solutions? (2) Is there a universal *model* for effectively organizing the people, tools, properties, funds, and other resources needed to make renewal happen?

The answer, somewhat to my amazement, was "yes" to both questions. Three universal processes emerged for creating solutions such as plans, policies, and projects. Those renewal processes are *visioning, culturing,* and *partnering.*

What's more, a single model emerged over and over as the ideal way to institutionalize those processes and create actual revitalization. That model, which I dubbed a *renewal engine,* was the "golden goose" I'd been seeking: a community revitalization organization that would keep on laying the golden eggs of successful renewal partnerships until the community was fully revitalized. The largest, most productive rewealth activities around the planet these days usually take the form of public-private partnerships. I refer to them as renewal partnerships, but they're called regeneration partnerships in the United Kingdom.

How I Found the Golden Goose

I had a rather unique advantage while researching this book. As mentioned in the preface, for six years, from early 2002 through early 2008 (when this manuscript was finalized), I spent my entire professional life keynoting restoration and revitalization conferences, conducting workshops for communities and regions seeking revitalization, and consulting on renewal projects, programs, and plans worldwide.

All the while, I was reading and writing articles about regeneration, renovation, reuse, and redevelopment. Everything was "re" this, and "re" that. I was earning *re*wealth, and was constantly surrounded by others who were doing so.

Thus, I was involved in, witnessed, studied, or heard about countless attempts at renewal. Some failed. Some achieved modest success. But some resulted in *spectacular* reversals of misfortune. Cities and regions that were at death's door suddenly were reborn and bloomed in a *stunning* manner. I realized that mine was a unique vantage point from which to track down "universal" factors that were usually present in successes, or absent in failures.

The goose wasn't really that hard to find, because she was always hiding in the same place: communities that had been in terrible shape, but that were now enjoying dramatically renewed prosperity. Not just higher income levels: that can be temporarily achieved by artificial, unsustainable means (like sprawling or buying an employer with tax incentives).

I sought stories of economic renaissance that also enhanced quality of life. They did this by reversing the decline of their natural environment, their built environment, their culture, their social services, and more. As with my search for the renewal rules, I mentally reviewed the thousands of renewal stories I'd been exposed to over the years. I tossed in a little inductive reasoning, and *voila!* As philosopher Dale Jamieson says, "the plural of anecdote is data." (In other words, don't expect a tabulated list of communities analyzed according to the three renewal rules, three renewal processes, and the presence of a renewal engine. I'll leave the painstaking work of quantifying what I know to be true to the grad students and pros in academia.)

As I spoke with the leaders of those super-successful efforts, the goose gradually emerged from her hiding place. Over and over, I heard variations on the same story: "Well, we created a permanent, nonprofit, public-private organization that engaged all of our stakeholders in the creation of a shared vision for the renewal of our community and our natural environment. We worked on making our policies more supportive of redevelopment, and less open to sprawl. We provided a forum for the public and private sectors to craft partnered approaches for the renewal projects our community needed."

The "goose" thus turned out to be a new type of community revitalization organization that has been struggling to emerge all over the world: what I'm dubbing the renewal engine. It continually pumps out renewal partnerships that are guided by a shared vision of the community's future; partnerships operating in an environment that nurtures rewealth. Properly structured and managed, renewal engines powerfully enhance a community's capacity to renew itself.

I reverse-engineered those renewal organizations to reveal the commonalities that made them succeed or fail. None were perfect, since all of these pioneering communities had created their renewal engines on-the-fly, often haphazardly and in isolation. They didn't know others were taking a similar approach, because this model has never before been documented. All were missing a component or two. But when all the stories were aggregated, the same rough model, the same three rules, and the same three processes emerged over and over.

Does Your Community Have a Renewal Engine, a Redevelopment Corporation, or a Renewal Coalition?

Many communities have established some sort of official group or agency to think about their future, and maybe even to actively work toward improving it. Such community renewal groups almost always yield important benefits, but seldom produce our ideal goal of rapid, resilient renewal. When I use the term "renewal engine" here, I'm not speaking generically about such organizations. It's called an "engine" because it generates funded action, not just talk, meetings, and reports.

The most common missing factor in the incomplete renewal engines was the "culturing" process. They had forgotten the importance of making their community more attractive and supportive to redevelopers and investors by renovating their public policy and governance.

When the three renewal processes take place within a renewal engine, and both citizens and leaders make their decisions in accordance with the three renewal rules, then a community has both the golden goose and the holy grail. Miraculous things can happen.

You'll read about those miracles in Part III. For now, let's pull the renewal engine apart, examining the structure and processes that make it tick. With this information, and with what you learn from the stories in the third section of this book, you should be able to assemble a renewal engine of your own.

We'll look closely at the three processes that vehicle must perform, in order to be a true renewal engine. But first, we need to revisit what turned out to be the "universal goal." I wasn't looking for any such thing—it sounds silly, after all—but it revealed itself as I researched the processes and models.

The Universal Goal

This phrase "universal goal" always provokes cross-eyed looks. How could communities across a world as diverse and conflicted as ours possibly have a common goal? But there is one, and I used it to uncover the three renewal rules, as described in Chapter 2. We're revisiting it here because striving for it is what has caused communities to invent renewal engines.

Rapid, resilient renewal is that universal goal, and I have yet to encounter a community that doesn't desire it. That doesn't mean such a community doesn't exist, but it's universal enough for me to feel comfortable putting it forward. Let's break it down.

Rapid

There's always a need for speed, even in cultures that don't share Americans' addiction to constant, frantic busy-ness. The urgency might come from a politician who needs to see tangible results in time for the next election. It could come from redevelopers who are paying interest on the millions they borrowed. It could come from a government agency that needs to show progress in order to retain their funding. It might come from a recent disaster. Or it could come from the desperation of the businesses and citizens in a depressed economy. Whether a community is flush or desperate, rapidity of results is usually a constant in their goals. Your entire renewal program doesn't need to be delivered quickly, of course. But some low-hanging fruit should be identified to produce some early wins . . . To boost confidence and produce momentum.

Resilient

Too many renewal initiatives skip this element of their strategy, even though it's more important than speed. All responsible citizens and businesses want their renewal to last a long time.

So, if resilience is universally needed and desired, why isn't it universally pursued? If an initiative is too dependent on elected officials, it will often focus exclusively on the speed of results. Spending big money on grand "magic bullet" projects in the absence of an overall strategy—or without a lasting entity charged with following through—is symptomatic of the vote-getting approach to renewal. But magic bullet projects can also be symptomatic of hit-and-run developers who specialize in a certain type of project, and who roam the world looking for opportunities to do them. Resilience is also damaged when good projects of a previous administration are cancelled when a new party comes into power.

People concerned about their historic neighborhood, their watershed, their ecosystems, their rural way of life, or their children's future all have at least one thing in common: they want their community to remain on a revitalizing trajectory. No matter who is in office, no matter what disruptions or disasters hit, not matter what happens in the world around them, they want their community to survive and thrive. Like the three-legged emblem of the Isle of Man, no matter what you hit them with, they should always land on their feet.

Renewal

This will seem like a big "duh" if you've read this far, but let's be sure we're clear on what "renewal" is and isn't. The goal isn't "rapid, resilient *growth*." Ever-increasing size in anything is freakish and unsustainable.

But renewal doesn't mean more, it means better: better quality of life, just to be specific. Granted, you will need *more* of something (jobs, food, water, cleanup, justice, affordable housing) to achieve that higher quality of life. But all of those things can be achieved through renewal of your natural, built, and socioeconomic environments. Increasing both standard of living (income) and quality of life means relying primarily on renewal, not on expansion, not on simply creating additional stuff.

After a certain point in a community's initial development, dewealth-based expansion (sprawl) reduces quality of life by increasing commute times, increasing pollution, decreasing green space, and destroying cultural heritage. There's no such downside to basing economic growth on renewal.

The Universal Renewal Processes

As mentioned at the beginning of this chapter, decision-making rules need solution-creating processes to make a difference in the real world. And processes need to be housed so they can operate efficiently, and be sheltered from disruptive influences if they are to continue long enough to achieve the goal of rapid, resilient renewal.

Renewal processes turn renewal rules into renewal solutions. Those solutions are such things as policies, plans, programs, and projects.

Again, the three universal processes are *visioning, culturing,* and *partnering.* Together, they produce a renewal vision (which drives strategies and plans), a renewal culture (which attracts and nurtures redevelopment via policies, regulations, incentives, and support services), and renewal partnerships (which fund and implement projects and programs).

The three processes help your community achieve something that's of known value in the corporate world, but that is seldom applied at the community level: strategic alignment. Strategic alignment is what you have when your organizational systems (processes) support your organizational strategy. It's depressingly rare.

The three processes and three rules together comprise a system for action. You *engage* all the stakeholders to create a shared *vision* that *renews* your natural, built, and socioeconomic environments in an *integrated* manner. You imbed the renewal rules into the *culture* and governance of the community. Your public-private, public-public, and private-private project *partnerships* should likewise be based on the three rules. Let's now look at each of the processes individually.

The Visioning Process

Where there is no vision, the people perish.
—Holy Bible, Proverbs 29, Verse 18 (King James version)

To produce rapid, resilient renewal, a community requires a shared *renewal vision* of its future. Everyone knows they need a strategy and a plan, but they often get a bit uncomfortable when asked about their vision. Maybe it's because visions have often been associated in our culture with mysticism, mind-altering drugs, or mental illness.

The three major reasons communities proceed blindly are (1) creating a good vision statement is difficult, and few know how to do it; (2) many people assume they already have a vision (but can seldom put it into words); and (3) they simply don't understand what a vision statement is, how it differs from a strategy, and how a strategy relates to a plan.

When communities *are* finally convinced they should have a vision statement, many make the mistake of copying a good-sounding one from another community. (That's why I'm not including a sample vision statement here.) They don't realize that the process of creating the vision statement is at least as important as the statement itself.

This holds true for strategies, as well. Honest business and military leaders will tell you they seldom follow their strategies all the way through. Reality tends to intrude somewhere along the way. Despite that, they will also tell you that the *process* of strategizing is invaluable, even if you never look at the strategy again.

Whatever the underlying reasons, most communities are flying blind, with no vision underlying their strategies and plans. In fact, many don't have strategies, either. Just plans. That's like coming up with detailed activities for each day of your vacation, but forgetting to figure out where you're going.

Simply having a vision isn't enough. To be effective, a vision must be shared by all key stakeholders, it must be communicated to all citizens and institutions, it must be housed securely, and it must be occasionally updated if necessary. But don't update it too frequently: part of the vision's purpose is to provide confidence via continuity and coordination.

A vision shared by all stakeholders inspires confidence among the investors, employers, and redevelopers who are looking for opportunities. All other things being equal, resources will flow toward communities that know where they're going.

Broad public buy-in also tends to yield faster, more reliable project approvals, which increases the redevelopers' (and lenders') safety.

A good vision statement requires only a few sentences. A good strategy can be done in one or two pages; the longer it is, the harder it is to adhere to day-to-day. A plan, on the other hand, can fill a book. Take a look at the master plan for the Noisette Project in South Carolina, and you'll see why people have paid over $100 for a copy: it bridges the line between plan and book (a beautiful and enlightening book, at that).

The Los Angeles River Revitalization Master Plan is another impressive read. This $2 billion public-private partnership's goal is to turn a dry, ugly concrete ditch—with many ugly, crime-ridden neighborhoods and industrial wastelands along its 32-mile stretch—into an urban paradise. Tetra Tech, Inc. (an engineering, environmental, and planning firm based in Pasadena, CA) was the plan's lead consultant to the City of Los Angeles' Bureau of Engineering. The consulting team included Civitas, Mia Lehrer + Associates, Wenk Associates, and eight other firms. A cursory glance makes one think the plan is just about revitalizing neighborhoods and boosting property values by creating attractive greenspace. But a closer look reveals many wildlife habitat, water-quality, and water-based recreation goals. The funding for that watershed restoration will come from the commercial and residential real estate enhancement. The bottom line should be a spectacular increase in the local quality of life.

It's important to remember that a vision is not a design or prescription; it's more like a high-level performance specification. If we lack a vision, we might do everything else competently and responsibly, yet still not meet our objective, since we never really knew what our objective was.

This describes most communities today, especially those who think revitalization starts with planning. Planning is the third stage, not the first, and the vision should never come from the planners. In fact, it's often dangerous to let the planners facilitate the creation of a community's shared vision. The exception might be if the planners are thoroughly grounded in—and committed to—the three renewal rules, and are working within the controls of a renewal engine.

Simply put, your vision should describe the type of place you'd like you community to become, the direction you wish to pursue. It describes the qualities and image you want your waterfront, your downtown, your city, or your region to have, not the specific functionality or structures that will achieve it: those belong in the strategy and plans.

If your downtown or overall community is competing for residents or commerce with other places, your vision should describe what your community will do that's different from or better than the others . . . how living and/or working there will create a higher quality of life than the others.

Your vision statement should be comprehensive enough to address all the elements of your community that require renewal (from sewers to policies). But it should also have boundaries, since the visioning process can sometimes get a bit giddy. Boundaries will help reduce the inclusion of elements that won't contribute significantly to rapid, resilient renewal, and that might even retard it by being unattainable.

Your vision statement should be clear enough so that those who are involved in day-to-day programs can remember it, and instantly tell how what they are doing is contributing to the vision's fulfillment. Your vision should be grand enough to inspire, while also being achievable: it shouldn't be wishful or pie-in-the-sky.

Of the three key planning components—vision, strategy, and plan—the vision is least-often updated. Along with the three rules, your vision guides decision making. Visions should not be confused with goals. Goals and milestones are the province of strategy, which executes the vision. A plan is an integrated collection of projects that, in turn, executes a strategy.

Strategies are next in line on the frequency-of-updating scale. But strategies also shouldn't be updated too often: redevelopers need to be able to make certain assumptions about your future in order to make safe investments. Good plans, on the other hand, should be updated constantly.

The same diversity of stakeholders—though usually not the same participants—should be represented at all three stages; vision, strategy, and plan. Business, for instance, could be represented by the chamber of commerce. Academia could be represented by a school board member, plus a representative from both a technical/community college and a university. Nonprofits and citizen groups should have representatives who can address environmental, heritage, and social issues. Government could be represented by one person from each of the jurisdictions involved in the partnership (city, county, and maybe state and federal).

The Culturing Process

A vision without resources is a hallucination.
—old saying at the Pentagon

Attracting and nurturing investment in the renewal of a community means providing the right kind of environment. It has to be a better environment for that investment than is offered by the communities that are competing with you for that money. You need a *renewal culture*, in other words.

A renewal culture boasts policies, regulations, codes, support programs, and incentives geared toward renewal, rather than sprawl. Ideally, they should be geared around all three renewal rules: *renewing* your assets, *integrating* your natural, built, and socioeconomic environments, and *engaging* all your stakeholders.

But it's not just about governance. Culturing also means helping the populace come to grips with a future that might be very different from their past. Culturing helps them shift from basing their wealth on depleting and degrading natural resources to replenishing and restoring them. It helps them understand what's really standing in the way of a revitalized future, such as by performing a renewal-oriented strengths, weaknesses, opportunities, and threats (SWOT) analysis.

> *Cursed before the LORD is the man who undertakes to rebuild this city, Jericho:*
> *At the cost of his firstborn son will he lay its foundations; at the cost of his youngest*
> *will he set up its gates.*
> **—Joshua 6:26, New International version of the Holy Bible**

Without proper policy support, redeveloping a city can feel a lot like rebuilding Jericho. A community whose policies reflect the three renewal rules should be a paradise for redevelopers to work in, compared to those whose policies are still primarily dewealth-based.

We're not going to spend any time describing *how* to imbed the renewal rules into your public policies. While doing so is of crucial importance, we'll gloss over it for two reasons. First, you already know the renewal rules that should be at the heart of enhancing your policies. There are only so many ways to say "embed those rules in your policies, and weed out the policies that conflict with the rules," so I won't belabor it.

Second, the process of policy revision varies hugely from place to place. Policy changes are suggested, implemented, and enforced via legislation in a very different manner in an open democracy than they are in a monarchy, a police state, a dictatorship, a military junta, or a socialist system. But all want and need renewal.

When people are suffering from inadequate food, water, or shelter, rapid resilient renewal of their built, natural, and socioeconomic environments is their rallying cry.

Politics can wait. Politics can *always* wait as far as wildlife is concerned: the critters just want sufficient clean food, clean water, clean air, and appropriate shelter.

Rapid, resilient renewal is what the leaders generally want, too. (The exception being parasitic hit-and-run regimes, whereby elected officials buy asylum in other countries, escaping with bags of cash when popular outrage indicates that the time to run has come.)

Imbedding the renewal rules into policy will thus be in everyone's best interest, but it can be done in a variety of ways. It can be done unilaterally by a benign dictator or monarch. It can be voted on by an electorate. It can be agitated for by NGOs or citizens' groups. It can by mandated externally by multilateral lenders, or by international bodies such as the United Nations (UN). However it's done, adding policies that nurture the renewal rules while deleting policies that frustrate renewal, is essential to the resilience of your recovery.

Without policy support, local stakeholders (universities, nonprofits, planners, redevelopers) face an uphill battle when advancing rewealth projects. The government agencies they need to deal with simply don't "get it." Or, if they do "get it," they can't do anything about it. Too much education and wheel-reinvention is needed to move each project forward. Too many dewealth-based regulatory barriers (building codes, zoning, sprawl subsidies) stand in the way of those who wish to revitalize their communities.

Most of the current policy, planning, and budgeting tools found around the world are designed for deconomies and dewealth projects. They are designed to address assets in isolation; brownfields, historic buildings, roads, sewers, ecosystems, and fisheries. They often promote a command-and-control environment; decree rather than consensus. And many of these policy environments actively discourage both public-private partnering and innovative renewal funding tools like tax increment financing (TIF).

Imbedding the three renewal rules into all phases of the revitalization process—from vision and strategy; to policy and legislation; to the design, implementation, review, revision of your plans—will decrease the cost and increase the speed, quality, and safety of your renewal. Having a simple, reliable basis for decision making inspires private investors and redevelopers with confidence that their projects will be supported at each stage of the process by every public entity involved.

The renewal engine is where most of this policy and regulation reform should start. Even if policy, bureaucratic, and regulatory barriers didn't exist, redevelopers and public leaders often don't know how to implement the three rules. How do you inventory, manage, and *integrate* the *renewal* of all of an area's natural, built, and socioeconomic assets? How do you effectively *engage* all of the stakeholders? Then they discover the magic of renewal engines.

A renewal engine is the best way to accomplish this "culturing" process, since sustained effort is required to transform a dewealth culture of sprawl and extraction to a rewealth culture of renewal and replenishment. The governance side of the process (policies, regulations) also requires lobbying. One of the key functions of a renewal engine is to give comprehensive revitalization a voice. The coalition of interests represented by a renewal engine becomes, in effect, a lobby for rapid, resilient renewal.

The Partnering Process

> *What's been characteristic of city innovation is that it's almost always a public-private partnership. Politicians are working with tax dollars, so they don't want to be reckless. But then private citizens foment and support revolutionary thought.*
> —Larry Keeley, president, Doblin, Inc, quoted from
> "How CEOs Can Improve Cities" by Reena Jana in
> *BusinessWeek Online,* June 16, 2006

Just as rewealth is the key rule, so too is partnering the key process. Revitalizing a community usually requires major projects like infrastructure renewal, waterfront redevelopment, and natural resource restoration. Done on a large scale, any one of them might require more funding than public agencies can raise on their own. Partnering is the proven solution. Without partnering, your community is unlikely to accomplish many of the things called for in your vision.

But, you might ask, is it really important to do things on a grand scale? Can't we just do a long series of small projects? The long-term, incremental approach to renewal will sometimes work in a community that already has a stable economy and a decent quality of life. For distressed communities though, large and fast is often the ticket. You need to do things on a scale that draws new attention to your city, that changes perceptions about its future, and that builds critical mass quickly.

"Critical mass" usually refers to the number of residents when the subject is downtown revitalization. This is a tricky proposition, since few retailers will move in until there are enough residents to support them. But few residents want to move into a place with no retail. After all, one of the most popular reasons for moving downtown is to reduce automobile dependence.

Without a strategy for hitting critical mass at the right time, and then maintaining the momentum, cities risk abusing their renewal partners. Tactics such as increasing residential density gain much of their value only within the context of a strategy. Too many people get "religious" about revitalization tactics, believing certain ones are always good or always bad. Free parking is an example. There's a time to initiate free parking, and a time to end it. Free parking can help bring a dead downtown back to life, but it can send that downtown back into decline later on, if it's left in place so long that it produces irritating traffic congestion.

As described in the next chapter, some communities use TIF to subsidize retail. The idea is to enable shops to open before the critical mass of residents has been reached, thus ending the chicken-or-egg quandary. It's a dangerous practice. However, if the mixed-use development is being done on a large enough scale, the point at which critical mass will be reached becomes more predictable. In such situations, subsidies might be the right solution. The key is to keep the focus on increasing the number of residents; too often, public officials fool themselves into thinking the area is revitalized just because it has a lot of subsidized retail. It's a commercial ghost town in the making if the timing is off.

Size doesn't just matter with downtown redevelopment: it's also important when restoring natural resources. Most ecosystems don't like to be small, nor do they like to be disconnected from other ecosystems. Restoring on a viable scale, and reconnecting a sufficient number of these restored or conserved ecosystems to bring them back to health can involve hundreds of thousands—even millions—of hectares.

Partnering is the key to being able to do all kinds of renewal at a scale that will produce the results you desire. Partnering is so important, in fact, that the next two chapters are devoted to this one subject. Thus, we won't go into detail here; we'll just make a few general observations.

Partnering is how you assemble sufficient resources and knowledge to do enough of the right things to make a difference, and to do the right things right. Partnering can be public-public, public-private, or private-private. Partnering is where vision meets money. It's where the public good meets private goals. Partnering is where business helps government manage risk.

A new generation of public-private partnerships (P3) is fast emerging. They provide not only the resources and risk management communities desire, but can also help supply communities with the technical sophistication needed to properly design and run their renewal processes. Designing, funding, and implementing projects via public-public, public-private, and private-private partnerships is the only way

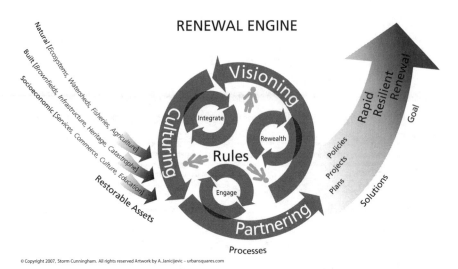

RENEWAL ENGINE

Figure 2 This artist's conception shows how a renewal engine "takes in" restorable assets, subjects them to the 3 renewal processes (which implement the 3 renewal rules) performed by the stakeholders, and produces solutions that yield rapid, resilient renewal. (See color plate.)

you're likely to achieve rapid, resilient renewal (R3?). When a P3's goal is R3, astonishing things can happen. But a *project*-oriented P3 can only contribute to R3, not achieve it. Achieving R3 requires the constant effort of a renewal *program*, and that's best designed and implemented via a renewal engine.

Again, all three processes—visioning, culturing, and partnering—should have a home, one that's safe from changes of political administration, and safe from excessive influence by big-money interests. This helps capture renewal momentum, so each new project doesn't have to start from scratch. That ideal home is a renewal engine (See Figure 2). We've already described it as a permanent, non-profit organization that houses your renewal processes. Now let's examine it in a bit more detail.

Renewal Engines: The Universal Model

Renewal engines enhance a community's capacity to envision, design, fund, and implement its renewal on an ongoing basis. Renewal engines have three major functions:

1) To form the vision and strategy that drive the area's renewal.
2) To foster a renewal culture that attracts reinvestment and supports the renewal strategy.

3) To establish the bonds of trust and shared values needed for public and private entities to work together. It provides a forum where public and private entities can agree on goals, and where they can partner on innovative, win-win projects that help achieve those goals.

Without such an organization, renewal tends to be sporadic, reactive, divisive, and inefficient. Without a way to provide continuity, revitalization initiatives seldom generate much confidence or build real momentum. As a result, they seldom inspire major investment from outside the community. The renewal engines I've encountered displayed a broad morphological diversity (shapes and sizes) from community to community and country to country, but shared a basic "genetic structure": the renewal rules and renewal processes.

It's through a renewal engine that communities create *and maintain* a shared vision of rapid, resilient renewal. It's through a renewal engine that communities embed the renewal rules into their public policies. And it's through a renewal engine that communities create the project partnerships that translate vision into reality.

More importantly, a renewal engine produces the right *kinds* of partnerships: the right projects, at the right time, in the right place, involving the right people and organizations. By "right," I mean advancing the community toward its shared renewal vision, via relationships that build its sense of community.

Let's pause from all this talk of universal success principles for a deep breath of reality. In Chapter 2, I cautioned readers not to think of the renewal rules as the solution to everything; they "merely" increase your capacity to create such solutions. The same goes for the renewal processes and even the renewal engine.

The three renewal rules won't revitalize your community. The three renewal processes won't revitalize your community. Not even a renewal engine will revitalize your community. These are all ways of enhancing your community's *capacity* for renewal. The actual revitalization plan needs more than guiding principles, generic processes, or an ideal model. You'll still need design, planning, and economic redevelopment professionals to make these tools work.

Why Did the Renewal Engine Model Emerge?

In recent years, it's become popular for communities to create some kind of diverse, independent group of citizens and other stakeholders focused on envisioning their mutual future. The good ones are seeking the Holy Grail: sustainable economic growth that renews their assets without destroying any valued assets. The best ones are able to raise the money to put those dreams into action. To paraphrase John Steinbeck, it is the nature of cities to rise to greatness if greatness is expected of them.

Until now, such "visioning coalitions" haven't had a proven model on which to base their structure and functions. At best, they studied other successful communities that had created such a coalition. But even those role models had created their solution from scratch, so they had weaknesses. What's more, they were molded to their particular needs: certain features wouldn't be universally needed.

Communities need to free themselves from reinventing the wheel (renewal engine) so they can immediately start resolving community problems. They need to spend a fair amount of time defining goals and creating a vision statement; they shouldn't have the additional burden of inventing processes and organizational models.

Many of these groups were formed in reaction to what they perceived was abuse by their public leaders, by private developers, or even by their own planners.

How to Abuse a Planner

Teamwork is a lot of people doing what I say.
—**Marketing Executive, Citrix Corporation**

At this point, some readers might be saying, "Hold on, why do we need a renewal engine when we've got a professional planning department? Isn't that what they are there for?" The short answer is no, that's most definitely *not* what they are there for.

Planners plan. As described in the visioning section, a plan is how you execute a strategy. A strategy is how you execute a vision. A community should no more leave it to their planners to come up with a vision and strategy, than you should hire someone to think up your life's dream. Renewal is personal.

The relationship citizens have with their planning departments has gone through three stages over the past century; what might be called receptive, reactive, and proactive. The receptive stage might also be called the "victim" stage, and was epitomized by Robert Moses: the tyrant planner from on high. That stage came to an end (though there's no shortage of laggard communities and nations still practicing it) via citizen outrage against the excesses of planners, led by the likes of Jane Jacobs.

The United States was fortunate in that World War II never came to our shores. But it seems that the U.S. government—with the willing assistance of professional planners—determined that we too should have some bombed-out cities. I refer to the urban renewal craze as "urban removal," since it was a gross misuse of the word "renewal." The urban removal hysteria started three years after World War II and lasted into the 1970s. It seemed to draw inspiration from Allied bombing missions over Germany. This dewealth-based approach to renewal accomplished much of what Germany and Japan only dreamed of doing to U.S. cities.

Urban removal left huge swaths of devastation in major cities across the nation, and many of them, like Philadelphia and Detroit, still haven't recovered. You can plainly see the dead zones where our own government subsidized the "bombing" of these cities decades ago. Adding insult to injury is that those cities paid professional planners to do this to them. Jane Jacobs gave citizens their voice, and the "reactive" period of planning was born.

The U.S. "freeway wars" erupted nationwide in the 1970s and stopped massive highways in their tracks (which is why Interstate 395 in Washington, DC, doesn't connect with 1-295, as it was supposed to). No longer were citizens going to allow planners to ram freeways through neighborhoods, or raze beloved buildings for the sake of sameness and modernity.

Newly enlightened planning departments and economic development agencies now started running major projects past the public "for approval." These requests for citizen input were sometimes rather low profile, as in "hey, you had your chance to comment . . . what do you mean you never heard about it? We had a two-inch invitation for public comment in the legal notices column of the newspaper."

That didn't work, so the "proactive" period was born, and the renewal engine is its highest expression. The renewal engine addresses one of the greatest problems of communities: the vision-strategy-plan process deficiency. Because the community hasn't been properly engaged, planners must either plan in a vision vacuum, or supply a vision of their own to plan around. Both scenarios are recipes for disaster.

With an effective renewal engine in place, planners are less likely to get off track. With a vision-strategy-plan process in place, environmental, heritage, and neighborhood groups won't have to waste time organizing protests against their own community's destructive plans.

It's dangerous to put too much power in anyone's hands, no matter how well qualified they may be. Planners are human, and humans are subject to all sorts of aberrations. Look at the way Washington, DC, planners tried so hard to tear down one of the city's most beautiful buildings—the Old Post Office—just because it didn't fit the idealized homogeneity they wanted in the Federal Triangle area.

Twentieth-century planners often used what might be called a Blitzkrieg-Monoculture style of development: they wanted to have a tabula rasa, so they destroyed what was in place. They did this also because too many planners prefer to leave their own mark on the world, rather than renovating and reusing the plans of others. This leads to monoculture development and redevelopment.

Without the restored Old Post Office, walking through Federal Triangle (where my office is) would be like walking through a tree farm, as opposed to a forest. It took a huge amount of effort by citizens—led by Nancy Hanks, chairperson of the National Endowment of the Arts—to protect Washington, DC, from its planners. A tribute to her heroic efforts is in the free public museum at the top of the clock tower of the Old Post Office.

So, yes, use professional planners. You need them. Some of the most brilliant, responsible, and holistic-thinking people I've ever met are professional planners (often the younger ones). The annual conference of the American Planning Association is one of my favorite events. In fact, an online directory of private planning firms that use the renewal rules—and who know how to help communities build renewal engines—is forming as I write this: check www.Rewealth.com for a link to this resource as it becomes available.

Don't abuse planners, and they (probably) won't abuse you. You abuse planners when you ask them to do things that are outside of their job description, and that are, in fact, *your* responsibilities as a community. You abuse them when you ask them to plan in a vacuum, without a vision or strategy to guide the plan. You need a shared vision of your renewed future, you need a strategy to get you there, and you need a way to form the partnerships that fund and implement your projects. A renewal engine can fulfill all of those vital functions.

Renewal Engines Versus Renewal Partnerships

Don't confuse a renewal engine with a renewal partnership. A renewal partnership (as I use the term) is usually focused on a project. Projects have beginnings and ends. Renewal engines embrace the great multitude of agendas and goals that define a community's future. Renewal partnerships, on the other hand, are focused on accomplishing one or more of the steps toward that future.

The renewal engine's multifaceted agendas and goals tend to make it relevant to everyone, and that equates to broad support. A renewal partnership's narrower focus makes it more open to controversy. While everyone can agree on increasing their quality of life, they don't always agree on what should be done with a particular building or piece of property. That's why renewal partnerships have to be outgrowths of the community's shared vision.

Renewal engines are "soft," relationship-based entities. Renewal partnerships are "hard," contractually-based entities. The renewal engine is program based, whereas the renewal partnerships are project based.

The purpose of the renewal engine is to be a forum in which the community forms a shared vision of their future, develops a strategy to achieve that vision, a plan to achieve that strategy, and policies to support that strategy. It's also a forum whereby the various public and private stakeholders perceive opportunities for interacting in a mutually beneficial manner. Those "opportunities for interaction" are what turn into renewal partnerships of all three kinds: public-private, public-public, and private-private.

Revitalization tends not to be linear. Like evolution, it tends to alternate between periods of incremental progress and great bursts of progress. But bursts can be dangerous. As your revitalization gains speed and you accumulate more and more renewal projects, two kinds of bursts are likely.

The first scenario is that you hit critical mass, with many positive feedback loops that bring in more funds and projects, which attract more funds and projects. The second scenario is that you hit critical *mess* (as the brilliant William Humber of Toronto's Seneca College puts it). Your disconnected projects start conflicting with each other, citizens start feeling overwhelmed by all the last-minute changes they're being asked to approve, and a moratorium on redevelopment might be called for.

Building a renewal engine is probably the best way to ensure the first scenario. A renewal engine helps communities give manageable *form* to their revitalization process.

Immortal Renewal Engines

Renewal partnerships have defined life spans, whereas renewal engines are (theoretically) immortal. Partnerships are sometimes long lived, but they are formed and defined by contracts. The contract might bind them for one year or thirty, and might even be renewable in perpetuity, but a lifespan is usually defined.

Why should a renewal engine be permanent? Diplomat William Eardley, IV once said, "Ambition is the path to success, persistence is the vehicle you arrive in." It's not enough for the renewal engine to establish a shared vision: it must stick around long enough to make that vision reality.

Saying the downtown Somerville redevelopment is going to be a terrific example of mixed use, (Richard F.X.) Johnson gave kudos to the public-private alliance of the Somerset County Business Partnership. . . . A frequent barrier to successful redevelopment is the "disconnect between the needs of the population and new political groups that shift" before a project comes to fruition, (attorney Thomas Jay) Hall said. "One generation's solutions can become the problems of the next," Hall said, "but some solutions take sustained, long-term investment and planning. It gets messy when people's sentiments change."

—**staff writer Lois Heyman, "Urban Planning Group Pushes Smart, Green Growth in State,"** *Courier-News,* **Bridgewater, New Jersey, United States, June 18, 2007**

Even if rapid renewal is achieved, an ongoing renewal engine is needed to turn it into resilient renewal. As researchers Karen Mossberger and Gerry Stoker said in a 2001 paper, "[the key to revitalization is] the capacity to mobilize a long-term coalition that is capable of achieving change on the ground."

The Value of Reduced Transparency

The heading of this section is, no doubt, a shocker. But it's not a teaser. There's a time for transparency, but there's also a time for secret discussions, even when the topic is the future of a community. A renewal engine is the best way to prevent that necessary secrecy from getting out of hand, as it tends to do.

As long as redevelopment conversations are held within public agencies, those proceedings are required to be made public (in open, democratic societies, anyway). That sounds like a good thing; you can't have too much transparency, right? Wrong. Partnerships often begin during "water cooler conversations." One of the reasons—possibly the primary reason—that communities create private nonprofit redevelopment agencies is to *reduce* transparency. They want to bring public and private players together in a way that encourages spontaneous, unfettered water-cooler discussions.

In the old days, redevelopment tended to be almost entirely planned and executed by the public sector. Or, if the community lacked effective planning capacity, it was left almost entirely to the private sector. In the former case, maximum transparency was desirable. In the latter case, transparency wasn't expected; folks hoped for the best, but seldom got it.

Now, with public-private partnering firmly established as the mode *du jour*, transparency and privacy have to be combined, and—hopefully—balanced. Why? Because the process of exploring potential partnerships is about developing trust, and of exploring a variety of paths to win-win.

It's not just a matter of forming a functional relationship: there are practical and legal reasons these conversations can't be conducted in public. The most obvious is to prevent predatory speculation. For instance, as soon as a company with deep pockets publicly expresses an interest in redeveloping a brownfield site or restoring a large historic building, a bidding war will begin as speculators try to grab it and flip it (and the properties around it). The project thus loses much of its profitability, and the city will likely lose the potential partner.

> *What we find is that there is no such thing as optimized in the absolute sense.*
> *It often depends on a balance between individual and social good.*
> **—Michael Gastner, Santa Fe Institute postdoctoral**
> **researcher (complex systems)**

So, how does a public-private redevelopment agency balance the need for serving the public good with the need for private negotiations? As Lucien Gosselin, Executive Director of the Lewiston-Auburn Economic Growth Council (LAEGC) told me, "that's the magic we have to pull off."

Their formerly depressed town of 36,000—which lost most of its heavy industry over the past four decades—has seen a 24% decrease in crime over the past three years alone. They've also attracted some $300 million worth of public-private renewal partnerships. It's now the greatest revitalization success story in the state of Maine, and *Inc.* magazine cited Lewiston as one of the top 50 cities in America to do business. It seems the LAEGC members are good magicians.

Gosselin also points out that when occasional (and probably inevitable) controversy does arise, it's not the LAEGC that catches flak over secrecy. After all, everyone knows they are a private organization. The ones who attract negative attention from the media and from citizen's groups are the city council members. They are usually briefed on pending deals during executive session. In most places, an "executive session" does not need to be recorded or reported.

So, if citizens suddenly learn that a big-box store is about to spring up on the outskirts of town and drain the life out of their historic main street, they tend to get upset that they weren't told sooner. Walmart, for instance, is well known for demanding complete and utter secrecy before they will enter into negotiations. So, if the city council members believe a Walmart will be good for the city, they are over a barrel regarding transparency.

> *Confucius advised that if we hoped to repair what was wrong in the world, we had best start with the "rectification of the names." The corruption of society begins with the failure to call things by their proper names, he maintained, and its renovation begins with the reattachment of words to real things and precise concepts. So what about this much-abused pair of names, sustainable and unsustainable?*
> —Michael Pollan, "Our Decrepit Food Factories,"
> *New York Times*, December 16, 2007

This is just one reason that the number one renewal rule is *rewealth*. Very few people object to bringing a blighted, previously developed property back to life. Many people object to losing green space and devitalizing their downtown. Renewal is thus far safer, politically, than more divisive, harder-to-define strategies like "smart growth" or "sustainable development." But when properly focused (meaning, on rewealth), both smart growth and sustainable development programs have produced some excellent results.

One of the biggest problems with smart growth is its dumb name. "Smart" is a matter of opinion, and calling one's self smart has never been a path to popularity. Rewealth, on the other hand, is both quantifiable and universally appealing. It might be measured by the amount of contamination removed from soil, the quantity of invasive species replaced by natives, the number of derelict buildings now in productive use, or the quality of water from a watershed. It's usually easy to tell when something has been renewed. Determining when it's been made smarter or more sustainable is something else again: "smart" compared to what? . . . "sustainable" for how long?

Communities shouldn't have to rely on Gosselin's "magic." Surely there must be a process or structure that allows necessary privacy when potential partners want to safely float ideas, and that also provides sufficient transparency and public engagement. There is. It's called—as you might have guessed—a renewal engine.

Most magic tricks are simple once the technique is revealed, and so it is with the magic of the renewal engine. The old model of nonprofit, public-private redevelopment companies is one that devises projects largely on its own, and then runs (mostly larger) projects past the public for approval. The primary difference between that and a renewal engine is the visioning component, powered by the renewal rules. The formation of that shared vision is a totally transparent, totally engaged process.

Renewal engines emerged at the intersection of two trends: the public-private partnering trend, and the trend toward greater transparency. Within a renewal engine, project partnerships will still come together with a large degree of confidentiality, but the public's shared vision guides projects from conception through delivery. In that way, the public is "engaged," even in private sessions.

The shared vision, and the renewal rules, act as filters for possible projects. Thus, when potential partners meet in the private forum provided by that renewal engine, the shared vision and the three rules—both of which are inscribed in a simple, easily referenced document—should automatically eliminate inappropriate proposals before they progress too far.

When renewal partnerships based on the community's vision reach the point of being "done deals" in private, they can be announced to the public with an expectation of enthusiastic public support. This announcement should also be done via the renewal engine, which enables all stakeholders to be informed simultaneously. Any discomfort the partners feel at that point will usually be in direct proportion to how far the project digresses from the shared vision and/or from the three renewal rules.

Creating Your Renewal Engine

> *The process of regenerative design is a process of continually enriching dialogue among the designers, the community or organization, and the system the design is a part of. Dialogue among the stakeholders is an essential aspect of sustaining sustainability. This dialogue is a process of growing an understanding and relationship with the place—economic, natural, cultural relationships. This dialogue should go on and evolve forever—just as life does. Since you won't be around that long, a core team is established with key stakeholders whose job it is to hold and develop the understanding of life in that place—the evolving story. Their job is not to manage but to receive the feedback from the system and respond to it along with helping the stakeholders understand the implications of the feedback.*
> **—Bill Reed, American Institute of Architects (AIA), LEED, principal, Regenesis, Inc., Santa Fe, New Mexico, United States**

Almost any credible, trusted existing group, institution, or agency can be the starting point of your renewal engine, if you don't want to start from square one. Many community renewal groups are formed around a far more limited agenda, such as education, pollution, and transportation. Nothing wrong with that, as long as there's also a renewal engine to encompass the whole of the community or region.

Just as the three renewal rules can be used to evaluate revitalization programs and projects, so too can you use them to design true renewal engines. The engines' mission and values should be based on rewealth, integration, and engagement. If the renewal engine passes that test, check the core activities: visioning, culturing, and partnering. If you can check off all six factors—and it's a permanent, not-for-profit, public-private organization comprising businesses, government, academia, NGOs, and citizen groups—you've got a real renewal engine.

It's not necessary for a new renewal engine to address all 12 sectors of restorable assets (see Glossary) from the very beginning, as long as all 12 are in its scope. But all five stakeholder groups (ibid) should be engaged from day one. One college, one government agency (or political leader), one business group (such as a chamber of commerce), one or more NGOs, and a citizen's group (such as a neighborhood coalition) should be enough to start.

Or, you might want to try finding a preexisting home for your renewal engine. If you don't want to start from scratch, find a trusted organization within your community that already exemplifies one or more of the three renewal rules.

For instance, you might have an environmental, heritage, affordable housing, sustainability, or smart growth group that already does a good job of engaging all the stakeholders and that already takes an integrative approach to the natural, built, and/or socioeconomic environments. They might only need to add a primary focus on "re" activities to become the seed of your renewal engine.

Or you might have a university or government agency that really "gets" the purpose and value of a renewal engine. They could volunteer to provide initial staff and offices for it, and even to legally form it. Creating a new legal nonprofit entity is especially important when a single organization (like a university) is going to be the primary "sponsor" of the renewal engine. The renewal engine must have the freedom to cover a scope that's beyond the charter of the sponsoring organization, and must have the ability to form alliances that might be inappropriate for the sponsoring organization.

Be very careful of this approach, however. I'm offering it as an alternative, but am not recommending it. As a general principle, working with the assets you already have (which includes institutions) is usually best. But well-established institutions tend to be highly resistant to change. They are very likely to fall back into old missions and behaviors. Starting from a clean slate should be your first choice.

What do call your renewal engine? Whatever works . . . Rock Hill, South Carolina, for instance, called their (partial) renewal engine "Community Builders." You'll encounter other, very different sorts of names in later chapters. The lack of standardized naming has the good effect of encouraging flexibility, so that communities don't feel forced into rigid, possibly inappropriate structures. But it has the negative effect of obscuring the renewal engine trend, thus reducing communities' ability to learn from each others' best practices. Again, watch www.rewealth.com for the announcement of an online resource to rectify this situation.

Barriers to Creating Your Renewal Engine

Why would a community need a renewal engine to bring them together? After all, everyone already agrees that more jobs, more money, and higher quality of life are good things, right? Thus, you'd think that government agencies, professional societies, environmental groups, historic preservation groups, universities, private landowners, and business leaders would automatically come together harmoniously and productively to guide their shared future, right?

I can almost hear the uproarious laughter of readers who have been involved in such initiatives. The reality of functionally organizing diverse stakeholders—especially from multiple jurisdictions—can be incredibly frustrating. It gets worse when people aren't clear about the organization's intended values, functions, and outcomes: some are intimidated by the creative process, while others try to control it.

Three common barriers to the creation of renewal engines are (1) fear that creating it will disrupt current programs or projects; (2) turf wars, where various agencies or professions worry that a renewal engine will dilute their control of the situation; and (3) hidden agendas, whereby parties used to secretive deal making worry about the transparency of real renewal engines.

Politics, differing priorities, sovereignty issues, and the tension between public good and individual rights are just a few of the factors that can divide people who are otherwise united in their desire to enhance their quality of life. While these issues can slow the creation of a renewal engine, their presence also confirms your need for one. At Resolution Fund, we are professional trespassers. One of the biggest challenges to integrated approaches is professionals—planners, economic development officials, public works agencies—protecting their turf. Building a community's capacity for renewal forces us to tread on everyone's turf.

One beauty of a well-designed renewal engine is that all public and private players can partner to find their highest and best role within the revitalization process.

Trust is the key, but that doesn't spontaneously arrive with the creation of a renewal engine. A shared commitment to a shared vision starts a community down the road to building trust. It's the completion of your first project together that's often the point at which trust is greatly heightened, and the wheels of your renewal engine become well-lubricated. That's why rapid results are important.

Who Should Renewal Engine?

> When a community sets out to address complex problems, such as economic stagnation, sprawl, and failing schools, the effort usually ends up going nowhere. . . . like org charts, "most powerful" lists reveal nothing about the human qualities of those who occupy senior positions, the web of personal relationships upon which they can draw, and the trust they inspire (or don't inspire) in other people. . . . people simply will not put themselves on the line for a sustained period of time unless they trust and feel connected with the leaders of the initiative. . . . the most effective local initiatives engage people whose informal networks reach broadly and deeply across sectors and organizations. Such people are often unsung heroes in a community.
>
> —Karen Stephenson, professor, Erasmus University (Rotterdam), and CEO Netform International, "The Community Network Solution," *Business + Strategy* magazine, Issue 49 (Winter 2007)

One of the keys to effective engagement is choosing the right people to represent those assets and stakeholders in your renewal engine, rather than just the usual suspects. The "right" representatives are well-connected people who enjoy the trust of the community.

I use the term "community leaders" a lot in this book, but I'm only occasionally referring to official or authoritative leaders, whether private or public. When Dr. Karen Stephenson (quoted above) helped Philadelphia map the most valuable influencers to recruit for their revitalization initiative, officials were shocked to find few of their own kind. There was only a 1% overlap with their "Philadelphia's 100 Most Powerful People" list. They hadn't even heard of the vast majority of the candidates. That research also yielded the superficially-counterintuitive insight that—while universities are a powerful environment for producing diverse networks—academics comprised only 6% of these "true" community leaders.

As for leadership of your renewal engine itself, don't think adherence to the renewal rules will make up for bad people skills. Hire your renewal engine leaders with great care; they will likely have to work with difficult citizens and obstinate leaders. As a wise philosopher once put it: "Everyone is entitled to be stupid, but some abuse the privilege." Or, as another wise guy said: "Some people are like Slinky toys: not good for much, but they bring a smile to your face when pushed down the stairs."

You can assemble your renewal engine in whatever manner works for your community: top down (from the mayor's office), bottom up (from a neighborhood group), or something in between. How heavily should a renewal engine engage elected officials? Enough to obtain their support, but not so much as to be vulnerable to the withdrawal of that support. People often forget how to be useful as they rise in political rank, to the point where they think they've accomplished something just by showing up. With the exception of lobbyists who come bearing gifts, productive meetings with top-level officials primarily occur when they are called by the official. In other words, when you are seen as a resource, not as a supplicant. Add in their high turnover rate (in democracies and coup-prone nations), and it becomes obvious why you should include political leaders in your renewal engine, but shouldn't become overly reliant on their support.

Managing Your Renewal Engine

Many renewal engines aren't tightly managed, in the sense that everyone involved has a specific job. Aligning people around the goal of rapid, resilient renewal—and giving them the three renewal rules to guide their decisions—tends to be far more productive than specifying everyone's exact responsibilities.

Keep in mind though, that a renewal engine isn't meant to be yet another layer of decision-making and managerial burden: it's there to speed and improve decision-making among your many public and private stakeholders. You should have a project review team, as part of your partnering forum. They would help match-up potential partners on the front end, and vet project proposals on the back end, to make sure the renewal partnerships remain true to the community's vision. This should be a collaborative process, not just a yes/no function. That said, the project review team needs to have the power to say "no"; otherwise they'll risk being the only ones at the table.

It's important that the renewal engine remain apolitical. That's one reason it needs to be permanent. If you disband your renewal engine after you're successfully revitalized, its functions will probably be picked up by an agency that is political, or politically vulnerable. Once that happens, you might be on your way back to the bad old days of dewealth, symptomatic solutions, and poor engagement.

It never ceases to amaze me how many places invest vast resources in their regeneration, yet don't think to establish baseline data at the beginning of the process. This impedes their ability to effectively monitor and report on progress, reducing opportunities to increase public support over time. It's like forgetting to take a "before" photo prior to launching a major restoration of your Victorian home.

A local college or university might be a perfect partner in such a baseline-documentation project. The resulting data—and its analysis—can provide great research fodder for students looking to position themselves for careers in the global reconomy. And, they'll be contributing to real-world revitalization while pursuing their academic goals.

The flip side of tracking the "before" numbers (and images) is communicating them. I frequently encounter cities that have made tremendous progress for five or 10 years, but don't know it. They've got dozens of examples of restored historic buildings, reused industrial buildings, remediated/redeveloped brownfields, revitalized streams or wetlands, and renovated infrastructure. But no one is in charge of aggregating and sharing that good news with the citizens. As a result, the common perception is that they are still in a downward spiral, or maybe in stasis at best.

This is one of the signs of a community affliction I've been calling "reblindness" in my workshops for the past four or five years. Reblindness is the inability to perceive restorable assets, and the failure to measure and report restorative development (rewealth). This situation is most common in those cities whose reconomy has emerged "organically," rather than as a result of government stimulus or overt private leadership. Effective communication of your vision and progress is an essential role of a renewal engine.

What else should your renewal engine do? You should create a team to develop model partnering contracts, so you'll be prepared when the partnership opportunities start to emerge. You should establish a legal team that's up to date on what your community can and can't do regarding renewal, and what legal/financial tools are available to it. For instance, some U.S. states, such as New York, are way behind the rest of the country regarding the use of TIFs. Such a legal/policy team will be a key part of your culturing process. If many communities were to show the state how TIF is essential to their revival, the state would likely modernize its policies.

[Note: New York state isn't opposed to P3s or TIF, per se. Their problem derives from much-needed rules that were put in place after the massive New York City corruption crises of the early twentieth century. It was felt that rigidly separating public from private was the best way to reduce political abuse. Maybe it's time New York gave their public leaders a second chance.]

The Feminine Principal (No, That's Not a Typo)

Restoring, integrating, and engaging are all qualities we tend to associate with feminine strengths. These are the core decision-making factors of rapid, resilient renewal. Therefore, all other qualifications being roughly equal, it's logical to hire a woman as the executive director of your renewal engine whenever possible.

Why not stack the odds of success in your favor? You can train any intelligent person in the technical disciplines of renewal: it's much harder to turn a person into an integrative, engaging personality when that's not in their nature.

We don't seem to have much trouble accepting the logic of hiring men as soldiers when we need someone to specialize in isolating and destroying an enemy (human, wildlife, or geophysical), so men shouldn't feel put-upon by this advice. What your renewal engine needs is a generalist (integration) who nurtures relationships (engagement) in the cause of nursing a community back to health (renewal).

My guess is that forensic investigations of failed revitalization plans would find little evidence of the three renewal rules at work, and even less evidence of feminine leadership. The military command-and-control style of planning is present to no small degree in planning agencies throughout the United States and elsewhere. The three renewal rules can be used as a hiring filter. If you use them in that manner, my guess is that relatively few (straight) men will survive the process.

It's no accident that allopathic doctors, who wage war on the body with their cutting, removing, and poisoning, have traditionally been male. Nurses, who support the entire person with their care, compassion, and counsel, have traditionally been female. Our communities have similarly been cut (by misplaced highways), had vital parts such as historic buildings removed (by the urban "renewal" disaster exposed by Jane Jacobs), have been isolated (by waterfront highways and single-use zoning), and have been poisoned (by dewealth/sprawl) for too long.

It's time to heal and renew the entire body of our communities. That might be a job best left to a woman. The right woman, of course: some women leaders can be just as uncompromising and dictatorial as men. Margaret Thatcher, Indira Gandhi, and Golda Meir come to mind . . .

How Renewal Engines Deteriorate and Die

Properly designed and managed renewal engines should, in theory, last forever. Other than problems with incompetent or dishonest employees, when they get into trouble, it almost always follow the same pattern.

The universal dynamic of renewal engine birth and death seems to be as follows. They start off with tremendous amounts of public engagement during the visioning and strategizing process. This is understandable, since it's usually a crisis that precipitates the revitalization initiative; people are feeling significant amounts of both pain and passion.

The crisis does two things: it draws people together who might not normally want to be together, and it motivates political leaders to become more inclusive. The politicians need access to private resources, and they need solid public support if they are going to launch a grand new program. Under such conditions, all three renewal rules find a ready and willing reception.

Communities need to grab that opportunity with both hands, and use it to rework everything that's wrong with the community, because the moment won't last. Once renewal has been achieved to any significant degree, people will become comfortable and complacent. Change has an inverse relationship to comfort, so imbed the rules of renewal firmly during the crisis. Those rules will be your primary protection against the deterioration of your renewal, and your renewal engine.

As noted earlier, updating visions doesn't happen very often. In fact, it's important to formally stop the visioning process in between updates. That way, projects won't be delayed or disrupted by a changing vision. Communities can easily get stuck in both the visioning and the planning processes. When the process of creating or updating a vision stops, the process of using that vision as a filter begins. In other words, the vision doesn't just sit on a shelf, as they usually do: it becomes a tool to vet new projects.

That said, just because a city has achieved an agreed-upon vision doesn't mean the visioning process should stop at all scales. It might stop for the city in general, but continue at smaller (neighborhood) or larger (regional) scales.

What's more, the people who contributed to or facilitated the vision shouldn't expect to be consulted when projects are being designed. They've done their job. If they've done it well, the vision should speak for itself, and renewal partnerships shouldn't need any help interpreting it. A key ongoing function of the renewal engine is to review those project designs to make sure they did, in fact, adhere to the vision. But that doesn't necessarily mean being involved in the design process itself (unless the project designers invite such input).

Updating strategies is more frequent, but updating them doesn't require as much effort as creating them. Thus, the natural progression is that the day-to-day work of project partnering becomes the star of the show. There's nothing wrong with that: such activities are, in fact, what everything else is meant to foster. But having a star doesn't mean firing the rest of the cast.

Public-private partnering involves money . . . lots of it. As noted in our discussion of transparency, exploratory partnering discussions need to take place in private.

This is the danger point, where leaders put the vision aside, rather than making it an essential part of designing a project partnership. When that happens, partners sometimes try to free their project from the constraints of the community's vision.

If the renewal engine's management fails to force all project designs through the filter of that vision, the renewal engine has begun its deterioration into just another public-private development corporation. The vision is the manifestation of public engagement. If it starts becoming less central to the partnering process, citizens—especially those of lower incomes—will start seeing the renewal engine more as a cabal of the wealthy, and less as "their" organization. The resulting outrage can be ugly.

The most likely time for these tensions to go from a simmer to a boil is during mayoral and city council elections. A populist politician might run on a platform of dethroning the elite, symbolized by the partnering component of a malfunctioning renewal engine. If the election is heated or close, the newcomer will start exaggerating the situation, to scare voters into his or her camp. As the rhetoric intensifies, the renewal engine can morph from simply not doing a good job of engagement into being the epitome of evil; the source of everything that's wrong in the community.

When a renewal engine's partnering arm has its reputation damaged in this manner, it loses much of its ability to build consensus for projects. At that point, it has lost one of the qualities redevelopers and restorative investors desire most: a supportive, predictable environment for their projects. No longer can they count on public support for the partnerships created via the renewal engine. That will scare them toward safer places, those with renewal engines that are still firing on all cylinders.

The solution is to design *and maintain* a complete renewal engine, not just a redevelopment agency/company that tries to do a good job of stakeholder engagement.

*Re*solution: The Reliable Recipe for Rapid, Resilient Renewal

> *Do not wait; the time will never be "just right." Start where you stand, and work with whatever tools you may have at your command, and better tools will be found as you go along.*
> —**Napoleon Hill (1883–1970)**

Until now, most revitalization efforts have taken one of four approaches:

1. They focused on the renewal of just one or two sectors (such as brownfield redevelopment, historic restoration, or infrastructure renovation).
2. They focused on design issues, such as new urbanism or green building.

3. They focused on one narrow tactic or theory, such as attracting a "creative class" of residents, or fixing their "broken windows."
4. They assembled collections of best practices based on intelligent philosophies such as sustainable development or smart growth.

Such approaches are well meaning, but lack both rigor and comprehensiveness. Most leave gaping holes in the community's renewal. Many are so fuzzy as to make it hard for people to know what they should be doing at any given moment.

The solution to these challenges is what I call "the *re*solution," and you already know what it is. It's simply the combination of the three renewal rules, the three renewal processes, and the renewal engine model. Just as applying all three rules produces results greater than would be expected from the sum of the three, so too are powerful synergies unleashed when all of the rules and processes come together in an effective model for action.

I call it the *re*solution for brevity's sake: it's a lot easier to tell folks they need to base their regeneration on "the *re*solution" than on "the combination of the three renewal rules, the three renewal processes, and the renewal engine model."

Many of the revitalization initiatives I see—especially those led by traditional economic development agencies—are actually "inertiatives." This recently-coined word elegantly combines "inertia" and "initiative" to describe programs that champion doing the same thing we've been doing all along. That describes most economic development. The *re*solution is the best way to overcome the inertia of dewealth, which has been the default for so long.

Not surprisingly, more than a few renewal initiatives and coalitions die in the process of being born. Some lose public support because of a lack of perceived relevance and value (insufficient integration or engagement). Others run out of enthusiasm and/or money as members and sponsors get discouraged by the lack of progress (insufficiently rapid results). Any number of internal and external factors can interrupt a community's renewal.

But the *re*solution isn't just a framework for community renewal. The presence of all seven *re*solution components in a community's revitalization program can—and I think should—be used by private investors and public agencies as an investment filter; a way to determine which communities are best prepared to put their money to good use.

Another (as yet untested) use for the *re*solution is as a predictive tool: money is always looking for assets whose value is just about to begin an upward trajectory. Buying the asset (or moving to the community) just before that trajectory begins is the key to buying at the lowest point. Community investors are like technology buyers in reverse: in technology, early adopters get the fewest features at the highest prices. Rewealth investors who buy based on early indicators—such as a community's use of the *re*solution—will get lower prices and more glory than those that come in after a revival has been documented to be underway.

First Steps: Education and Analysis

How do you move from reading this book to building a renewal engine? A good first step is to raise the community's awareness of its renewal potential. If citizens don't believe it's possible for the community to come back to life, they will likely see renewal efforts as a waste of time. Making them aware of their renewal potential is best done through a combination of education and analysis.

The education portion should comprise seminars or workshops that familiarize both citizens and leaders with (1) the universal goal (rapid, resilient renewal); (2) the universal rules (rewealth, integration, and engagement); (3) the universal processes (visioning, culturing, and partnering); and (4) the universal model (renewal engine). This education can be sponsored by local businesses or a foundation, and can be hosted by the city government, by a local college, by a nonprofit, or (preferably) by a partnership of all.

The analysis portion helps citizens understand their specific situation. It should begin with a SWOT analysis (strengths, weaknesses, opportunities, threats), which is a common, well-established tool. Few communities will have trouble finding folks in their ranks with SWOT analysis experience. Even if no such person is found, it's a simple process; plenty of books have been written on the subject and web-based training is available.

A generic SWOT analysis of your community would be valuable, but far more productive would be one using the taxonomies you've learned in this book. All 12 types of restorable assets should be examined, as should all five stakeholder groups. Analyze each of them according to the three renewal rules and the three renewal processes. This *re*solution-based SWOT analysis should give your community a strong shove down the path to rapid, resilient renewal. It does so by increasing citizens' awareness of the community's renewal potential, and their understanding of what's inhibiting its renewal.

The other form of analysis that makes a great first step is a policy review. Simply auditing your current public policies (and the legislation, regulations, and incentives that have ensued from them) according to the three renewal rules would likely yield valuable insights into how your policy environment is helping or hindering your renewal.

Doing this up-front education and analysis will likely make assembling your renewal engine far easier, and will help it hit the ground running.

Last Steps: Building Your Access to Resources

No matter how good a community is at partnering, sometimes it simply doesn't have all the financial resources and partners it needs within its borders. After you've created your renewal engine and you're busy culturing your community into a money magnet, you might need to connect with investors, redevelopers, and other key resources outside your community. Maybe even outside your country.

The cruel-but-obvious reality is this: the more a community needs revitalization, the fewer resources they have to achieve it. Money is attracted by prosperity, and is generally repelled by desperation. The flip side is that the more a community revitalizes, the more renewal resources are attracted to it.

Desperate communities should be warned that there's no shortage of predators and scavengers that seek out aged, crippled, and dying communities. They sometimes offer "partnerships" that promise renewal, but that only bring further heartache. These experiences tend to further deplete and demoralize the community, and often end political careers to boot. A reliable source of financing and partners is needed, some kind of filter. The three renewal rules can be that filter.

There's a large and fast-growing legion of enlightened, responsible redevelopers and rewealth investors. All are looking to put their projects and money into equally enlightened, responsible communities. The ideal is for both private and public sectors to operate according to the three renewal rules. That sort of celestial alignment can produce heavenly results.

But the simple existence of potentially perfect partners isn't enough: they need some way to come together in a productive manner at the right time. Some will be found in your community, while others might be on the other side of the world.

The world is covered in restorable assets and renewable communities: how does a rewealth investor know which ones are ready to be revitalized now, as opposed to five years from now? Decrepit buildings, dilapidated infrastructure, degraded natural resources, and a declining economy are all potentially profitable opportunities for restoration, but timing is everything.

An otherwise-excellent project can fail if not preceded or followed by another rewealth project, such as when a revitalized area is not served by adequate infrastructure. Come in to a revitalization effort too early, and you can lose your shirt. Come in too late, and you miss the best of the buy-low, sell-high opportunities.

The best overall guidance I can offer is to seek-out investors and redevelopment partners who share your commitment to the renewal rules. More specific resources can be found in Appendix 3.

How to Stop Being a Victim of Developers

> *The winning design for a 40-acre park that would unfold across the southern half of Governors Island is not the kind of grand public-works project the city once championed. But in an age when developers regularly usurp the government's planning role, it reflects the kind of imaginative, civic-minded thinking that can restore our faith in city and state leaders. The park's informal landscape of undulating hills and voluptuous marshes is a refreshing departure from the crass commercialism that infects so many public projects today. . . . it could well become the most inspired public park built here in generations . . . How refreshing to see government not only take back some responsibility for the public realm, but also to do so with such care.*
>
> —Nicolai Ouroussoff, "A Landscape's Isolation Is Turned Into a Virtue," *New York Times*, December 20, 2007

Let me end this chapter with a tragic story that illustrates what can happen if your community doesn't implement the *re*solution. I was recently invited to be an expert witness in the government-imposed legal hearing (projected to last the better part of a year) regarding a proposed redevelopment in a city with an historic waterfront. A developer has bought all the key properties, and is proposing to tear down some historic buildings to make room for a tower of condos that many local citizens feel will ruin the look and feel of this neighborhood. Politicians and neighborhood leaders have expended vast amounts of time fighting or supporting this project over the past four years. Folks are now both bitter and exhausted.

The developer's proposal and website use all the popular buzzwords such as "new urbanism," "heritage," "revitalize," and "density." There's no mention of restoration, renovation, or reuse though. Citizens took me on a tour, showing evidence that the developer had been purposely letting the area go to seed over his four years of ownership, in order to undermine arguments that there was anything worth saving. Leaving aside appropriateness issues and solutions, my cold-blooded analysis of the situation is this: the city was asking for this kind of trouble.

Waterfront property is in great and increasing demand all over the world (excepting maybe in some low-lying areas that are increasingly concerned about rising global sea levels). They had to know that a developer or redeveloper (one destroys to create new value; the other restores/reuses/renews to create new value) would start eyeing it hungrily, sooner rather than later. But they didn't have a vision for their waterfront, much less their city. They didn't have policies in place that would put some controls on what happened there. And they didn't have a partnering forum. In other words, they not only lacked a renewal engine: they lacked all three of the processes that are normally housed by a renewal engine.

Little wonder, then, that when a developer came to town, he had to supply his own vision, he had no guidance or constraints on his project design, and—lacking a partnering forum—he simply bought-up the property and moved ahead on his own. The city had put itself in reactive mode, simply waiting for something to happen, and then responding to it. Others would call it victim mode. The sad thing is that this is the norm, especially with smaller communities.

You might be wondering, if the citizens are so enamored of their waterfront, why did they sell their properties to this developer in the first place? Because he had a vision, and they didn't. He saw what that waterfront could be, and offered them twice what they thought their property was worth. If the city had had a credible vision and strategy for a revitalized waterfront, the property owners likely would not have sold out so cheaply. But now, with the waterfront owned by the developer, the only hope those who oppose the development have of regaining control of their community's future rests with the decision of the judges running the legal review. All for wont of a renewal engine.

There's nothing capital-intensive about creating a renewal engine. These folks could have done so with less than half the time and effort they've invested in fighting this developer (or fighting their own citizens, in the case of those who are in favor of the project). Had they put their time into forming a renewal engine, they'd have something lasting and worthwhile to show for their work, rather than just hard feelings (which are running so high that some citizens fear the developer will torch the properties if the project is squelched).

Renewal engines should create a "flywheel effect," capturing the momentum of each successful project to make the next one easier. This gives communities more control over their future, turning their redevelopment from a buyer's market to a seller's market. This momentum attracts more investors and redevelopers, and the resulting competition gives the city more leverage at the bargaining table.

Chapter 5

Good Partnerships: How to Renew on a Grand Scale When You're Broke
A new generation of public-private partnerships plays by the renewal rules.

Partnerships succeed. When you go it alone, you fail.
—John Flicker, President, National Audubon Society, in a speech
at 2007 National Conference for Ecosystem Restoration,
Kansas City, Missouri, United States

Why do some communities find all the money they need for major redevelopment and restoration projects, even when they are broke? Seemingly impossible projects have been funded and implemented via creative partnering over the past two decades. These successes gave rise to a proliferation of public-private partnerships worldwide. P3s take so many forms today that there's much confusion over what they are, and what they are not.

Growing recognition of the $100 trillion global shortfall in renewing our built, natural, and socioeconomic assets has collided with the rise of politicians promising tax cuts (there's nothing new about the promise, but some have actually been following through). The resulting budget crises have put community renewal financing front and center. Each time a bridge or levee collapses . . . each time a fishery or ecosystem collapses . . . each time a city or nation runs short of water or power . . . the pressure increases to find more money—and innovative delivery solutions—for renewal projects.

Partnering occupies two entire chapters because it's the primary way in which large-scale rewealth projects get funded. As stated in the previous chapter, rewealth is the key renewal rule, and partnering is the key renewal process. Without funding, most of the lessons of this book are useless. But proper partnering can even bring visioning and culturing capabilities to the table, not just money. This is what makes it the crucial process. This chapter discusses the benefits of partnering, showing how powerful a tool it can be. It describes the essential elements of good public-private, public-public, and private-private partnerships.

Good partnering tends to significantly increase both the size and quality of projects. Partnering overcomes the three resource hurdles faced by most communities in their quest for renewal: how to gain access to sufficient funding, property, and expertise. A study in the United Kingdom recently showed that billion-dollar renewal P3s are becoming almost commonplace. Any time billions of dollars (or their local equivalent) come together, the potential for danger increases. Chapter 6 will thus serve as a caution against some of the deadly P3 traps that still await the unwary.

These two chapters are only overviews of key trends and issues. Readers wishing to take their knowledge to the next level are directed to *Public Private Partnerships* by Grimsey and Lewis (Edward Elgar Publishing, 2004) for a more detailed examination of the issues, and for an introduction to best practices from around the world. It contains a history of partnering, such as when the Romans partnered with the Salassi tribe to build and maintain a toll road through a mountain range. It explains why the French don't have a specific agency to promote P3s: because there, P3s have been a normal, natural way to provide public services for over a century. This excellent book is written in a style that's accessible to all.

What Is a Public-Private Partnership?

> *A P3 is a partnership between the public and private sectors where there is a sharing of risk, responsibility and reward, and where there is a net benefit to the public. Specifically, a P3 is a partnership for some combination of design, construction, financing, operation and/or maintenance of public infrastructure which may rely on user fees or alternative sources of revenue to cover all or part of the related costs of capital (debt servicing and principle payment and return on equity if applicable), operations and capital maintenance. A spectrum of partnership models exists. . .*
>
> —British Columbia Ministry of Science,
> Competition and Enterprise

What is a public-private partnership? This question will be asked and answered repeatedly in this and the next chapter. First, let's be clear that partnering is a process, like visioning and culturing.

That means there's no standard model for it, as there (now) is for a renewal engine. Partnering is the process of developing a trust-based, mutually beneficial relationship to achieve a clearly defined objective. The relationship is captured in a contract, and many "standard" P3 contracts exist, but the relationship can really take almost any form.

The trust factor is one reason application of the *re*solution (see previous chapter) is so important: the more values and expectations shared by the partners, the better things will go. It's far easier to draft a contract than it is to instill trust, so it's best for there to be a natural foundation for the requisite trust. Partnering is hard for both public and private institutions that were born and developed in an adversarial and/or litigious environment. Rather than wait for an institutional evolution that might never come, communities in need of revitalization are creating new institutions that are built on trust from day one. By now, you know what they're called: renewal engines.

P3s take more time to create than traditional contracts, but the time spent in the research and risk analysis (both of which are minimal in most non-partnered public contracting) can pay dividends for decades to come via the better solutions that often ensue.

P3s Can Solve Two of the Greatest Barriers to Creating Greener Communities

As a general rule, the more of the asset's lifecycle that's provided by the private partner, the better the project is likely to turn out. For example, one of the major barriers to creating healthier and more efficient commercial buildings is the disconnect between the designers/owners of a building and those who pay the utility bills. If someone else is going to occupy the space, and someone else is going to pay the utilities, what motivation does a developer have (other than conscience) to use less toxic and less wasteful designs and materials if they cost more up front and aren't required by law?

But what if a community partners with a firm to finance, renovate (or design, if new), operate, and maintain a public facility? Such contracts usually run for 25 to 35 years. In that case, it's in the best interests of the P3 to design or retrofit the facility with the greenest (most efficient/least toxic) materials and technologies. After all, the public partner's citizens or employees will inhabit it, and the private partner will be paying the water and electricity bills. Under those circumstances, lifecycle costing makes sense, so the use of highly efficient components that cost more up front is no longer a problem. Thus, we no longer have to rely on conscience, public relations, or even regulations to motivate green building techniques. This same argument applies just as well to power or drinking water utilities as it does to schools and office space.

Such lifecycle integrity solves another problem, as well, one that is specific to infrastructure. The adoption of many highly efficient and environmentally friendly power and water technologies has been retarded in recent decades by the opposite problem: they cost too little. Public utilities are usually contracted on a cost-plus basis: the engineering firm is guaranteed a profit based on a percentage of the project's cost.

If your company's revenue were, say, 5% of a project's budget, how much motivation would you have to go with designs or technologies that cut the cost of the project in half? But, if the city only wants the *service* of power or clean water from you, your job is now figuring out how to deliver it in the most efficient way possible. That's a very different proposition.

Such a shift from owning assets to contracting for services is at the heart of many P3s. Again, a partnership isn't just a transaction: it's a relationship designed to achieve a mutually agreed-upon goal, such as providing a community with all the high-quality drinking water it needs.

P3s could help resolve the debate that is currently raging over bottled water. The plastic wasted in packaging—and the energy expended in transporting—bottled water is immense.

Unfortunately, in their zeal to end such waste, many environmental groups have resorted to whitewashing very real concerns over the safety and palatability of tap water. It's a return to the bad old days when early environmental groups didn't hesitate to put nature's needs over those of humans, and didn't even try to find solutions that benefited both. This adversarial approach greatly limited their effectiveness then, and it's doing so again now on the bottled water issue.

The inconvenient truth is that most consumers don't like the taste or toxicity of chlorine. Many also know that there are over 10,000 toxic or potentially toxic human-made chemicals circulating in our world. Most public drinking water facilities test for just a few, and most "modern" technologies can't remove many of them. Ask the managers of most drinking water utilities how well they monitor contaminants, and their answer will usually focus on how often they test, not on how many substances they test for. As a result, cities tend to discover they have a problem only when a disease cluster emerges. I mentioned that in *The Restoration Economy*, but it bears repeating. Add to that the threat of biological, chemical, and heavy metal contamination from ancient infrastructure (or from sabotage), and green consumers are forced to choose between nature and the nurturing of their own health.

P3s can solve that dilemma by eliminating the lifecycle disconnect that leads to waste in the form of energy-intensive, non–ecologically sound water purification technologies. P3s can similarly eliminate the cost-plus contracts that block low-cost technological innovations. In some cases, greening is simply a matter of retrofit. For instance, algae-based and biological community-based systems (such as the approaches pioneered by Walter Adey and John Todd almost two decades ago) can polish and oxygenate drinking water, making tap water *better* than bottled water, because it won't contain leachates from the plastic bottles.

Constructed wetlands also polish and oxygenate water from sewage plants. Since much of our drinking water comes from rivers and lakes that upstream communities and industries are using as toilets and waste dumps, their use results in ecological restoration, as the discharged water is cleaner than the uptake. We've been chlorinating and fluoridating the world's oceans and waterways long enough. What's more, those constructed wetlands can provide a badly needed supplement to natural wildlife habitat.

Both people and wildlife end up with healthier water, and the bottled water industry goes down the toilet (sorry guys: I really appreciated you while you were needed). Until that happens, though, I'm going to continue filtering my water at home, and drinking bottled water on the road. Another point I made in my first book that bears repeating is that I'd rather buy a filter than be a filter.

A lifecycle partnership for the renovation and operation of a toll road is not a purchase of a road, but of a transportation *service*. How is the public welfare protected from abuse? Primarily through payments related to performance and availability. The private partner agrees to be penalized when the quality of the service falls below certain levels, or when it's not available at all (such as during maintenance and upgrades). It's not adversarial: the private partner knows up front that failure is not an option when dealing with vital public services. The price of entry into the P3 market is the acceptance of responsibility—risk, in other words.

Is the public always protected from abuse? Not by a long shot. A taxi driver just last week complained bitterly to me about how a publicly owned toll road to the airport had been sold to a private contractor. He said that toll increases were supposed to be regulated, but that they had gone up three or four times—to about $10 for just a few kilometers—and the private firm was making obscene profits. More about such dangers in the next chapter, but I'll ask a question now, for you to ponder. If the taxi driver's complaints are legitimate (I don't know if they are, which is why I didn't name the city), who is more at fault; the city for not protecting the public interest, or the private firm for taking advantage?

At the moment, Canada and the Europeans—and the United Kingdom in particular—are far ahead of the rest of the world in the design and delivery of true partnerships. The United States has developed leading-edge expertise on the legal, financial, and technical side, but the relationship side—our partnering process—is still in a very primitive state. The trust factor on both sides is very low.

This might be a result of our traditional distrust of big government. It might be due to the fact that our construction industry is hugely adversarial and lacking in integration, or the result of abuse of the public good by huge corporations, or simply because of our litigious nature. Whatever the reason, the United States is behind the curve. This is probably why the vast majority of my work is abroad.

The United States is especially weak in applying the third renewal rule: effective engagement of stakeholders. This same weakness makes us less adept at the third renewal process: partnering. The solution for us will most likely be found (surprise!) in adopting the *re*solution, which—among other benefits—results in the creation of community and/or regional renewal partnerships.

Most P3s are formed and implemented in a way that doesn't significantly enhance the community's expertise in partnering. Nor do they improve the overall culture to better support partnering in particular and renewal in general. In other words, communities aren't increasing their renewal capacity as a result of these experiences. This is partially because most P3s are project based (rather than program-based): and are often confined to the silo of the primary asset involved. The other reason is that most communities don't have a mechanism for increasing their renewal capacity. A renewal engine solves both problems by capturing both the lessons and the momentum of each successful project to make subsequent projects easier and better.

A transportation P3 tends to involve primarily transportation, finance, and legal people. A wastewater P3 tends to involve primarily wastewater, finance, and legal people. While the community often has to approve the initiative at some point, it's not really *their* process. Each individual agency increases its partnering expertise when they do a P3, but the community itself isn't developing any such expertise.

A renewal engine, on the other hand, should be the starting point for all P3s. It should also be where the subsequent designs are vetted against the community's shared vision of their future. That way, a new sewage treatment plant isn't located on a waterfront the community intends to revitalize in 10 years. That way, an old sewage treatment plant on a waterfront slated for revitalization isn't renovated, it's replaced by a facility in a more appropriate location.

"The wave of the future is a public/private partnership to run parks," [Cathy McNair, executive director of Shenandoah National Park Trust] said. *"Parks are just getting more expensive to run."*
—Carlos Santos, **"Shenandoah Rebuilding Skyline Drive portions,"** *Richmond Times-Dispatch,* December 9, 2007

The two primary motivations for partnering from the public side's point of view are (1) to acquire a level of public service that the community could not afford to provide on its own, and (2) to shift risk to the private sector, since citizens expect uninterrupted provision of essential services. The two primary motivations for the private side are (1) to create and expand into new markets, providing services that are logical extensions of their core expertise, and (2) to acquire long-term contracts that provide reliable cash flow for decades (rather than merely during a one- or two-year construction phase).

Public-private partnerships thus enable the creation, operation, or renewal of public services or facilities to be funded and implemented in whole or in part by for-profit companies.

In some cases, the public sector taps tax revenue to pay for contracted services from a private firm. In other cases, the public side of the investment is in the form of transferring assets to the private partner; an abandoned (and contaminated) industrial waterfront property, an old government building, a power generating system, or an aging bridge.

In yet other cases, such as private finance initiatives (primarily a UK term), the private firm makes the entire initial investment, on the basis of the expectation of recouping it through a long-term service contract with the government. For instance, in the case of the expensive renovation of an aging hospital, a private consortium will often form a "special purpose vehicle" (SPV) to restore and maintain the building.

Such a consortium might include a constructor, a maintenance firm, and a lender (often a commercial bank). This SPV enters into a contractual relationship with the local government, and usually hires subcontractors to do the renovation and maintenance work. The hospital would then be owned by the SPV, but they would often lease it to a public healthcare agency. The private partner is basically the landlord and housekeeper, and all medical services are provided by the healthcare agency.

A P3 can be applied to a broad variety of public needs: property development/redevelopment, educational facilities, social services, transportation, water/wastewater services, public safety, parks and recreational facilities, national defense, telecommunications, and financial management are some of the more common. Public assets are usually involved and public employees often are as well.

In most cases, the goal is cost savings and/or quality improvement. Private firms are often seen as being less prone to bureaucratic red tape, while being more efficient and innovative. The motivating assumption is that the private sector can bring more sophisticated design/management expertise to bear on the situation, while assuming some or all of the risk if the project encounters problems.

Thanks to the gross (and growing) mismatch between the $100 trillion of public "re" needs and the paucity of public financial resources, a lot of creativity has been stimulated over the past decade or two. The goal has been to figure out how the public sector can gain access to private funding while maintaining some semblance of control over the results. In other words, harnessing the profit motive without sacrificing the public good.

There have been three basic drivers of this move toward public-private partnerships: (1) the aging of public facilities and infrastructure (combined with deferred maintenance), (2) population growth and resulting resource shortages, and (3) renewed interest in urban living.

The renewed interest in urban lifestyles is directly related to the constraint crisis. It's driven in part by the reconomies that have made downtowns more livable, in part by growing disgust with the sterility and disconnection of suburban/exurban lifestyles, and in part by demographics. Young people find urban environments more stimulating and "cool," while older people find the ability to dispense with their car and walk to food, fun, and friends more convenient, more economical, more enjoyable, and far healthier.

As a result of the urbanization trend, renewal partnerships have been proliferating. In this book, I'll refer to any P3 that has a rewealth focus as a "renewal partnership." But even renewal partnerships cover a broad spectrum of quality standards, which is why we need to screen them according to *all three* renewal rules, not just rewealth. Even good goals can be pursued badly.

Good Partnerships Reduce Public Risk

Currently, "public-private partnership" is used to describe a bewildering array of relationships, contracts, legal entities, and financial vehicles. So, there's a great deal of confusion as to what a P3 really is. In fact, even the abbreviation is changing: P3 is increasingly accepted as the global standard, but you'll frequently come across the older "PPP." (If you want muscular lips, try saying "PPP" 100 times per day.)

Definitions and labels aside, there's also a great deal of confusion over how to do a P3 "right." While the theoretical advantages of public-private partnerships are obvious, what isn't obvious is how to create one. The fact that some are phenomenally successful while others are outright disasters leaves public leaders with mixed feelings about them.

The bad publicity emanating from corrupt, inept, fake, and/or destructive P3s has made life difficult for honest, competent, real, restorative P3s. This has catalyzed the appearance of new terminology—such as public finance initiative in the United Kingdom or "alternative financing and procurement" in Ontario—as folks try to tap the positive qualities of P3s without dragging along the negative baggage that has attached itself to the label.

> *Our definition of a public-private partnership is, "A cooperative venture between the public and private sectors, built on the expertise of each partner, that best meets clearly defined public needs through the appropriate allocation of resources, risks and rewards." There must be a transfer of risk evident in the arrangement. A contribution from the private sector in kind or actual payment (a sponsorship for example) with no risk obligation would not meet the test in our organization's definition.*

—Jane Peatch, Executive Director, Canadian Council for Public-Private Partnerships (April 9, 2007, private communication with author)

Jane Peatch's definition (above) offers the simplest way to determine whether a P3 is a true partnership, or is just a sweetheart deal for a well-connected company. If the private sector is taking a risk the community is not willing to take, that company is providing the community a real service, and deserves to be appropriately rewarded.

Without that risk factor, such deals are just privatization of public assets, which often creates effective monopolies. This is ironic for two reasons: (1) most government procurement processes emphasize competitive bidding, and (2) companies specializing in the privatization of public utilities claim they will be more efficient because of the competitive pressures that typify the private sector. The effect of these abusive contracts, unfortunately, is usually to shield the winner from competitive pressures, thus neutralizing both of those factors.

Partnering isn't always needed when risk needs to be transferred to the private sector. This is especially true for short-term projects. On April 9, 2007, a gasoline tanker truck burned beneath a span of an important artery road in the San Francisco Bay Area, causing a 55-meter section to collapse. The California Department of Transportation (Caltrans) needed the road fixed fast, as many thousands of commuters depended on it daily.

Caltrans determined that it would normally take about 50 days to repair such damage. They issued an RFP (request for proposal) stipulating a $200,000/day penalty for each day after 50 days that the road remained closed. But they also offered a bonus for each day less than 50, up to a maximum of $5 million.

Construction firm C.C. Myers won the contract with a bid of $867,075, finished 32 days early, and got their $5-million bonus. Everyone was happy, especially the commuters. There was no time or need for a public-private partnership: the situation demanded a more expedient way to transfer risk. But even that project had some partnering characteristics.

In the article "Early Opening Earns Highway Contractor $5-Million Bonus" by Mike Nolan and Robert Carlsen (in the June 4, 2007, *Engineering News Record*), Donald Reeve, president of Reeve Trucking (a subcontractor) said "A project of this size would normally take two or three months to complete, and most of that would be waiting for Caltrans approval for different parts. But [Caltrans] had the motivation to work with [C.C. Myers]. This was an emergency." Often, the most valuable thing the public sector can contribute to a partnership is getting its own bureaucracy out of the way.

How to Recognize a Desirable Partnership

Besides transfer of risk, the three renewal rules provide the quickest and easiest way to distinguish good P3s from bad. For instance, the de/re perspective is one way to evaluate partnerships. A dewealth-based partnership combines public and private resources in a destructive or depleting activity that might have some short-term economic benefits, but which undermines both the economy and quality of life in the long run.

Examples would be ramming a new highway through a rainforest, building a new industrial park on farmland, and damming a river. Many people suffer immediate damage from massive dewealth projects, as we've seen with the Three Gorges Dam in China. This wasn't a P3, but it displaced millions of people and is causing billions of dollars worth of environmental and economic damage.

That suffering makes public-private partnering on such a project especially inappropriate, especially in democracies. It's bad enough when your own elected officials make monumental mistakes, but far more controversial when private companies are profiting from your suffering. That's not good for political careers, as you'll see in the following chapter.

A rewealth-based partnership (what we're calling renewal partnerships) combines public and private resources to accomplish an activity that enhances the health or capacity of an asset the community already possesses. It often undoes damage done by earlier dewealth projects. Examples would include cleaning and redeveloping a brownfield, replacing or restoring an old bridge, removing a waterfront highway, and renovating/expanding a sewage system. Regardless of any other characteristics, that one factor, dewealth versus rewealth, should be a go/no-go decision.

"De" versus "re" isn't the only determinant of whether a partnership will help or hinder your community, though. Our growing global population means that some sprawl is sometimes necessary. (I'll let braver souls address the issue of whether a growing population is necessary). New infrastructure is sometimes necessary even in the absence of population growth.

For instance, a city with no sewage treatment system—like Halifax, Nova Scotia or Victoria, British Columbia—will be doing themselves (and the world in general) a favor by building one, as Halifax is finally doing. Even Victoria—a beautiful city with filthy habits, sewage-wise—is seriously considering it, under pressure from the provincial government. This will bring both cities into the twentieth century before the middle of the twenty-first.

Looked at from the angle of the distressed harbor or sound that has long received the raw sewage, those new treatment plants are part of the effort to restore that body of water. So even new infrastructure can be restorative.

One can only hope that both cities will take advantage of the long delay to leapfrog to the cutting-edge of sewage treatment design and technology. They won't combine sewage and storm water, of course: no one in their right mind does that any more. But they might make the mistake of going with ancient, energy-and-chemical-intensive processes in centralized facilities, as opposed to the more efficient ecologically-based or biomimetic water purification (or polishing) technologies, combined with smaller facilities distributed to the most appropriate locations.

In other cases, new utilities are replacements for obsolete systems. Replacement is a legitimate element of restorative development—our bodies are replacing old and damaged cells all the time, for instance—so these projects should also be done via renewal partnerships.

Sometimes, due to population growth and development patterns, it's no longer appropriate to have the replacement system in the same location. A renewal engine would—thanks to applying all three renewal rules—help ensure that the new system is located and designed in a way that doesn't impede an area's regeneration, doesn't destroy ecosystems or cultural resources, and doesn't pollute (with toxins or noise) low-income or ethnic neighborhoods.

Embedding the three renewal rules in a community's decision-making would automatically guide a new sewage system in a restorative, non-destructive, and socially just direction. Sewage treatment (for example) would no longer be planned in isolation. It would become an integral part of the area's vision of restoring natural assets, enhancing quality of life, and revitalizing the economy. A fringe benefit is that those additional agendas make funding a state-of-the-art system more feasible.

For instance, you might have an ugly brownfield in a depressed area that's undesirable for any kind of residential or commercial redevelopment. Putting that new sewage plant there would provide an economic justification for cleaning up a site that might have otherwise continued to leak toxins for decades. The sewage facility thus restores the value and functionality of that property.

Putting that same facility on top of a pristine wetland, on the other hand, would destroy an asset of long-lasting and multifaceted value, not to mention being a rather nasty thing to do to the creatures living there. A planning department or public works department won't always care about the frogs, but a well-run renewal engine certainly will.

While the de/re test is a key determinant, the other two renewal rules are what really distinguishes the new breed of P3 from the old. The integration and engagement rules affect how the P3s are formed, funded, and managed. The mistakes the *re*solution can prevent are often of the brain-dead variety, the kind that—years down the road—makes people say, "What were they *thinking?*" An example would be a community that donates land for a suburban shopping mall when they are trying to revitalize their downtown, or that renovates a waterfront garbage transfer facility, rather then relocating it. Citizens and tourists have no desire to spend their recreational time around a power generation or sewage treatment facility.

Projects that demonstrate concern for the welfare of the community aren't designed in silos: they will look for ways to *integrate* the main focus of the project (infrastructure, brownfield, waterfront, or whatever) until it becomes a catalyst for renewal. They will also look for opportunities to *engage* everyone who will be affected by the project to seek ways to do it better. This engagement will often reveal the integration opportunities they were looking for. A renewal engine provides them with a venue for doing so.

How Smaller Communities Can Successfully Partner with Giant Firms (or Agencies)

Sometimes, a public-public partnership with a federal program will provide all the funding and risk management a community needs, and there will be no need tap the private sector's resources. In the United States, as federal funds are increasingly devoured by overseas misadventures, this is becoming less common. The federal government increasingly requires states to deliver new or expanded services without providing the means to do so.

So, the most common situation will be that some private sector contribution is needed to make the community's dreams come true. If a community seeks to renew its natural, built, or socioeconomic assets, and needs to tap private capital to fund it, then a renewal partnership is needed. That's simple enough.

The tricky part is how to do it so that the public good is maximized. After all, many communities—especially smaller ones—have never done a P3 before. They end up partnering with giant redevelopment and engineering firms that do P3s all the time. How can a tiny community's part-time leaders and small-time attorneys hope to come away from such a negotiation without finding themselves holding the smelly end of the privatization stick?

The Ontario Ministry of Public Infrastructure Renewal (PIR) is a world leader when it comes to tackling the challenge of designing and managing P3s responsibly. In May of 2005, they established a set of five principles and guidelines for P3s: (1) The partnering process must be fair, transparent, and efficient; (2) The public interest must remain paramount; (3) There must be a demonstrable value received for the public money; (4) Appropriate levels of public control and ownership must be retained (such as to prevent the privatization issues described earlier); (5) Accountability must be maintained.

Apply those five criteria to projects that are based on the three renewal rules, and you should have a formula for spectacular success.

Creating Renewal Partnerships

To praise the growth of public-private partnerships to meet public needs is not to criticize government—federal, state or local—as being unable to meet those needs. Rather, applause is due to innovative public officials who are seeking creative means to meet public demands and expectations. Government leaders face a "perfect storm" of economic and social dilemmas and demands. . . . The nation's infrastructure is aging and needs replacement and revitalization. A growing and aging population is placing greater pressure on federal, state and local services of all kinds. The public has made it clear at the ballot box that it is reluctant to increase taxes as a potential answer to these problems.

—*For the Good of the People: Using Public-Private Partnerships To Meet America's Essential Needs,* **a white paper by The National Council for Public-Private Partnerships (2002)**

As we'll see in Chapter 6, some P3s—such as water privatization schemes—provoke a level of public outrage that has to be suppressed by riot squads, killing the partnership and even ending political careers. For now, let's skip directly to preventing such situations.

The most common engagement technique of community redevelopment programs is to invite public comment whenever a major new project is about to be approved. This is just a token: if the public's opinion really mattered, their opinion would be sought much earlier. But confidentiality considerations during the early days of a proposed partnership can prevent that. How to reconcile the conflicting constraints of confidentiality and transparency?

One solution, as described in Chapter 4, is to have a shared vision in place. If that vision is shared by all stakeholders, the project can be vetted against the vision in private, thus serving the goal of public engagement and confidentiality. Then, when the project is presented to the public just prior to being approved, it's no longer just a thin veneer of engagement.

There is such a broad spectrum of renewal partnership types that no standard process for creating them could be documented here. You'll be exposed to a wide range of partnering solutions throughout the book, and most of the stories will give you some insight into how they came about.

There's no shortage of literature on the legal and financial aspect of creating public-private partnerships, and it's beyond the scope of this book to get into such details. Suffice it to say that if your partnerships are spawned by a well-designed, well-run renewal engine, many of the key success factors will be addressed automatically; factors such as transparency or integration with your community goals.

There seem to be three fundamental factors behind the disastrous P3s, and none of these factors is getting sufficient attention. The first problem is terminology. Far too many different types of activities are being crammed under the P3 label:

long-term coalitions, short-term ventures, and specific categories of business transactions (such as outsourcing). As long as "public-private partnership" remains such an imprecise catchall phrase, confusion will reign, and communities will be hobbled in their ability to use these tools effectively. Jane Peatch's risk-based definition (mentioned earlier) weeds out many pretenders quite nicely.

A unique (though not necessarily recommended) example of melding the public and private domains is found in the town of Sandy Springs, Georgia (a newly-created suburb of Atlanta). They turned over management of virtually the entire community to the United States-based multinational engineering firm CH2MHill. Everything except government "core competence" areas such as fire, police, and judiciary are run by CH2MHill. Whether that contract can legitimately be considered partnering boils down to one factor: how much risk did CH2MHill take on? If none, or very little, then it was just outsourcing. That would be a vendor relationship. There's nothing wrong with that, but it's not a partnership.

P3 Contracts

Renewal partnerships take a vast diversity of forms, as do P3s in general. Almost any generic form of P3 can be focused on rewealth activities, thus becoming a renewal partnership. The renewal partnerships category is actually larger than the public-private partnerships category, since renewal partnerships also include public-public and private-private partnerships. Let's look at some of the forms of contracts typical to P3s (renewal and otherwise).

In April of 1999, the U.S. Government Accounting Office published *Public-Private Partnerships: Terms Related to Building and Facility Partnerships*. Here's their list of P3 types used primarily for individual buildings and facilities: Lease/Purchase; Sale/Leaseback; Tax-Exempt Lease; Turnkey; Build/Operate/Transfer (BOT); Build/Transfer/Operate (BTO); Build-Own-Operate (BOO); Contract Services (Operations and Maintenance or Operations, Maintenance, and Management); Design-Build (DB); Enhanced Use Leasing (EUL); Design-Build-Maintain (DBM); and Design-Build-Operate (DBO).

Here are three additional forms of contracts often used by P3s. These three are most commonly used on rewealth projects for public buildings, facilities, and infrastructure:

- Buy-Build-Operate (BBO): BBOs are primarily used where a public entity sells an asset to a private redeveloper so as to rehabilitate and operate it.

■ Developer Finance: This is where the private sector pays for the construction, renovation, or expansion of a public facility in exchange for the right to add residential, commercial, or industrial facilities to the site.

■ Lease/Develop/Operate (LDO) or Build/Develop/Operate (BDO): These relationships are created to enable a redeveloper to lease or purchase an existing public facility and then renovate, modernize, and/or expand it. The private party then operates the facility under contract. This is often used to revive or enhance municipal transit operations.

Those are just terms in use in the United States. The United Kingdom has a similar list with some differences, and it's at least as long. If that profusion of contractual and legal relationships indicates to you that this is an area of great activity, you'd be right, but it only scratches the surface. More importantly, those examples are primarily used in projects of fairly limited complexity. I don't mean small: many of the larger neighborhood redevelopment and infrastructure-related P3s run into the billions of dollars.

The trend, however, is toward greater complexity, not just size. That means including natural resource restoration and socioeconomic renewal. Such projects are normally focused primarily on renewing buildings, contaminated lands, and infrastructure. No small task, but incorporating natural and social renewal agendas ratchets up the potential payback to the community tremendously.

Four Short Stories from Washington, DC

Most of the stories in this book are in Part III, but the best way to illustrate the power of public-private partnering is with some real-life examples. So, here are four stories from our hometown (the Resolution Fund office is three blocks from the White House). They are offered in chronological order: Union Station (1988), Washington, DC Bureau of Parking (1999), Oyster School (2001), and the New York Avenue Metrorail Station (2006).

Let me start by pointing out that Washington's comfort with the concept of public-private partnering probably started with visionary architect Arthur Cotton Moore's phenomenal revitalization of the Georgetown waterfront. Born in 1935, Princeton-educated Moore was one of the pioneers of the renewal trend in the United States. He was certainly the trend's private-side leader in Washington, DC. I consider him the grand old man of the restoration economy in the United States, though he's more physically graceful and mentally agile than many who are much younger.

Moore's path to specializing in renewal probably began in 1976, with his work redeveloping the Nashville, Tennessee, waterfront. Virtually his entire career since then has been based on the restoration of grand old buildings (such as the recent $81-million renovation of the Library of Congress), the renovation and reuse of generic industrial buildings into places of beauty, and the revitalization of waterfronts. His projects can be found in three dozen cities around the world.

Moore is still at it. In his Watergate studio, he showed me proposals for connecting the Kennedy Center to the Potomac and for extending the National Mall. Both were seamless weddings of beauty and common sense. Of his Georgetown work in the 1980s, he told me "I felt like we were pioneering a trend. Nobody else was doing this, and it looked like it would keep us in business." He was right on both counts.

Moore is not a fan of the new urbanism panacea, saying it should be called "new suburbanism." One of his favorite quotes is "Authenticity is the power that comes from being real without trying." True urbanism (using existing buildings) versus new urbanism, in other words. After I posited that restorative development is far more sustainable than most of what's labeled sustainable these days, he said "You're right to say that reuse of an old building is far more sustainable and responsible then just greening a new building. There's still a basic bias in government against reuse. I don't know why that's true."

The gorgeous "industrial baroque" style Moore invented for the 1986 Washington Harbor redevelopment skillfully harmonized the new buildings erected on this brownfield site with the old industrial buildings he was renovating and reusing in the surrounding area . . . without simply mimicking them, as lazier architects often do. That project required partnering with the District, mostly on issues regarding infrastructure renewal. Today, Washington Harbor—formerly the ugliest, most crime-ridden spot in Georgetown—is a lively, must-see destination for every visitor to Washington. It wasn't a P3 as we know them today, but it certainly was a P3 in spirit. To learn more about Moore, find a copy of his 1998 classic, *The Powers of Preservation: New Life for Urban Historic Places*, which is currently out of print.

Among the following four stories, you'll encounter examples of many different aspects of P3s, including outsourcing, privatization, joint venturing, design-restore-operate (the rewealth version of design-build-operate), and creative mutual problem solving.

Union Station

Any readers who have strolled in awe through Washington, DC's lovely Union Station have viscerally experienced the power of a renewal partnership. In the early

20th century, when railroads ruled the terrestrial transportation universe, most people entered and left Washington through Union Station. Being the primary portal of our nation's capital, it was a regal structure, located just a few blocks' walk through tree-filled parks from the U.S. Capitol building.

As airlines and automobiles gained supremacy after World War II, the recently built National Airport (across the river in Arlington, Virginia) was expanded, and U.S. passenger rail service went into a steep decline. Union Station paralleled that decline, and by the 1970s, it was a shameful relic. Massive holes in the roof made mushrooms, toadstools, and pigeons the only life to be found in the Grand Foyer.

Congress sealed the building in 1981 to prevent any further vandalism, and to avoid lawsuits from injuries. But they could hardly countenance having such a symbol of blight and decrepitude sitting in plain sight of both the public and our national leaders. As a result, they almost unanimously passed the Union Station Redevelopment Act. The act authorized the use of a public-private partnership to restore the building, both visually and functionally. The stated goal was to turn Union Station into a viable mixed-use transportation center, while restoring the historic building to its original glory.

The $160-million restoration and adaptive reuse project began in 1985 and finished three years later. Washington, DC was in dire economic straits at the time, so it was no small benefit that the project cost the taxpayers not one penny. The U.S. Department of Transportation currently owns the structure, but the private company Jones Lang LaSalle actually operates the building, and services the more than 100 restaurants and retailers who together generate over $70 million annually in sales. The rent paid by these businesses covers 100% of both the operating budget and maintenance of the debt incurred during restoration, not to mention a nice profit for the private partner.

As a local resident, I can't begin to express how much pleasure and value this wonderful building adds to my life. Taking the train to New York City is a joy, thanks in large part to this renewal partnership. Now, all we have to do is restore our shabby U.S. passenger rail service, whose condition wouldn't be tolerated in many countries we consider "lesser-developed."

Washington, DC, Bureau of Parking

The sight of thousands of headless meters on the city's streets had severely tarnished the District's image, giving it the look of a war zone. In a city like DC that hosts millions of visitors every year, the new meter program has dramatically improved the aesthetics of the city streets. . . .While maintaining control of the elements central to parking management regulation and policy decision, the District has creatively used the capital resources and operational expertise of its private-sector partner to restore a program to its former world-class status.

—from a case study by the National Council for Public-Private Partnerships, which gave the Washington, DC, parking services project one of their annual awards in 1999

This next story deals with one of the most mundane of subjects: parking meters. This is primarily an outsourcing story. Although we don't normally consider pure outsourcing contracts to be partnerships, they are often important components of them. It's seldom a black-and-white situation, so I'll leave it to you to determine whether the following story is just a business deal, or whether it contained elements of partnering.

Back in the 1960s and 1970s, Washington, DC, was seen to be on the forefront of public parking operations. By the late 1990s, however, vandalism and old age had rendered over half of their 40-year-old meters inoperable. Monthly meter revenue had dropped from over $1 million to under $200,000. This created a monthly loss of $800,000, since it didn't come close to paying for the Bureau of Parking's overhead and maintenance.

The city was broke, so the only chance of renovating their meter system was to tap private resources. Their use of a P3 to solve the parking meter problem once again made them a national leader. The District of Columbia Bureau of Parking Services became the first public entity in the United States to use the private sector to restore their parking system, both physically and operationally.

They selected ACS State and Local Solutions (a division of Fortune 500 company Affiliated Computer Systems of Dallas) and Lockheed Martin IMS to not just replace the meters, but to run the entire parking operation. In other words, they privatized it.

Soon, 99 percent of the city's meters were working at any given time, and users were very happy with their state-of-the-art electronic, vandal-resistant hardware, which allow them to use quarters, dimes, or nickels. Complaints from drivers over meter malfunctions fell off precipitously. The meters were installed 60 days earlier than the contract required, and can be retrofitted to use "smart cards." Revenues bounced back to over $1 million monthly almost instantly.

By way of full disclosure, I should probably end this story by mentioning that I just returned from a lecture at the beautifully restored National Building Museum in Washington, DC. I fed $2.00 worth of quarters into a nearby meter, and the meter dutifully showed an additional 15 minutes as I added each coin. But, when I hit the maximum of two hours, it suddenly displayed "FAIL," forcing me to move (you get a ticket for parking at a broken meter: this discourages purposeful jamming via slugs). I first banged on the meter to knock a little sense into its head, and discovered that others had probably been doing likewise for some time: it was so loose it almost fell off. So, maybe this particular partnership is starting to unravel . . .

Oyster School

Public schools in low-income neighborhoods face numerous challenges, including: erosion of the tax base supporting school budgets; high rates of student mobility and absenteeism; buildings that lack the infrastructure to support modern teaching methods; a parent population struggling with employment, housing, and health issues; declining enrollments; and a high proportion of students with special needs. At the same time as they are challenged by neighborhood conditions, poorly performing public schools may accelerate neighborhood decline by hindering the preservation or creation of stable residential communities. . . . Coordinated investment in neighborhood revitalization and school reform has the potential to reverse this downward trend. . . . a neighborhood revitalization strategy that includes a school improvement component will be more successful and more sustainable than a strategy that focuses only on the neighborhood.
—Jill Khadduri, Heather Schwartz, and Jennifer Turnham,
Reconnecting Schools and Neighborhoods: An Introduction to School-Center Community Revitalization (Enterprise Community Partners, Inc., 2007)

Sometimes, a renewal partnership springs from a brilliant moment of creative thinking. After the last two stories, you might be thinking that renewal partnerships are for boring stuff like parking meters and water mains. But providing better schools for our children is every bit as appropriate an application.

The Enterprise Community Partners report cited above offers five criteria for integrating educational renewal with economic renewal. They say, "What makes a community revitalization effort 'school-centered' is its focus on five core elements: 1) Improvement of one or more schools in the neighborhood; 2) Housing that is safe, affordable, and attractive to families with children; 3) High-quality child care and early childhood education programs; 4) Affordable health services for children; 5) Workforce and economic development programs."

Here's a renewal partnership story that hits those first two criteria square on the head, and it wasn't even part of a community revitalization effort. In 1995, Washington, DC's James F. Oyster Bilingual Elementary School Building was suffering from overcrowded classrooms and a dilapidated structure. It was considered to be poorly delivering its innovative English/Spanish dual-language immersion program. The school was not in compliance with federal requirements for access by the disabled, but the school lacked the money to renovate, even though the District's economy was on the upswing at the time.

Meanwhile, LCOR Incorporated, a private real estate developer based in Bethesda, Maryland, was looking to build another multifamily building somewhere in the greater Washington, DC, area. The best location for a family-oriented apartment building, of course, is close to a desirable public school. But no land was available near Oyster School, so no apartments had been proposed.

When the city announced that the school was scheduled to close, the founder and executive director of the nonprofit, Washington, DC-based, 21st Century School Fund, Mary Filardo, came up with a brilliant idea: swapping some of the school's real estate for a new school. They sent out an RFP, to which LCOR successfully responded. LCOR had never built a school before, but they were willing to participate in what looked like a wonderfully creative opportunity.

Their mutual needs were met via an innovative partnership with District of Columbia Public Schools, whereby the school system financed the replacement of the 42,000-square-foot school by issuing a 35-year, tax-exempt bond. The bond was designed to be repaid entirely with revenue generated by the 210,000-square-foot Henry Adams House apartment building that LCOR built on 35,000 square feet of land on the school grounds. 21st Century School Fund played the vital role of intermediary, providing a trusted third party for Washington, DC's school officials to deal with in this politically risky and highly unusual experiment.

In June of 2001, Washington, DC, residents opened the doors on an $11 million school with a gym, library, computer lab, and classrooms designed specifically for their bilingual education. It was their first new school in two decades, and it had cost taxpayers nothing but some of their creative, open-minded public leaders' time.

LCOR, for its part, was able to build an apartment complex right next to the most desirable "new" public school in the city. It's near both a Metro station and the National Zoo, and is in an attractive part of town that had no real estate available for such a project. LCOR invested approximately $26 million in the project, and sold the residential building two years later for $56 million, after it was fully leased. This extraordinary payback was due—according to LCOR—primarily to their having underestimated the value of two factors: (1) the rental market in that area, and (2) the value of having a nonprofit as an intermediary.

That second factor should be a lesson to all, because speeding good renewal partnerships through the negotiating and bureaucratic processes is a key value of a renewal engine. Redevelopers usually are working on borrowed money, so anything that accelerates agreements and approvals contributes to the bottom line.

In fact, 21st Century School Fund was so happy with the Oyster School outcome that they are currently working to replicate this success in lesser-developed countries. Most of them have even less public funding available for education or affordable housing. Part of this solution is to implement support for partnering in public policy. Different situations require different solutions, so they are also exploring how a similar success can be achieved via public-*public* partnerships.

A few citizens later experienced sellers' remorse, complaining that they could have got an even better deal if they had known how much profit LCOR would earn on the deal. But most don't begrudge LCOR their rich rewards when they see the benefits this partnership generated for the neighborhood in general, and the children in particular.

This sort of win-win-with-no-downsides outcome is the norm for renewal partnerships. In case you're wondering, Oyster School *is* a "re" project, even though the school building was new construction. As noted earlier, replacement is a legitimate aspect of rewealth when the existing asset is not worth renovating.

What's more, the project was built entirely on the existing footprint, so no destruction of natural land or historic buildings took place. There is such a thing as "destructive redevelopment," such as in redevelopment projects that don't use the three renewal rules. The urban removal disasters of the 1950s and 1960s bear painful testament to the possibility of doing more damage than good when redevelopment is carried out by decree, and doesn't take all three environments into account.

New York Avenue Metrorail Station

Marc Weiss is currently executive director of the nonprofit Global Urban Development. But back in the fall of 1997, he was in government. He was looking from his office window at a great empty spot in Washington, DC, just north of Union Station. The

Metrorail system's Red line ran through the area, above ground at that point, but there was no station. Marc had just heard local planners explain that it was obvious why the Metrorail system's designers had not built a station in this area: because there was nobody there. To Marc, that sounded like the best justification for *building* a New York Avenue Metrorail station; . . . *because* nobody was there.

In 2006, the Washington Metropolitan Area Transit Authority and a private consortium called Action 29 won the National Council for Public Private Partnerships' (NCPPP) annual award for best transportation infrastructure project. Action 29 was formed in 1999 by Marc Weiss shortly after he left Washington, DC, government.

I took a walk through and around the station a few days ago. The renewal potential is so pervasive and obvious, you can't help but feel it in your bones. The many new and under-construction buildings only under score the feeling. The "build it and they will come" philosophy doesn't always work with ballparks, but it's a pretty safe bet when it comes to public transit. It's especially safe when it's a location near the heart of a city, and it's creating a transit stop on an already-functioning system. In this case, no new subway lines were needed: it was just a matter of connecting the neighborhood to the existing service. But let's back up a bit, so you can better understand this achievement.

Washington, DC, went bankrupt in 1995. In response, Congress created the Washington, DC, Control Board, which took over the running of the city from then-Mayor Marion Barry. Congress didn't want the Control Board to focus only on cutting spending, so they demanded a redevelopment plan for the city. They passed the National Capital Revitalization Act in 1997, and Bill Clinton signed it into existence.

The Act was designed both to bail out the city from its debt, and to set it on a new course. The city was bankrupt partly because of corruption and mismanagement, but mostly because the federal government had created an impossible situation. All other cities have a state government to support them, but the District is a city without a state. Making matters worse, huge portions of the city are taken up by federal property and universities, neither of which pay property taxes. Clinton and the Congress fixed the situation by allowing the federal government to function as a state government.

Marc Weiss had been a senior official in the Clinton administration from its beginning, and was currently special assistant to the Department of Housing and Urban Development (HUD) secretary Andrew Cuomo (and Henry Cisneros before him). With Clinton's second term in office coming to an end, and the Republican

Party resurgent, Marc accepted an offer to be hired as a private consultant to the newly formed Control Board, functioning as a de facto city official. He specifically assisted Richard Monteilh, who was Washington, DC's director of the Department of Housing and Community Development.

Marc's new office was on Massachusetts Avenue, facing the northeast, so that it directly overlooked the vacant area known as NoMa (North of Massachusetts Avenue) running along the New York Avenue corridor. His first day on the job, Marc asked Richard Monteilh, "Why is there no station there?" The run from Union Station to the Rhode Island Avenue station was the largest gap in the system.

Around the same time, the District of Columbia partnered with some federal agencies such as the Economic Development Administration and Fannie Mae. Together, they researched, wrote, and published in 1998 *The Economic Resurgence of Washington DC: Citizens Plan for Prosperity in the 21st Century* with assistance from the World Bank and the nonprofit organization Local Initiatives Support Corporation (LISC). Its goal was to envision and plan the long-term revitalization of a city that was then a checkerboard of neighborhoods of immense wealth or dismal poverty, often with little or no buffer between them. The city's infrastructure was shot, as were many of its citizens (literally).

A major part of the District's economic revitalization strategy was to grow the private sector. As it turned out, the redevelopment of the NoMa area was one of the core elements in that strategy, so Marc's question about the missing station couldn't have been more relevant. The New York Avenue Metrorail Station was quickly adopted into the "Citizen's Plan" as the key to revitalizing the area. Today, the area is barely recognizable. After decades of failed attempts to bring the New York Avenue corridor back to life, residential and mixed-use projects are sprouting like mushrooms after a rain.

But where did the cash-strapped District of Columbia find the $90 million that the new station was expected to cost? You guessed it: a public-private partnership was created to leverage the many public and private revenue streams that renewal of the area was expected to create. The partnership included the Washington, DC Government, the Washington Metropolitan Area Transit Authority (WMATA), the federal government, private redevelopers, and the NoMa community. Together they created an "out-of-box" solution that combined funding from the District, the federal government, and the private sector.

The partnership created a Dedicated Tax District for the area around the proposed station. Property owners agreed to pay a "Metro Benefit Assessment Fee," which enabled $25 million in bonds to be sold to investors at the market interest rates. This is a technique called tax increment financing (TIF), which was mentioned in Chapter 4 and will be explained later in this chapter. Once those bonds have been repaid, the TIF assessment expires.

In addition to that $25 million in private backing, the District of Columbia put $59.9 million into the partnership (derived from general funds). The federal government contributed $25 million, but would only contribute that money as a match, after an equal amount had been raised from the private sector.

One more key element was needed to make the project happen though: private property owners generously donated key parcels to the city for the station site itself. With that, the New York Avenue Metrorail Station—and the revitalization of the entire area—transitioned from dream to reality. It opened November 20, 2004, having cost a total of $109.9 million over a five-year design and construction period.

Using a design-build delivery process, the project might represent the first time in the United States that a new subway station was constructed between two active stations without interrupting passenger service. The project enjoyed an enhanced level of stakeholder engagement; much greater than with previous stations, which were designed, funded, and built entirely by the public sector.

New York Avenue set new standards for the Washington, DC Metrorail system in terms of how well the station was integrated into the neighborhood, such as creating a bike trail link. Borrowing from the example set decades ago by Mexico City (one of the world's largest and finest subway systems), they brought artwork into the station design; a first for the Washington, DC, area. Metrorail ridership through this station has exceeded projections, generating revenue far in excess of the station's operating costs.

As a result of this public-private partnership, some $94 million of tax revenue is projected from this former NoMa "dead zone" from 2004 through 2014, with about $975 million expected in the 20-year period from the station's completion. When fully built and occupied, at least $1 billion of public and private investment will have flowed into the area, creating at least 5,000 permanent jobs in NoMa. The $350 million Washington Gateway project is due to be completed in 2010. It will put two office towers and a residential tower directly on top of the station. My guess is that, by 2012, this former dead zone will start feeling fully revitalized.

As exemplary as the private sector's contribution was, visionary leadership on the public sector's part is what enabled those private contributions to do their magic. The Washington, DC Department of Housing and Community Development, the Washington, DC Department of Transportation, and the WMATA, the lead public partner, all contributed vitally to this extraordinary success. It was only with such strong public partners that the enabling legislation (for the TIF financing) was created and passed in an expeditious manner.

I should point out that, while these Washington, DC stories were chosen to illustrate some very positive aspects of partnering, they shouldn't give the reader the impression that P3s are in any way unusual. There are literally thousands of outsourcing, privatization, and "real P3" programs at work in the United States alone. The size of these deals is going in two directions at once; both larger and smaller. Larger P3s are being carried out as cities gain more confidence in the process, and smaller ones are also being done as big cities create tools that can be adopted by smaller communities. As a result, the tools become safer and less experimental.

Some observers claim that the smallest viable size of a P3 is $100 million. Even if once true, the figure is now plummeting. One of our goals at Resolution Fund, LLC is to create easier, more efficient ways to make renewal partnerships practical for smaller projects and smaller communities, and to connect them with potential private partners from outside of their community when necessary.

Meanwhile, huge P3s in larger communities around the world seem to emerge weekly. The new International Arrivals Building at New York's Kennedy Airport was one of the first renewal partnerships to exceed a billion dollars in the United States. Los Angeles is currently launching two massive renewal partnerships, each exceeding $2 billion: the Frank Gehry-designed Grand Avenue redevelopment to revitalize downtown L.A., and the Los Angeles River Revitalization program, which will span 25 to 50 years.

Land Readjustment: A Partnered Alternative to Eminent Domain

> *The specter of condemnation hangs over all property. Nothing is to prevent the State from replacing any Motel 6 with a Ritz-Carlton, any home with a shopping mall, or any farm with a factory.*
>
> **—Justice Sandra Day O'Connor**

The recent legal and ethical crisis in eminent domain was triggered by the confluence of the rewealth trend and the P3 trend. With the trend now shifting from development to redevelopment, private companies are now a crucial element in downtown revitalization. This has led to a new form of taking, in which the city takes private property so they can give or resell it to another private party.

When governments take from the poor and give to the rich, what do you call that? I know most of you said "normal," but the correct answer was "a recipe for danger."

Champions of eminent domain say that being able to assemble large parcels of unencumbered property is one of the keys to attracting redevelopers, and they are right. Opponents say the potential is too great for wealthy individuals and companies to influence city hall so that the rich can usurp the land rights of the poor, and they are right, too.

On June 6, 2007 a federal judge dismissed a lawsuit brought against the $4-billion public-private partnership that is behind the Atlantic Yards project in Brooklyn, New York. The project includes a Frank Gehry-designed sports/entertainment complex, a hotel, retail and office space, plus more than 6,400 residential units. The suit was brought by a group of 13 residents and local businesses.

They claim that the city unconstitutionally used eminent domain to assemble the site. They said the project did not serve the public good, and that the only beneficiary would be the private partner, Cleveland-based firm Forest City Ratner Companies. Forest City is one of the largest privately held firms in the United States that specializes in downtown redevelopment and the restoration of very large old buildings.

I don't know enough about the project—or how well it engaged the stakeholders—to comment on the suit, but it shows that even projects that seem to be an obvious win for a blighted neighborhood can get into trouble with the citizens. The use of eminent domain in this manner—where the state forces citizens to sell their property and then gives it to a large corporation—is asking for a fight these days. It often can't be avoided, though, partly because of the ubiquity of public-private partnerships, and partly because of the ubiquity of irresponsible property owners who stifle renewal by sitting on unused eyesores.

P3s can certainly be abused, or at least badly applied. In the United States, this was most prominently displayed in the recent—and very public—dialog and court proceedings regarding the use of eminent domain for community revitalization. The taking of private property for the public good goes to the heart of eminent domain, but now that the reuse of that property is being done via P3s, the tricky question arose of whether it's appropriate for the government to take (actually, a forced purchase at fair market value) property from one private owner and give (again, sell) to another private entity. The potential for corruption is more than enough to create controversy, even where everything is above board.

The most interesting stories aren't those of a private redeveloper doing good things in isolation. The real magic often happens where public and private entities focus on rewealth together, looking to creatively combine their resources and agendas for mutual benefit. A high-quality partnership will find ways around sticky issues such as eminent domain, either by using the tool properly and transparently, or by adopting (or even creating) a new tool.

For instance, an alternative to eminent domain that is gaining in popularity is "land readjustment." The primary goal of eminent domain in most situations is to assemble an appropriately located land parcel that is large enough to accomplish the community's goals. Land readjustment allows such an assemblage to be accomplished without taking property.

It's done by offering property owners a stake in the redevelopment project, rather than just removing them from the equation. It might be an equity stake, or simply a vote in the public-private partnership entity. It usually involves their receiving a similarly valued parcel of land in the immediate area. This enables them to retain their business and/or personal connection to the neighborhood, while still allowing the project to redesign the area.

In other words, land readjustment turns the potential "victims" of eminent domain into stakeholders in the revitalization effort. Another advantage of the land readjustment approach is that it is far less capital-intensive than the buyouts of eminent domain. It thus reduces the community's up-front cash needs while promoting greater harmony via a more inclusive partnership.

This new tool is already in use in Europe, the Middle East, and Asia. Yu-Hung Hong, a fellow at the Lincoln Institute for Land Policy is co-author of the 2007 book *Analyzing Land Readjustment*, which explores this and other closely related partnering alternatives to eminent domain.

Public-Public Partnerships and the Problem of Having Too Much Money

We've focused primarily on public-private partnerships so far, and you'll find some examples of private-private partnerships in Part III. But public-public partnerships are becoming increasingly common, and some noteworthy things are happening because of them. Earlier in this chapter, I mentioned that public-public partnerships sometimes yield all the funding needed for a renewal project, so no private-sector component is needed. But there's a wrinkle in that rosy scenario: they sometimes produce *too much* money.

Most readers will look at that problem and say "bring it on," but it's not a joke. When I say "too much," I'm specifically referring to having too much funding *too soon*. Having overflowing coffers before you're prepared to spend it wisely can severely diminish a renewal initiative's effectiveness, and resulting in such bad publicity that the initiative suffers an early death.

Effective renewal engines can help prevent this problem, because one of the most common situations in which they arise is in the creation of public-public partnerships. A newly created partnership that's sitting on vast quantities of ready-to-spend funding is almost certain to head straight into trouble. Unless, of course, the coalition formed by the renewal engine is there to provide the scientific data, management expertise, or general awareness needed to perceive why rushing into action is a bad thing.

For instance, when two or more federal or state agencies come together to accomplish something, they often bring copious amounts of ready money to the table. The funds have already been allocated to achieve a certain goal, and when two or more agencies discover they have the same goal, partnerships can emerge. This is generally a good thing, but the confluence of all those ready-to-spend budgets can distort decision making, seldom in a good way. It can also attract "partners"— known in Washington as "beltway bandits"—whose primary expertise is relieving government agencies of their money.

The tendency in such situations will be to start spending that money immediately, especially if the agencies suffer from the "spend-it-or-lose-it" annual budgeting process. This can result in projects being designed—and contracts let—before sufficient research has been done.

The giant CALFED Bay-Delta Program—designed to restore San Francisco Bay and the Sacramento/San Joaquin River delta—is a recent example. CALFED bills itself as "the largest and most comprehensive water management and ecosystem restoration program in the nation." As a public-public partnership of 25 state and federal agencies pursuing a 30-year plan to manage and restore the largest estuary (about 1,000 square miles) on the west coast of the United States, that claim is probably accurate. While they've only spent about $4 billion to date, tens of billions more will be needed to achieve their goals.

The Sacramento/San Joaquin River delta is a source of drinking water for some 23 million people in California, contains 1,600 miles of levees (many of which are in need of renovation or removal), and supports $31 billion of agriculture per year. It's also home to some 750 animal and plant species, many of which are listed as threatened or endangered, such as Delta smelt, Chinook salmon, and steelhead trout. It was obvious that no one agency could ever address all of the issues needed to manage or restore such a massive water system effectively, so this monumental partnership was created in 1996.

Not surprisingly, this incredibly complex program developed some major problems, and they reached crisis levels as CALFED neared its 10-year mark. Many of their technical problems (as opposed to problems such as federal monies being diverted to Iraq) can be traced to an initial rush to action that lacked adequate scientific backing. As one long-time, high-level CALFED leader commented, "we had too much money, too soon."

The basic problem is that CALFED started as a renewal partnership, rather than creating a renewal engine first. A renewal engine—by definition—would have effectively engaged not only government agencies, but also academic, nonprofit, citizen, and industry stakeholders prior to designing and funding projects. While CALFED did have advisors from most of those other stakeholder groups, that's all they were. As a result, the projects were designed and funded in a relative vacuum, and each project had to deal with issues that should have already been addressed and resolved by a broad-based coalition.

It's not that CALFED needed to tap private scientific resources in industry or academia: the amalgamated agencies possess more than enough expertise themselves. But a public-private partnership would have added more NGO, university, and business partners, in addition to the necessary public-public partnering. This probably would have lent a more realistic, practical management mindset to the situation, rather than relying purely on the leadership perspective, strategic skills, and management expertise of government bureaucrats.

Interestingly, CALFED itself is now being renewed at the beginning of its second decade: a 10-year *Revitalizing CALFED* action plan was released in 2006. You know the global restoration economy is coming into full bloom when we have restoration programs so large and long-lived that they themselves require revitalization. CALFED is using on itself the adaptive management that is so important in its projects.

The Little Hoover Commission was created to evaluate CALFED, and made the following comment in their recommendations: "At the core, CALFED was envisioned as an inter-governmental effort that would resolve conflicts and allow state and federal agencies to accomplish together what they could not accomplish separately. That purpose, and hope, survives. Creating a performance-based management system, however, will require rethinking how the shared effort is organized and managed." The taxonomies developed by the Revitalization Institute were designed to provide a structure for organizing exactly that kind of complex restoration effort, and the three renewal rules form the ideal basis for the creation of performance specifications.

A major part of this 10-year revitalization plan involves expanding the partnership to include leadership and oversight from a broader spectrum of stakeholders. This will be accomplished through the creation of a CALFED leadership council, a public advisory committee, and an agency operating council. For instance, the 10-year plan states: "The Public Advisory Committee is designed to provide the broadest possible opportunity for stakeholder recommendations to the CALFED Leadership Council and be the conduit through which the public interest and input is channeled to Program decision makers."

Before we leave CALFED, it should be noted that the Sacramento-San Joaquin River Delta—which feeds San Francisco Bay—is another Katrina in the making. The New Orleans situation was a levee failure disaster, not a hurricane disaster, despite the media spin encouraged by an administration intent on denying federal responsibility (and, more important, financial liability).

Families are being sold bay-delta area homes (many of them mobile homes) in places that are from five to 25 feet below sea level, and that are protected by levees every bit as substandard as those in New Orleans. They all assume—and the real estate agents don't discourage them from this fantasy—that "the authorities" wouldn't let them live here if it were dangerous. The scientific community, on the other hand, is virtually unanimous that this is a disaster waiting to happen.

These were all wetlands a century ago, when they were drained and when dikes were built for farming (only occasionally for residential development). The restoration of the delta wetlands and related ecosystems desperately needs to be integrated into a strategy for either strengthening or dismantling the levee system. To address these issues in silos is a recipe for yet another "Katrina." If any urgent multiple agenda ever called for a massive public-public and public-private partnership, this is it. Maybe adding a rigorous disaster prevention component—along with a public-private solution for moving inappropriately located residents—is what CALFED needs in order to enter its own period of renewal.

Governments are quickly learning the value of public-private partnering, and are creating programs to encourage it. The simplest and most direct way to do so is by offering matching grants. For instance, the North American Wetlands Conservation Act (NAWCA) of 1989 provides matching grants to organizations and individuals who have developed partnerships for the "long-term protection, restoration, and/or enhancement" of wetlands in the United States, Canada, and Mexico to benefit migratory birds and other wildlife. Mexican partners are also encouraged to integrate technical training, environmental education/outreach, organizational infrastructure development, and sustainable-use studies into their programs.

Between 1990 and 2007, over 3,230 partners were involved in 1,612 NAWCA-funded projects affecting almost 24,000,000 acres of wetlands and associated uplands. Over $791,300,000 in NAWCA grants have leveraged about $1,600,000,000 in matching funds, plus $913,400,000 in nonmatching funds. The program—which is administered by the Division of Bird Habitat Conservation at the U.S. Fish and Wildlife Service—thus triples the power of their federal monies via partnering.

The bottom line is that public-public partnerships among government agencies are good, but generally work better if guided by a renewal engine. Likewise, private-private partnerships among companies, investors, and private landowners can often achieve some wonderful things, but tend to serve the public good better when forged within a renewal engine. Seeking private-sector partners isn't just about money. They also bring expertise, ideas, property, and much more to the table.

TIF: The Ultimate Form of Rewealth Financing?

An economic revolution such as the shift from dewealth to rewealth can't be completed until practical financial tools emerge that are specifically designed to discourage dewealth and facilitate rewealth. Good news: such tools already exist. I'm not just talking about old tools adapted to restorative purposes, such as tax credits, bond issuance, and the like: I'm talking about brand new rewealth tools.

The most important rewealth funding tool is tax increment financing (TIF), but it's actually been around for over half a century. TIF was invented in California in 1952, but didn't start spreading into other states and countries (such as Canada) until the reconomy caught fire in the 1990s. As of this writing, every U.S. state (and the District of Columbia)—with the exception of Arizona (which is still deeply dependent on dewealth)—has passed laws allowing TIF, though some (like New York) are very restrictive.

What's especially shocking (but little known) about the advent of TIF is that it was an outgrowth of the post-World War II "urban removal" debacle. When the federal money that was underwriting the self-destruction ran out, California invented TIF as a way to generate the money needed to demolish an area in anticipation of the arrival of the renewal fairy. The fairy did make a few rare appearances, but then went into retirement, leaving most urban removal victims crippled for decades to come.

TIF was likewise mothballed to some degree. But the idea—that you can borrow against future revitalization—had been planted. It was ready to spring into full flower when the dewealth/rewealth shift began, and the wonderful global epidemic of restoration contagion began.

What was considered an innovative, leading-edge tool just a decade or two ago is now mainstream, thanks to the explosive growth of rewealth. But it's not just the growth of the reconomy that has fueled the use of TIF. Federal and state funding in the United States has been in short supply recently, so communities have been forced to be creative, and to focus on building their own internal renewal capacity.

Tax increment financing is simple enough; you just follow these steps: (1) Establish a baseline of tax revenues from a specific area (referred to as a TIF district); (2) Estimate how much tax revenues will likely rise to after you enhance the area via some kind of renewal project or program; (3) Borrow against that incremental increase; the difference between current and projected postrevitalization revenues; (4) Use that money to finance the renewal effort now.

Do you see the key difference between this approach and the old approach? TIFs are based on an increase in the *quality* of an area (an increase in its productivity and property values), whereas the old school methods are based on an increase in *quantity* of stuff (people, houses) in an area. That increase in quantity—which is the major driver of traffic jams, pollution, and habitat destruction—will very likely decrease quality of life.

Here's a rule of thumb to guide community growth strategies. Borrowing against a dewealth-derived increase in tax revenues stimulates more dewealth (quantity-based economic growth). Borrowing against rewealth-derived increases in tax revenues stimulates more rewealth (quality-based economic growth).

TIF is a powerful tool that is evolving in many forms. Like any tool, TIF can be both misused and overused. Those details are beyond the scope of this book, so I'll save them for a more application-oriented sequel. For now, here's just one example of TIF misuse.

> *Retail is not economic development; it's what happens when people have disposable income. We do not have more money in our pockets because we have more places to shop. Building new retail space doesn't grow the economy, it just moves sales and lousy jobs around. When we subsidize retail, it costs taxpayers three ways: the bricks and mortar subsidies going to the new big boxes; the losses caused by main street and*

mall abandonment; and the massive hidden costs of public assistance to low-wage workers.

—from the policy reform recommendations of Good Jobs First [www.GoodJobsFirst.org], a non-profit dedicated to exposing counter-productive economic development practices (which describes the vast majority of them)

Some communities use TIF to attract and subsidize retail development. If increasing retail capacity is the core of the strategy, it will almost certainly fail. Retail should be attracted by residents; we should never try to attract residents with retail. A resident can survive a lot longer without a nearby coffee shop or grocery than those businesses can survive without customers.

Retail will come automatically once you have the residents and employees to sustain it. Retail is a sign of revitalization; it's not revitalization itself. Using TIF to accelerate retail presence is likely to cause retailers to move into an area too early, which can be disastrous for them. It's also likely to damage nearby retailers outside of the TIF district. Worse, if the retailers you artificially produce via TIF go out of business just as you reach a critical point in the renewal process, the sight of those dead businesses can undercut confidence in the area, sabotaging all your hard work.

Use TIF instead to create the circumstances that will attract high quality jobs (retail jobs don't qualify) and residents. Don't let the high visibility of retail fool you into thinking it's a cause of revitalization: it's only an outcome, a sign that you've been successful.

Using TIF to stimulate retail is like buying yourself a trophy for your mantle, rather than waiting for someone to award one to you. It's like putting your homeless citizens in fancy clothes to make them less of an eyesore, rather than finding them jobs and homes. Retail subsidies are often driven by short-term political agendas, the need to show visible results, even if they are phony and misleading. Don't fall for it.

All that being said, there *is* a legitimate way to use TIF to attract retail to an area you wish to revitalize, as you learned in Chapter 4. It overcomes the timing challenge of attracting residents without retail, and attracting retail without residents.

TIF Is the Way To Go When an Historic Neighborhood Needs Infrastructure Renewal

Without TIF, one is forced to take the slow, steady approach, which requires uninterrupted government support. Maybe the best example of this "pay-as-you-go" approach to revitalization is the brilliant work of Eusebio Leal, Ph.D.

Leal is the City Historian of Old Havana, Cuba and Ambassador of Good Will to the United Nations. He also runs Old Havana's restoration program. It's the only government program in Cuba that is directly based on business revenues, and that gets to keep those revenues all to itself. Old Havana is a treasure trove of gorgeous colonial buildings, most of them in a horrendous state of repair.

Dr. Leal's restoration agency has restored over 300 of them, using a special tax imposed on restaurants and retail businesses within the historic section. Unlike a TIF, though, he wasn't able to borrow against those anticipated revenues, so Old Havana's restoration is on a pay-as-you-go basis. The businesses are happy to pay this tax, since all of the money comes back to them in the form of more restoration. This kind of earmark is another characteristic of a TIF. Such rewealth reinvestment further boosts tourism, which increases their business, which generates more taxes, and so on, in a happy loop. Unwavering government support has allowed the program to flourish since shortly after Old Havana was named a UNESCO World Heritage Site in 1982.

The major downside to this pay-as-you-go approach is that you don't have the major funding you need up front to address infrastructure issues. It's usually best to renew the infrastructure before the buildings, since infrastructure work often involves tearing places up. Old Havana has never had that investment, so these wonderfully restored buildings are sitting on a base of equally historic infrastructure . . . and that's not a good thing. While some attractive above-ground infrastructure (such as bridges) can get away with being old fashioned, it's not a desirable trait in underground utilities dealing with water, wastewater, telecommunications, and power.

Natural Resource TIFs?

You've seen how TIF works for urban neighborhoods. Could TIF work for natural resource regions as well? With a bit of creativity, I believe so. The TIF concept has a lot of untapped potential. While it was designed primarily for urban settings, who's to say that it won't someday be used to finance the restoration of an estuary? If it can be made to work, it opens up the possibility of multibillion-dollar partnerships for the restoration of natural resources.

TIFs are currently based on property or retail sales taxes: why couldn't they be based on resource extraction taxes, or simply sales taxes on fish (or timber, or even water)? If the estuary restoration adds significantly to recreational use, then tourism taxes (hotels, restaurants, boat rentals) could also be part of the mix

For instance, Chesapeake Bay is only producing between 1 and 10% (depending on the species) of the seafood it used to, and even that paltry remnant still amounts to some 100 million pounds annually. If we were able to restore it back to just 50% of its historic levels, that would mean an increase of 400 million pounds of seafood annually, using the more conservative 10% base. Clearly a total of 400 million pounds of seafood should have a value worth borrowing against.

Granted, it would be vastly more complicated than collecting property taxes, but consider how a restored Chesapeake Bay would also boost coastal property values, tourism, and revitalize fishing communities in Maryland and Virginia.

I'd be surprised if someone hadn't already thought of creating a TIF-like tool for financing natural resource restoration—given the trillions of dollars worth of ecosystem services they provide—but I've never heard of such a thing. Consider that dams prevent runs of valuable anadromous fish (those that spawn in freshwater but spend much of their life in saltwater), such as salmon. Experience with dam removals has already shown that fish populations quickly explode as soon as that spawning habitat is once again made available to them. Why not borrow against some of that increased economic activity—both from the seafood industry and from sport-fishing licenses and related tourism industries—to help finance dam removals?

Those are just two fishy examples, but the TIF principle should hold for watershed restoration (based on the value of the increased quantity and quality of water), agricultural land restoration (based on increased farming or ranching yields), and even ecosystem restoration (based on increased ecotourism or sustainable agroforestry). Granted, it won't always be a tax-based payback mechanism, but where there's significant increased value or economic activity, there should be a way to tap that value to restore the region's natural capital.

Large-scale renewal partnerships involving public (federal, state, and local) and private landowners (individual and corporate) might be one way to aggregate the productivity and property value in a way that any enhancements could be measured, extracted, and borrowed against. An equally large-scale renewal engine could take on the challenge of envisioning and creating such a partnership.

Money for Renewal Sometimes Goes to Waste

The de/re shift has been a long time coming, but it really gained momentum in the 1990s. Many times, visionary leaders created programs that were ahead of their time. They saw the need to shift into renewal mode back when almost everyone else was still in the thrall of sprawl. As a result, renewal funding sometimes went untapped. The following two examples show how the three renewal rules go hand in hand.

Think how much better the faltering $10.5 billion Everglades restoration program might have been run if most of that money were private. That would certainly have made it far less vulnerable to political influences that have undermined its goals at every turn. This wasn't even a public-public partnership, much less a public-private partnership. It started as a federal program to restore ecosystems, and ended up as a state program to provide water for sprawl and agriculture. Had a renewal engine been created for the project, it would have been far less vulnerable to the shameful abuse it has suffered: if nothing else, this would have produced a shared vision to guide it, all the stakeholders would have been properly engaged, and a renewal culture would have been created not just in South Florida, but throughout all parts of the state that should be involved.

Sometimes, renewal funding is created by integrating the natural, built, and socioeconomic environments. For instance, in 1999, California's state treasurer, Philip Angelides, decided to stop funding infrastructure sprawl projects that damaged the state's natural environment or that hurt communities. He decided instead to direct infrastructure funding toward enhancing capacity via renewal and redesign, and focus the projects on distressed communities in a way that would help revitalize them. He called these "smart investments." Just a year later, $1.4 billion of low-interest infrastructure renewal loans were flowing.

Other times, a renewal-funding shift is triggered by a move toward better stakeholder engagement. An example in the United States is the Community Reinvestment Act (CRA), which was passed in 1977, but which was apparently before its time. The CRA was designed to rechannel public revenue back into low- and moderate-income neighborhoods to aid in their revitalization.

For over a decade, it was barely used, chalking up less than a billion dollars of activity in its first 15 years. Then, the National Community Reinvestment Coalition was formed in 1992 to properly engage stakeholders (via a network of neighborhood citizen groups) in its implementation, and the CRA suddenly went from near dormant to a frenzy of activity. In the following five years alone, it exploded into $353 billion worth of reinvestment.

The Washington, DC partnership stories demonstrated how enamored I am of public-private partnering. The following chapter will provide some balance, showing how suspicious I am of them, especially the first generation of phony partnerships that are still fighting to survive.

Chapter 6

Bad Partnerships: How *Not* to Revitalize Your Community

Beware: the first generation of public-private "partnerships" hasn't disappeared entirely.

This is one of the great economic debates of our time that will affect policy for the next 50 years. [Federal transportation officials are] tremendous proponents . . . of public-private partnerships.

—**Tyler S. Duvall, Assistant U.S. Transportation Secretary for Policy, at the Construction Business Forum in Washington, DC, October 24, 2007**

Some P3s aren't just bad partnerships, they aren't partnerships at all. Proposing or implementing a P3 these days evokes a wide variety of reactions.

Some trigger gunshots. Others are nonevents, where the citizens are largely unaware of any changes. Still others produce a level of public joy that becomes an inspiring story of social, economic, and ecological renewal for the world to celebrate and emulate.

This chapter is about the first type, where public and private "partners" sometimes have to wear bulletproof vests. Literally. The problem is usually that it's not a P3; it's privatization.

As with any innovation at the business-government interface, the P3 trend's initial lack of ground rules has led to some significant abuses. A new generation of P3 is now emerging, and they play by the rules. Not just any rules: the renewal rules. Policymakers worldwide agree with Duvall's claim, quoted above: they say that properly defining public-private relationships in the financing and implementation of community projects (especially infrastructure renewal) is the number one policy issue of our time.

Much of the best work in resolving this issue is coming from Europe and Canada, where blind trust in the boundless altruism of corporate leaders isn't as commonplace as it is in the United States. I'm exaggerating the level of that trust, of course. But most of the world does see us as having far too much faith in the ability of the free market to correct all manner of environmental and social ills. They feel this leads us to abdicate responsibility for governing many aspects of our economy and society that sorely need governance.

The legitimacy of the community's voice is taken far more seriously in Europe. Exposed to decades of corporate whining about "onerous" and "anticompetitive" government regulations related to protecting the environment and society, we Americans have been conditioned to equate protecting the public good with disruption of sacred market mechanisms, and with government waste.

It's not that government waste is a rarity; it's commonplace. Many recent studies in both the United States and Europe have shown that the norm for publicly financed infrastructure projects is to overschedule and overbudget. A 2002 study by Mott MacDonald, *Review of Large Public Procurement in the UK*, was commissioned by their national treasury. It showed that P3 projects averaged 1% cost overruns, and were delivered early. Conventional projects were usually late and were 47% over budget on average. So, the trend toward P3 isn't just about the public sector's not having enough money; it's also about spending what money they have more efficiently.

Is It Right to Profit from Solving Community Problems?

Let's start with the most philosophical/ethical aspect of the issue. Should business earn a profit providing life-or-death services like drinking water, disaster response, and national security? Coming from the only country in the western world with an almost entirely profit-based healthcare system, this American author might not be best qualified to comment. I'm going to anyway.

The fact that a private company will make a profit from assets in the public domain is often the sticking point when a P3 is used to create, renovate, improve, or expand an essential public service. If significant rate increases are needed to pay for the project, the dialog can get very heated.

For instance, Northern Ireland will have its first privatized water utility come on line in September of 2008. Dalriada Water, Ltd. is a consortium comprising the private firms Earth Tech, Kelda Group, and Farrans. They have a 25-year design-build-finance-operate contract to deliver water to about half of Northern Ireland's citizens. In return, they are investing $207.4 million (US) in renovating the existing drinking water system up to European Union (EU) standards.

Recouping this investment will involve introducing direct charges for water for the first time, which has led to significant public protests. The "We Won't Pay" campaign argues that citizens are already indirectly paying for their water via other taxes. Such protests can occur even when a well-designed renewal partnership is at work, but that's usually the result of their having not properly engaged all the stakeholders.

Suspicions of political corruption are only exacerbated when the public learns, as they did in Northern Ireland, that one of the private partners is owned by a firm pilloried in the international press for greed-related scandals. The parent company of Earth Tech is the $40 billion/year Bermuda-based global conglomerate Tyco International.

There are three fundamental ways to answer the antiprofit argument. Each is based on one of the renewal rules. The first is what might be called the "de/re filter": ensure that the project is nondestructive at the least, and preferably restorative. Objections to a project will be more vociferous if private profits are based on purposely destroying natural or cultural assets. Profit based on restoration and renewal is far more likely to be viewed as a win-win.

As mentioned in the previous chapter, some P3s are pure dewealth. They might fund and build new highways through a rain forest, resulting in massive deforestation for short-term gain. They might fund and build new dams on pristine rivers, inundating ancient historic sites, killing vibrant communities, and destroying valuable farmland and ecosystems. When a private firm profits from such activities, public objection can be immediate and vociferous.

Other P3s are designed to revitalize an economic region and renew its forests, culture, farms, and economy. Some actually remove earlier public works, such as tearing down a dam to restore a river valley's ecology and farming communities. When a private firm profits from these activities, few people mind, and most applaud.

The privately owned Dulles Greenway toll road spurred hypersprawl in Loudoun County (northern Virginia). Most such sprawl-inducing P3s come from nonintegrated planning processes: they are public-private, but they aren't really partnered with communities, much less regions. Renewal partnerships spawned by renewal engines—or any good collaborative process—are less likely to produce tunnel-vision projects that are grossly out of sync with people's quality of life goals.

The truth, however, is that by far the majority of P3s *are* "re"-oriented (possibly in excess of 80%). Sprawl developers are already significantly (indirectly) subsidized by the public sector, so they don't need to resort to partnering as often as do renewal projects. This fact would seem to make "renewal partnership" a largely redundant term, but rewealth isn't the only defining factor. Having to comply with all three renewal rules to qualify as a "renewal partnership" significantly raises the bar.

The second answer to the profit objection is better integration. When the integration rule is ignored, the natural, built, and socioeconomic environments aren't considered as a whole. This sometimes leads to "accidental" destruction of valued assets, and always leads to lost opportunities. Some renewal projects get so focused on one asset (such as transportation infrastructure) that they destroy other assets (like ecosystems, or healthy low-income neighborhoods) through sheer sloppiness.

The project might have a renewal focus, but its "accidental" destruction of long-lasting, possibly irreplaceable assets makes it controversial. The flip side is that properly integrated strategy can lead to the project's renewing more than just infrastructure. It's often surprisingly easy to integrate various forms of natural, economic, or cultural renewal into a large infrastructure project—without increasing the cost—so as to win support from the public.

The third answer to the profit objection comes from adherence to the stakeholder engagement rule. A transparent partnering process—especially as it comes closer to being formalized—is essential (see Chapter 4 for the exception). The profit factor will be more explosive when citizens are left in ignorance to imagine the worst. But transparency isn't engagement. If trusted citizen representatives have been part of the visioning and strategizing process, they will understand if a P3 is the only way to get the healthy, efficient water (or other infrastructure) system they need. And they will share that understanding with the public.

In dewealth P3s, the private "partners" are often seen as villains and parasites, and might be the subject of lawsuits and even physical attacks. In rewealth P3s, the private firms are often seen as heroes, feted by citizens and political leaders alike. The difference is *not* that the former are run by bad people and the latter by good people: the difference is that the former examples were based on new development (dewealth, such as extraction or sprawl), whereas the latter were based on restorative development (rewealth). In the end, "de" versus "re" is the key.

Paying Taxes Versus Paying for Use

Another aspect of the profit issue is the trend toward charging the people who actually use certain infrastructure, rather than charging everyone for all infrastructure. Pay per use is very visible, so these projects must be especially careful that the private sector's return on investment (ROI) is reasonable. As we saw in Northern Ireland,

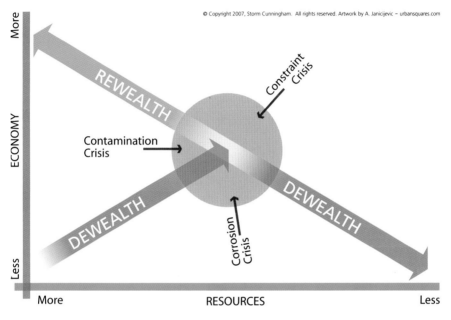

Figure 1 This "turning point" graphic illustrates how we have built our global economy on resource depletion, and how three global crises are forcing us into a mode of wealth creation that renews what we've built and replenishes our natural resources. If we turn "right" instead of "left," both our resources and economy decline. (See Chapter 3, page 51 for discussion.)

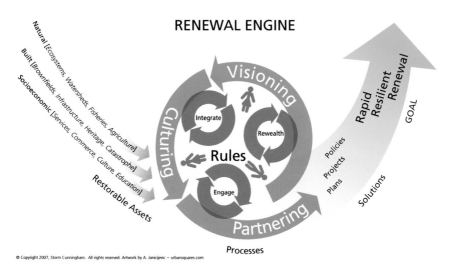

RENEWAL ENGINE

Natural [Ecosystems, Watersheds, Fisheries, Agriculture]

Built [Brownfields, Infrastructure, Heritage, Catastrophe]

Socioeconomic [Services, Commerce, Culture, Education]

Restorable Assets

Visioning

Culturing

Integrate

Rewealth

Rules

Engage

Partnering

Processes

Rapid Resilient Renewal

Policies

Projects

Plans

Solutions

GOAL

Figure 2 This artist's conception shows how a renewal engine "takes in" restorable assets, subjects them to the three renewal processes (which implement the three renewal rules) performed by the stakeholders, and produces solutions that yield rapid, resilient renewal. (See Chapter 4, page 96 for discussion.)

people have a hard time accepting charges for infrastructure services when they think they are already paying for them through general tax revenues.

> *In California, birthplace of the freeway . . . the free ride may be coming to an end. There is emerging consensus in the Capitol that the state should follow the path already blazed elsewhere and look to tolls to help bankroll new roads, public and private. Local and state transportation agencies are already planning several such projects on busy urban corridors, and some of the world's largest investment firms are lining up with proposals that could leave them in control of some major new roads. Voters last November approved billions in borrowing for roads, but that was only a start; the money won't meet all the state's transportation needs and never was intended to. Nor would anything short of a major increase in the gas tax — one for which voters appear to have no appetite. That leaves tolls. "The existing way of paying for these projects is not going to work," said Senate Transportation Committee Chairman Alan Lowenthal (D-Long Beach). "We're used to free roads and everything being free. That is a 1950s model. If we want to move forward, we are going to have to head in a different direction."*
>
> —Evan Halper, "Voter-Approved Bonds Won't Bankroll All of the State's New Roads. Up Ahead: Public and Private Tollways," *The Los Angeles Times*, **February 13, 2007**

The above quote shouldn't be interpreted as an indication that California's legislators are universally in love with P3s, or with pay per use. As a pioneer of transportation-related P3s, California has experienced its share of high-profile disasters.

Orange County, for instance, made the mistake of promising their private partner on the 91 Freeway project that the county would not improve any of the surrounding roads that might compete with the toll road. This was blatantly designed to maximize profits of the company (called California Private Transportation), and was in conflict with the public good.

The resulting congestion outraged the citizenry, and protests climaxed in the state's repurchase of the toll road. This is a process known as municipalization, which—like nationalization—is the opposite of privatization. Had the partnership been formed through a renewal engine—rather than in a smoke-filled room of political leaders and company executives—it's unlikely that such an egregious provision would have been suggested, much less approved. Such provisions are a vestige of the Wild West days of public-private partnerships (the 1980s and 1990s).

Some bad experiences with P3s simply derive from honest mistakes made because of a lack of familiarity with the tool. After a long series of delays and lawsuits, San Diego's new private toll road opened in the summer of 2007 at a price of $683 million: 70% higher than estimated. The original plan was for the state to take back the road and (possibly) eliminate the tolls after 35 years. This has now been bumped to 45 years to give the private partner more time to recoup the extra costs.

The *Los Angeles Times* article quoted officials in the governor's office as saying such setbacks are minor bumps in the road. "We have learned a lot of lessons," said Sean Walsh, a senior policy advisor to the governor. ". . . people who keep going back and looking at [the mistakes] . . . ignore the fact that it is a model now being used successfully around the world."

The state of Indiana recently turned over its famous 157-mile turnpike—known in the central United States as the "Main Street of America"—to a consortium of foreign private firms and investors. The state of Illinois did something similar to renovate their Chicago Skyway, and both Pennsylvania and New Jersey are considering similar arrangements to upgrade and maintain their extensive turnpikes.

Texas is looking to do a P3 to enhance their road system in grand style. Their plan is to make virtually every major road currently under construction into a toll road. In fact, they want to create a 4,000-mile network of toll lanes to feed an expanded port. Their goal is to better compete with California for Asian cargo ships.

Only 26 U.S. states currently have toll roads, so private transportation companies are seeing a growth opportunity in the pay-per-use trend. The current pay-per-use leaders are Oklahoma, New York, and Pennsylvania, each having over 500 miles of tolls. Citizens usually hate tolls, but some green strategists see pay per use as a step toward getting Americans out of our cars and onto public transit. The best way to stop wasteful, polluting behavior is to stop subsidizing it. London learned this lesson with their highly successful "congestion fees," whereby those who drive through the crowded heart of the city pay for the privilege.

The First Generation of Public-Private "Partnerships" Hasn't Disappeared Entirely

Most people not familiar with the subject can be forgiven for assuming that anything called a "public-private partnership" would automatically engage all the stakeholders. That's what partnerships do, right? This is why the term has been so abused, used as a smokescreen to create what often amount to legal private monopolies.

The same thing has happened with "sustainable development" and "smart growth," and other "warm and fuzzy" monikers. They are all warm because they contain a friendly, desirable word (partnership, sustainable, smart), but they are all fuzzy because they are multifaceted, still evolving, and were never well defined in the first place. People tend to feel good about activities that fly under those flags, but they often aren't clear on exactly what it is they are supporting.

The fuzzy definitions leave plenty of room for abuse. For instance, "new urbanism" (walkable communities) is considered an aspect of smart growth, so sprawl developers are adopting it. As a result, many of them label their projects—which might destroy hundreds of acres of wildlife habitat or farms—as "smart growth." Others slap some photovoltaic panels on the roof, or some porous paving on the driveways, and call their sprawl "sustainable."

The World Bank and its sister institution, the IMF, are frequently criticized for forcing debtor countries to sell their public utilities to a small group of private corporations at bargain-basement prices. The companies end up with monopolies on essential public services as a result. Both institutions defend the practice by claiming there is a worldwide consensus for public-private partnering. That's true enough, but it's only people's fuzziness on the meaning of the phrase that allows them to get away with using it in this context.

There are two problems with the World Bank's claim: (1) If there's a consensus on anything, it's on the general concept of partnering, not specifically public-private partnering (though support for the latter is growing fast); (2) the projects offered by the World Bank and the IMF as examples of public-private partnering are often just privatization deals. There's usually very little, if any, partnering involved. In fact, many (probably most) of the public-side players didn't want to be at the table at all. We've got to define our terms clearly to progress.

Privatization Versus Nationalization: Two Sides of the Same Coin

When private assets (such as a railroad or oil company) are forcibly turned into public assets, it's called nationalization. Sometimes, such moves are a reaction to excessive greed or bad management on the part of the private sector. Other times it's an attempt to correct a past injustice, whereby a firm obtained public resources via corrupt or violent means.

Still other times, it's purely a political move by a populist leader, designed to win votes, and an entrepreneur who might have devoted his/her life to building the enterprise unfairly loses everything. The people of Cuba overthrew a corrupt, bloody, right-wing dictator (General Batista), going to the other end of the spectrum and adopting Soviet-style communism. Private assets were nationalized in one fell swoop, from foreign-Mafia-run casinos to honest family farms and businesses. A major problem was cured, but at the cost of many thousands of smaller tragedies.

Nationalization comes in flavors ranging from an outright taking of all assets to a partnered approach. For instance, Hugo Chavez told the multinational oil companies operating in Venezuela that he wanted them to share more of their revenues with the Venezuelan people. He claimed they had sweetheart deals struck with earlier corrupt regimes, and that Venezuelans deserve a bigger cut of this dewealth pie, since they are selling-off nonrenewable assets.

Chavez even allocated a portion of that extra income to reforesting the country, as we saw earlier. In other words, he proposed using dewealth profits to fund rewealth activities. Oil lobbyists "forced" U.S. politicians to decry this demand for a bigger share of the revenues as being communistic or socialistic, which "forced" Chavez to cancel some oil company leases and take the assets. Strangely, those same politicians didn't call Louisiana governor Kathleen Blanco a communist or a socialist when she demanded a greater share of oil revenues from their offshore wells. The restoration of Gulf Coast wetland damage—most of it inflicted by oil operations—will require between $15 and $20 billion.

When public assets are taken over by businesses, it's called privatization. Like nationalization, it can be done in a coerced or a partnered manner. Privatization comes in two basic flavors, with many variations. There's "service privatization," or outsourcing, such as CH2MHill's previously described community management services for Sandy Springs, Georgia. Then there's "asset privatization," whereby buildings, natural resources, or public utilities are sold outright to a private firm.

Both contain the seeds of danger to public interests—not to mention political fallout—when corruption, greed, incompetence, or poor stakeholder engagement are added to the mix. Here are a few recent examples of problematic privatization in the United States:

- The city of Atlanta, Georgia outsourced its public water infrastructure to United Water Services, but terminated the contract because of reports of poor service.
- The citizens of Larkfield, California are trying to regain ownership of their water system from California American Water (Cal-Am), a subsidiary of American Water and parent company RWE. Larkfield citizens are forming

a Community Services District that would be responsible for providing water to residents, amid charges of excessive profiteering by Cal-Am.

- The U.S. subsidiary of the French Suez Corporation, United Water, recently acquired another water firm, Aquarion-New York. With this purchase United Water became the second largest private water firm in the United States, the largest being American Water. Immediately after the acquisition, the Argentine Popular Commission for Reclaiming Water warned Aquarion-New York's 667,000 customers about their experience with French Suez Corporation. Argentineans called the firm "abusive," saying it puts profits over public welfare. They claimed the company had raised rates excessively, refused services to poor neighborhoods, and had failed to perform the infrastructure renovation promised. The Argentine contract was legally dissolved after massive public discontent.

Privatization Can Be an Element of Partnering, but It's Not Partnering

Social movements are humanity's immune response to political corruption, economic disease, and ecological degradation.
—Paul Hawken

P3s are not synonymous with privatization. Privatization of poorly run or dilapidated public assets can sometimes be a good thing. But it can also mean offloading valuable public assets at fire-sale prices to politically connected firms or individuals.

In Mexico, the publicly owned telephone utility (Telmex) was privatized in 1990. Telmex's monopoly was maintained for six years after the privatization deal, so Mexicans ended up paying some of the world's highest rates for local calls, while enjoying some of the world's worst service. Now that competition has arrived, Telmex is starting to behave like a regular telephone company, even expanding beyond Mexico.

(A note of rewealth interest concerns Carlos Slim, who purchased Telmex from the government and is now Telmex's honorary president. He's also one of the three wealthiest men in the world. Over the past decade, Slim has become the foremost donor in support of heritage restoration projects in Mexico, a country with a wealth of magnificent buildings and historic sites in need of rehabilitation.)

Partial privatization of public infrastructure is a legitimate aspect of many P3s. Even full privatization might occasionally be warranted when the public sector is dysfunctional, such as following civil war. Surgery is sometimes a necessary part of healthcare, but few would claim that surgery is synonymous with healthcare. The relationship between privatization and public-private partnering is similar: the former is a drastic tool that's only occasionally necessary. The latter is a strategy that can and should be used on a regular basis, if done right.

Nowhere is the potential for abuse of public trust greater than in issues related to water. The most common form of abuse is using the term "public-private partnership" to describe a water infrastructure renewal project that is really privatization of public water resources. So, let's go to the city of Cochabamba, Bolivia, for an example of how *not* to do a P3, and how to recover from doing it wrong. This story will be told in considerable detail because the lessons to be learned can help national, community, and business leaders avoid embarrassing—even catastrophic—mistakes.

Cochabamba: Ground Zero of the Water Wars

Cochabamba is the third largest city in Bolivia, with a metropolitan population of about 800,000. The Cochabamba valley has been inhabited for over a millennium, thanks to its highly fertile soils. The city is known throughout South America as the "City of Eternal Spring," because of its year-round mild climate, and sometimes as "The Garden City," because of its many beautiful parks.

Though it was called a P3, Cochabamba's first attempt to renovate their water system with private partners was more a case of extreme privatization than partnership. Worse, it was coerced privatization. The resulting protests were so intense that the military was called in to quell them. The story is told in the 2007 book *Thirst: Fighting the Corporate Theft of Our Water*.

For over three decades, Cochabamba's water supply was managed by a public utility called Servicio Municipal de Agua Potable y Alcantarillado (SEMAPA) . . . but not very well. Half of the citizens weren't served at all, and the other half were served poorly, with frequent outages and contamination problems. About half of the water was lost to leakage and illegal connections.

The pricing scheme was designed to benefit wealthy land and factory owners, so discounts were offered for high levels of usage, which encouraged waste. What's more, they had trouble collecting payments from users . . . not just from the poor, but from government agencies, as well. Thus, the poorest people paid the highest rates, and the 50% percent not served by the system were forced to buy their water from the trucks of entrepreneurs, often at exorbitant rates. Given such a situation, there's little wonder that the government was open to an entirely new approach.

Meanwhile, the World Bank was lending money to this desperately poor country. One of the key conditions of those loans—as with many of the World Bank's loans in recent decades—was privatization. The countries were coerced into allowing private corporations to take over publicly owned utilities and key infrastructure. Partly as a result of this policy, privatization became a trend unto itself. Privately owned water utilities served about 50 million people in 1990, but that number had rocketed to 300 million by 2002.

In 1999, the woeful performance of SEMAPA—combined with privatization pressure from the World Bank—led to Bolivia's Drinking Water and Sanitation Law. This established a legal framework for public-private partnerships to address water problems. The privatization process was fast tracked, but their first RFP failed to recruit an acceptable bid from a single company.

In response, an international consortium comprising the U.S. firm Bechtel, which contributed 55% of the capital, the Spanish engineering firm Abengoa (25%), and four Bolivian firms (5% each) was quickly formed, called Aguas del Tunari (AdT). Unconfirmed sources say that International Water Limited (UK) was also a partner.

In October of 1999, AdT "won" (there were no other bidders) a $2.5 billion, 40-year concession to run the Cochabamba water system. Since the stated purpose was to renovate and better operate the water utility, this was an ideal opportunity to create not just a P3, but a renewal partnership. This AdT "partnership" was deeply flawed, however. Auditing their experience using the three renewal rules, we find that AdT failed on all three counts.

Factor Number 1: Failure to Renew

The first major failure was fundamental, in that the focus of AdT was *not* primarily on renewal of assets, as it should have been. It started off well enough: the first thing AdT did was to start renovating the dilapidated water mains. The reduced leakage boosted the available water supply by 30% in just 60 days. So far, so good, but it was all downhill from there.

The built environment wasn't the only environment that needed to be restored: the watershed suffered from massive deforestation, which exacerbated natural floods and droughts. Renewing the decrepit water infrastructure was a great beginning. The next step should have been to focus on watershed (and related agricultural restoration) that would address the water supply issues over the long term.

Instead, the engineers slipped into dewealth mode. While there's plenty of money to be made from the sorts of restorative activities just listed, there's also easy money in building new stuff, like dams. AdT was contractually guaranteed a net profit of 15% on anything they did.

> *The privatization of water is just the latest in a decade-long series of sales of Bolivian*
> *public enterprises to international private investors, the airline, the train system, the*
> *electric utility, as government officials carefully toe the neo-liberal line that 'private is*
> *better'. While the promises have been about an injection of new investment, the more*
> *obvious results have been a weakening of labor standards, increases in prices, and*
> *reductions in services (the train service is gone altogether).*
> —Jim Shultz, *In These Times*, April 17, 2000

In this case, the Bolivian government (possibly via pressure from the World Bank, though they deny it) required AdT to build the $214 million (US) Misicuni Multipurpose Project (MMP). This was a 120-meter (400-foot) dam to divert water from the River Misicuni into the Central Cochabamba Valley for electricity generation, irrigation, and water supply to the city. While the private partners were happy to do so, they demanded that significant rate increases be built into the contract to pay for it.

So, rather than restore the watershed, the plan was to destroy the Misicuni watershed to get fast-but-unsustainable results. In a few decades, the dam would be silted beyond usefulness, and they would once again not have enough water for the city. But the situation would then be far worse, as they would have killed the ecology and communities of the valley where the water used to flow. So, AdT failed the test of the rewealth rule miserably. It's hardly surprising that just about the only good things that have ever been said of the project were related to its restorative aspects (fixing the leaks).

Factor Number 2: Failure to Integrate

> *The formula for resolving conflicts is that the solution should meet the minimum needs*
> *of everyone, but the maximum needs of no one, since that sets up a feeling of*
> *victor/loser.*
> —Unknown (Overheard at a Conference on Public-
> Private Engagement)

The renewal projects that could have provided a long-term solution for Cochabamba would have included such things as watershed restoration, renovation of agricultural irrigation systems, or renovating the water utility to integrate the drinking water and sewage treatment systems to allow for greater water reuse.

In other words, they should have focused on renewing the natural environment (watersheds and agricultural lands), on renewing the built environment (primarily water and sewage infrastructure), and on renewing the socioeconomic environment (using a regional approach that not only revitalized the metro area, but integrated the enhancement of the nearby rural communities).

This would not only have resulted in a healthier regional economy, but would have prevented the inundation of communities, ecosystems, and farmlands behind the new dam, and also the desiccation of communities, ecosystems, and farmlands in front of the dam. In other words, an integrative approach that considered all three environments would have revealed the folly of building the dam in the first place. (This gets back to the "hidden agenda" barrier to P3s mentioned earlier.)

Factor Number 3: Failure to Engage

The failure of AdT can by no means be laid solely at the feet of the private sector. For instance, the investment in infrastructure improvements—but primarily the exorbitant cost of the new dam—was designed to be repaid by raising the price of water by 35%. Part of the rate increase was due to AdT's assumption of SEMAPA's outstanding debt.

The local government contractually agreed to inform the populace about the upcoming increase, and to educate them as to the need for it. The administration failed to do their part, so the sudden, unexpected price increase only confirmed the public's worst fears about the unsavory nature of the privatization.

> *Many of the problems that arose could have been avoided early in the process, through effective stakeholder consultation and communication. . . . as a result, the terms and conditions of the concession eventually established in the Cochabamba project were not suited to the cultural, political and economic situation in the area. . . . Under the Agua Tuya (Your Water) program, the [new] ApT partnership is part of an initiative to unite stakeholders, and improve coordination and efficiency by combining the resources of the various partners.*
>
> **—Cochabamba case study for United Nations Development Program. Primary author: Rick Norment, executive director of the National Council on Public-Private Partnerships (NCPPP)**

It's the role of government to ensure that all citizens have access to the basic means of existence. Someone who is unemployed and/or far below the poverty line will be in no position to handle a major price hike for water. It was the government's job to make sure that the urban poor were not victimized by this initiative. They failed to do that, as well.

Having a basic natural resource in private hands is a difficult sell even in countries where capitalism is effectively a state religion. In countries like Bolivia, it clashes headlong with some of their cultural mores and spiritual beliefs. Access to water is considered a basic human right in most cultures. For an individual or firm to claim ownership of it is no different from their claiming ownership of the air.

Maybe the most serious of many flaws was greed. Bechtel (AdT's lead partner) wasn't satisfied to merely own the water treatment and distribution infrastructure; they ended up effectively owning the water itself . . . all of it. As sole bidder, Bechtel and friends were able to dictate the conditions, and some say they took everything they could get.

Besides boosting the rates for the people hooked up to the public water system (which was necessary), they even charged people for taking water out of their own wells, in their own backyards. Bechtel had negotiated exclusive rights to deliver water in Cochabamba: no one else was allowed to provide water; not even Mother Nature. Not surprisingly, this had severe political repercussions for local leaders.

Bechtel did do some things right. For instance, the new water fees were higher for wealthier people, a badly needed reversal of previous policies. While poorer folks saw rate hikes as low as 10%, wealthier and high-usage customers saw their bills more than double. It should also be noted that the higher bills people received were partly the result of their using more water, since more was now available owing to pipeline repairs.

Uprising and Aftermath

Just as "renewal by decree" is the wrong way to go about revitalization, so too is "partnership by decree." In this case, it was the World Bank's far worse "privatization by decree" that put AdT on the wrong footing.

Despite AdT's initial success in repairing some of the leaks in the aged water mains in only 90 days, significant public opposition started emerging. It took the form of the Coalition in Defense of Water and Life. The protests intensified to the point that AdT employees fled their offices and the military was called in. The protestors were victorious, however. The government cancelled the rate hikes, sent out refunds, and eventually cancelled the contract altogether. Those remedial actions didn't save many of the leaders (including the president) from being voted out of office, however.

The anger spread beyond Cochabamba. On February 4, 2,000 protestors were opposed by troops and police in Oruro and La Paz, where similar water privatization efforts were underway. Over a period of two days, about 200 demonstrators were arrested and some 70 protesters and 51 police were injured. In November 2001, AdT filed a request for arbitration with the International Centre for Settlement of Investment Disputes (ICSID), regarding the assets expropriated by the Bolivian government when the contract was cancelled.

Cochabamba's Coalition in Defense of Water and Life was founded by shoemaker and union leader Oscar Olivera. The coalition's victory spawned action across South America via Red Vida (Web of Life). Olivera has since expanded the fight against water privatization throughout the world. To date, the movement has stopped AdT-style water privatization schemes in Argentina, France, Germany, India, and Tanzania. This global movement was first brought to the attention of the public in industrialized countries via a 2004 video documentary called *Thirst*, which led to the previously mentioned book of the same name.

> *Everyone from farmers to hotel owners opposed the privatization, and even the World Bank pulled out. But only when Olivera's coalition organized massive strikes and, finally, a virtual insurrection, did the Bolivian government throw out Bechtel and hand the utility over to a community-based organization accountable to the residents. . . . Canada's lakes and rivers, as well as many U.S. rivers and streams, may be the ultimate stakes in the fight over the privatization of water utilities. It will be oil-company-sized water conglomerates aligned with pipeline giants like Bechtel and Halliburton [that will be] lobbying in international trade talks to define water as a product to be sold to the highest bidder.*
> —from *Thirst: Fighting the Corporate Theft of Our Water*
> (John Wiley & Sons, 2007) by Alan Snitow,
> Deborah Kaufman, and Michael Fox

The Coalition in Defense of Water and Life wasn't merely a grassroots group of Cochabamba's peasants and urban poor, either: it included a number of professional associations, business leaders, and civil rights groups. In other words, rather than using stakeholder engagement to design a good public-private partnership, stakeholder engagement was used to bring a bad one to an end.

Stakeholder engagement was also used to bring a new, improved P3 into being. Since it was too late to stop the dam by that point, the new P3 fails the environmental integration test. The ongoing environmental and socioeconomic damage being done by the new dam means that the improved P3 is still a long way from being a renewal partnership.

Cochabamba Today: Learning How to Renew, Integrate, Engage . . . and Partner

So, what became of Cochabamba's water situation? Upon cancellation of the AdT contract, the Bolivian government reappropriated the water system, which might have been the first major nationalization of a privatization.

> *The success or failure of any public-private partnership is dependent on six key factors: the political and legislative environment, a skilled dedicated unit to oversee the partnership, a viable contract, a clear, dedicated revenue stream, strong communication with all interested parties, and careful selection of the private sector partners. In the case of the first Cochabamba PPP, there were significant problems in each of these areas.*
>
> —Cochabamba case study for United Nations Development
> Program (UNDP). The primary author was
> Rick Norment, Executive Director of the NCPPP
> (the full report can be found at
> www.ncppp.org/undp/cochabamba.html)

As a result, Cochabamba made another attempt to solve their water problems via the P3 model. They didn't have much choice, since they were now more aware of the poor condition of their infrastructure than ever before, and were equally aware of their inability to fund the needed renovation on their own. This time, they were determined to avoid the mistakes of their initial attempt.

Two years later, (December 2004), a new partnership called Agua para Todos (Water for All) abbreviated ApT, was created, and it's obvious that many lessons had been learned. ApT consisted of a nonprofit foundation, the affected local communities, two microcredit providers (CIDRE and Pro-Habitat), SEMAPA, and a new locally-based private sector consortium called Plastioforte/Agua Tuya, which designs and builds water systems and provides training in their maintenance. This partnership is supported by the United Nations Development Program (UNDP), rather than the World Bank.

Large rate increases were avoided in two ways: (1) The preexisting SEMAPA debt of $30 million (US) was not assumed by this P3, and (2) the inappropriate

$214-million dam project was initially abandoned, but was (unfortunately) later revived via powerful lobbying, though at much lower cost.

In 2006, ApT won a Supporting Entrepreneurs in Environment and Development (SEED) Initiative Partnership Award for Sustainable Development partnerships. This was in recognition of creating a truly participatory P3 driven by actual stakeholder needs. Less than a year after its creation, ApT was addressing the unserved half of the population via seven new extensions of the existing water system.

These enhancements are serving over 5,000 people, and the cost of water has been reduced by 50%. Goals for the following five years are to add 17,000 more connections, which will serve some 80,000 people. Overall, though, people are far from satisfied with their service, and ApT lacks the funding to tackle their major renovation challenges.

Phony P3s: An Endangered Species?

"Privatization," [former Stockton, California mayor Gary Podesto] said, "you have to be careful with that word." The Urban Water Council and a host of conservative think tanks have created a more appealing public relations alternative: "public-private partnerships." This euphemism became all the rage during the 1990s as both conservative Republicans and Clinton Democrats competed to grant subsidies and concessions to business. "A public-private partnership is privatization because it's taking a municipal function that has municipal employees and is turning it over to the private sector," said Dale Stocking . . . "This idea that bringing a private business model into a municipal operation brings the benefits of competition is an oxymoron . . . The only competition is at the bidding over who is going to get the spoils."

—from *Thirst: Fighting the Corporate Theft of Our Water*
(John Wiley & Sons, 2007) by Alan Snitow,
Deborah Kaufman, and Michael Fox

As the above excerpt indicates, the confusion over privatization and public-private partnerships rages. On July 17, 2007, the citizens of Stockton cancelled their $600 million water privatization contract with OMI-Thames, which they felt had been rammed down their throats by former mayor Podesto without proper research.

If the most vehement P3 critics are correct, and the term public-private partnership was invented as a smokescreen for privatization, one could make the argument that there's been a silver lining. The controversy has forced governments around the world to closely examine the public-private interface. This has resulted in the creation of some innovative and productive new relationships. It should be kept in mind that the book *Thirst* dealt only with the most controversial application of P3s: water. Most P3s don't involve water.

Thanks to the water wars, local groups protesting new projects can now tap legal and publicity-related resources to help in their fight against privatization masquerading as partnering. Food & Water Watch (www.fwwatch.org) is one of the leading such organizations.

Sometimes, privatization of a public utility will be honestly and openly examined as an option for renewing and operating it, and will be rejected. For instance, on May 8, 2007, the Knox (Pennsylvania) City Council voted against turning over their water and wastewater systems to private firms. The two largest U.S. water companies—American Water and Aqua America—had both bid on the project. A grassroots opposition group, Knox Friends of Locally Owned Water (FLOW), emerged and successfully called that model into question.

The May 2007 issue of *Currents*, the newsletter of Food & Water Watch, quoted former Knox mayor (and FLOW founder) Carol Weaver as saying "We figured, if we're paying for the upgrades anyway, we might as well own the system in the end."

Communities that have had bad experiences with privatization are particularly suspicious when real P3s are proposed, and understandably so. Many of the worst experiences have taken place in lesser-developed countries, where the government was too desperate, too weak, or too corrupt to protect the public welfare. Their inability to cope isn't surprising: the corporations with whom they dealt sometimes had larger annual budgets than the nation itself.

As noted in Chapter 5, the sophistication of the private side's lawyers is often light years ahead of the government's legal team. After all, the private team is employed full time to put together privatization deals all around the world. The public sector team is often dealing with the issue for the first time. But you now know how communities large and small can ensure that they don't end up on the losing side of what should be win-win: create a renewal engine.

You Want It All, and You Want It Now: A Shortcut to Rewealth

You say you're tired of sprawling your quality of life into the toilet, and don't want to wait for a global economic paradigm shift? You say you don't want to wait for a salesperson from a giant rewealth company to walk through your door? You say you want to revitalize your community now? No problem. You can get it all now. Just ask for it.

The solution is in how you write your RFPs and requests for qualifications (RFQs), and in how you measure project outcomes. RFPs and RFQs are how communities and agencies solicit private vendors and partners. While there's no shortage of legal boilerplate designed to ensure enforceable contracts, there's a paucity of guiding principles for specifying an ideal renewal partner.

Communities have a lot more control over their mode of growth than most realize. In fact, you can start your shift from a deconomy to a reconomy without a single policy change . . . without any legislation. All you have to do is start specifying the three renewal rules in your RFPs and RFQs. Request partnered solutions that *renew* your assets in an *integrated* manner on the basis of a vision derived from *engaging* all your stakeholders and that's what you should receive.

Granted, you'll likely receive fewer bids, because most architectural/engineering/construction (AEC) firms and redevelopers aren't up to speed on such approaches yet. But the quality of those that do respond will likely be far higher, and will really help revitalize your community. Many will even vie for the honor of giving you the money to do so. I'm not recommending it as an alternative to creating a renewal engine; just offering it as an expedient shortcut if you've got an RFP going out next week.

Redevelopers and AEC firms want to do business with you. Their business development model is to respond to RFPs. Embed the renewal rules in your RFPs, and you will not only get renewal, you'll get the cream of the crop of private partners. Why? Because, while many firms know how to renew assets, only the very best, leading-edge firms know how to integrate the renewal of natural, built, and socioeconomic assets . . . and only the very best, leading-edge firms know how to properly engage the stakeholders.

If an RFP asks for dewealth, the AEC firm delivers dewealth. If it asks for rewealth, they're more than happy to deliver. There aren't any publicly-owned AEC firms (that I know of) that *only* do rewealth . . . that would not respond to a dewealth RFP. That would be bypassing a profitable opportunity, which would violate their legal requirement to maximize value to their shareholders. There are, however, quite a few *private* firms that do exclusively rewealth.

When most cities adopt the three rules in policy, and are issuing renewal-rule-based RFPs, you'll likely see a mass migration of design and construction firms toward rewealth, toward integrative strategies, and toward engaged approaches. Many firms won't be able to handle that radical shift in thinking, which will likely trigger a new round of mergers, acquisitions, and divestitures.

> *Public-private partnerships continue to see expanding acceptance in institutional building worldwide, particularly in Europe. . . .New York-based Bovis Lend Lease is part of a consortium . . . for the $882-million redevelopment of the Royal Children's Hospital in Melbourne . . . the largest hospital redevelopment in Australia.*
> —Bruce Buckley, *ENR Sourcebook*, December 24/31, 2007

Many bad public-private partnerships had their provenance in economic development programs based on wooing employers with incentives. This outmoded model is a zero-sum game for regions (when communities within the region "steal" employers from each other), for nations (when states do likewise), and for the world as a whole when nations do the same. As Greg LeRoy, Executive Director of Good Jobs First, says: "city officials feel trapped in subsidy competition."

The end result is the presence of employers whose devotion to a community often ends when the subsidies run out, rather than one attracted by the quality of life. Such programs pervert the public-private relationship, and leave communities without the tax revenues they need to cope effectively with growth and change. Public-private partnerships built on such relationships seldom turn out well.

> *We are seriously deluded if we think peer review can lead to innovation and scientific progress . . . the way is open for creative funding efforts . . . exploring the idea of public-private partnerships . . . to help us find those 400 or so scientists who will transform the 21st century.*
> —Donald W. Braben, Visiting Professor, University College London, Author of *Scientific Freedom, The Elixir of Civilization* (Wiley, 2008), Quoted in *New Scientist*, February 23, 2008

Once your community has a renewal engine, you should be highly suspicious—and should slow-track—project proposals (P3 or otherwise) that try to bypass being vetted by the renewal engine's project review team. But if a proposal passes the renewal rules test and is compatible with the community's vision of its future, the community should reward that firm by fast-tracking the project's approval.

A well-run renewal engine will turn out a constant stream of good partnerships. Even a barely adequate renewal engine—such as a brand-new one that hasn't quite coalesced—will probably be able to at least help you avoid bad partnerships. And that's no small thing, as anyone in Cochabamba will be happy to attest.

Part III

Stories

Career, Investment, and Business Opportunities Renewing Farms, Fisheries, Forests, Communities, and Countries

Proof that you can earn a living reversing crises in energy, food, water, poverty, disease, species extinction, heritage, and climate change.

. . . hearing stories acts as a kind of mental flight simulator, preparing us to respond more quickly and effectively.
—Chip and Dan Heath, *Made to Stick* (Random House, 2007)

Parts I and II have been "concept-rich." Their primary purpose was to plant the seeds that government agencies, businesses, nonprofits, and individuals could nurture in the real world. Those sections were also intended to provide academia with the basis for new research, curricula, and community outreach programs.

The chapters of Part III are mostly the opposite: we'll only occasionally stray from storytelling mode into analysis, theory, or commentary. In this section, you'll discover both enormous companies and small entrepreneurs who are earning their living restoring the world.

The purpose of these stories is partly to provide examples of the concepts in the first two sections, but mostly to provide inspiration, showing others (you perhaps?) how they can "go forth and do likewise." In other words, how you too, can restore the world (or at least your own piece of it) for a living.

Chapter 7

The Tom Darden Story

An anthropologist becomes a billion-dollar rewealth entrepreneur.

Tom Darden might be the epitome of a rewealth entrepreneur. In 1976, he received his bachelor's degree in cultural anthropology at the University of North Carolina (UNC-Chapel Hill). Over the years, his reading of the *Whole Earth Catalog* and *Limits to Growth* had convinced him that the earth was on a path to environmental ruin. He had no idea what he could do about it, though. Nor did he know what he wanted to do for a living, although he thought he might follow his father's path into law.

Fast-forward to 2006. When Tom went to Wall Street and asked investors for money to restore damaged land and revitalize communities, they gave him $1.2 billion. That's not something most *Whole Earth Catalog* readers can claim. Certainly not this writer: I can't remember the last time someone gave me a billion dollars.

Let's now fill in that 30-year gap.

As an undergraduate, Tom wrote an honors thesis on the impact of capitalistic economic growth in Kenya. His master's thesis at UNC-Chapel Hill was on the legal dimensions of interstate acid rainfall. He received his JD in 1981 from Yale Law School, with the idea of focusing on environmental law. In 1992, he finally completed a master's degree in regional planning at UNC, for which he had begun studying in 1976.

He interned at the Hunton & Williams law firm in Richmond, Virginia. During this period of on-the-job training, two things happened simultaneously in 1981: he graduated with his law degree, and he lost interest in practicing law. He was rescued by Bain and Company in Boston, a major business-consulting firm. Despite knowing almost nothing of business, Tom found himself excited by it. He even found a niche that might help save the world: he became an energy efficiency consultant.

That might well have been the end of his story, career wise. After all, there's no shortage of demand for energy consultants these days. But Tom has a rewealth soul: he's powerfully attracted to taking what others damage or throw away and restoring its value. The picture frames in his office were made from scraps left over from building the wooden deck on his house. At 15, he bought a "worthless" 1959 English Ford Consul convertible for $50, restored it, and sold it. Five years later, he had repeated the process 20 times over with both cars and motorcycles.

It might thus have been inevitable that he'd eventually find a way to restore the world for a living. It just required the right opportunity. That opening came in 1983, when someone threw a brick through Tom's career window . . . almost literally.

Tom's father-in-law, William M. Ragland, purchased the Cherokee Brick company back in 1957. After many years of running it, he asked his lawyer/business consultant son-in-law to help him structure the sale of the business to one of his employees. It was doing about $6 million annually in sales, and he was willing to sell it for $5.5 million.

After Tom had invested a lot of time and energy in valuing the business and learning about the industry, the prospective buyer decided to leave and buy a lumber mill instead. Maybe he was scared off by the fact that their biggest competitor, nearby Sanford Brick, was more than twice their size, but was losing $2.5 million annually.

Tom's research revealed there were two primary ingredients required for making bricks: clay and energy. The cost of both had been rising steadily. Brick manufacturing requires vast amounts of heat, much of it obtained from coal and oil in those days. Air pollution laws were forcing many to change over to natural gas; cleaner, but increasingly expensive.

Tom knew nothing about clay, but he was an expert on energy efficiency. He decided to buy four brick plants, Cherokee Brick, Sanford Brick, Chatham Brick, and Stanly Shale, which had combined annual sales of $21 million and losses of 12 million. Tom had $30,000 in the bank at the time. He pulled off not only the purchase, but the restoration of profitibility. Tom switched the plants from burning oil to burning wood scraps, becoming nearly carbon-neutral, and the bottom line jumped considerably.

His waste-to-wealth strategy was so successful that he purchased four other struggling plants in Maryland, North Carolina and South Carolina. They became the Cherokee Sanford Group (CSG). It looked like Tom had finally found his niche.

Or maybe he hadn't. In 1985, the EPA tossed some toxic sludge through Tom's career window. The property at his Chatham brick plant had been poisoned by fuel oil and gasoline. This happened before he bought it, of course, but Cherokee was now liable. North Carolina's state regulators told Tom to dig up the poisoned soil and dump it in a landfill.

But using all that energy just to move the problem elsewhere offended Darden's sensibilities. He had heard that brick makers in England sometimes used clay that had coal particles in it, and that the coal simply burned away in the process of firing the bricks in the kilns (which takes place at over 1,000 degrees Celsius). He suggested the same approach with this petroleum-ridden clay, and it worked perfectly. *Voila!* He was now able to clean his property without the expense of trucking heavy dirt around the country, and he got "free" clay for his bricks in the process.

Tom created Cherokee Environmental Group (CSG) in 1986 to focus exclusively on this aspect of the business. With his mindset now well-entrenched in rewealth, Tom realized that leaking underground storage tanks (USTs) were being discovered by the tens of thousands all over the country. To him, the next step was obvious: CSG should be in the business of receiving and remediating contaminated clay from underground storage tank cleanups. CSG quickly became the largest soil remediator in the mid-Atlantic region of the United States, decontaminating some 15 million tons of toxic dirt. No longer was Tom receiving free brick-making material: now he was being *paid* to take it.

Now heading full speed in a "re" direction, Tom the found that the sludge left over from processing drinking water made an excellent amendment to brick, another free source of raw material. Then he discovered that the ash from incinerators burning magazines was full of clay, a major ingredient of coated paper. Tapping these additional "free" resources boosted profitability still further.

Profits from its "re"-oriented efficiency enabled CSG to purchase three more plants in 1989 and an eighth in 1991, making CSG the largest privately held brick manufacturer in North America. But by then, Tom had long since decided his future was in rewealth, not in making bricks (even though they were "rewealth bricks").

It turned out that the baking technique didn't work for all kinds of contamination found in the clay. Darden started working with professors at Virginia Tech to develop bioremediation processes. A friend of his from Bain and Company, John Mazzarino, had left Bain to start a business buyout firm in Raleigh. Tom put up some of the buyout capital, and soon found himself in a familiar position: one of the companies they purchased turned out to have contaminated its land.

The process of dealing with yet another cleanup made Tom realize that he was far from the only person saddled with polluted property. The most conservative estimate says there are at least half a million brownfields in the United States. He also realized that a poisoned property is basically just another form of "waste" waiting to be reused. So it didn't take him long to come to the conclusion that his newly-developed cleanup technologies positioned him nicely for the ultimate buy-low-sell-high real estate scenario.

In 1992, he started doing purposely what he had previously done accidentally: buying and remediating polluted properties. This struck him as more potentially profitable than simply cleaning dirt for a living. And he was right.

Some companies have failed in the brownfields business because they focused only on making money from the cleanup process. Tom takes a more strategic approach, buying properties that have great intrinsic value, such as a good location. He then goes out of his way to find responsible buyers who will put the site to a really good use for the community.

In 1993, Darden and Mazzarino created the predecessor company of Cherokee Investment Partners and started buying polluted properties, beginning in California and Connecticut. In 1994, they formed an affiliate to focus on risk management advisory services, and in 1996, they created Cherokee's first vehicle (Fund I) for receiving institutional investments, which attracted $50 million.

All of that funding came from a private chemical and oil company, Koch Industries of Wichita, Kansas. But Tom knew a diverse pool of institutional investors, like pension funds and university endowments, would be more reliable long-term. He went after them, and 1998 saw the creation of Fund II, which drew $250 million in private equity. The year 2002 yielded the $620-million Fund III, with 28 investors (in addition to investments by Cherokee employees). The most recent (as of this writing) was Cherokee's fourth fund, Fund IV, which raised $1.2 billion in 2005.

These brownfield investment funds are perceived as riskier than normal real estate transactions, so they have to offer "opportunity fund"-level returns in the double digits. "Normal" real estate fund returns are usually in the high single digits.

Today, Cherokee has purchased more than 525 contaminated properties for more than 50 projects in 35 states, including North Carolina, South Carolina, California, Rhode Island, Connecticut, Alaska, Georgia, Texas, and Colorado. Cherokee has expanded internationally, with projects in Italy and Canada. It operates with about 100 employees, most of whom focus on assessing sites and on environmental planning.

A half dozen or so of those 100 employers are LEED-accredited professionals. These LEED-accredited designers focus on upfront early stage planning, land use, and future green buildings. Cherokee sometimes gets involved in the "vertical development" of their sites too, and works with the firms that redevelop the sites after they have been cleaned. This helps ensure that the sites and buildings are as "green" as possible. With some $10 billion worth of buildings being constructed on Cherokee's properties, they exert no small influence on the green building trend. Their reuse of damaged land greatly magnifies the greenness.

"Billion" is a word that pops up often around Cherokee's offices in Raleigh, North Carolina. This isn't surprising, since every dollar invested in a site normally generates about 10 times that in redevelopment activity. Their redevelopment of the former Gates Rubber Company site in Denver will be a billion-dollar project when built out. Cherokee also has billion-dollar projects in Charleston (South Carolina) and Boisbriand (Quebec).

Considering the vital links among cleaning/reusing land, community/human/ wildlife health, and economic growth, you probably won't be surprised to know that Tom has created a nonprofit with a similar focus. Cherokee Gives Back gets Tom back to his roots in the 1970s, when he was researching and writing about the challenges of Kenya, and other lesser-developed countries. His dream is that someday, Cherokee Gives Back will be larger than his investment funds.

Cherokee Gives Back focuses on underserved areas around the globe, which includes significant work in Africa, and also some in Bhopal, India. It is trying to help clean up the still-horrendous aftermath of the 1984 explosion of the Union Carbide pesticide factory. Forty tons of methyl isocyanate spilled out of the facility, killing more than 22,000 people so far.

Cherokee has offered remediation assistance free of charge and up to $1 million to help the people affected by this disaster. To date, the Indian government is still paralyzed by the extent of the Bhopal disaster. Their infamous bureaucracy hasn't allowed Cherokee to help begin the assessment, much less assist with the actual cleanup.

Most of the work of Cherokee Gives Back is performed by volunteers from Cherokee's staff, plus an estimated 100 volunteers from outside the firm. Sam Whitt is its director. Tom has pledged 10% of the company's annual profit for charitable works, and the firm has so far given about $20 million to charity.

Darden tries to weave that community sensitivity into his for-profit projects, as well. For instance, Cherokee's Magnolia project in Charleston encompasses the historic black community of Rosemont. I'll probably tell the story of this project in a follow-up to this book. Magnolia is almost next door to John Knott's Noisette Project, featured in Chapter 9. I didn't want to overexpose the Charleston area in this book, even though its story deserves telling, since it's home to another rewealth superstar: long-time mayor Joe Riley.

Cherokee's Magnolia project is based on brownfields surrounding most of Rosemont. A sudden rise in real estate prices—as ugly, abandoned waterfront industrial sites are transformed into market-priced town homes—was almost certain to disrupt the low-income Rosemont community. Most redevelopers (and communities) simply throw up their hands when the subject of gentrification-displacement arises. They say, "Hey, it's a natural outcome of revitalization: higher real estate prices are exactly what we're trying to achieve here!" When long-time, low-income residents are forced to sell because of rising property taxes, the common assumption is that it's the inevitable price of progress.

Cherokee and its local partners didn't think so. After trying and failing to get the city or state to do something about it, they set up a nonprofit called the Stay Put Foundation, whereby Rosemont residents would be refunded any incremental increases in their property taxes by the foundation. In the end, the state came through with its own program to keep the Rosemont community whole, so Cherokee's solution became a backstop program.

Tom is no longer making bricks, having sold Cherokee Sanford Brick for $81 million in 2000. But he made—and is still making—the metaphorical bricks that helped lay the foundation of the global brownfields industry. Cherokee is now one of the largest private investors in the world specializing in the remediation and revitalization of brownfields.

At only a little over a decade old, brownfields redevelopment is an industry still very much in its infancy. Out of the 500,000 to 1,000,000 brownfields in the United States (depending on who's doing the estimate), fewer than 2,000 have been remediated and redeveloped. It's an industry that is only well established in the United States, Canada, and Europe, so the global growth potential is immense. Australia is starting to get serious about its potential, boasting (if you'll excuse a perverse use of the word) an estimated 80,000 to 100,000 brownfield sites.

Tom's commitment to good business practices pays off; for Cherokee, their partners, and the eventual property owners. Not a single buyer or seller of their properties has ever incurred unexpected environmental costs or liabilities, beyond what was in their Cherokee contract. This approach adds significantly to the bottom line. It also won the firm adulation, including a Phoenix Award (the "Oscar" of the U.S. brownfields industry) from the U.S. EPA, and an Excellence in Public/Private Partnership award from the U.S. Conference of Mayors. In 2003, Cherokee became what they believe is the first private equity fund in the world to have an ISO 14001:2004-certified Environmental Management System (EMS), which is the global standard for environmental management.

An internal 2006 assessment of five Cherokee projects in the United States and Canada revealed some interesting estimates. The total development value of the five projects currently underway is estimated at $5,649,000,000. Those five projects have the potential to generate 35,947 construction jobs, 10,851 permanent jobs for the communities, and enhance local property tax bases by a total of $70,052,250.

Of course, sprawl developments can also generate impressive numbers. That is, until you factor in the destruction of green space, natural resources, cultural assets, productive agricultural land, and quality of life. Then you have to deduct the lost productivity due to driving times, the cost of new infrastructure, and so on. The difference is that the numbers generated by Tom's projects were net enhancements to the community. There were no dewealth-style trade-offs for this economic growth.

More important than profits is the precedent Tom and his partners have set. They've shown that it's possible to build a profitable international business recycling land that others consider worse than useless . . . a liability. They've shown Wall Street and institutional investors how to make money restoring the world. Old-style, socially responsible investment funds focus on not destroying the world. This approach has been problematic, as there's no rigorous, easily definable method of distinguishing responsible companies from irresponsible ones.

The new wave of responsible investors isn't satisfied with not being destructive, they are not satisfied with fuzzy standards, and they want the higher returns that come with growth industries. The dewealth/rewealth shift solves all three problems: (1) Their investments will restore the world, not just slow the rate of its destruction; (2) There's nothing fuzzy about distinguishing dewealth from rewealth . . . a five-year-old child can do it; and (3) The reconomy is where most of the growth of the twenty-first century will take place.

Dewealth won't go away, but it's already in rapid decline as a percentage of the global economy, vis-a-vis rewealth. It has almost completely disappeared in cities that have run out of room for sprawl. Those cities are a window on the future, as the planet itself runs out of room for sprawl. Until space exploration becomes practical, the only direction the deconomy can possibly go is down.

Given that, where should responsible investors be putting their money in the twenty-first century? Ask Tom Darden, automobile restorer, environmentalist, Morehead Scholar, cultural anthropologist, planner, business consultant, attorney, brick maker, philanthropist, CEO of Cherokee Investment Partners, and a model rewealth entrepreneur. If the *Whole Earth Catalog* were still being published, Tom would probably be on the cover.

Tom's backing into the reconomy is probably the norm. Many rewealth companies and entrepreneurs begin by restoring an asset of their own. In the process, they develop a restorative skill or technology, and then realize that similar restorable assets exist all over the world. A similar dynamic can happen with communities: They revitalize themselves, and become a global center of rewealth training and technologies.

Although I had been reading about Cherokee for years, I didn't meet Tom until early 2004. He and visionary redeveloper John Knott kindly agreed to guest lecture at a restorative development workshop I was doing at Harvard University. Tom flew up in his own plane (piloting it himself), and it struck me then that—with John also in the room—I was in the company of two rewealth superstars. Darden and his wife, Jody, have three children. Their grandchildren might someday read in their history texts how granddad helped birth the global reconomy.

Tom's Greatest Challenge

Lest anyone get the impression that remediation and redevelopment is all white hats and adulation, let me add a cautionary story, one that's complete with decomposing mobsters.

At the end of the 19th century, the marshes at New Jersey's Meadowlands, across the Hudson River from New York City, became the preferred legal and illegal waste disposal repository of the region. You've probably seen the Meadowlands many times in movies about organized crime in New York City, since it was a traditional dumping ground for those who annoyed them. But far more toxic substances than crime victims found their way into the Meadowlands.

What was once a productive and natural system grew into one of the most widely recognized environmental hazards in America. By the 1990s everyone wanted the Meadowlands cleaned up, but nobody did anything about it. Neither the state of New Jersey nor the federal government had the funds available to remediate the area. The New Jersey Meadowlands Commission recognized that the only way to fix the mess was to partner with the private sector. Allowing for some redevelopment on the upland areas of the Meadowlands could generate the funds to pay for the cleanup. This type of public-private partnership is now a common practice at similar large-scale sites across the nation.

In 1999, EnCap Golf Holdings, a firm whose principals had successfully developed a landfill golf course in Houston, Texas, was selected as the master developer of the Meadowlands Redevelopment project. At the time of EnCap's selection, Cherokee Investment Partners had no ownership of, and had made no investment in, EnCap. A year later, Cherokee began to invest in EnCap, which owns the Meadowlands project. Over the years, Cherokee continued to invest more, and today is the largest EnCap investor, with a majority interest in the project. EnCap Golf Holdings has served as the day-to-day operator of the project, but EnCap has no employees. It had a manager originally, William Gauger, who works for his own independent management company. All the other people working on the Meadowlands either were independent contractors or worked as employees of Guager's management company.

The Meadowlands Redevelopment includes 785 acres located in a number of local New Jersey jurisdictions. The project includes addressing three landfills in Lyndhurst and one in Rutherford, protecting and restoring wetlands, improving water quality, enhancing recreational resources, and developing a smart growth community that is economically beneficial to the state, the Bergen and Hudson counties, and the local municipalities.

The Meadowlands Redevelopment is one of the world's most visible and complex projects of its kind. As such, there have been a number of articles in the papers that have described the project's challenges, not all of them accurate. As with many projects of this magnitude, unexpected challenges and problems abounded. In the Meadowlands, Cherokee learned that the cost of cleaning up the site was dramatically greater than originally projected. What's more, the manager and operator of the redevelopment plan—EnCap—misjudged both the market and the changing political climate, which led to significant financial and operational difficulties.

When Cherokee learned that EnCap was running into these problems, it took a series of corrective actions to ensure that the original goal of cleaning and restoring the Meadowlands was achieved. Cherokee has changed the management of the project and invested considerable time and money to address the EnCap-related difficulties. At the end of the summer in 2007, Cherokee announced that they were seeking a new partner with the operational expertise and financial strength needed to see the project through.

As a result, Cherokee allowed the Trump Organization to take over day-to-day operational control of the Meadowlands project from EnCap. Cherokee recently made an additional $5 million investment in the cleanup of the site and it will remain involved as a major investor in its redevelopment. With Trump Organization's years of project management experience and a track record of successful redevelopment initiatives, Cherokee is convinced they are the right partner to ensure success in the Meadowlands.

Tom and the Cherokee team learned some painful-but-valuable lessons from their experience in New Jersey, and they are applying them to other projects. For example, Cherokee now plays a greater role in the oversight of project implementation. They also focus on creating strategic long-term relationships with operators and redevelopers, ensuring that they share Cherokee's values.

But the lesson from the Meadowlands that Tom Darden most often speaks of is the importance of never giving up, even when the odds seem stacked against you. The Meadowlands has been a great corporate challenge, and personally difficult for Tom. He is very proud that his company never gave up. The project has new life today because Cherokee never abandoned its vision of a clean, safe, and revitalized Meadowlands. With Trump's help, Cherokee is optimistic that the vision will become a reality. As Cherokee continues to finance some of the largest and most important environmental remediation projects in the world, its perseverance in the Meadowlands will probably benefit the company for many years to come. Communities want private partners who won't run when the going gets tough.

Additional Lessons from the Tom Darden Story

Most of the lessons one might glean from Tom's success are fairly obvious. So let's ignore generic factors such as turning waste to wealth, or having rigorous processes and quality standards. We'll focus instead on how Cherokee (or a firm like it) might grow in the years to come, based on what's been learned so far.

Continuing to expand internationally offers one obvious growth path. My suspicion, however, is that Tom's more interested in boosting the rate of return (ROI), rather than simply doing more of the same. Quality over quantity, in other words.

Tom tells me the biggest factors affecting their ROI is "entitlement issues." The entitlement process is the legal method of obtaining approvals for the right to redevelop property, usually for a new use. A catastrophic entitlement problem would be when a community changes its mind about redeveloping a site after a company (like Cherokee) has already incurred the expense of cleaning it up.

An example might be when an environmental group, heritage preservation society, or neighborhood association that wasn't properly involved in the project objects to it at the last minute. If you read Chapter 4, you'll know that a renewal engine should prevent such problems, because of its shared vision, project review team, and broad-based stakeholder engagement.

Entitlement problems can also be the result of a change in political administration: the incoming mayor alters his or her predecessor's projects in order to take credit for them, or cancels them outright out of spite. An effective renewal engine can reduce this risk as well, by making it a community project, rather than just a private deal. One of the key aspects of a renewal engine is safeguarding the community's vision of its future from externalities. This helps to maintain renewal momentum, and creates a safer environment for folks like Tom to do their work.

Entitlement problems are primarily rooted in poor stakeholder engagement. Sometimes, a community already has a shared vision of its future, and possibly even a strategy based on that vision. If that strategy is rewealth based, it might be an ideal community for a Cherokee project. He says that about half the communities he works with already have a good plan with passion behind it, which usually makes his work easier.

Very often, Tom has to rely on a locally-based deal partner for the stakeholder engagement. In such cases, the quality of that engagement can be hit-or miss. Tom is thus using his internal team to improve the process by developing stakeholder engagement (and other process) guidelines.

If a last-minute protest or lawsuit against a project is launched, there's often very little a redeveloper can do to resolve it quickly. Since they are usually working on borrowed money, delays often spell death for the partnership.

But there's a lot that can be done to prevent such situations in the first place. In August of 2007, when I first told Tom about how Resolution Fund, LLC, had been created to help communities create renewal engines, he told me he'd like to channel *all* of Cherokee's future investments into communities that have one.

Why? Because it's just too painful and expensive to have projects killed at the last minute by communities that haven't effectively engaged citizens in their future. There are tens of thousands of communities around the world with brownfield (and other rewealth) opportunities. Rewealth investors can easily afford to cherry-pick those that have created a better environment for revitalization by forming a renewal vision, a renewal culture, and a renewal engine. By implementing the *re*solution, in other words.

A properly functioning renewal engine should boost the bottom line of redevelopment projects. This is accomplished both by accelerating approvals, and by creating value-adding connections to other projects; past, present, and—most importantly—future. Working with a renewal engine can give redevelopers heads-up on projects that are only just being envisioned. This can greatly boost the value of present projects that are designed to integrate with that future reality.

When communities lack sufficient renewal capacity, it would be in a wise redeveloper's best interest to help them create a renewal engine. They could directly underwrite all or part of the cost, or help recruit a sponsor who will. There's nothing capital intensive about the process of creating a renewal engine: it's mostly people's time, plus facilitation. Sponsoring the formation of a renewal engine would be a small price for a redeveloper to pay for eliminating entitlement problems.

When you consider the plethora of long-lasting benefits the community would enjoy—and the positive effects these revitalized communities would have on the national economy—you might wonder why there isn't a federal agency specifically designed to help communities create renewal engines. Why should communities have to rely so heavily on the private sector to help them get a handle on their future? Wonder no more: in Chapter 13, you'll discover a country that does have such an agency.

How else might Tom boost ROI? If I were in his shoes, my next fund wouldn't be narrowly focused on brownfield remediation; it would be a revitalization fund. In other words, it would integrate the renewal of natural, built, and socioeconomic assets. You'll remember that one of the ways Tom achieves higher returns is by taking a more strategic approach to projects. Rather than just focusing on cleanup revenue, he looks at location and other factors that would affect the resale value. But many of those "other factors" are uncontrollable when the project's footprint is too small.

A strategic alliance with an infrastructure firm could, for instance, produce the kind of private partner cities crave: capable of taking on huge old industrial zones, many of them waterfronts whose primary big-dollar issues are infrastructure renewal and brownfield remediation. In many of the public-private renewal partnerships to date, the private partner takes the brownfield risk and the public partner takes much of the infrastructure risk. But some cities aren't capable of that, and need a private partner who can do both, leaving the city with the less-capital-intensive aspects like police, fire, education, or health services (the latter two can also be done as P3s, as we've seen in earlier chapters).

It's often the quality of the infrastructure coming into a brownfield site that imposes the most limits on its uses, and thus its potential. The buyers of high-end residences won't put up with low-grade roads, absence of nearby parks, or poor

Internet connectivity. In recent years, those "external" value-enhancing factors have been addressed via public-private partnering: the private redeveloper agrees to take on a brownfield, provided the public partner enhances the surrounding neighborhood. There is nothing wrong with that scenario, if that public partner has the planning and funding capacity.

As the global reconomy expands, and the cream is skimmed from inventories of redevelopment opportunities in larger cities that have competent planners and redevelopment agencies, rewealth investors will increasingly look to smaller communities. But small-to-mid-sized communities don't always have top-flight design professionals on staff, and local the money to contract them.

At the same time, redevelopers will be looking for opportunities that allow them more control over the enhancement of the area around their project, and the public services within the project area. This can result in a tremendous win-win situation, as the community gets access to "free" master-planning expertise, and the private partner gains insight into—and some influence over—what goes on around their project.

Chapter 9 story about John Knott will illustrate the concept: the city of North Charleston, South Carolina offered him their mothballed 300-acre military base (at fair market value) in exchange for creating an integrated revitalization plan for the entire 3,000-acre community. As a result, the city benefited from a world-class team of architects, engineers, restoration ecologists, and planners. Knott, meanwhile, boosted the value of his military base property by enhancing the neighborhoods surrounding it.

My suggestion is that this approach could lend itself to the next generation of rewealth investment. The same companies and institutions that coughed-up $1.2 billion for Cherokee's fourth fund could provide $10 billion or even $100 billion for a fifth fund that goes beyond brownfield remediation/resale into neighborhood and community revitalization.

Moving to the community level involves more focus on infrastructure renewal, where the market—as we've seen—is measured in the trillions. This model offers a more cohesive and comprehensive approach to redevelopment; it taps the many efficiencies and synergies that emerge when the natural, built, and socioeconomic environments are renewed in an integrated manner.

The obvious danger of this model for the community is losing too much control over their future to the private sector. The obvious solution is to channel all of this through a properly designed renewal engine. If the private partner funds the process of creating the renewal engine, it should probably be done through a neutral third party. This would generate trust and goodwill from day one, as the citizens quickly come to realize that the public engagement is real, not just a public relations facade.

There's nothing I know of in current business contract models—or in current governance models—that could serve this purpose. This, I believe, is the next generation of public-private partnerships. But it's largely dependent on the existence of a renewal engine of some sort. Otherwise, balancing private gain with serving the public good in a transparent way that inspires citizen support isn't likely to happen.

Such a strategy would converge the leading edge of four trends: the partnering trend, the engagement trend, the integration trend, and the rewealth trend. If you'll excuse the phrase, it could create a perfect storm of opportunity, maximizing private returns and public good simultaneously.

There are three keys to making this model work: (1) Ensuring that both public and private partners are thoroughly familiar with the three renewal rules; (2) Imbedding those rules into public policy to advance a renewal culture; (3) Creating a renewal engine—a forum for project partnering around a vision of the community's future that's shared by all stakeholders. That, of course, is the *re*solution, the reliable recipe for rapid, resilient renewal you encountered in Chapter 4.

Activating the *re*solution in thousands of communities worldwide will require a level of funding that makes Cherokee's $1.2 billion fund look like chump change. But if anyone can scale up Tom's proven process from brownfield renewal to community renewal, it's probably either Tom himself, or someone inspired by his example. You, maybe?

Chapter 8

The James Aronson Story

An American living in France works in Africa to help shift the global economy toward rewealth.

You'll like the following story if you want to restore the world for a living, but you don't want to run a business . . . you don't want to move dirt (or decontaminate it) . . . you don't want to breed animals or plants . . . you don't want to manage complex projects . . . you don't want to plan cities, design buildings, or crawl through old sewer pipes. In other words, you'll like this story if you're a creature of the mind. You'll like this story if you're a citizen of the world. You'll also like this story if you're a student in search of a career that will excite and satisfy you.

It's a story of France, South Africa, Israel, and Missouri. It's a story of nature, economics, and people. This book is full of communities, programs, projects, and organizations that embrace and practice the three renewal rules. This is a story about an individual whose entire *life* seems to be based on rewealth, integration, and engagement.

The Tom Darden chapter was a story of an ambitious, business-wise man who was concerned about the future of our world. He "stumbled" into a billion-dollar business via a passion for reuse, recycling, and remediation.

The James Aronson story is very different. He's an American living in France, and working in Africa. He's got a basic aversion to business for business' sake. Tom owns his own company, while James has a steady job with a government scientific agency. James is an academic at heart, and controls no great financial wealth, but his influence equals Tom's. They've never heard of one another as of this writing, but both are restoring our world for a living, and both are doing it on a grand scale.

Tom Darden restores the world from the cockpit of either his personal plane or his corporate plane. James Aronson does his thing from a gorgeous, 200-year-old farmhouse in the south of France. With his wife and children, he's been restoring virtually every aspect of the building and grounds for 15 years. A local Kung Fu teacher helps him with some of the heavy labor.

He's renovated virtually every aspect of its seven or eight acres, including the ancient rainwater harvesting/distribution system and the century-old olive grove. The sheepfold became his office and guestroom (where my wife Maria and I stayed). Combining the traditional rainfall harvesting techniques of the area's farms with modern drip-irrigation, he's been able to add fruit trees, berry bushes, table grapes, and a pond and ornamental garden areas, without any piped-in water. Solar energy and wood are gradually replacing gas and electricity for energy supply.

James Aronson grew up in St Louis, Missouri but—by age 16—wanted to see the world. He went to France for a school year abroad, and discovered the multiplicity of languages, landscapes, and cultures to be found on this planet. He decided then and there to find or create a profession that would let him travel and learn for a living. Thanks to the Missouri Botanical Garden, he discovered a passion for plants and the way people use them, so he began to study botany.

He started to focus his studies on how people transform vegetation and landscapes, often in unsustainable ways. He worked for two years in Chile and two in the Peruvian Amazon, but found he was happier and healthier in dry places. He then lived for eight years in Beer Sheva, capital of the Negev desert in Israel, where he worked at the Applied Research Institute as plant introduction officer. His job was to visit the driest and saltiest places on earth in search of arid land plants of potential economic value in agriculture, horticulture, industry, or forestry.

While working in Beer Sheva, he obtained a Ph.D. at the Hebrew University of Jerusalem in plant ecology. Learning to think and ask questions that concern ecologists, he found it impossible to go back to the institute where—at that time—sustainability was not yet on many people's minds. In the mid-1980s he went to Montpellier, France, as a visiting researcher at the Centre d'Ecologie Fonctionnelle et Evolutive. This is the largest ecology lab of the French national centre for scientific research, called the CNRS (Centre National de la Recherche Scientifique). There, he had already built contacts with a group of arid land ecologists working on pastoral systems in Africa, the Middle East, and Latin America. They were very practical folks, focused on the rehabilitation and sustainable use of degraded rangelands in those areas.

Aronson was aware that in the United States, during the same period, the Society for Ecological Restoration was starting up. They were developing—or, more accurately, reinventing—the art and science of ecological restoration, which has been practiced by humans longer than most of us realize. The ancient Persians restored their lands, as have inhabitants of the Mediterranean region and many parts of Europe since the 19th century.

For the first time in human history, the need for such knowledge had become planetary. Fortunately, advances during the past two or three decades allowed the more holistic and science-based approach on which the modern ecological restoration movement has been founded. The majority of this emerging restoration ecology work was taking place in the United States, Western Europe, and Australia, but along different paths.

Europeans placed emphasis on the renovation of drastically depleted lands and unproductive landscapes, which they sought to rehabilitate to a functional condition. They were not much interested in the idea of recovering a primeval ecosystem or landscape, owing in large part to the overwhelmingly cultural matrix of Europe consisting of working rural landscapes, rather than any kind of primeval landscape.

In the United States and Australia, the emphasis was divided. Most restorationists were enraptured with the ideal of restoring a primeval landscape, such as the one they imagined occupied the North American and Australian continents prior to European settlement. Others were engaged in more European-like reclamation of mined lands and the functional renovation of degraded forests, wetlands, and rangelands. Europeans, Americans, and Australians were all aware of each other's work but continued to work independently until they began to see the value in common goals that incorporated the best elements from each camp. The multilingual, globetrotting Aronson was instrumental in arranging this "marriage" of ideas.

James made it his job to start engaging them with each other, and to find ways to integrate the many component disciplines. By the early 1990s, he was in the vanguard of the fast-growing, soon-to-be global science and practice of ecological restoration. He had found his ideal role in the future of the planet.

He helped convince Americans that their penchant for restoring a nostalgic presettlement landscape was, at best, provincial, and that such restoration would never be taken seriously elsewhere in the world. He convinced Europeans that a focus on function alone was inadequate, and that degraded ecosystems could be returned to a contemporary condition that was compatible with their historic developmental trajectory. Those are "loaded" words that may not mean much to a nonecologist, but they shook up the reigning complacency, and got a worldwide restoration movement percolating.

Aronson's niche is partly to be a communicator and bridge-builder, identifying and overcoming as many geographical, linguistic, political, conceptual, and cultural barriers as possible. He is especially concerned with how ecological restoration could be employed in poverty-stricken, lesser-developed countries, where the advice of foreign conservationists and economic developers frequently conflicts with cultural traditions.

In 2002, although still fully employed as researcher at the CNRS, Aronson took on the unpaid position as editor of the Society for Ecological Restoration International and Island Press Book series on ecological restoration. Since then, he has coauthored and edited several books on restoration and related topics and published numerous articles in scientific and popular journals. His most recent books are the best yet. One is *Ecological Restoration: Principles, Values, and Structure of an Emerging Profession* (2007), coauthored with Society for Ecological Restoration International cofounder and president emeritus, Dr. Andre "Andy" Clewell. It comprehensively and thoroughly describes this newly conceived discipline and industry.

The second is *Restoring Natural Capital: Science, Business, and Practice,* coedited with Suzanne Milton and James Blignaut, also published in 2007. Both books are part of the Society for Ecological Restoration International (www.ser.org) and Island Press Book Series (www.islandpress.org). The latter book prepares the way for merging ecological restoration and economics, provides 19 case studies, and provides tactics and strategies to implement the restoration of natural capital on regional, national, and international scales.

It was while working on *Restoring Natural Capital* that Aronson's conviction that economics—and private business—were going to be a big part of ecological restoration's future was translated into a convincing thesis. He realized that environmental and economic development efforts had to go together, even blend into one. "We need an economy in which nature matters and an ecology in which people matter." This line, which paraphrases E.F. Schumacher, is now the motto that restoring natural capital (RNC) specialists use in describing their work.

Restoring Natural Capital

Some of the best reconomics thinking taking place in the academic world is coming from the restoring natural capital group, whose key members are James Aronson, Andy Clewell, James Blignaut, and Suzanne Milton. Some of their most important contributions include adoption of a taxonomy of four types of capital, a typology of five basic motivations for ecological restoration, and a call for greater integration among all of those factors.

Their four types of capital are:

- Natural capital: The planet's nonrenewable resources—such as fossil fuels, uranium, and diamonds—plus its renewable resources, which are primarily ecosystem based.
- Cultural (social) capital: knowledge and traditions related to decision making, survival, and exploitation of the Earth's resources, including the creation of products and the valuation of goods and services.
- Cultivated capital: crops, tree farms, ranched meat, and aquaculture.
- Manufactured capital: buildings, infrastructure, machines, and materials. This form of capital is not able to reproduce itself, and so is considered "sterile."

I can't paraphrase their five basic motivations for ecological restoration any more elegantly or succinctly than they did in the following abstract for a recent paper, so I'll simply reproduce that here, almost in its entirety. Although it was written specifically for ecological restoration, try reading it from the perspective of whatever kind of "re" activity you are involved with. You might find their thinking surprisingly applicable to the other 11 sectors of restorable assets in our natural, built, and socioeconomic environments:

The reasons ecosystems should be restored are numerous, disparate, generally understated, and commonly underappreciated. We offer a typology in which these reasons—or motivations—are ordered among five rationales: technocratic, biotic, heuristic, idealistic, and pragmatic.

- *The technocratic rationale encompasses restoration that is conducted by government agencies or other large organizations to satisfy specific institutional missions and mandates.*
- *The biotic rationale for restoration is to recover lost aspects of local biodiversity.*
- *The heuristic rationale attempts to elicit or demonstrate ecological principles and biotic expressions.*
- *The idealistic rationale consists of personal and cultural expressions of concern or atonement for environmental degradation, reengagement with nature, and/or spiritual fulfillment.*
- *The pragmatic rationale seeks to recover or repair ecosystems for their capacity to provide a broad array of natural services and products upon which human economies depend and to counteract extremes in climate caused by ecosystem loss.*

We propose that technocratic restoration, as currently conceived and practiced, is too narrow in scope and should be broadened to include the pragmatic rationale whose overarching importance is just beginning to be recognized. We suggest that technocratic restoration is too authoritarian, that idealistic restoration is too overly restricted by lack of administrative strengths, and that a melding of the two approaches would benefit both . . . The biotic and heuristic rationales can be satisfied within the contexts of the other rationales.

—Andre F. Clewell and James Aronson, "Motivations for the Restoration of Ecosystems," *Conservation Biology,* Volume 20, Number 2, April 2006

The primary lesson to be drawn from such work is this: programs that effectively integrate as many of these motivations as possible are more efficient, more likely to succeed, and those successes are more likely to yield better-than-expected results. The three renewal rules neatly capture all five of these motivations in a way that's simple enough to be applied in the real world.

Back to James

Aronson is thus engaged full time in ecological restoration, in a variety of ways. He is on full salary as a researcher at the CNRS in France, and is a long-time research associate of the Missouri Botanical Garden. Both are exceptional institutions that give great liberty to researchers.

But research and publishing are not enough to get the job done. Together with his South African colleague, the economist James Blignaut, ecologist Andy Clewell of the United States, and bushland manager Bev Debrincat of Australia, Aronson was instrumental in establishing the Restoring Natural Capital (RNC) Alliance, an international network based at the Missouri Botanical Garden.

The alliance brings together individuals, nongovernmental organizations, private companies, and government organizations. It seeks to develop, demonstrate, and offer locally appropriate solutions to resolve environmental and economic development problems simultaneously, in underdeveloped countries and industrialized countries alike. The RNC Alliance (www.rncalliance.org) has projects in the Mediterranean Basin, Africa, Madagascar, Australia, and Latin America. Related programs are under development in China and India as well.

What makes the natural capital concept effective is its binocular vision, capturing the insights of both economics and ecology. "No one actually lives in the isolated silos in which these two disciplines have been academically confined," says Blignaut. "We all live between them. Economists and ecologists both intuitively understand the concept of capital. Any economist will tell you: 'If you don't invest in your capital stock, you are going backwards, my friend.' And ecologists will say the same. So natural capital provides a common platform for the two disciplines, because the terms underpinning the concept are familiar to all of us." "Restore" is the verb that turns two nouns into a strategy relevant to today's challenges.

Aronson sees that the world faces the interlinked challenges of global climate change, desertification, poverty, ocean decline, ecological overshoot, and loss of bio-diversity, and simultaneously the need to develop a sense of dignity among the world's poorest people. "The logical approach to resolve these interrelated chal-lenges," he says, "is to tackle them all simultaneously – through the application of the RNC strategies. The upbeat message is that there are many ways in which restoration can improve people's lives and increase resilience to the tide of climate change and other profound global changes breaking over our heads right now. This is fundamentally an optimistic, positive, and can-do message, unusual in environ-mental thinking, which tells us that unprecedented losses of natural capital and biodiversity, which we have brought upon ourselves, can be rolled back."

To help pay the bills and get involved in interesting projects, Aronson does occasional freelance consulting. For example, he and Clewell participate as inde-pendent reviewers in the program financed by the United Nations Compensation Commission (UNCC) to help "restore" Kuwait, following the 1991 invasion of that country by Iraq. Much of the budget provided by the UNCC will go to rebuild-ing the damaged, human-made infrastructure of the country, but a certain proportion is for natural environments as well. Coordinated by Kuwait's National Focal Point, Aronson is part of the international team selected to supervise the Implementation of Projects Related to Environmental Remediation in that country.

Aronson is also attempting to launch a triangular relationship among the RNC Alliance, the International Union for the Conservation of Nature (IUCN), and the World Business Council for Sustainable Development (WBCSD). The goal is to introduce the WBCSD's staff—and CEOs from the mining, cement, energy, and automobile companies represented in the WBCSD—to discover and understand the restoring natural capital approach to business. The IUCN is already working with the WBCSD, and poised to be an active partner in this three-way interaction as well.

Large financial and development prospects for large-scale eco-restoration lie ahead, in relation to the emerging markets for carbon credits and payments for ecosystem services. The main issue is no longer about remediation or mitigation, but rather about adaptation and rethinking development. Many challenges lie ahead for the disciplines and industry of ecosystem restoration. These issues are regularly discussed (quite passionately) in journals such as *Ecological Restoration* (primarily in the United States), *Restoration Ecology* (international), and *Ecological Management and Restoration* (Australia).

If you're wondering about the similarity of those titles, let me point out that "restoration ecology" is science, whereas "ecological restoration" is practice, which includes vital—yet less quantifiable—social, cultural, economic, and aesthetic factors. The former is rigorous and largely academic, whereas the latter is (ideally) holistic.

There's a subtle but substantial difference in approach between the restoration ecology scientists and the ecological restoration practitioners. Many (certainly not all) scientists believe that restoration ecology can be reduced to a rigorously predictable and controllable discipline via greater understanding of basic laws and mechanisms. Most practitioners, on the other hand, argue that ecosystems are far too complex to be reduced to such a formulaic approach, and that there are far too many nonbiological factors—for example of a cultural or political nature—to design and manage in that manner.

Since new academic research tends to reveal previously unknown levels of complexity, and since many ecosystem (as with human health) dynamics are emergent phenomena that defy prediction, my guess is that the practitioners are right. Besides, the restoration need is far too urgent for us to wait for anything approaching perfect knowledge before taking action.

How this rift will become resolved will depend partially on the pervasive influence of government agencies that are instrumental in funding and shaping restoration programs. On the one hand, governments depend, sometimes inordinately, on science. On the other hand, there is an incipient trend for governments to relinquish their command-and-control authority in favor of local, community-based control of restoration projects. Local projects are generally more pragmatic and less theoretically based, and more in step with restoration practitioners.

Regardless of how this drama plays out, practitioners depend on fundamental ecological science that improves their craft. In addition, and in a real sense, practitioners are also researchers at heart, as they try to elicit new ecological knowledge in all that they do at a project site. Every project doubles as a research project that helps improve our insights of ecological dynamics. In spite of their penchant for theoretical science, most academic researchers in restoration ecology are sensitive to pragmatic issues.

For example, several authors provided much insight in recommendations that emerged from articles in a single issue (September 2007) of *Restoration Ecology*, which had a special focus on river restoration. Viewed from the standpoint of the three renewal rules, integration and engagement appear frequently (rewealth is a given). There are many calls for quality improvement via better monitoring. This could—in a stretch—be seen as an extension of the engagement rule, since engaging all stakeholders will tend to increase both oversight and the demand for high standards:

- River restoration projects that seem to have failed can be turned into successes through the application of adaptive management. (My suspicion is that this also applies to troubled community revitalization projects).
- Ecological restoration projects need to identify quantifiable success criteria up front, and monitor them rigorously.
- Comprehensive watershed plans must place each waterway restoration project in both its present and future contexts.
- Project scale is of extreme importance to waterway restoration. It must encompass the entire riparian area, not just the stream channel, and should address floodplain connectivity.
- If your project lacks sufficient funding for proper monitoring, it isn't yet fully funded.
- A study of 860 stream restoration projects in Georgia, Kentucky, and both Carolinas showed that only 30% were carried out as part of a larger watershed plan. While the southeast United States generally monitors its restoration projects better than the rest of the country, North Carolina only monitors about 36% of theirs.
- A survey of 2,247 ecological restoration projects in the state of Victoria, Australia revealed that only 14% involved any form of monitoring. (An old business management maxim says that we can't achieve what we can't measure. We need to get out of restore-and-run mode).
- According to a telephone poll of 317 restoration managers across the United States, ecological degradation is usually the primary motivator of river restoration projects, yet post-project aesthetics and positive public opinion were the most common measures of success. Fewer than half of the projects had measurable objectives, yet two-thirds of the interviewees called their projects "completely successful."

The dozen authors of that article recommended the creation of a "national program of strategic monitoring." Not a bad idea when you consider that well over a billion dollars is spent in the United States annually on river-related ecological restoration alone. That figure doesn't include combined sewer overflow redesign projects—and the renovation of other waterway-related infrastructure—which runs into the tens of billions of dollars.

In collaboration with South African economists James Blignaut and Martin de Wit, Aronson is working to develop restoration NGOs and RNC businesses in several African countries. Together with the Missouri Botanical Garden's conservation science staff, he is developing similar initiatives in Madagascar and the tropical Andes. In South Africa, Aronson, Blignaut, and de Wit have three companies—JABENZI, JAINSA, and ASSET–International working on these projects, which closely follow the renewal rules. (The acronym ASSET stands for Africa's Search for Sound Economic developmenT).

Many of Africa's rural areas are heavily degraded. The restoration of natural capital not only aims at restoring the land, but also at removing the pressures and poor management practices that caused the degradation in the first place. The RNC Alliance envisions a national and regional restoration project as a public works endeavor together with private concerns. Under this scenario, restoration could employ many thousands of people while "selling" these invaluable ecosystem goods and services to those living on commercial farms and in cities, thereby contributing to income security.

They have a three-year-old project in the World Heritage region of the Drakensberg Mountains of eastern South Africa. It aims to restore and maintain indigenous vegetation cover to retain soil, paying for the restorative work by developing a market for water services. This project recalls the well-known Delaware-Catskills watershed restoration project linking New York City to upper New York State and adjacent lands (described in *The Restoration Economy*). The Drakensberg mountain range occupies less than 5% of the total surface area of South Africa, but produces 25% of the country's surface runoff, and it has a "water footprint," or reach, covering approximately 60% of the country.

The watershed restoration project's prospects are bright because of the convergence of four critical factors: (1) an imperative for water, (2) the emerging markets for carbon credits and payments for ecosystem services (PES), (3) its profundity of unique and endangered biodiversity, and (4) its wealth of cultural assets. It's one of the richest areas in the world for prehistoric art, hosting more than 40,000 Bushman (Khoisan) rock art paintings at more than 600 locations.

Aronson stresses that restoration of natural capital is an economic development strategy, not a conservation strategy. This is a key point in developing countries where poverty makes the classic ecological arguments seem a luxury. Foreign-bred ecological programs can sound like a new form of imperialism. The developed world demands that its former colonies do not commit the very ecological sins—such as deforestation and wetland drainage—that Europe and the United States have already profitably committed on their own territories. Aronson and his colleagues avoid this conundrum by emphasizing that humans are themselves an essential part of what he calls "socio-ecosystems." This perspective is epitomized by South Africa's Working-for-Water program that you'll discover in Chapter 13.

With James Blignaut and others, Aronson is also working on the idea of establishing a carbon, water, and biodiversity credit-trading center, which could bundle the credits from a range of large, medium, and small-scale RNC projects throughout southern Africa. They would then sell those credits in bulk to buyers in Europe. The carbon market is well established internationally but very few projects in Africa are yet qualified, and there is also a great problem of the carbon producers not enjoying a fair share of the benefits. The water and biodiversity markets are less developed, but Blignaut, Aronson, and their colleagues think the future is going that way, especially if bio-banking grows significantly.

They are in discussion with a Dutch carbon broker in this regard and hopefully these talks will lead to the establishment of such a trading center. Both this effort of JAINSA and the interrelated Working-for-Water program are outstanding rural examples of the "renewal engine" model: permanent, nonprofit, public-private entities fostering natural and socioeconomic renewal. James Aronson says "all three renewal rules are fully embraced by the RNC Alliance."

Restorative Lifestyles

Many persons have a wrong idea of what constitutes true happiness. It is not attained through self-gratification but through fidelity to a worthy purpose.
—Helen Keller

One thing I've noticed in my travels is that rewealth tends to restore its practitioners. That doesn't mean you don't have to deal with nastiness, incompetence, corruption, and other stress-inducing factors, of course. But it *does* mean that the satisfaction of restoring our world for a living goes a long way toward offsetting those challenges in terms of one's mental, emotional, and spiritual health.

One might say that rewealth can be a path to a restorative lifestyle. We tend to get so wrapped up in everyday life that we put our dreams on hold. Rewealth can be a way of integrating our ultimate dreams into our daily reality. Of course, whether we resist challenges and produce distress, or calmly flow with them is still key. Restorative activities in restorative surroundings aren't entirely stress free: people can probably get ulcers restoring the world, too. But joy seems to prevail.

A good example of a restorative lifestyle are the hundreds—maybe thousands—of Americans, Canadians, and Europeans who have been buying and restoring run-down, historic haciendas and other buildings throughout Mexico, Central America, and South America. In the process, they beautify the community, help to revitalize its economy, and create a place for themselves in what they consider paradise. This is often done in the latter third of their lives, which really puts the "re" in retirement. I'll probably feature at least one such story in my next book.

As you've seen, James Aronson personally embodies the three renewal rules. His work is entirely based on *rewealth*: restoring natural capital. He *integrates* the renewal of both natural and human communities. He acts as a bridge among European, African, and North American restoration ecologists, *engaging* them with each other to enrich and accelerate their research and practice.

He does all this from a lovely restored farmhouse near the French-Spanish border, halfway between his American roots and his African passions. As James and I sat by his fireplace, sipping the local wine, I couldn't help but admire his lifestyle and life mission.

Adaptive Reuse of Ecosystems as a Global Climate Change Strategy

We've mentioned global climate change several times in the course of the Aronson story, so this is probably as good a place as any to bring up how it might affect global ecological restoration.

The dream of visionary restoration ecologists has long been to not just restore individual ecosystems, but to restore the connections among them, so as to restore regional—and even continental—ecosystems. One of the many challenges posed by global climate change is the way it will likely disrupt or even undo ongoing and completed conservation/restoration efforts. For instance, rising sea levels could turn a newly-restored freshwater Everglades ecosystem into a salt marsh.

Climate change will likely be an unmitigated catastrophe for isolated ecosystems. However, an inter-connected system of conserved and restored ecosystems offers wildlife migration paths and other opportunities to take adaptive measures. To put it in urban redevelopment speak, wildlife can "adaptively reuse" ecosystems abandoned by other refugee wildlife, just as industrial workers move out and families move in when factories are adaptively reused as condos.

Nothing new about that, of course: species have been jockeying for their niche in nature for millions of years. But anthropogenic climate change is likely to make the adaptive reuse of abandoned properties—and entire climatic zones—the key factor of species survival. Whether species—and the entire wildlife communities upon which they depend, and whose context often defines them—can adapt at the hyper-accelerated pace of the anthropogenic change being inflicted on them today is another story.

Chapter 9

The John Knott Story

A for-profit renewal engine pioneers integrated rewealth strategies in the world's largest rapid, resilient urban renewal project.

O f all public-private rewealth partnerships I've encountered around the world, the Noisette Project leads the way both in quality and quantity. It's the largest example of what I would call truly integrated, fully engaged rewealth. It is already producing *rapid* renewal, and—despite the severe downturn in the U.S. real estate market—shows every sign of producing *resilient* renewal. Noisette is still seeing escalating demand for residences—along with increasing prices—even while sprawl projects in the area are slashing prices right and left.

At a ceremony celebrating a military base transfer on July 1, 2003, North Charleston Mayor Keith Summey told a crowd of 200 city and Noisette Company employees and other guests: "It's taken a lot of stamina to get where we are today. You're standing in a building that hasn't been on the tax books since it was built [in the early 1900s]. Now, it's time to take it back to private development" [quoted from a July 2, 2003, article by Terry Joyce in the Charleston *Post and Courier*].

Knott told me he hopes to create a global prototype for the sustainable redevelopment of inner cities. He says Noisette has the potential to become a transformative project for American cities, and maybe beyond. Let's see if he's living up to that ambition.

North Charleston, South Carolina

Americans historically have a low regard for the public realm, and this is a very unfortunate thing, because the public realm is the physical manifestation of the common good. And when you degrade the public realm, as we have, then you degrade the common good. This is what lies behind a whole range of social problems, from crime to municipal bankruptcy. Our disregard for the public realm has especially impaired our ability to think about public life, or civic life, let alone civic art. We built a nation of scary places and became a nation of scary people.

—James Howard Kunstler, *Home from Nowhere: Remaking Our Everyday World for the 21st Century* (Touchstone Press, 1998)

Located on the North Charleston peninsula, the city is adjacent to U.S. Highway 26, between the Cooper and Ashley Rivers. It sits directly above its wealthier and more famous neighbor, Charleston, whose residents have long called North Charleston by a derisive nickname: "Upchuck" ("up" because it's upcounty, and "Chuck" for "Charles"). For many years North Charleston has been a community without a core, having lost whatever vision and community cohesiveness it might have once had over decades of neglect and decay. It regularly qualifies in annual lists of the top 10 most dangerous cities in the United States.

North Charleston's mayor, Keith Summey, had identified what he called "five cancers" in the city that needed to be cured: The Garco asbestos and rubber plant; the Century Oaks and Calhoun Homes (World War II temporary military housing areas); North Park Village (the largest public housing project in the state, now being redeveloped under the Hope VI program); and the closed navy base and adjoining areas. All of these "cancers," of course, were also restorable assets, when looked at through the eyes of rewealth.

There's also a restorable cultural and historical aspect to the city; the Gullah-speaking, African-American neighborhood of Liberty Hill, founded in 1865 by the newly emancipated "freemen."

The Noisette Project

Noisette has been called "the largest sustainable redevelopment project in the U.S.," as well as "the largest and most comprehensive urban redevelopment project in the United States."

People refer to the Noisette Project as a 3,000-acre redevelopment, but it's actually a 340-acre redevelopment project being done in a manner that integrates with—and revitalizes—about 2,700 acres of contiguous, mostly private property. About 13,000 people currently live within the project area.

Noisette is expected to attract about $1 billion in private and public investment in the near term, and about $3 billion over 15 years. In the process, 7,000 new housing units will be created, 3,000 existing housing units will be rehabilitated, and six to eight million square feet of commercial and retail space will be built or renovated.

The project includes a redeveloped naval base (closed in 1995), new parks, numerous brownfields, renovated infrastructure, renovated housing, and much more. But the spiritual heart of the project, in many ways, is the restoration of the polluted, eroded Noisette Creek into a protected, 135-acre wildlife-rich tidal estuary.

There are two key geographic components to this unique public-private collaboration between the city of North Charleston and the Noisette Company, LLC:

- Revitalizing the Noisette "Footprint." This is the 3,000-acre area that comprises the original boundaries of the city of North Charleston. The city takes leadership on this aspect, with the Noisette Company's support and advice. This "support and advice" is no mere token, either: the area's master plan—the best this author has ever seen—was developed at no cost to the city whatsoever.

- Redeveloping 340 acres of the former navy base under the project name *The Navy Yard at Noisette*. The base includes a wide variety of restorable assets: historic admiral's homes, reusable office buildings and residential units, waterfronts, brownfields, and degraded streams. The Noisette Company takes leadership on this aspect, with the city providing support and advice.

The financing is being done through the city as a public-private partnership. The Noisette Company won't actually perform much of the actual deconstruction/redevelopment work, subcontracting some to various engineering and contracting firms, and selling other plots outright to redevelopers who will work in accordance with the Noisette master plan.

Here are the 10 chapter headings from the 140-page Noisette Master Plan: (1) Vision and Process, (2) Regenerative Land Use, (3) Restoring Natural Systems, (4) Restoring Connections, (5) Neighborhoods as Catalysts for Change, (6) River Center at Noisette, (7) Project Phasing, (8) Initiatives and Strategies, (9) Benchmarks for Success, and (10) Synthesis: The New American City. Other cities would do well if some of those subjects inspired and structured their own plan.

About 250 acres of the naval base was appraised at $9.6 million: that property was deeded to North Charleston from the federal government at no cost, and the city then sold it to Noisette. The remaining 90 acres had "issues" (don't ask . . . let's just say that South Carolina and Louisiana share some governance challenges) that required more time. Demolition and asbestos removal on the base alone will run around $8 million.

Once the sites have been prepared, Noisette sells parcels to other redevelopers, thus spreading the risk and tapping into far more sources of funding. A press release issued by the Noisette Company on July 1, 2003, said: "The Noisette Master Plan involves an ongoing, unprecedented community participation in the development of plans to restore ecologically damaged areas, and economically revitalize blighted neighborhoods. The Noisette team hopes to create the most comprehensive sustainable redevelopment project in the United States, as a fulfillment of the City's Garden City history and Frederick Law Olmstead's Chicora Park, which were drawn in the early 20th Century."

It continued: "As a public-private venture, the Noisette Company will arrange bridge financing for public infrastructure, which will be ultimately funded by the Tax Increment Financing district established on the former base. Under the TIF, the City of North Charleston will not issue bonds until the infrastructure is complete. All of the project's urban redevelopment plans and designs are privately funded by the Noisette Company, LLC."

Dewees Island: Restorative Residential Development in Paradise?

Dewees Island is an environmentally sensitive, 1,206-acre barrier island off the coast of Charleston. In January of 2003, I was in South Carolina investigating the Noisette Project and talking to some folks at Clemson University (more on that in a moment). John Knott invited Maria (my wife) and me to spend a few nights at his tranquil Dewees Island project. What John had done there won the Urban Land Institute's 2001 Award of Excellence, one of the country's most prestigious real estate development awards.

You wouldn't think a high-end residential development on an undeveloped island could ever be considered "sustainable," much less "restorative," but John pulled it off. An earlier, aborted attempt at development had done considerable environmental damage. John restored the ecosystems, and the island now feels more like a state park than a housing project.

He also undid some misguided coastal engineering that had led to erosion of the island's beaches. When I arrived in 2003, home owners who had purchased— less than a decade earlier—waterfront lots with just 100 yards of beach now had up to a quarter of a mile of gorgeous dunes and beaches in front of their homes. They actually had far more real estate than they had purchased. This added not only to the beauty of the place, but to the security of their homes (by buffering storms).

Note that this was accomplished by working with nature, allowing nature herself to restore the beaches. Not a single bucket of sand was dredged from another beach and dumped here, which is how communities usually "renourish" their abused coastlines.

How the Noisette Project Came to Be

Kurt Taylor, the mayor pro tem of the city, invited John into North Charleston in December 1997. He looked at the area around the E. Montague business corridor and then toured the area as a whole. He was invited thanks to his work at Dewees, which was attracting much acclaim. Emboldened by that island success, John had been floating the concept of a "Dewees in the City." Taylor thought North Charleston might be an ideal candidate.

Mayor Summey, in March 1998, asked John to look for renewal opportunities in the city. Each time John came up with one, Summey asked for more. This went on for about three years. Over time, the current comprehensive model emerged, bringing (as John puts it) "the skills of sustainable master community developers to the urban world with a new partnership model."

As you've learned earlier, the whole point of adopting the renewal rules in your decision making—and of creating a renewal engine—is to enhance your community's renewal potential. Capacity building doesn't usually consist of inviting a redeveloper to town to do as he/she pleases, no matter how "visionary" they might be.

But, even if North Charleston had given him a free rein, John Knott isn't the type to do things in the sort of top-down, cookie-cutter manner that typifies so much redevelopment in the United States these days. Although I've never heard John use the term, I believe he's practicing what could be called "true urbanism." This approach follows Alexander Pope's advice to "consult the genius of the place . . ." as John is fond of quoting. In his case, "the place" includes the people, not just the natural and built heritage.

Where does the name Noisette come from, you might be asking? It is in honor of famed French botanist Phillip Noisette, who—in the late 1700s, while on an expedition in Haiti—fell in love with and married a black woman, and brought his new family to Charleston. South Carolina's racial laws made his Haitian wife and children legally his slaves—a situation he wasn't able to rectify until he was on his deathbed. He moved to the North Charleston area in part to escape social persecution.

Today, people are moving to North Charleston to escape high real estate prices, and to enjoy watching—and being a part of—a historic community's rebirth.

A For-Profit Renewal Engine?

While all of this leading-edge renewal of the natural and built environments has been taking place, the Noisette Company has been serving as the area's renewal engine.

What makes this story especially unusual is that this public-private renewal engine was inspired, designed, and run not by a mayor or an NGO or a citizens' group, but by a private redeveloper. You know . . . the guys that citizens often have to protect themselves from . . . the guys who seem to love demolishing historic buildings and neighborhoods so they can have a blank sheet of paper on which to do their thing? But this one's different . . . *very* different. So, different, in fact, that a citizens' group has been formed to make sure that city officials support his efforts.

What's even more unusual is that the renewal engine is not just housed in a private firm, it *is* a private firm: the Noisette Company, LLC. I'm certainly not recommending such a model; after all, there aren't many John Knotts in the world (despite the fact that he has an identical twin brother, Frank).

Granted, the firm is based on a public-private partnership, but it's a for-profit firm nonetheless, so that departs from the renewal engine model, since they are usually nonprofit. But the Noisette Company operates according to the three renewal rules—rewealth, integration, and engagement—to a degree that any nonprofit community group should envy.

It also performs all three of the renewal processes—visioning, culturing, and partnering—extremely well. This illustrates the importance of understanding the basic drivers of a renewal engine, and not getting hung up on who sponsors or runs it, or what kind of organization houses it. They engage the entire community on an ongoing basis regarding vision and strategy, to the point where it's the community's own vision and strategy.

One only has to look at some of the grand schemes—some of them very green—that have gone nowhere in recent years to see why all three processes are so crucial. Many celebrated architects (sometimes called "starchitects") and redevelopers are long on vision but short on engagement and/or partnering skills; prima donnas who don't play well with others. A burst of enthusiasm and initial funding is often followed by an embarrassing loss of support. It's "rapid" without "resilient" or even "renewal."

Noisette's visioning process has been geared toward helping the citizens understand their heritage and appreciate the value of the place. At dozens of meetings in schools and churches during the early years, John constantly asked, "What do you like about your community?", "What don't you like about it?", and "What would you like it to become?". This helps build a renewal culture.

As proof, in 2005 a neighborhood group called the Progressive Neighborhood Alliance arose spontaneously to help ensure that the city follows through properly on the Noisette Master Plan. The group is growing fast, and their presence at city council meetings is making a big difference. It's a perfect example of what happens when a community has developed a renewal culture.

John didn't take a passive approach to culturing, though. He has formed a number of community organizations to embed values that will help heal the community. Remember, he's working with an existing community here; it's not just a redevelopment project.

Here are some of the nonprofits the Noisette Company has formed or helped form: Sustainability Institute (1999); Michaux Conservancy (2003); Noisette Foundation (2004); Navy Yard Community Association (2006); Navy Yard Business District Association (2006). Let's take a brief look at each, as they offer tremendous insight into what makes the Noisette Project so unique.

Because he will have no authority over what the surrounding private property owners do with their homes and businesses, Knott formed the Sustainability Institute. The Sustainability Institute educates local residents about renovating their homes in a healthier and more energy/water-efficient manner. One of their first projects was to buy (for $30,000) and renovate (for $55,000) a dilapidated 900-square-foot home using the latest "green" materials and technologies.

This "green house" demonstrates how to retrofit green components into an older home. Thousands of residents have toured the green house and over 1,300 have participated in workshops. These activities have yielded over a quarter of a million dollars in energy savings in local homes. The Sustainability Institute also encourages community gardens, which restore value and beauty to vacant lots while boosting both nutrition and neighborliness.

The Michaux Conservancy supports the restoration of the 135-acre Noisette Creek Preserve and its 1,400-acre watershed. It has already attracted over $750,000 in support, in large part because the Michaux Conservancy is itself a partnership. Some key partners include Audubon South Carolina, Clemson University Restoration Institute, Project Oceanica at the College of Charleston, South Carolina Sea Grant Consortium, The Charleston County School District, The Heinz Center for Economics, Environment, and Science, and The Heinz Endowment. New partners in the process of coming aboard include the National Oceanic and Atmospheric Administration's (NOAA) Community-based Restoration Program, the Trust for Public Lands, the North Charleston Sewer District, and the North Charleston Progressive Neighborhoods Alliance.

The Noisette Foundation's mission is to achieve long-term social, environmental, and economic equity in the neighborhoods surrounding the navy yard. Besides charitable donations and grants, it's funded through real estate transfer fees. Their programs focus on environmental leadership, social justice, lifelong education, human health, economic opportunity, plus arts and culture. It puts its mission and goals in the form of creating three "pathways" for local residents: healthy pathways, restorative pathways, and 21st century career pathways.

One of the Noisette Foundation's programs is the Lowcountry HUB Academy Consortium. Its goal is to help North Charleston residents create their own construction-related companies, so more of the money will stay in the community. To date, 33 graduates are now growing their own businesses. The academy is supported by most of the redevelopers and construction companies working at the Noisette Project, such as Bovis Lend Lease, as well as by South Carolina State University. The Noisette Foundation is also a partnership, with about a dozen major partners including Soros Foundation and Delancey Street Foundation (which specializes in prisoner reentry programs).

The Noisette Company doesn't just engage stakeholders; they engage them in a way that encourages stakeholders to engage each other. For instance, the Navy Yard Community Association and the Navy Yard Business District Association work collaboratively on almost everything. This is both sensible and highly unusual: most communities' citizen and commercial groups seem to exist in different worlds, and many of them are at loggerheads.

John refers to this culturing process as "building an institutional framework to support a 'green culture' in the city." It's been yielding some spectacular results. For instance, inspired by the green standards being promulgated by the Noisette Foundation, the Charleston County School District raised its own standards. In 2005, they completed North Charleston Elementary, the first LEED-certified school in the entire state, and LEED certification is now mandatory for all future county schools. Charleston County School District bonds were recently approved to raise $200 million for the renovation of 13 existing schools to LEED standards.

LEED wasn't good enough for John, though. The city of North Charleston and many of the major redevelopers building within the Noisette Project have adopted the Noisette Quality Home Standard, which exceeds the LEED home certification. All of the other major redevelopers are using either LEED or EarthCraft. (LEED is managed by the U.S. Green Building Council. EarthCraft House is a green residential building program created by the Greater Atlanta Home Builders Association.)

Such culturing also attracts the "right" kinds of businesses. Noisette now has the first "sustainable" brewery in South Carolina: it runs on biodiesel, sources sustainably grown grains and hops, and is—of course—housed in a renovated building.

Noisette has a recycling business that doesn't just turn out raw materials; it adds value to them in the form of finished products.

No Good Deed Goes Unpunished

My 2003 trip to the area coincided with one of the many political crises that afflicted the early years of the Noisette Project. There's been no shortage of dangerous moments, ranging from bickering between local and state governments to nervous local politicians unfamiliar with restorative development. At one point, the state tried to take the navy base from the city (unheard of in Base Realignment and Closure (BRAC) practice), no doubt to bestow it on a "special friend."

During this particular crisis, an important deadline was being sabotaged by wealthy, well-connected local forces that had been hungrily eyeing the base property. They had no intention of letting an outsider have his way with it, and launched a smear campaign through friends at a local newspaper. The situation was extremely tense.

While I have all the respect in the world for redevelopers like John Knott and Tom Darden, I would never for a moment want to be one. It takes a level of courage, persistence, and sophistication I could never measure up to. That said, I'd much rather be a redeveloper like John, than a sprawl developer. I like to sleep at night.

The stresses of John's trials and tribulations have been Job-like, but I'm sure his heart and soul rest easy. This personal renewal, in John's case, no doubt derives not just from what he's accomplishing for the people and wildlife of North Charleston, but from the example he's setting for the world. I'm honored (and personally renewed!) to be among those who are bringing that example to light.

Nothing this big in a small town is going to happen without controversy and fear. An April 27, 2003, article by reporter James Scott in the Charleston *Post and Courier* included the following passage: "'I have said it from day 1 this project will never get completed,' said (City Councilman A.C.) Mitchum, one of the city's more conservative leaders. 'We'll spend lots of tax dollars and then all of a sudden the project will be abandoned.'"

The article continued, "The other council members argue the risk is worth taking. Noisette, they say, gives North Charleston a chance to create a thriving city center. 'There is a risk in everything,' [North Charleston Mayor Keith] Summey said. 'This is a risk we take because we want improvements in our lives. . . . This is a once-in-a-lifetime opportunity. To bypass this and let it escape us would be unforgivable.'"

After five years of planning and negotiating, the key naval base property was officially transferred to the Noisette Company on July 1, 2003. The Noisette

Company describes this project as "a modern-day regeneration . . . a public-private financial partnership, a community-based development process." Knott describes the redeveloper's role as "an integrator of community vision." What's more, he claims, "I'm not in the land business. Not in the sticks-and-bricks business either. I'm in the business of rebuilding community."

Rewealth Genes?

Here are the official values and principles of the Noisette Project, but they started life as the values and principles of John Knott: (1) experience our heritage, share our vision; (2) respect individuals, community, and the natural environment; (3) reweave and strengthen the city tapestry; (4) rekindle the city as a great place to grow; (5) restore and enhance the environment; (6) rediscover opportunities for sanctuary, spiritual renewal, and inspiration; (7) regenerate places for people to live, work, and learn.

That list alone should be enough indication that John Knott is a reconomic leader. But the Noisette Project breaks new ground in so many other ways that their master plan should probably be sold in bookstores. Make a list of the leading-edge practices from around the world that are considered restorative—or simply environmentally and socially responsible—and you'll probably find all of them at work in the Noisette Project.

Those "re" values and principles are all geared toward enhancing "the health of the economy, the health of the environment, and the health of the social fabric of the community" to put it in John's words. He refers to economic, environmental, and social *durability* (rather than "resilience") but we're talking about the same thing.

Knott has a genetic advantage for competing in the global reconomy: he's a third-generation redeveloper, with the family now in its 83rd year of restoring historic buildings and revitalizing cities for a living. The H.A. Knott Company was founded in Baltimore, Maryland in 1908, by John's builder/craftsman grandfather, Henry A. Knott. The Knott Company worked on contract with the late James Rouse of Baltimore, one of the pioneers of restorative development throughout the world.

As the Knott Company grew, it became one of the leading restorative builders in the Washington, DC-Maryland area, landing exclusive projects like the restoration of the historic governor's mansion in Annapolis, Maryland. The firm restored townhouses, built new residential structures in Washington, DC, and Baltimore City, and completed many quality projects for both the Maryland state government and the University of Maryland.

John's father, John L. Knott, Sr., was CEO of H.A. Knott Company, and John, Jr. worked for him until 1990, when he moved to Charleston to work on the Dewees Island project. John, Jr., has now been restoring the world for 33 years, and Noisette will likely be his magnum opus. He doesn't use the "Jr." much, so neither will I.

The rewealth genes haven't stopped with John, Jr., either: John, Jr.'s, son, John L. Knott, III, is taking restorative development into the fourth generation. He works for EQA Landmark Communities, in Pittsburgh, Pennsylvania, whose projects include Playa Vista in California, Somerset in Pittsburgh (a restored strip mine with neotraditional housing), and even the Noisette Project (John III is not a part of the Noisette project, however).

Furthermore, Knott's daughter, Melissa Knott, is director of sustainability at Forest City Stapleton, the largest redevelopment project in Denver's history. Forest City Enterprises, a Cleveland-based firm known nationwide for its redevelopment of historic downtown buildings, is redeveloping the defunct Stapleton Airport property. In the process, Forest City is restoring wetland ecosystems and wildlife corridors and adaptively reusing about half a dozen airport buildings, such as the control tower, a hanger, a terminal, and a cargo building. Denver simultaneously has two large-scale air-related projects, the other one being the redevelopment of the 1,866-acre Lowry Air Force Base.

Readers of *The Restoration Economy* will remember that the Resource Appendix listed three memberships as being the "basic three" that anyone involved in restorative development should join as an absolute minimum: the Society for Ecological Restoration International (www.ser.org), the Urban Land Institute (www.uli.org), and the National Trust for Historic Preservation (www.nthp.org). John Knott belongs to all three, and has been a leader in the latter two.

The Noisette Team

Noisette's master plan was created between 2001 and 2003 (and updated ever since) by an all-star rewealth team. It includes lead design firms Burt Hill Kosar Rittelmann (led by Harry Gordon) and BNIM out of Kansas City (led by Bob Berkibile). The landscape architecture is led by Ralph Sauer of Philadelphia.

LS3P (led by Tom Hund) is the local design firm partnered with Burt Hill and BNIM, and Tom Penny, LS3P's president, is the current national president of the AIA. Both Harry Gordon and Bob Berkibile are founding members of AIA's Committee on the Environment.

In addition to these designers, Knott's team includes those who know the restorable assets best. James Augustin, vice president and cofounder of the Noisette Company (and incurable punner) is one of them. Augustin was director of base closure for the U.S. Navy Civil Engineer Corps, and was a national leader in making the U.S. Navy's operations more sustainable. Shortly after retiring from the military, he got rescued from retirement by John Knott.

Reconnecting People to Their Water

As you'll see throughout this book, one of the most powerful catalysts of urban revitalization in recent decades has been the reconnection of citizens with their waterfront. Throughout most of the eighteenth, nineteenth, and twentieth centuries, waterfronts were blighted zones of warehouses, factories, and polluted ports. As the first land to be settled, they've been subjected to the longest abuse. But their location makes many of them buy-low, sell-high goldmines.

Many of the cities where these zones were located forgot to leave themselves any publicly accessible waterfront green space. Cleaning up waterfront brownfields and redeveloping them as parks is a strategy that is today turning around many depressed communities. The Trust for Public Land has been a powerful facilitator of this trend.

North Charleston, too, has a waterfront that few of its citizens ever saw up close. And if they had seen it, they probably wouldn't want to repeat the experience. Both industry and the military had denied residents access to their Cooper River waterfront for as long as any living person can remember. North Charleston's citizens have never had a place to relax, picnic, or party on the river. Now they do. The Riverfront Park opened July 4, 2005, with 15,000 citizens in attendance at the unveiling ceremony.

One aspect of their public-private collaboration is that the city will even-tually reimburse the Noisette Company for the cost of cleaning, replanting, and redeveloping a three-quarter-mile stretch of the riverfront. This is what has now become The Riverfront Park, with strolling trails, public dock, and amphitheater. Around the entire perimeter is a biking trail.

Using the "pocket park" concept that is so popular in this part of the south— whereby small public parks are within a block or two of almost any point in the downtown—Knott is giving aesthetically challenged North Charleston a feel similar to that of Charleston. Many streets will end at the water, and attractive commercial buildings—offices, restaurants, and retail—will be immediately accessible from the sidewalks.

Higher quality of life often involves a higher-than-normal quantity of public green space. Grand spaces like Central Park are wonderful, but pocket parks often provide more quality-of-life boost per acre. This is now well documented. It thus comes as a shock to see Detroit's recent announcement. They proposed to sell 92 of their pocket parks "to position the land for redevelopment." If there's one thing Detroit already has too *much* of, it's land available for redevelopment (thanks to the urban removal fiasco). If there's one thing Detroit has too *little* of, it's quality of life. One justification offered is that the money saved on maintaining neglected parks in neighborhoods that have lost many residents will help them renovate others. But if those 92 parks are run down, they aren't being maintained, so where are the savings going to come from? And how will those neglected neighborhoods ever come back to life without public green space? Many local experts agree: " . . . there's enough vacant land without hitting the publicly owned parkland," said Abe Kadushin, principal of Kadushin Architects Planners Inc., in an October 26, 2007 *Detroit Free Press* article by Zachary Gorchow. He continued, "Parkland is a very important and necessary resource in a revitalized neighborhood." It's not the kind of strategy a renewal engine is likely to generate . . . it more resembles the lovechild of a desperate city accounting office and a bargain-hunting real estate speculator.

Loft apartments will be above many of the commercial establishments in order to form the diverse, round-the-clock activity that's so necessary to successful urban revitalizations. Housing prices will be reasonable, ranging from condominiums costing approximately $65,000 to single family homes around $250,000. Knott claims that "When the project is done, it will feel like it has been there forever."

Rapid, Resilient Results

"The Noisette Project, just talking about it and all the optimism it has created, has definitely affected the market in a positive way," said (local real estate broker, and North Charleston's first mayor, John) Bourne. "Prices are up, values are up, and sales are up."

—April 27, 2003, article on Noisette by reporter
James Scott in the Charleston *Post and Courier*

John has taken tremendous personal risks, and—as a relative newcomer (known locally as "come 'eres" as opposed to "been 'eres")—has endured innumerable attacks from the old boy network. To virtually everyone else, he's a local hero.

The Noisette Company put over $6 million into planning this project, money that would have been completely lost had the deal fallen through. The local real estate market had taken a downturn since the project was first envisioned, which added to the uncertainties and risks. But the resilience of John's integrated, engaged approach to renewal is helping to weather that storm.

When John arrived, the median income of North Charleston was half of South Carolina's mean income, and the state has one of the lowest in the country. The percentage of home ownership was only 32%. Property values were flat or declining: housing sold for an average of $54 per square foot, and spent an average of 270 days on the market. Commercial real estate sold for $40,000 to $50,000 per acre. The East Montague business district was 70% vacant. The local schools had a 50% dropout rate in the 6th through 8th grades, and a 70% drop-out rate in the 9th through 12th grades. Seventy percent of North Charleston's crime emanated from those "five cancer" neighborhoods.

Today, all five of these priority areas have now been largely "cured" and are under redevelopment. Home ownership has shot up to over 45%. Housing is now selling for an average of $170 per square foot, and spends an average of only 45 days on the market. Commercial real estate now averages $300,000 to $500,000 per acre. The East Montague business district is now 90% leased, and contains two spas, seven restaurants, plus artist galleries.

The Noisette Master Plan is now complete, has been accepted by the city council, and has won the American Institute of Landscape Architects (ASLA) Award of Excellence. An off-navy-base TIF plan has been approved to raise $78 million. As of this writing, the Noisette Company has over a million square feet of tenant demand to offer redevelopers.

John Pharis, president of the Olde North Charleston Neighborhood Association, has lived in the area for less than a decade. But, those years began before the Noisette Project, so he's in a position to see the difference it's made. In the same *Post and Courier* article quoted above, he said Noisette has given residents new hope and reason to invest in their homes and the community. "More and more young folks are moving in," said Pharis. "Property values are definitely going up. You can see it."

Recent investments in the Noisette Project include the Oak Terrace Preserve residential development at $80 million; the Mixson Avenue mixed-use development at $180 million; Horizon Village redevelopment at $200 million (including $30 million of Hope VI funds); and Noisette Preserve restoration at $30 million. That's almost $700 million to date, which doesn't even include the navy yard.

The navy yard is the portion that the Noisette Company directly owns. To date, 305 of the 340 acres have been legally transferred to the Noisette Company; the navy yard cleanup and reuse plan has received federal approval; an on-base TIF has been approved to raise $300 to $500 million; 80,000 square feet of offices have been renovated and released; the American College of Building Arts (ACBA) is an anchor tenant, with some 40,000 square feet leased; the Arts & Design Center has a million square feet of old warehouse space leased; and some 61 companies, NGOs, government agencies, and schools are now tenants, totaling over 800 employees.

For decades, we've been trying to figure out how to solve our social, economic, and environmental ills, while perpetuating a deconomic model that mostly exacerbated them. The above numbers—indeed, the entire John Knott story—proves that economic growth can actually heal social and environmental problems, but only if it is based on rewealth. However, the comprehensive cure only comes when the renewal of the natural, built, and socioeconomic environments are properly integrated, and when all stakeholders have been properly engaged. As John has done—and is still doing—in North Charleston.

Lessons from John Knott and the Noisette Project

Strategic planning is done no more frequently than every three to five years in most cities (if at all). At Noisette, they do it constantly. They know that there's no more efficient chaos inducer in the world than delayed feedback, so they respond to their changing environment like the living system a community really is . . . not like the semirigid structure many city leaders seem to think they're in charge of.

The city of North Charleston is using TIF in a way that helps encourage homeowners and business owners to invest in renovating their property. These might be generic renovations inspired by the area's revitalization, or green retrofits inspired by the Sustainability Institute.

North Charleston designated Noisette neighborhoods as TIF districts. Done properly, TIF prevents residents from being penalized (tax-wise) for the increase in their property values that results from their renovations, and from the area's overall recovery.

In many places, the increased property taxes collected from reinvigorated neighborhoods go into the general funds of the community. Thus, the people who bore the brunt of the renovation expenses see relatively little benefit. In South Carolina, by law, all incremental increases in tax revenues within a TIF district go into a special fund. That fund is earmarked for the renovation of public infrastructure and green spaces within that area only. In other words, they get their money back, which eliminates one of the downsides of gentrification. This is an excellent policy that should be adopted by all states and countries.

North Charleston plans to put a quarter of the TIF funds into the local schools, and the rest into planting trees, refurbishing roads and sidewalks, and demolishing unsalvageable structures. In this manner, the renewal of private property and public infrastructure within a given area is linked via a simple, measurable mechanism.

This is the sort of intelligent city management—along with other revitalization tools like smart codes, historic tax credits, brownfield tax credits, and the like—that attracts both redevelopers and redevelopment capital. North Charleston's TIF districts are expected to generate about $350 million over 30 years, and that's just internally. Add in the outside redevelopment funds that tend to flow into areas that are seen as being on a path to increasing health and wealth, and the payoff could be huge indeed. This is the policy/legislative side of creating a culture that attracts and nurtures renewal.

You've seen how the Noisette Company integrates the renewal of the natural, built, and socioeconomic environments in a way that engages the business, government, NGO, academic, and citizen stakeholders. This covers the three renewal rules. You've seen how it performs two of the three renewal processes: visioning and culturing. But what turns all of these values, principles, and rules into actual rewealth is the third renewal process: partnering.

As stated earlier, one of the key functions of a renewal engine is to provide a neutral forum for partnering. Here, public and private entities can form public-private, public-public, and private-private partnerships; partnerships that follow the three renewal rules, and that are guided by the community's vision of their future. You've also seen that most of the nonprofits that the Noisette Company has catalyzed to create a green renewal culture in the community are partnerships. The Noisette Company itself operates in that same partnered manner when forming the projects that bring North Charleston's neighborhoods back to life.

When I say a "forum," I'm not talking about a physical room where you throw public and private players together and hope for a partnership. A designated room and a planned partnering event can be useful, but the process should be similar to by the way they do it at Noisette. Partnering is considered a basic mode of operation there. Everyone on staff looks for opportunities for productive partnerships, and helps make them happen. The entire company is a forum for partnering . . . it's embedded in the firm's DNA.

The Role of the Individual Champion

By now, it's no secret that I believe virtually all cities would benefit greatly from creating a renewal engine. However, there are some great revitalization success stories that can be traced to the sustained leadership of a single individual.

The primary reason neighboring Charleston, South Carolina has been a long-term national leader of restorative development is due to its "strong mayor" form of government. This has allowed its famed rewealth mayor, Joseph P. Reilly (in office since 1975), to move forward expeditiously with his restorative vision for this lovely city. His leadership in the successful revitalization of downtown Charleston is, in fact, the key to his political longevity.

Chicago, Illinois (under Richard M. Daley) and Guayaquil, Ecuador (under Jaime Nebot Saadi) are two more examples of cities that are reconomic leaders *sans* renewal engines. Guayaquil won the Model City for Human Development award from the United Nations in 2003. As with Charleston, Chicago and Guayaquil have strong, multiterm mayors with a rewealth orientation. All three cities are restoring their natural, built, and socioeconomic assets to a degree that most other cities envy. (Now, if Chicago could just figure out how to pay for renovating their elevated train system . . .)

Their strength in the first renewal rule, rewealth, is undisputable. But there's a downside to such centralized leadership. All three cities could get a much bigger bang for their buck if they focused more on the other two renewal rules; integration and engagement. Those rules add efficiencies and synergies to rewealth.

Now that Charleston, Chicago, and Guayaquil are well established on a regenerative trajectory, the ideal next step would be to start weaning the cities from this strongman model. The quickest, easiest, and safest way to do so is by creating a renewal engine. Only in that manner can they be assured of truly resilient renewal when these dynamic mayors leave office. If Reilly, Daley, and/or Nebot were to build local renewal engines before stepping down, it would assure their place at the forefront of global reconomic leadership, even while in retirement.

Clemson University's Restoration Institute Comes to Noisette

I've been telling the John Knott story in my keynotes and workshops since 2003. In March 2004, I saw an obvious connection between John's work and the consulting work I was doing with Clemson University, on the other side of South Carolina. A core group—comprising Dean Jan Schach, former director of development Mendal Bouknight, former professor Jeff Burden, professor Barry Nocks, and professor Mickey Lauria—had read *The Restoration Economy* and wanted Clemson to lead the way.

After helping Clemson raise their first round of matching funds from the state to create the institute, I recommended the Noisette Project as a living laboratory of leading-edge revitalization and restoration techniques and technologies for their students. After some four years of strategizing, fundraising, politicking, and real estate negotiating, the Clemson University Restoration Institute is finally coming to fruition. It looks like it will be well worth the wait.

They are building an 82-acre campus in the navy yard at Noisette. Clemson is also partnering with Noisette on the creation of the Center for Urban Coastal Ecosystems, a restoration-oriented research institute. The Clemson side of the Noisette story might be featured in the sequel to this book.

Silicon Valley of the Global Restoration Economy?

During my first trip to the Noisette project in January of 2003, I told John that I thought the Greater Charleston area had the potential to become "the Silicon Valley of the global restoration economy." I've since issued the same challenge to several other places around the world that had similar potential, such as southern Ontario. John has been using that theme ever since. More importantly, almost everything necessary to turn that theme into reality is actually happening in North Charleston.

Tom Darden's billion dollar Magnolia Project is right across the river from the Noisette Project. Joe Riley's Charleston is at the heart of the entire region. With a trio like that at work—plus Clemson's Restoration Institute—what could stop the greater Charleston area from becoming the Silicon Valley of the global restoration economy? Well, a paucity of integration and engagement at the regional level comes to mind. Now, if they were to create a *regional* renewal engine . . .

Chapter 10

Four Short Stories of Postindustrial Evolution
Waukegan, Youngstown, Winooski, and Louisville take surprising paths to recovering from the loss of factories.

W aukegan, Illinois, wants to grow by running long-time employers out of town. Youngstown, Ohio wants to grow by shrinking, by "undeveloping." Such counterintuitive strategies fly in the face of common wisdom. But all four of this chapter's stories are about growing economies by boosting quality of life. Three of them are about revitalizing by reconnecting citizens to their water. Those strategies are just plain common sense.

So, before telling them, let me reiterate the important difference between quality of life and standard of living. Initiatives to raise the standard of living focus primarily on recruiting jobs and increasing income. While both jobs and money are desirable, they make lousy goals. As we saw in Part I, such shortsighted goals drive unwise behaviors that undermine your quality of life. And that undermines economic resilience.

Initiatives aiming for enhanced quality of life also try to elevate incomes, but they encompass the renewal of natural, built, and socioeconomic assets as well. If one defines "renewal" in a holistic manner, then the "universal goal"—rapid, resilient renewal—moves a step higher, with quality of life being just one of its component goals.

We've seen other such "sub-goals" of rapid, resilient renewal in these pages, such as reconnecting to water and enhancing green space. The following two stories—Waukegan and Youngstown—show how pursuit of those goals can lead to rethinking some of our most basic assumptions about revitalization. The second two stories—Winooski and Louisville—reveal innovative approaches to partnering, and to making things happen.

Waukegan, Illinois: Reducing Employment for Economic Growth

As many other cities have done in the past two decades, Waukegan, Illinois, (population 90,000) has somewhat belatedly decided that their Lake Michigan waterfront is the key to their revitalization. Also like many other Great Lakes cities, Waukegan has endured many decades of economic and environmental deprivation.

Most of their dirty, heavy industries have gone bankrupt, or have moved to countries that value jobs over quality of life (which usually means they'll eventually have neither, as happened here in Waukegan). You'd think such cities would treasure their remaining industries, but instead Waukegan is inviting them to leave.

As did most waterfront cities, Waukegan has long considered their industrial waterfront their back yard, and has tried to isolate it from residential and commercial areas as much as possible. Now, they want their four-mile coastline and port to be redeveloped into their *front* yard.

Two major things stand in their way: the half-century-old wallboard factory of the National Gypsum company, and the cement distribution plant of Lafarge, SA. The former employs about 60 people at around $19/hour, and the latter about 12 people (in the 1950s, Waukegan's lakefront hosted some 35,000 jobs). Both plants are unsightly, and the city now considers these employers far more of a liability than an asset, because of their location.

To accelerate their departure the city is suing both companies to clean up the harbor. Now-bankrupt former employers like the Outboard Marine Corporation had dumped PCB-laden hydraulic fluid directly into the lake on a regular basis for many years. Compared to such companies, National Gypsum and Lafarge are relatively clean industries, but still inappropriate for a residential and retail waterfront.

A September 12, 2007 article by Ilan Brat in the *Wall Street Journal* quoted Bill Hudnut, Senior Fellow at the private developers' association, Urban Land Institute, as saying, "There is a great jewel, and that is the lakefront. That jewel should be burnished to its brightest effect. To our way of thinking, that does not mean heavy industry."

Local resident Tim McDonald isn't wasting any time waiting for the industrial evictions to be finalized, even though those companies aren't moving without a fight. His ZOOM Real Estate group is spending $6 million renovating and reusing the Chateau Waukegan hotel on the waterfront into a 54-unit condominium. They already have over two-dozen signed contracts. It's going so well that they've lined up their next project two blocks away: converting the 81-year-old Karcher Hotel to condos.

In May of 2007, the city council unanimously voted to approve a harbor cleanup plan, but only if the federal government transferred responsibility for the waterfront to the city (from the Army Corps of Engineers), and only if a barrier was built to keep commercial ships away from their harbor. The propellers from these large vessels stir up the PCBs and other pollutants lying in the bottom. This barrier would effectively shut down both plants, which rely on ships.

Lafarge has another half a century left on its lease, and has no plans to move. Such are the unique—and sometimes painful—dynamics of the dewealth-rewealth transition.

Youngstown, Ohio: Shrinking for Renewal

In nearby Ohio, the city of Youngstown has also lost most of its industrial employers over the past 40 years. Unlike Waukegan, though, Youngstown has no industrial waterfront to revitalize. Also unlike Waukegan, they aren't trying to remove any employers. But like Waukegan, they are basing their future on enhancing quality of life.

The city population is half what it was 50 years ago. While this former steelmaking giant is by no means a ghost town, some areas of Youngstown have lost more than half their residents in recent decades, effectively rendering them "ghost neighborhoods." In such situations, most cities would indulge in frantic resuscitation measures, such as publicity campaigns that burnish their image or tout their low housing costs. Youngstown has decided on a more creative approach.

Recognizing the ebb and flow of all things, they have decided to allow the city to revert to the size of a more rural town. They are going to allow the declining neighborhoods to continue their decline. This strategy will allow them to do two things: (1) spend what little money they have on maximizing the quality of infrastructure and public services in the city's urban center and other more densely populated neighborhoods, and (2) convert abandoned neighborhoods to parks and green space . . . maybe even add some semiurban farms and ranches.

Rather than trying to grow their population, they are trying to grow quality of life . . . what a concept. Abandoned buildings lacking in architectural or historic value would be demolished. Some 1,000 of these visual blights are already slated for destruction. In some cases, they would be replaced with the kind of large-lot residences you normally find only in rural sprawl areas. In other cases, nature will be allowed to return.

In a wonderfully titled article called "Shrink to fit" in the May 3, 2007, *Wall Street Journal*, reporter Timothy Aeppel said this approach is ". . . considered blasphemy in most cities, where officials are taught to promote growth and development and fight against population decline. Accepting that a city is going to shrink goes against conventional wisdom that a bigger city means more jobs, more taxpayers, more revenue, better education, and better services."

The *Wall Street Journal* article went on to quote one of the strategy's designers, Hunter Morrison, director of the Center for Urban and Regional Studies at Youngstown State University, as saying, "It's un-American. It seems like you're doing something wrong if you're not growing." But, he continues, it's "not really about growth or shrinkage, it's about managing change." Aeppel also quoted Frank Popper, a Rutgers University land-use planner, who commented on the challenges of such an approach, "The one thing you always run up against is that Americans don't want to be told about decline."

It's the poorest, mostly African-American neighborhoods that are most subject to abandonment, so the political implications of this a strategy shouldn't be underestimated. Such political courage—not to mention innovativeness—is a rare commodity among mayors. Politicians usually step outside of the mainstream either at the very end of their career, displaying the false courage of having nothing to lose, or at the beginning of their career, when they are trying to make their mark.

Thus, it might not surprise you to learn that Youngstown's mayor, Jay Williams, is just 35 years old. He told me that "restoring greenspace is crucial to enhancing our quality of life." He asserted in the "Shrink to Fit" article that "we're focused on clearing decades of blight that had built up." Restorative housecleaning, one might say. Planner Bill D'Avignon of their community development agency explained, "We have to break the downward cycle. There's a mindset in Youngstown that says, 'It's coming my way, the blight is moving this way.' We have to put a stop to that."

Downsizing cities might seem strange, considering that the overall global trend is toward urbanization. But, as with people or companies, the world's tens of thousands of cities display a broad diversity of ages and health issues. In fact, during the 1990s, over 25% of large cities all around the world actually lost population. They were, of course, primarily industrial cities that had degraded their natural and socioeconomic environments, and thus their quality of life.

Europe has led the way on thinking about how to cope with the natural cycles of expansion and contraction. This has produced what some refer to as a "smart decline" movement, to mirror the American "smart growth" movement. Community leaders who don't know how to deal with ebb economies are like stock market players who don't know about "short selling" and other tactics for making money in bear markets.

Each community must look first to what's appropriate for their unique situation. In February of 2007, the University of California, Berkeley recognized that this countertrend had arrived in the United States. They held a symposium entitled *The Future of Shrinking Cities* that drew attendees from five continents. The title is a bit misleading, since cities like Youngstown—which covers 35 square miles—have no intention of shrinking physically. The goal is simply to become cleaner and greener by adjusting their strategy—and self-image—to a smaller population.

Germany has also recognized the value of demolishing bad or dead developments to create green space (a very different model from the "urban renewal" fad that demolished healthy neighborhoods to create vacant lots). They have budgeted almost $3.5 billion (U.S.) to convert ugly, dysfunctional Soviet-era apartment complexes in the former East Germany into parks. This is in response to the evacuation of these cities, as the citizens continue to move toward the higher quality of life in the cities of western Germany.

It should be noted that Youngstown arrived at this innovative approach to revitalization via effective public engagement. The "revitalization via shrinkage" comprehensive plan is officially called "Youngstown 2010." Some 5,000 citizens participated in the planning, which involved 11 neighborhood meetings in 2004. The process was jointly sponsored by the city and by Youngstown State University.

Youngstown 2010 was praised as one of the "74 best ideas" in the *New York Times Magazine*. Besides the front-page article in the *Wall Street Journal*, Youngstown's strategy has been featured in *USA Today*, and in both *Metropolis* and *Governing* magazines. It has won a number of state and national awards, including the *2007 National Planning Excellence Award for Public Outreach* from the American Planning Association. The city council formally adopted the plan in 2006.

The Louisville Story: A Public-Public Partnership for Waterfront Renewal

David Karem spent 33 years in the Kentucky legislature, so he knows the limits of relying on politicians for a long-term strategy. How can you pin your future on people who are likely to lose their jobs every four years or so?

Nonetheless, when Louisville, Kentucky decided they needed to revitalize their ugly, defunct industrial waterfront, they didn't start off with a public-private partnership, as you've seen throughout this book. They layered politicians on top of politicians, forming their renewal engine around a public-public partnership. Imagine: city, county, state, and federal governments working together productively for over a decade . . . what a concept (city and county have sinced merged).

The Louisville Waterfront Development Corporation started as a white paper, which became a public-public partnership, and finally a public-private partnership. But even today, it's a lot heavier on the "public" than most of the stories you'll find in this book. That's primarily because the waterfront is first and foremost a public space, and the focus wasn't on maximizing property values (or tax revenues) per se.

The Waterfront Park *is* dramatically enhancing adjacent private property values, turning some of the city's least desirable land into its most valuable. Several new condo projects bordering the park are already sold out. In the very recent past, nobody wanted to look at—or be close to—the ugliness of a decrepit industrial waterfront. Now, it's the best view in the city. But again, that wasn't at the heart of this effort.

The immediate goal of this partnership has always been to dramatically enhance the community's quality of life. Louisville was apparently wise enough to know that economic renewal is an almost-automatic outcome of quality of life renewal. They didn't make the all-too-common mistake of spending their time and money trying to steal jobs from other communities. Nor did they take the simplistic approach of focusing everything on the creation of an iconic building.

They didn't risk millions of public dollars on a major-league sports gamble, either, despite their cultural link to baseball: "Louisville Slugger" bats have been manufactured there since 1894, and their manufacture in the city goes back another 10 years, before the name was invented. The city *did* build a baseball stadium on the waterfront, but it's a very pleasing minor-league stadium that's the right size for the community. What's more, it's on a cleaned-up brownfield, and it reuses a beautifully renovated historic warehouse.

The dominantly public sector leadership of Louisville's waterfront revitalization initiative reveals itself in many ways. For instance, the Jefferson County public schools use the Waterfront Park as a teaching tool. They have curriculum guides for the elementary, middle, and high school levels. These guides help teachers use the park to impart lessons in community history, nature, writing, poetry, culture, engineering, art, math, and the Ohio River (which carries more shipping tonnage than any other river in the United States). What's more, students from Purdue University, the University of Louisville, Ball State University, the University of Kentucky, and other institutions hold classes on community redevelopment at the waterfront.

In fact, the waterfront is a living laboratory, introducing students to the principles and practices of community revitalization. Now, *that's* a community that understands that its future, and the future of its children, will be based on rewealth.

Of course, with the exception of David Karem, no one in the city had even heard the term "rewealth" prior to May of 2008 (when this book was published). As described earlier, the dewealth/rewealth transition is the world's largest undocumented trend. Despite its multitrillion-dollar status and explosive growth, the lack of rewealth metrics has shrouded it in reblindness. They might not have ever heard terms like "restorable asset" or "restorative development," but Louisville's leaders slugged a rewealth ball out of the park nonetheless.

As of this writing, visitors might find portions of Louisville's Waterfront Park a bit stark. That's because it's about to enter its third and "final" phase of renewal.

In 1986, Mayor Harvey I. Sloane asked a group of four or five people to write a white paper on the future of the city's waterfront. That white paper led to the forming of a quasi public coalition, the Louisville Waterfront Development Corporation. This has been the city's closest approximation of a renewal engine, although it's focused solely on the waterfront. Kentucky allows governmental entities to spin off quasi public corporations for redevelopment purposes. They are tax exempt, but not in the 501 (c) (3) category.

The original form of the Louisville Waterfront Development Corporation had fifteen members: five at the city level (the mayor, a member of the city council, plus three at-large citizens), five at the county level (the county executive, plus members of the county legislative body), and five at the state level (someone from the governor's administration plus four at-large members). Federal representation was left out purposely at this stage to keep things manageable.

Nongovernmental stakeholders were represented via the at-large members. They ranged from leaders of environmental NGOs to entrepreneurs and bankers. The selection of these at-large members was based more on their personal interest in the project, rather than arbitrarily trying to make sure all stakeholder niches were represented. This recruitment strategy ensured true engagement, versus having the team populated with midlevel people assigned by an organization because they had time on their hands. Their membership in this incipient renewal engine allowed them to interact with the government agencies as partners; a very different—and far more effective—relationship than the norm.

Each layer of government was asked to support one-third of operating funds (not the capital investment). The Waterfront Park project has a capital budget of approximately $100 million, of which 38% was privately donated.

Why didn't the city try to keep things simple, and go it alone? It wasn't all a matter of believing in innovative, collaborative leadership: that urban stretch of the

Ohio River was under county government, so not much could be accomplished by the city without the county's involvement.

Louisville's strategy is unique in another way, as well. They have what I refer to in my workshops as a "WIHNAR (Waterfront Isolation Highway/Neighborhood Annihilation Road) problem" called Interstate 64. It dominates their riverfront, both visually and aurally. With a waterfront isolation highway (WIH) like that in place, you'd think they would join the global WIHNAR-removal trend and bury or reroute it. Instead, Louisville apparently had no option but to leave it in place, and they've managed to be successful nonetheless. True, their waterfront will never have the calm or charm it could achieve without that smelly, noisy behemoth, but sometimes WIHNAR removal just isn't politically or economically feasible.

[For those of you without WIHNARs (pronounced like the hotdog), let me give you some idea of how overbearing the presence of a massive waterfront isolation highway can be. One of the largest and most expensive WIH's in the world is Toronto's Gardiner Expressway. When leaving a government building downtown recently, I asked a woman at the security desk in the lobby how to find a certain street. Her answer? "It's in the direction of the Gardiner." She could have said it was in the direction of the waterfront—or Lake Ontario, the fourteenth largest lake on the planet—but the Gardiner came to mind first. That's just sad.]

Yet another brilliant aspect of Louisville's waterfront renewal effort was that citizens were told up front that it would be seven to eight years before they enjoyed any significant benefits. Most U.S. elections take place on a four-year cycle, so it's highly unusual to see longer horizons. What's more, citizens were told up front that this quasi public renewal entity would be effectively permanent. It wasn't just in charge of designing, funding, and implementing the Waterfront Park: it was tasked with maintaining it and periodically renewing the vision for the park ad infinitum.

As you know by now, permanence is an essential characteristic of a renewal engine. Only when the vision is safe from changes of political administration and safe from being hijacked by moneyed interests will investors, employers, and potential private partners feel enough confidence to invest for the long term. The initial tasks of this team were to solicit public input, select a design team, and monitor implementation. They have since created their own maintenance crew, owing to the heavy park usage.

The Louisville Waterfront Park comprises 85 acres. It was created from abandoned rail lines, three old scrap yards, a concrete plant, a defunct bulk storage facility for aggregates and salt, several abandoned (or barely functioning) warehouses, and two asphalt terminals. Bringing it back to life is having the usual "restoration contagion" ripple effect, such as the $60 million renovation of the historic waterfront Galt House hotel, completed in late 2007.

How did they come by all this wisdom? Why did they base their strategy on quality of life, and on reconnecting citizens to their water? City leaders decided that the first step should be to visit other cities to see what was *and wasn't* working. They looked at Toledo, Minneapolis, Detroit, Cincinnati, Miami, San Francisco, Baltimore, Chattanooga, Boston, New York City, Washington DC, and more. Today, cities like Memphis, Buffalo, and Pittsburgh are using Louisville's waterfront corporation as a model.

Their research showed that communities that focused heavily on commercial development (jobs, retail, and tax revenues) tended to get into trouble, or failed outright. They decided to focus instead on park development. The city has a strong park tradition. In fact, they have the most Olmsted parks of any city (18). As he did in Buffalo, New York, Frederick Law Olmsted envisioned a necklace of parks with the crown jewel on the waterfront. Also like Buffalo, Louisville never got the waterfront park, because industrial users held too much sway at city hall.

Louisville has never had to do a true public-private partnership real estate project on the waterfront. The park is completely public, but retailers, redevelopers, and investors have been drawn to the private properties around the park like moths to a flame. The original design actually planned for two P3s: two destination restaurants within the park. They decided instead to bring restaurants to the park via long-term ground leases. They now generate nearly $300,000/year from those leases and other concessions.

In a way, though, even those ground-leased restaurants are a form of P3. Remember the earlier quote from Jane Peatch (of the Canadian Council for Public-Private Partnerships)? She said the test of whether a P3 is a true partnership is risk: if the private partner is at risk, they are providing a real service to the community. If there's no risk, it's probably something the community should be doing for itself.

Most people wouldn't think of a lease as being a public-private partnership, but it could be if sufficient risk is involved. A ground lease is just what it sounds like: the city is leasing only the land. It's up to the private entity to build the facility. That's speculative: they could lose their shirts if the park (and business) fails.

The waterfront experience will be significantly enhanced if visitors have access to nice restaurants, so the public is benefiting. Thanks to the business owner, the city is getting this enhancement with zero cost or risk. In fact, the revenue from the leases will pay a portion of the park's maintenance. Even better, the city knows in advance that rent will be coming in for 10 to 20 years, so they can budget with confidence. That sounds like public-private partnering to me, whatever the legal agreement might be called.

Although the redevelopments around the park are purely private, the city offered some low-interest loans, along with other incentives and assistance in order to stimulate the area's revitalization. Again, that's not a legal public-private partnership, but it's one in spirit.

The biggest missing element in all of this is a formal ecological restoration program. While not ecological restoration per se, the remediation of contaminated sites and the replacement of paved surfaces with parkland certainly improved the natural environment. Even better, the city has just negotiated a ground-lease deal with a redeveloper doing a residential project adjacent to the Waterfront Park. They will be required to construct on portions of a brownfield site, and restore a wetland area.

Winooski, Vermont Dismantles Its Renewal Engine After It Did Its Single Job

Readers in very small communities might be wondering whether the renewal engine model applies to them. In the following chapter, you'll find stories of how two cities—one medium-sized and one large—pioneered the renewal engine model. For a town of a few thousand (or even a few hundred) people to replicate what Chattanooga and Bilbao created would be like going squirrel-hunting with a bazooka.

The good news is that a renewal engine is defined primarily by the rules that govern its decisions and by the processes that create its solutions; not so much by the size or structure of the organization. Effective leadership is also key. Creating a permanent non-profit organization might be inappropriate if the community is too small.

If a single person dedicates him or herself to guiding a community's future according to the renewal rules, and creates projects via the three renewal processes, then it's theoretically possible to have a one-person renewal engine (or, as you saw with the Noisette Company in Chapter 9, a one-firm renewal engine). The Winooski story comes very close to that.

But Winooski's size wasn't the only factor affecting the size or lifespan of its renewal engine. Sometimes, a small community contains only one key property or neighborhood that needs to be revitalized, and lacks the resources or desire to keep their renewal engine running. That's what happened in Winooski after they successfully revitalized their tiny, economically strapped town. I'm not recommending this strategy: maintaining a capacity for renewal is a healthy thing for a community. But small-town dynamics are different from metropolitan dynamics, so judge for yourself whether Winooski did the right thing.

Young redeveloper Bill Niquette had spent his whole life in Winooski. He'd had a lifelong dream of seeing the town reconnected to their waterfront on the riffle falls of the Winooski River, where he fished as a child with his grandfather. They had a beautiful old mill building on the waterfront; the sole survivor of the urban removal madness of the 1950s through the 1970s, which destroyed the entire neighborhood behind the mill.

This town of just 6,500 residents had gone through decades of failed attempts to bring that vacant, blighted 21-acre property back to life. They thus had little enthusiasm for yet another waste of time. Nonetheless, they formed the Winooski Community Development Corporation (WCDC). It was a purely grassroots removal engine comprising local congressional representatives, doctors, lawyers, and concerned citizens. It didn't have the kind of all-encompassing structure we recommend for larger communities, whereby individuals or teams are assigned to each of the 12 sectors of restorable assets. Nor were all five stakeholder groups represented. All of that was contained in the WCDC's overall mission of revitalizing the town, and in the mind of its sole employee: Bill Niquette.

The WCDC proposed the Winooski Falls Riverfront Downtown Project to the city (a committee-derived name, by their own admission). Mayor Clem Bissonnette got solidly behind it: despite his $1,000/year salary, Bill says the mayor often put in 60-hour weeks helping to make this happen. (In a small enough town, sometimes the public-private partnership essentially comprises two individuals . . .) The city issued a formal resolution in support of the waterfront project about six months after its launch.

The first step was to find the right private partner, a master redeveloper and property manager for the entire project. The WCDC issued an RFQ that attracted Pizzagalli Properties of South Burlington, Vermont as the master developer to bring private-sector capacity and experience to the project. As part of their proposal, Pizzagalli committed to interview and bring on board an experienced mixed-income housing developer, Norwood, Massachusetts-based HallKeen LLC.

City manager Gerry Myers was brought in to lead the city team as the city became financially involved with bond-anticipation financing. The city planned to issue TIF bonds backed by tax increments from the project, by parking revenues from the new parking facilities, and by proceeds from sales and leases of land. Bond-anticipation notes financed the remaining planning and design services. Public support arrived after WCDC had raised some $2 million in private financing, which inspired confidence that *this* waterfront project wasn't just another pipe dream.

The WCDC held at least a dozen meetings with local citizens over an 18 month period, but didn't bother doing a design charrette with local residents. Bill feels that people tend to get too attached to the design they produce during charrettes. This locks the redeveloper into a particular schema, reducing the flexibility needed to attract the variety of investors and builders needed to complete a large site. He notes that many communities do endless charrettes, spending a great deal of money to end up with lots of pretty pictures (cartoons, he calls them) that end up sitting on a shelf without meaningful follow-up.

More important, he feels, is to focus on the design and quality of the infrastructure . . . how well the site connects to the community. In other words, create an ideal environment for regeneration, and investors will come, just as flora and fauna will quickly populate a newly restored piece of habitat. Niquette says, "It's more important to build support for renewal, than for a particular project." I couldn't agree more. What he's talking about, of course, is creating a renewal culture with a renewal vision. The renewal partnership(s) will take care of design.

The city wasn't putting a single dollar of its nonexistent money into the project. All the city government could offer was support, and they provided an ample amount of that. The WCDC wasn't asking the citizens how their tax dollars should be spent, so Bill engaged them to an extent he felt was appropriate, and no more.

Winooski's redesign of the intersection of three state highways maintained the same quantity of traffic flow, but greatly increased the quality of that flow in terms of the balance between vehicular and pedestrian needs. Remember the flow-based definition of infrastructure in Chapter 3? It can be expanded to include the chemical flows that keep us alive. Our green and blue infrastructure—watersheds, oceans, farmlands, and ecosystems—provide the flows that recycle wastes, nutrients, and elements, making it possible for us to continue eating, drinking, breathing, and excreting. Winooski restored their *built* infrastructure flow to reconnect people with the *green* infrastructure flow of the river.

Another reason it was probably wise to avoid a design charrette was because most of the citizens thought the town had too much housing stock already. They had homes, and couldn't understand why market demand studies in the region said they needed more housing to revitalize the community. (As corporate research and development executives like to say: "Asking your customers what they need is often like staring into a rearview mirror.") That's why the renewal rules say "engage" and not simply "ask" stakeholders. If they don't want or need to be truly engaged, it's sometimes better not to bother asking.

When I asked Bill how he overcame local objections to his plan for more residential capacity on the site, he said there were two key factors. The first was the mixed-use nature of the project, which has something for everyone to like. Those who might not have seen the value of apartments might value the coffee shop, the grocery store, the covered parking (it's a snowy place), or the office space.

His second "secret" to obtaining community support was the public promenade along the river. Sitting on the public waterfront benches facing the rapids, local residents have made comments like "I've lived in Winooski 50 years and never knew this spot was here." Reconnecting people to their water is, again, one of the most powerful elements of urban revitalization, and Bill harnessed its power to make his project attractive to everyone.

As mentioned elsewhere in this book, failure to include public access when redeveloping a waterfront is one of the worst mistakes a community can make. It's a mistake they're likely to regret for a long time, and that regret will likely grow over time as additional renewal of the area makes the value of such access increasingly obvious. Thanks to Bill's grandfather, Winooski's citizens were reconnected to their most precious and beautiful natural amenity, their unique riffle falls.

The site was currently in use as an ugly parking lot, combined with an equally ugly commercial strip center that isolated the citizens from their waterfront. (One of Bill's proudest moments during the project was watching the demolition crew tearing that eyesore to shreds.) But parking was needed: none of Bill's plans for the site would work without adequate parking, and—given Vermont's wealth of snow—covered parking was the order of the day.

Working with the city and the state, Niquette got the city to build an ugly, seven-story parking garage. Why make the garage ugly? Because it's invisible. Bill's thinking was this: the money saved on not making the garage aesthetically pleasing could be put into creating a mixed-use "wrapper building" that would hide it. It worked perfectly. The narrow strip of land surrounding the garage was ground-leased to the Collegiate Housing Foundation (CHF) of Mobile, Alabama. They created a wrapper building with five floors of student housing, In keeping with the goals of the project, the ground floor of the building was developed as small retail spaces that were to be developed and owned by HallKeen as part of their commitment to the mixed-use project.

Bill used TIF, initially via HUD Section 108 loans, which were guaranteed by the state of Vermont. These HUD loans were quickly repaid via private TIF notes, which saved the city hundreds of thousands of dollars annually in interest expense. The TIF money was primarily used to build the 930-space public parking lot, and some of the money was combined with state and federal transportation funds to redesign the highway.

The state's redesign of the busy highway running past the site created a calmer, more pedestrian-friendly roundabout with green space and public seating in the center. Besides reducing the NAR-effect (remember Neighborhood Annihilation Roads?), this redesign helps reconnect the site to the neighborhood on the other side of the highway.

You might be wondering if this quasi-renewal engine really followed the rule of engaging all five stakeholder groups. The citizen, business, and government involvement is obvious, but what about academic and nonprofit? The answer is they're both present, but they got involved at critical times a bit later in the process.

For instance, the mixed-use wrapper building that masked the ugly garage needed an anchor tenant and development partner for the five residential floors. They found both in the University of Vermont (UVM), and the nonprofit Mobile, Alabama-based CHF.

UVM became a member of CHF, and used their help in solving UVM's need for more off-campus student housing. CHF became a partner in the renewal partnership and owns the residential component of the wrapper building. After 30 years (when the note is repaid), ownership will revert to UVM. This is CHF's basic model; serving as a bridge financier for the academic community's housing needs.

There was another aspect of academic involvement, as well. Sometimes, additional injections of confidence are needed at different points in the renewal partnership's project. For instance, Phase Three of the project involved a significant 210-unit riverfront condominium development. But before private financing could proceed for this phase, lenders required a confirmation of market interest in the project. The WCDC got that from nearby St. Michael's College, which needed faculty housing.

The Winooski Falls Waterfront Downtown Project has been a great success. When the final phase has been completed, it will have turned $19 million in public grants and $30 million of TIF into a $240 million public-private partnership. Not bad for a town with a part-time $1,000-per-year mayor. What was the largest, most visible blighted property in Winooski is now the most attractive and vibrant. The heritage mill building, the riffle falls access, the roundabout roadway, the mixed usage, and the critical mass of residents has proved to be a powerful combination. Only 20 of the 124 acres will be built on: the remainder is reserved for a community park and for a natural conservation area.

And what of the historic Champlain Mill? The 156,000 square-foot building dating from 1902 had been partially renovated and reused back in 1981. But two decades later, that low-budget renovation was itself in need of renovation, and the mill's offices were running over 50% vacancy. The owner was happy to sell the building to HallKeen. They are now doing a $10 million restoration of this community landmark, leveraging both state and federal historic tax credits.

Elsewhere in this book, we talk about how renewal engines and renewal partnerships can influence public policy and legislation, so as to make places more revitalization friendly. Here's another example: prior to the Winooski partnership, the state of Vermont had never participated in the HUD Section 108 program, which is focused on creating affordable housing. Thanks to the success of their Winooski experience, Vermont is currently in the process of guaranteeing several more such loans in other communities around the state.

Such partnering and financial backing from local and state governments inspires confidence in potential private partners, which garners additional support, which in turn inspires yet more confidence. Revitalization might thus be a positive version of a "confidence game," otherwise known as a con. In this case, the people being "conned" are those who don't believe in the community's future, and those who would compromise that future via the short-term profits of sprawl.

Would the project design have been improved with a broader-based renewal engine in place? No doubt. For instance, the presence of an environmental or green building group probably would have injected more environmentally sound energy technologies into the design. They might have insisted on the use of reused and sustainably sourced building materials, and might even have included some ecological restoration in the riparian areas. But the project is still greener than average. It includes a very expensive and well-executed stormwater treatment system. Water from roof drains and other impervious surfaces is collected and handled separately before being discharged into the river.

But there *wasn't* a fully formed renewal engine in place, and the tiny beginnings of one that they had (the WCDC) might have been exactly the right size for their purposes. In fact, the added burden of expanding their small coalition while trying to get this renewal partnership off the ground might have fatally complicated or delayed the project. All they really needed were the three renewal rules and three renewal processes, not the institution to house and perpetuate them (the renewal engine).

Unlike Chattanooga, (as we'll see next) Winooski probably won't regret having dismantled their mini-renewal engine: they might be too small to keep one going.

Besides, they've already renewed their one key piece of property. In one fell swoop, they increased the downtown residential population, reconnected their community to the water, restored their primary historic building, enhanced downtown commerce, and renovated both their transportation and water infrastructure. Unlike most communities, Winooski can probably afford to sit back on their laurels for a while.

A Partial Renewal Engine Is Sometimes Enough

I've used the term "renewal engine" loosely in this chapter. None of the "renewal engines" referred to in these stories—or *any* of the stories in this book—perfectly reflect the complete template described in Chapter 4. But they were close enough to that ideal model to accomplish excellent results. Most were more akin to what might be called a "renewal coalition." Coalitions can be wonderful, but sometimes accomplish little more than holding meetings that schedule more meetings.

Ten years from now, Chapter 4's "ideal" renewal engine will (I hope) seem dated. My goal with this book isn't to represent that model as the ultimate, just an ideal you can aim for here and now. I encourage you to experiment with this model and adjust it to the unique needs and dynamics of your community. And then I encourage you to tell me about your experiences, so I—and others—can continually evolve the renewal engine model in particular, and the *re*solution in general. And maybe write about your experience in a future book.

Until now, no renewal engine template existed. Each of those communities I studied invented their renewal engine in isolation, although some drew inspiration from the success of others. Those communities that dared to go where none had gone before should be celebrated; not just for their revitalization, but for the courage it took to innovate a new approach.

What all four stories had in common was a basis in the renewal rules—rewealth, integration, and engagement—and in the renewal processes: visioning, culturing, and partnering. Three of them had incomplete-but-functional renewal engines, to boot. Those engines were where the community's restorable assets (public and private) meet the renewal processes to create solutions. Such is the language of community and regional revitalization in the 21st century.

Chapter 11

Two Stories of Cities that Pioneered the Renewal Engine

Chattanooga, the United States' former "dirtiest city" and Bilbao—Spain's "city with no future"—pioneered a universal model for community revitalization.

Chattanooga: Birthplace of the Renewal Engine

The Chattanooga Choo-Choo was powered by a renewal engine. Not a perfect one, but possibly the first ever built. The engine was called Chattanooga Venture, and it was responsible for one of the most dramatic revitalization stories on the planet.

How is Chattanooga Venture doing today? It's dead, "accidentally" killed by the same people who created it. Why? Ah, now *that's* an interesting story . . .

In 1986, the renewal engine model emerged for the first time in Chattanooga, Tennessee. It was the result of two years of very active public engagement, brought about by a severe economic crisis. Leaders from other cities have been visiting Chattanooga ever since, hoping some of the magic would rub off. Chattanooga's leaders knew they had done something special, but probably didn't realize they had invented a universal (well, planetary at least . . .) model for community revitalization.

I'm writing these words in downtown Chattanooga, Tennessee, from my room in the historic 1926 Read House Hotel (now part of the Sheraton chain). In 2004, it was restored and expanded by the Chicago-based Falor Company, which specializes in reviving old hotels, at a cost of $11 million.

I really enjoy being in Chattanooga. It's a lovely city in a beautiful place, with friendly people. It's a magnificent story of renewal. But there's trouble in paradise.

Normally, I would have ignored the flaws. After all, what city doesn't have its problems? I really don't want to write anything critical of Chattanooga, for two reasons: (1) they have accomplished a truly spectacular turnaround over the past two decades: it's taken a lot of hard work, and they've got a lovely waterfront—and city—to show for it; (2) the folks in Chattanooga have been very open, always willing to reveal what they could have done better.

One shouldn't punish that kind of trust and transparency, and I won't. Many oh-so-gracious folks spent hours with me, before and after my visit, helping me understand the inner workings of Chattanooga's near-death experience and subsequent resurrection story. They wanted to make sure I grasped the essence of what they call "the Chattanooga Way" of renewal. Jim Frierson was chief among them, and Lori Dodd brought me to the city.

The trouble I discovered is directly attributable to the accidental killing of their renewal engine. Therefore, I *must* tell the full story, warts and all, because every other community that is attempting to create their own renewal engine is in danger of making the same mistake.

What happened in Chattanooga is emblematic of what seems to be the one universal threat to renewal engines. Ignore this story at your community's peril. The good news is that this problem is easily prevented, provided you understand it. Chapter 4 gave you some general insight into this threat. This chapter will show how it manifests in real life.

As important as these forensic insights into their difficulties are, the Chattanooga story is far more valuable as an inspiration than as a caution. From the depths of a stinking environmental crisis, an ugly social crisis, and a hopeless economic crisis, the Chattanooga rose bloomed into a fragrant, delightful flower of the American South.

A Warning from the Pentagon

My first visit to Chattanooga in August of 2007 started auspiciously. In the seat pocket in front of me, US Airways' national in-flight magazine featured an entire section on Chattanooga. Included was an excellent article about its revival, called *Re-Energized River City*, by Nancy Henderson.

But before the flight landed, I got my first hint that something might be wrong. My seatmate worked for the Pentagon. His first trip to the city had been six months earlier for a management conference, and he was returning for a follow-up event. When I told him I was writing about the city's world famous revitalization, he said "Really? I must have stayed in the wrong part of town. Seemed kind of dead to me."

I checked into the Read House hotel in early afternoon, when the neighborhood was bustling with shoppers and office workers. Around 7 p.m., I went out to pick up some snacks for my room, and walked into a virtual ghost town. Almost nothing was open, and the streets were nearly empty. "Uh oh," I thought, "maybe I'm wasting my time down here. Am I seriously considering promoting this place as a model of renewal?" Yes, I am.

Chattanooga actually turned out to be a fascinating story, and far more valuable to this book than I initially imagined. Their revival has been the subject of numerous articles and case studies, almost uniformly full of praise. Fortunately for this book, Chattanooga isn't a client of mine (as a speaker/workshop leader) nor of my firm, Resolution Fund, LLC. I'm therefore free to be more open, analytical, and even critical, as this information was not obtained in confidence. Several sources of politically sensitive insights asked to remain anonymous, which I've honored.

The section of downtown that seemed so dead that evening is actually next on the city's list of revitalization targets. From what I've seen of their plans, I expect it to come fully back to life in the near future. New residential capacity is being created as you read this, and it's selling out quickly.

The trouble I was referring to at the beginning of this chapter isn't downtown, though. It has to do with losing their way . . . the Chattanooga Way.

A Prime-Time Insult Brings Warring Factions Together

Discontent is the first step in the progress of a man or a nation.
—Oscar Wilde (1854–1900)

In 1969, Walter Cronkite announced on national television that Chattanooga, Tennessee was "the dirtiest city in America," according to the U.S. Department of Health, Education, and Welfare. The air was so filthy that drivers frequently had to leave their headlights on downtown in the daytime. Motivated by a potent combination of humiliation and regulation, the city spent the next decade remedying the situation.

The mayor appointed a citizen task force to oversee the clean up of the air, resulting in the Air Pollution Control Board. They forced the dirtiest industries to either clean up their emissions or leave town. Many switched from coal to natural gas, and all adopted the latest air pollution reduction technologies.

One firm was determined not to cooperate with those "pinkos" at the EPA. They moved just beyond city limits, where they could continue fouling Chattanooga's air in peace. That "valuable employer" is no longer in business, and few mourned its death. After about 10 years, the sky had turned from orange (its usual color) to blue.

Their current mayor, Ron Littlefield, likes to update Walter Cronkite by saying "Chattanooga is the most transformed city in the nation." He's continuing the air cleanup, supporting an initiative to make 2012 emission levels 7% less than 1990 levels. The difference in air quality is so spectacular that Chattanooga is often cited as a clean-up model, both nationally and internationally.

Chattanooga became the first city to win the EPA's Clean Air Award. They were also the first city to move from nonattainment to attainment of federal ozone regulations. The local medical community developed many of the nation's earliest public education campaigns linking air pollution to respiratory disease. This cleanup actually harked back to their heritage: Chattanooga enacted the first air pollution laws in the United States back in the 1920s, related to smoke abatement and boiler controls.

But it's what Chattanooga did *after* they cleaned their air that earned them star billing in this book. At the time of Cronkite's national shaming, air pollution wasn't the only Chattanooga crisis. The city was losing 5,000 manufacturing jobs annually, crime was high, racial problems were rife, and it was a divided place. The process of coming together to solve the air pollution problem gave the city the unity it needed to solve its other problems.

Wayne Cropp came to Chattanooga in 1977. He found that the federal program was largely toothless; there were no painful consequences for noncompliant cities. Wayne led the charge to toughen the controls and pushed for adoption of the latest technologies, which helped raise standards for the entire nation. Wayne also provided me with a keen insight into the genesis of Chattanooga's later leadership in community revitalization. He said, "Many of the leaders of the city's renewal 'cut their teeth' on the air cleanup: it developed their expertise and passion and confidence."

Bobby Davenport is a businessman whose family has been in the city since the 1860s. He now spends most of his time working for land preservation and quality of life issues. The March 2000 issue of *IIP Global Issues* (published by the U.S. Department of State), featured an article on Chattanooga called "It Takes Us All, It Takes Forever" by Charlene Porter. In it, Davenport said, "In order to create a place, an environment for attracting new activity, new jobs, new wealth, we had to remake Chattanooga." He was talking about what we're referring to as a renewal culture, but a lot of physical "remaking" was needed, as well.

John Parr wrote a case study called "Chattanooga: The Sustainable City" for a publication called *Boundary Crossers: Case Studies of How Ten of America's Metropolitan Regions Work* (Academy of Leadership, 1998). In it, he documented the key characteristics of the city's approach to solving its problems, an approach that was embodied and formalized by Chattanooga Venture. He suggested they call it "the Chattanooga Process." Here's his list, as told to him by local citizens:

- Any idea is worth exploring. At the beginning, all possibilities get a respectful hearing.
- Success will occur if we all sit down and put our heads together; that way, we can reach a common agenda.
- There must always be a specific, but open-ended, agenda for public participation.
- The collective good is always the goal, and that means the good of all citizens.
- Preventing future problems and creating systemic change are always priorities in the process.
- We always bring in the best people in the country to speak, advise, and participate.
- When necessary, we visit other communities that have been successful to find out the nuances of how and why a solution worked there, and what to avoid.

Moccasin Bend Task Force: Getting a Handle on the Future

The Moccasin Bend Task Force (MBTF) comprised five local citizens appointed by the city and county government (working together), and was funded by the Lyndhurst Foundation. Chattanooga started down the path toward a renewal engine when, in 1982, the MBTF hired Carl Lynch and Associates of Massachusetts to help them develop a waterfront revitalization plan.

They were wise (or fortunate) in that choice, as firm principals Kevin Lynch and Stephen Carr were oriented toward effective engagement of the public. (Carl died shortly before the MBTF was formed.) That trait was also championed by the MBTF chairperson, Rick Montague, who was president of the Lyndhurst Foundation at the time.

Eleanor Cooper, who later became executive director of Chattanooga Venture, was recruited to make that engagement happen. She certainly accomplished that goal: over 65 public meetings—and many more special-purpose and one-on-one meetings—took place during MBTF's three-year existence. But they weren't satisfied to merely invite people to meetings: they actively sought additional feedback, going out and visiting anyone they felt might offer a valuable perspective.

Simultaneous to MBTF's work, Bob McNulty of Partners for Livable Places (now Partners for Livable Communities) suggested that Chattanooga look beyond their own community for ideas. A small group took on the task of identifying cities they could learn from. Besides Rick Montague, the group included Mai Bell Hurley (who went on to serve several terms on the city council), and Gene Roberts (who later became mayor).

Their first choice was Indianapolis, then helmed by the visionary four-term mayor Bill Hudnut (now Senior Fellow at the Urban Land Institute). A study tour of about 50 participants was assembled to visit Indianapolis. It was so successful that study tours became a component of Chattanooga's knowledge-based renewal process. That initial group contained all five stakeholder groups: business, government, nonprofit, citizen, and academic.

The primary thing they learned from Mayor Hudnut was his basic philosophy, which he described to me as, "When you need to make great changes, involve more people, not fewer. In this day and age, stakeholders want to be included—and must be—in the decision-making process. Such transparency is a necessary ingredient of economic and community redevelopment."

Indianapolis didn't have a renewal engine, but they did have the Greater Indianapolis Progress Committee (GIPC), now over 40 years old. Founded during the earlier administration of Mayor John Barton, its effectiveness as a public engagement tool was hampered by its minimal diversity and its partisan orientation (each mayor appointed its members). Bill Hudnut expanded it to include both political parties, as well as more women and minorities. He also banned any discussion of politics. GIPC then became a dialog tool of tremendous value, used to resolve difficult issues such as desegregating education, and to respond to an infant mortality problem.

Dialog wasn't the only trick in Hudnut's bag, though. He says he was "always strumming the public-private partnering banjo" during the city's renewal efforts. This was in the early- to mid-1980s, which was the very beginning of the P3 trend, making Hudnut a true reconomy pioneer. In this manner did Indianapolis inspire Chattanooga.

Despite Hudnut's enthusiasm for partnering, GIPC was never a dealmaker; never a creator of public-private partnerships. Venture's genius was in putting GIPC's engagement rule under one roof with Chattanooga's visioning and partnering processes.

Chattanooga Venture: World's First Renewal Engine?

Chattanooga Venture was created in 1984 as a result of that trip to Indianapolis. The group that went on the trip continued to meet and hold open meetings, inviting citizens to learn from other cities. They perceived that Chattanooga needed a vision to harness their newfound spirit of cooperation, it needed a way to remake their culture to encourage revitalization, and it needed a way to turn that vision and culture into action. In other words, they needed a renewal engine.

The Lyndhurst Foundation agreed with that assessment, and provided the first year's operating budget. They saw that this was a critical moment in the city's history, so it wasn't a time for pinching pennies. Mai Bell Hurley was the first chairperson of the board, and Ron Littlefield was the first executive director. Rick Montague later took over as chairperson, and Jim Hassinger became executive director. Eleanor Cooper succeeded Hassinger for the remainder of Venture's life.

Chattanooga Venture's primary purpose was to engage the public in the creation of a shared vision of the community's future. Venture's visioning process was designed by Gianni Longo, president of Urban Initiatives. The resulting vision integrated the renewal of their natural, built, and socioeconomic assets.

Venture provided a home for that shared vision, to provide continuity that would allow renewal momentum to build. Having a safe home for the shared vision—one that is owned by the citizens (legally and psychologically)—is essential. This protects the vision from changes of political administration, and from excessive influence by big-money private interests, as mentioned more than once before.

Besides visioning, Chattanooga Venture evolved two additional functions along the way. The first was what I'm calling culturing. Via a series of field trips and lecturers from outside the community, it helped reshape public attitudes to better accept the changes that renewal would require. The second function was partnering: providing a forum—neutral ground—where public and private interests could convene. There, they would form partnerships to fund and implement the projects that would accomplish their shared vision. They were completely focused on rewealth, of course, and were committed to doing it in an integrated and highly engaged manner.

Thus, they obeyed all three renewal rules and performed all three renewal processes. In this manner, Venture became the world's first renewal engine.

How did their public-private partnering process work? Venture simply created a task force whenever new challenges and/or opportunities were identified. They selected people for these task forces in the hope that they would create a partnered solution. Decision makers from a wide range of public and private organizations—each possessing unique resources of potential value to the solution—comprised each task force. Those members could add other members as the project coalesced and as additional knowledge or resources were needed.

Over the past two decades, thousands of Chattanooga citizens have been involved in hundreds of meetings to envision a renewed community. They understood that revitalization isn't just job growth, or even just redevelopment. They addressed obvious subjects like brownfield remediation, historic building reuse, and downtown housing. But they also held intense dialogs and brainstorming sessions on how to remediate other community toxins, such as spousal abuse, racism, and loss of wildlife habitat.

Most Chattanoogans had never been invited to participate in their community's future before, so they enthusiastically turned out in force. The visioning process itself was periodically revitalized, carried out in phases in order to keep the focus on achievement, rather than navel-gazing. For instance, "Vision 2000," the first outcome of Chattanooga Venture, had a four-month visioning and planning process in 1984. It attracted about 1,700 citizens (at that time, 1% of the population). Those meetings produced 40 goals that, over time, yielded some 200 projects guided by numerous task forces and committees.

Fewer than 10 years later, in 1993, it was determined that nearly 80% of their goals had been met, earlier than expected. They reactivated the visioning process and produced the perfectly named "ReVision 2000" (a triple entendre). Over 2,500 citizens of all ages participated in these meetings, which yielded 120 project recommendations. Four more rounds of visioning took place between 1996 and 1999 (after Venture had been dismantled), each targeting a specific neighborhood.

While all of this was going on, Chattanooga was undergoing other major changes. The people who are chosen to run a renewal engine need to be comfortable operating in an ever-shifting environment. In Chattanooga during the 1980s, the form of city government changed from a commission form to a council form, which required the city to divide into districts and to hold district elections. This transformation had the effect of bringing the vote closer to the people, and resulted in a more democratic form of government.

The governance change also produced representatives who reflected the racial mix of the city. The city went from five white commissioners to nine council members who—as of this writing—comprise three women, one Hispanic, two white males, and three black males. This shift was a goal of Vision 2000, and was achieved by 1990. But it wasn't Venture that did it: it was a lawsuit brought against the city by black citizens, empowered by their shared vision.

RiverCity Company

Thanks to Chattanooga Venture, the city had created a vibrant culture of renewal and had proved that partnerships were the key to getting things done. Now, they need an ongoing mechanism for forming, funding, and implementing more and better renewal partnerships.

In 1986, eight local foundations and seven financial institutions funded the creation of the RiverCity Company, a private, not-for-profit corporation. The idea for RiverCity Company came from the MBTF, most of whose members later became heavily involved in Venture.

Venture was a public-private nonprofit P3 dedicated to revitalizing the entire city, which included all natural, built, social, and economic assets. The RiverCity Company, on the other hand, is a *private* nonprofit. Eliminating the public element from management removes the disruption caused by the constant turnover of elected leaders. Their declared mission is "dedicated to promoting economic development through the creation of great public spaces in downtown Chattanooga and along the riverfront."

The reason for that narrower geographic focus was that RiverCity's primary job was to create redevelopment partnerships, not to function as a community-wide economic planning body. They are primarily real estate driven, in other words. There is nothing wrong with that, but it explains a lot of what came later.

The primary partnering forum at RiverCity Company is the board of directors. The board meets in a glass-walled room that's open on two sides; a physical embodiment of the transparency they hope to maintain. Anyone passing by can see who's at the meeting and hear what they are saying.

As with many boards of directors, RiverCity's 20 members provide a lot more than 20 connections, since most members are on three or four other boards. So, besides the direct engagement of the institutions the board members work for, there are also direct connections to many other local, state, and national organizations on whose boards they also serve.

This sort of connectivity is also true of RiverCity's staff. For instance, RiverCity's staff counsel, Allen McCallie, is a long-standing board member of the San Francisco-based Trust for Public Land (TPL), which is one of the most important community renewal organizations in the United States. TPL is also represented at the RiverCity Company by a board member's connection with the organization. TPL has been of enormous value in Chattanooga over the years, especially in the creation of their RiverWalk and their riverfront parks.

Chattanooga's downtown is now the entire region's dining center, offering a range of fine dining, a microbrewery, family fare, and college-student nightspots. This is all in a neighborhood that barely hosted a burger bar 15 years ago.

Meanwhile, BlueCross BlueShield of Tennessee is building their new headquarters on Cameron Hill, a $300 million project overlooking not just the waterfront, but the entire city. Cameron Hill was the site of one of the most egregious crimes of the "urban removal" era. A historic neighborhood was bulldozed in 1960, and the top of the hill removed for fill material, drastically altering the traditional views-cape of the city. It was this cultural, humanitarian, and ecological disaster that caused Chattanooga to say, "No more!" and to take back the planning process from the professional planners. It was the catalyst of "the Chattanooga Way."

Jim Bowen was RiverCity Company's first executive director. That title was changed in 1987 to president, reflecting a shift of emphasis from planning to deal making, which required more real estate and business acumen. This is the strength of their current president, Bill Sudderth. After 21 years, Jim is still with RiverCity, now as vice president. Together with the Chattanooga Downtown Partnership—a closely related private nonprofit that shares its offices—RiverCity Company now has 13 full-time employees and a combined annual budget of about $2 million.

Following the opening of the Tennessee Aquarium in 1992, the Walnut Street Bridge (pedestrian) was renovated in 1993; the children's Creative Discovery Museum was opened in 1995; an IMAX theater opened in 1996; Coolidge Park opened in 1999; and the baseball stadium opened in 2000. They now have a 600-foot public pier with 2,800 linear feet of new docking space for both private and sightseeing boats. RiverCity Company has been central to all of these accomplishments, but we need to back up a bit to see how they came about.

Chattanooga Venture's Legacy

RiverCity Company is one of the most successful and best-known nonprofit rede-velopment companies in the United States. It's certainly the most visible organization to emerge from the Venture period, but it was far from the only one.

Chattanooga Venture's two biggest accomplishments were 1984's Vision 2000, and 1993's ReVision 2000. The partnering forum initially provided by Venture, and later by the RiverCity Company, turned these two visions into action. They've spawned over $2 billion worth of renewal in the downtown to date.

But Venture created (and inspired the creation of) a large number of valuable nonprofit organizations that thrive to this day. One was Chattanooga Neighborhood Enterprise, formed in 1986. Enterprise is a private, nonprofit organization that develops, finances, renovates, and manages affordable housing.

Enterprise currently obtains its financial support from the city of Chattanooga, the Lyndhurst Foundation, the U. S. Department of Housing and Urban Development, and the Tennessee Housing Development Agency, along with local banks and private citizens.

Venture launched the Chattanooga Neighborhood Network in the early 1990s to help neighborhoods organize themselves and to help integrate them into the overall city vision on issues such as housing. There are now about 100 neighborhood organizations in the city. This distributed leadership adds tremendously to the resilience of the city's renewal. After Venture folded, the city created a neighborhood services department to take over coordination of the network.

Never before had Chattanooga possessed a shared vision of their future, or a vehicle for creating and funding the projects that would achieve it (RiverCity). So, this newly developed capacity for renewal generated great excitement. The constant public meetings set a high bar for public engagement, and Venture kept raising it.

Venture had their facilitators professionally trained, and those facilitators trained others to lead meetings for church and neighborhood groups. (Most of this activity was spontaneous: neither the process nor the meetings were properly documented. Therefore, I conducted extensive interviews after my visit to access the city's oral history.) Effective public engagement became embedded in the city's culture . . . their renewal culture.

Not satisfied to "merely" engage, Venture also took a learning-intensive approach, never assuming they already had a handle on the situation. Engagement works much better when the people you're engaging can make informed decisions. They brought in a constant flow of lecturers to inform and inspire better approaches. For instance, 1984's Vision 2000 contained virtually no mention of the environment. But 1993's Revision 2000, thanks to exposure to leading-edge thinkers, contained over 25 goals related to environmental improvement.

Eleanor Cooper explained how Venture was able to incorporate environmental concerns: "Between the two visioning processes, the community held two conferences called The Environmental Forums, which brought together business, government and community leaders and resulted in numerous initiatives. I think the success of the Environmental Forums was due to two factors—one, it was truly community-based; we involved lots of people in the planning and got their buy-in early on. And secondly, the speakers were clearly chosen because they had practical, working solutions and results to show."

A thirst for learning became embedded in their culture, possibly as a result of this process. The city now has over at least eight lecture series on everything from development issues to Native American culture. The most recent addition is the George T. Hunter Lecture Series, inaugurated in September of 2007 with a lecture by former secretary of state Madeline Albright. It's funded by the Benwood

Foundation, and held at the spectacular Hunter Museum of American Art on the bluff overlooking the river.

Death of a Renewal Engine

Venture came to an end when the Lyndhurst Foundation—which had continuously funded them from the beginning—gave them their last grant ($1,000,000) in 1993. Lyndhurst felt that Venture had become bloated and had somewhat lost its way. If true, this shouldn't come as a surprise. Venture was created from scratch, with no real model or template to guide them. They invented the organization as they went along. All living systems tend to accrete excess structure over time, so it's not surprising that venture would hit a such crisis at some point.

While the dismantling of Venture broke some hearts, it didn't immediately cause any problems or interrupt the city's renewal. They had their brand-new Revision, which would keep them going for years. The trouble started in 2005.

Like Venture, the folks at Lyndhurst were operating without a renewal engine owner's manual. They had no way of knowing how crucially important it is to keep the visioning, culturing, and partnering processes together in one organization, and for that organization to be seen as being of the people, run by the people, for the people.

Venture's demise was messy. The chairperson announced that she would resign in a year, which left the organization in limbo for that period. A newcomer to the community was finally brought in as chairperson, and he fired most of the staff. Eleanor resigned in 1993 because of disagreement with the new chair's policies.

A Vision without a Home, or No Shared Vision at All?

Public engagement is still done far better in Chattanooga than in most other cities, but it's now part of the processes of many groups and agencies. What used to be housed within Chattanooga Venture is now distributed among the various city agencies.

For instance, one of the dozens of nonprofits spun off by Venture was the Chattanooga Neighborhood Network (which grew to include some 100 neighborhood groups). It has now been folded into a city agency called Community Services. Venture's visioning/strategizing function has been largely incorporated into the city's Planning and Design Studio. In theory, this evolution makes sense, since planning and design follow visioning and strategizing. In fact, Chattanooga's Planning and Design Studio has an excellent reputation, probably due to "the Chattanooga Way."

Typically, planning departments do an atrocious job of public engagement in terms of vision and strategy. The employees are used to working in a planning and design environment, which is a domain of experts (almost exclusively male): degreed architects, engineers, and planners. The culture is not conducive to effective public engagement. It's like going to a civil engineer for marriage counseling. Gerri Spring, a former Venture employee who ended up running Neighborhood Network, says, "Communities need a safe haven for ideas to germinate."

> *It's hard work no matter [how] you look at it.*
> *In retrospect, we often forget the labor, like birthing.*
> **—Eleanor Cooper, former executive director of**
> **Chattanooga Venture, and current president**
> **of Chattanooga's sister city program**

Although she disagreed with disbanding Venture at the time, in retrospect, Eleanor says it might have been for the best that other groups picked up the reins of visioning, and that it became a distributed process. The primary ones inheriting the function were the RiverCity Company and the city's Planning and Design Studio.

Eleanor's sentiments are generous, but can a vision be distributed like that, and remain a single, shared vision that you can audit potential projects against? Probably not.

On the one hand, embedding effective public engagement into the city's culture and institutions is a laudable accomplishment. On the other hand, there's the old saying, "When everyone is in charge, no one is in charge."

When I asked various citizen and city leaders which organization was responsible for housing and updating the community's shared vision of their future, the most common answer was something along the lines of: "Well, when you ask it in that manner, I'm not sure we *have* a shared vision of the future any more. If we do, I've got no idea where the heck it's housed."

What Chattanooga *Could* Have Done with Venture (Rather Than Kill It)

Lyndhurst had made an understandable but dangerous mistake. They decided that RiverCity Company could take over Venture's role. After all, partnering—and the outstanding projects it was creating—was now the star of the show. Visioning doesn't happen very often, so there's no need to maintain a separate organization for that function, right? Although Venture did a lot to create a renewal culture among the citizens, they never had a formal focus on improving policy and governance. That's probably the direction in which Venture should have evolved.

It probably would have been better to keep Venture—maybe after doing a little housecleaning to remove excess staff and overhead—and evolve it to focus more on culturing than visioning. Chattanooga needed, and still needs, some serious attention paid to culturing; specifically the creation of a policy and regulatory environment more conducive to renewal.

You might be surprised to hear that, given all the renewal that's happened in this city, but never underestimate the power of bureaucratic inertia. Most of the city's zoning and development policies are still sprawl friendly and make it difficult for rewealth investors to operate downtown. Chattanooga is finally starting to make some of the changes to their policies, codes, and zoning that should have been part of Venture's mission (had they known about the importance of the culturing process).

That's not to say there are no rewealth-oriented incentive or support programs. The PILOT Program is a downtown rental housing initiative established in 2004 to provide incentives for multifamily rental housing. The goal is to lower the cost of downtown projects for affordable housing redevelopers. Projects can be a rehab of an existing building or a new building on an infill site. The value of the construction or improvements planned must be 60% or more of the property's preconstruction value.

Property taxes are then frozen at predevelopment levels, according to the following schedule: 10 years for new construction; 12 years for the rehabilitation of an existing building; and 14 years for a certified historic restoration project. After the tax-free period, the program phases-in full property taxes during a four-year "thaw" period. The project owner pays 20% of full taxes in year one, 40% in year two, 60% in year three, 80% in year four. In year five, the Health, Education and Housing Facilities Board returns the title to the owner, and full taxes are payable.

The PILOT program has had limited success to date, primarily because the downtown hasn't quite hit the tipping point of becoming "the" place to live. My perception is that they are very close to achieving "critical mass" in quality of life. Housing projects downtown are doing well, but they've mostly been high-end units near the waterfront.

After all these years, in order to create a multistory urban infill building— especially mixed use or with pedestrian-friendly zero setback—you still have to get a variance. In other words, the default is still dewealth and single use, and the exception is rewealth and mixed use. After two decades of renewal, policies and regulations are still mostly stuck in the 1970s. Progress is finally being made, though. Chattanooga is creating new zones to facilitate urban redevelopment; one has already been adopted and a second is underway.

Much of downtown is in a Renewal Community zone, which is a federal program that provides tax incentives for urban redevelopment. However, the city itself has been slow in renovating their building codes and zoning, many of which are still geared to suburban sprawl. Such "culturing" work on the city codes and zoning could have been assigned to Venture staff during the breaks in the visioning work.

If Venture had been reborn to focus more on creating a better environment for renewal, it would, of course, have stayed tightly linked to RiverCity Company. This relationship would have enabled the partnering process to maintain an essential, *perceived* link to the public and their vision. I stress the word perceived because the medium is often the message: no matter how good a job of public engagement RiverCity Company might do, it's not a Venture: it's a private nonprofit redevelopment corporation.

Restoring Connections

Chattanooga understands the importance of connectivity. One of the many intelligent things the city did was to restore the historic Walnut Street Bridge. Built in 1890, it was designed for horses, not cars. It's now the world's largest pedestrian bridge.

It's in use constantly, not just by walkers and bikers, but for public parties, such as their Fourth of July fireworks. Another "bridge party" is Wine Over Water, which features wines from over 100 vineyards around the world. It takes over the entire bridge for a day. It regularly sells out all of the almost 3,000 tickets as folks rush to enjoy the sunset over the mountains, suspended above the river, sitting at their romantic table, full of good food and libations.

Another example of restored connectivity is their 12-mile (of a total of 22 planned miles) Riverwalk. This public promenade will continue to expand as additional waterfront brownfields are remediated and redeveloped. Speaking of brownfields, the Tennessee Aquarium (the world's largest freshwater aquarium, which now has a saltwater annex) was built on a brownfield. The spectacular twin aquarium is Chattanooga's icon of revitalization.

In an age when promoters of big-dollar redevelopment projects seem to feel free to make all kinds of wild projections, the Tennessee Aquarium almost instantly produced double the expected attendance. By the end of 2001, over 100 new stores and restaurants had opened on the 200 acres of brownfields surrounding the aquarium. Property value in the area rose almost 125% in less than a decade. Their very successful minor-league ballpark, AT&T Park, also sits on nearby redeveloped waterfront property.

21st Century Waterfront Plan

One key ingredient that has led to Chattanooga's downtown revitalization has been the effectiveness of public-private partnership. In many mid-sized cities, either public or private initiatives prevail over the other with the usual strings attached. In Chattanooga, the community has not only allowed, but embraced these public/private partnerships as a means to sustainable development.

—Rod Tyler, CEO of Filtrexx International,
"Chattanooga and Sustainable Development,"
Land & Water, Volume 50, Number 6

The 21st Century Waterfront initiative was created by Bob Corker when he became mayor in 2001. It expanded and renovated the aquarium, the Discovery Museum, and the Hunter Museum of American Art, and created pedestrian connections from the Hunter to the waterfront. By 2005, when the 21st Century Waterfront plan was finished, the Tennessee Riverwalk had been expanded to 11 miles of uninterrupted trail down to the Chickamauga Dam, and over 1,100 trees had been planted. Corker tasked RiverCity Company with implementating all of this.

Remember WIHNARs? Chattanooga was fortunate to have avoided any major NARs (neighborhood annihilation roads), since the two interstate highways both skirt the downtown. But they were plagued with a WIH (waterfront isolation highway), in the form of the five-lane Riverfront Parkway. Ten years after the Tennessee Aquarium opened, it was obvious that fully reconnecting the citizens with their waterfront would require a waterfront park. But that vision could never achieve its full potential with this wide, high-speed road in place.

The Riverfront Parkway was owned by the state, so the city officials had no power to narrow, reroute, or remove the obstruction. "After proposing several scenarios, we finally asked the state to give the Riverfront Parkway to the city, and TDOT [Tennessee Department of Transportation] agreed to that request," says

Tennessee senator Bob Corker (Republican), who was Chattanooga's mayor at the time, having taken office in 2001. Corker was a former head of finance for the state, so he was well placed to lead the effort.

Chattanooga's Public Works and Traffic Engineering departments supported the project. RiverCity Company was charged with the project management. With additional support by the city's Planning and Design Studio and the Chattanooga Hamilton-County Regional Planning Agency, the city wasted no time calling a public meeting to create a waterfront vision. In Chattanooga fashion, over 300 citizens attended. Hargreaves Associates was hired to turn vision into design.

This project was initiated immediately after Venture had been disbanded, so the waterfront was a great way to find out how well the publicly engaged visioning process had been imbedded throughout the city's agencies. "Suddenly, with the removal of that obstacle, our community had a 'blue sky' opportunity to transform our waterfront. Gaining control of Riverfront Parkway was like being handed a blank canvas," Corker continued. "The community responded with so many great ideas we couldn't wait to make them happen." And they didn't wait.

Corker immediately launched into an incredibly effective one-man funding and implementation program. A total of $121 million was needed to achieve the vision, and it was decided the public and private sectors would share the bill equally. Mayor Corker took care of both in short order, going on a whirlwind fundraising campaign that garnered $51-million worth of private contributions in just 90 days. To fully appreciate this achievement, remember that this was an economically struggling city, and there were only 311,000 people in the entire county.

They decided that the public half of the money would come from new revenue, so the effort wouldn't negatively impact any agency's current budget. They didn't use TIF, but they did finance the city's contribution via a tax increment. They raised their hotel/motel guest tax citywide, since the aquarium had done such a great job of boosting tourism. Hotel/motel guest taxes were bringing in $2.2 million in 1996; 10 years later, they had almost doubled to $4 million.

Downtown Housing, Schooling, and the Northside

During my first night's "ghost town" experience, I asked the Read House hotel staff where I could find a convenience store that was still open. Here's what they told me: "Take the free electric shuttle to the waterfront, change to the other shuttle line, and it will drop you off at the Walgreens on the other side of the river." Not quite the level of "convenience" I was expecting. No wonder so many folks who want to be close to downtown are choosing to live on the north side of the river (which is also Chattanooga).

Now that both the automobile bridge (Market Street Bridge) and the pedestrian bridge have been renovated and reopened, the Northside (as it's known) makes a lot of sense. It boasts beautiful waterfront parks and other public spaces created on its old brownfields. It has many charming old renovated buildings that give it a funky flavor.

The Northside is also home to the major example of ecological restoration in the area, the 23-acre Renaissance Park, which opened in 2006. This beautiful expanse of riverfront green space has caused prices of neighboring parcels to skyrocket, as new multifamily residences and offices vie to be as close to nature as possible. The 13 acres closest to the river comprise the "Flooded Forest" reserve. The park also has considerable cultural heritage value, being the site of many historic activities and events.

The national urban removal disaster destroyed the majority of Chattanooga's downtown housing in the 1950s. Some 240 homes—many of them lovely and historic—were bulldozed and turned into surface parking lots. Many downtown schools were likewise disposed of. The remaining school buildings, many of them badly deteriorated from years of disuse after the downtown removal was complete, were sold off in the 1990s. Some of these schools were renovated and reused as retirement housing, condos, and a community center.

Provident Insurance bought all of the parking lots and long refused to make them available for housing. Provident and UNUM merged in 1999, and the attitude toward community engagement changed markedly. They have swapped several key blocks with the city that will soon provide new housing options—both high-end town homes and affordable rental units—on the new Walnut Hill. City leaders hope that UNUM will choose to sell their remaining surface parking lots to help accommodate more people wanting to experience or live in downtown Chattanooga. Jim Bowen says, "UNUM has been very accommodating and seems to have the best interest of the community in mind. As soon as they can find a way to park the balance of their employees, they have agreed in principal to move their campus south of 4th Street Boulevard."

For decades, the downtown had no schools at all, and students were bussed to the suburbs. RiverCity Company created a partnership that included the university, the school district, and the Lyndhurst Foundation to create two downtown schools on infill lots around 2003 and 2004. One of them was privately funded with

$8 million in contributions. This was an educational experience for the school board itself, which only knew how to build schools on greenfields.

These schools now have access to a rich assortment of downtown museums and other educational resources. The suburban schools have to bus their children to take advantage of these amenities. There are two primary barriers to bringing more schoolchildren from the suburbs to the downtown schools: (1) the lingering perception of suburban parents that the downtown schools are for poor minorities, and (2) downtown repopulators tend to be singles, empty nesters, and retirees, which cuts demand for schools.

One program that enjoyed some success encouraged suburban parents who work in the city center to bring their kids to and from downtown schools during their commutes. This saved time and gasoline, and enabled them to spend more time with their children, which many of them actually wanted to do (go figure).

Vision 2000 identified downtown housing as a key goal, but they couldn't just start building houses: they had to first make the downtown a place where people wanted to live. Revitalizing the waterfront was the most effective way to dramatically boost quality of life in the downtown, so that's where most of RiverCity's efforts have been focused.

Bob Corker only left the mayor's office in 2005, which was the official end of the waterfront initiative, so there hasn't been much of a lag in focus on downtown housing, if any.

Those from communities with thriving downtowns won't appreciate how improved Chattanooga's downtown is over just a decade ago. By the end of 2007, eight new restaurants and a new grocery store will have opened in the downtown. The historic Tivoli theater has been restored and now hosts live events. A modern multiscreen theater on the main street packs them in, as people enjoy all the nearby before-and-after-the-movie restaurants, bars, and walking paths.

RiverCity has been working on downtown housing since 1993, when they helped create the RiverSet Apartments. This was the only project in which they took an equity interest: they felt it was a necessary catalyst to spark new housing on the waterfront, and they were right. Since then, 1,300 additional units have been built around the waterfront, and the time has come to start working in from the river.

New, mostly affordable housing is also appearing in Chattanooga's south side, a long-blighted neighborhood. If this area continues to come back to life, a "dumbbell" effect should appear, with concentrations of residents at each end of the main downtown street (Market Street). This should, in turn, result in a fairly natural process of infill that populates the 50-block central business district between the two. Indeed, some central business district housing is already underway, in advance of any future dumbbell effect.

The $11 million Mayfair at Market project, just two blocks from the Read House, was announced in 2006. It's a mixed-use eight-story project with 11,000 square feet of office space, 5,000 square feet of retail, and 50 apartments. Nearby, the historic 180,000-square-foot Loveman's Department Store was being converted into Loveman's at Market, offering commercial space on the ground floor with about 40 condos above. The roof of the six-story building boasts a garden, patio, and walking track, overlooked by a couple of 3,000-square-foot penthouse units.

As of 2007, over 1,100 new condos and apartments have recently been completed, are underway, or are ready to start in the central business district. This amounts to some $300 million worth of new projects, representing over 30 redevelopers. Meanwhile, almost half a million square feet of retail and office space is ready and waiting for reuse in the central business district. Now, if only the UNUM insurance company would hurry up and sell their remaining "urban removal" surface parking lot eyesores that are continuing to retard the downtown housing renewal . . .

Keep in mind that anything I say about RiverCity Company in the following section that sounds in any way critical is the result of comparing it to a complete renewal engine, which it was never meant to be. When compared to other private nonprofit redevelopment companies, RiverCity is definitely one of the best.

The Traumatic Election of 2005

> *Partnerships are a huge part of Chattanooga's success.*
> —Jim Bowen, vice president, RiverCity Company
> (conversation with author)

As noted earlier, when Venture was shut down, the visioning function separated from the partnering function, so there was no longer a renewal engine. Visioning was adopted as a basic process by a number of groups and agencies. Partnering, however, became the domain of RiverCity Company. Since the visioning function is the one that engages all stakeholders, RiverCity Company didn't inherit Venture's mantle as an organization of the public.

RiverCity Company has done many exemplary things for the city, much of which was guided by Vision 2000 and ReVision 2000. Over time, however, it has increasingly been seen primarily as a private group of wealthy interests who have the public good in mind. This role is certainly positive on the whole, but it's very different from a public entity.

Slowly, RiverCity became "them," rather than "us." The predictable result was that in the 2005 mayoral election, RiverCity Company became a political football. The better-financed candidate, Ann Coulter (no, not *that* one), was connected with RiverCity Company. The winner, Ron Littlefield, successfully positioned himself as the people's choice, painting RiverCity as a private club of aristocrats who held far too much power over the city's future. Interestingly, both candidates are certified planners, which might have been a national "first."

RiverCity Company has reportedly suffered for being associated with the loser, as have some of the renewal-oriented nonprofits and city agencies that work with it most closely. It's been a sobering time for Chattanoogans, as their prized unity has suffered a body blow.

This is why Chapter 4 recommended that renewal engines be safe havens for your vision; safe from politics, safe from excessive influence by wealthy outsiders (and insiders), and safe from anything that divides citizens. There might be arguments while creating that vision, but revitalization tends to be a unifying, nonpartisan issue of crucial importance, so any disagreements are generally in a good cause.

To Chattanooga's credit, the visioning and engagement functions were taken over by a host of public agencies and private nonprofits, each of which does a better job of engaging the public than their counterparts in most other cities. By most standards, RiverCity Company does a much better than average job of vetting their projects with the public. This communication is probably due in large part to the high standards of engagement that the citizens have come to expect from their Venture experience in the 1990s.

But, by their own admission, RiverCity only vets the larger projects with the public. And even that happens fairly late in the process, after they are designed and nearly ready to go. In other words, it's more approval than engagement. It's not RiverCity's job to create or house the community's shared vision, only to create projects that they perceive serve it.

Shutting down Venture wasn't the mistake. The mistake was in not recreating a complete renewal engine, with visioning and culturing functions. RiverCity

Company only provided the private venue that public and private players needed for partnering, but—as pointed out earlier—its focus was on economic redevelopment only in the downtown and waterfront areas. RiverCity would also have to alter its mission to become a renewal engine for the entire city.

The assumption was that visioning had become embedded in the culture of all the redevelopment-related institutions, both public and private. That's true enough, and that was a positive outcome, as stated earlier. But one reason that it's important to keep partnering and visioning together is to ensure not only that the projects achieve the vision, but also to ensure that the projects *inform* the vision (and strategy) in turn, in a co-evolutionary manner.

The best source of new insights into how your strategy can be improved is the actual work of renewing; that is, the projects themselves. Designing, funding, and implementing a renewal partnership is a learning process. Housing the community's shared vision under the same roof as its partnering function provides a natural conduit for those learning experiences to feed into the vision.

Since Mayor Corker left office in 2005, the absence of his dynamism, the lack of a renewal engine, and the damage done to community cooperation as a result of the divisive election, have combined to leave the city in what some see as a lull.

An alternate and more positive explanation is that the city is simply going through a much-needed process of consolidation and reflection after a couple of decades of frenetic, successful activity. Around the world, Americans are known for our compulsion to remain in active mode, and for our discomfort with moments of silence and contemplation. If this explanation is accurate, Chattanooga should be lauded for its wisdom . . . even if taking a "breather" wasn't a conscious decision.

You might wonder how a city with such a collaborative, harmonious atmosphere could have a nasty election. As we've seen, the polarization had a direct link to the dismantling of their renewal engine (Venture). Separating the public visioning function from the partnering function actually did two things: it reduced the transparency of the partnering process, and it greatly reduced the citizens' psychological ownership of RiverCity Company.

This was a one-two blow, because besides increasing the ability of political challengers to portray RiverCity Company as a club for the elite, it also reduced the likelihood that the public would come to the defense of "their" organization.

While RiverCity Company is still an effective builder of public-private partnerships, they have had to pull in their horns substantially, because of the pummeling of their image and credibility during the 2005 election.

Aftermath

Many organizations have picked up the reins on various aspects of the city's renewal, but the structure to support and coordinate that activity is in a bit of disarray. Some long-time citizens note that the sniping being endured by the RiverCity Company is very similar to that suffered when they championed the creation of Tennessee Aquarium, Inc. Today, you'd be very hard put to find anyone in Chattanooga who doesn't believe the aquarium was a godsend, but it was initially pilloried by many.

Now, Venture no longer exists, and both RiverCity Company and the Urban Design Center seem to be in the political doghouse. On the other hand, the mayor of the city is always on the RiverCity board, and Ron Littlefield shows up for all meetings. Of course, RiverCity, as a private entity, is not dependent on political support. This gives the revitalization program some resilience against such traumas. But Chattanooga is feeling a little wistful for the (possibly illusory) days of blissful harmony. The irony that caps this quarter-century of rapid, resilient renewal is that Ron Littlefield was the first executive director of Chattanooga Venture.

The October 2005 issue of *Metropolis* magazine documented the impact of Chattanooga's election pain in an article by Alex Marshall entitled "Chattanooga Crossroads." The subheading was "After completing an ambitious waterfront initiative the city recently changed leadership, raising the question: Is this the end of 20 years of urban enlightenment?" It states, "Since taking office, Mayor Ron Littlefield has essentially disbanded the influential design office that spearheaded many of the city's projects, and he has stopped other center city efforts."

The *Metropolis* quoted architect Stroud Watson, head of Chattanooga's Planning and Design Studio (now called the Urban Design Center) since its founding in 1981 thus: "After twenty years of positive change we had an election, and the candidate who won actually went on an anti-urban design kick . . . Right now power is being put into the hands of people who want to just build things and make money."

Littlefield retorted, "In elections things get distilled down and cast in one light or another. I talked about spreading the appearance of prosperity we have achieved downtown to the rest of the city. We have done a tremendous amount downtown, and we need to turn our attention to the neighborhoods and try to accomplish the same thing."

Many local leaders credit Stroud Watson with being the guiding light of Chattanooga's renewal from the planning and design perspective. The Design and Planning Studio was created by the Lyndhurst Foundation, then headed by

Rick Montague. The Studio was gutted following the election, starting with its leader, Stroud Watson.

At an event honoring Watson on the eve of his forced retirement in August 2007, Rick Montague's son, Tom, delivered a speech written by his father, who was in France at the time. Here's an excerpt: "All would agree that Stroud Watson has worked miracles in Chattanooga, and all would agree that Chattanooga was, before Stroud's arrival, not a very likely city to be a place where miracles were wished for, expected, appreciated or, perhaps, even tolerated. Stroud's greatest contribution may well be that now, in 2007, we may take miracles for granted."

That quote bolsters a point I've made before, and will probably make again: a renewal engine "only" builds a community's *capacity* for renewal. You'll still need professionals like Stroud Watson to make renewal happen.

The *Metropolis* article concluded: "Littlefield's election and his actions since have put an ambiguous note to the completion of the 21st Century Waterfront Projects."

It would be a mistake to assume that the citizens of a traditionally industrial city would unanimously and immediately shed that heritage, no matter how irrelevant it might be to their future. The *Metropolis* article interviewed resident Gary Scasbrick. He wants the city to focus more on industrial development and is nostalgic for the good old days, before Walter Cronkite and the EPA spoiled everything. He said: "I don't like the way this city's going at all. I worked twenty-nine-and-one-half years at the DuPont factory before taking early retirement, and I think other people ought to have that opportunity—to work at one place for a long time."

Alex Marshall offered another insight into a possible source of bitterness: ". . . Littlefield made a lot of his evangelical church affiliation and anonymous flyers labeled Coulter an atheist, which she was forced to deny." Little wonder that RiverCity, her previous employer, was portrayed as "evildoers."

The Lyndhurst and Benwood Foundations

Not even the most compressed version of the Chattanooga revitalization story could leave out the critical role played by the two largest foundations in the area, both of them built on the fortunes of independent Coca-Cola bottlers.

The Lyndhurst Foundation—funded by John T. and Alice Lupton, and currently led by Jack Murrah—funded and supported virtually every major initiative that has contributed to Chattanooga's renewal over the past three decades. Murrah has been on staff since 1978, and has been executive director since 1989. He announced his impending retirement around the time I came to town in 2007.

The Benwood Foundation—funded by the late George T. Hunter and led by Corinne Allen—has provided follow-on support for most of these renewal initiatives, with a heavier focus on arts and culture.

Lyndhurst is the best example of a foundation-based community revitalization champion I've ever encountered, bar none. Want proof? Here's a partial list of Lyndhurst Foundation revitalization programs during the critical decade from 1981 to 1991:

- MBTF: Lyndhurst partnered with the city and county to pay for this three-year study, which yielded the Tennessee RiverPark Masterplan;
- Tennessee Riverwalk: Lyndhurst offered challenge grants for about 20% of costs;
- Chattanooga Venture and Vision 2000 process: Lyndhurst provided full funding;
- Tennessee Aquarium: Lyndhurst provided $10,000,000 for the construction;
- Tennessee River Gorge Trust: Lyndhurst paid for the initial years of operation and provided partial ongoing support;
- RiverCity Company: Lyndhurst provided $10,000,000 for Aquarium property acquisition, as well as the operating costs of the organization in its early years;
- Chattanooga Neighborhood Enterprise: Lyndhurst provided the full operating costs for three years (beginning in 1986) and later partnered with the city to expand it, for a total commitment of about $25 million over 20 years;
- Tivoli Theater: Lyndhurst contributed to the capital campaign for the restoration of the theater;
- Creative Discovery Museum: Lyndhurst contributed to the capital campaign for building the museum;
- Chattanooga School for the Arts and Sciences: Lyndhurst led the effort to establish the school and provided support for the renovation of the building;
- Miller Plaza: Lyndhurst partnered with Tonya Foundation in the redevelopment of this space. It's now owned by RiverCity Urban Design Studio, which Lyndhurst established and supported for over 20 years (it evolved into the Downtown and Riverfront Planning and Design Center);
- Walnut Street Bridge: Lyndhurst paid for the feasibility study for the restoration and made a contribution to the capital campaign.

You might be thinking, well anyone could revitalize with a sugar daddy like Lyndhurst in the wings. Their financial support *was* a huge advantage, of course. But the universal lesson is in *how* the money was spent. There are many ways to attract investment from outside, if you don't have such internal resources. Spending it wisely is another matter.

Chattanooga spent it on *rewealth*. They spent it on *integrating* multiple agendas and properties. They spent it on *engaging* the public at both the city and neighborhood levels. They spent it on *visioning*. They spent it on creating a renewal *culture*. They leveraged their money by *partnering*. And the spent it on creating a *renewal engine*. Those three rules, three processes, plus the renewal engine model, are the seven characteristics of leading-edge revitalization—the *re*solution—and Lyndhurst did it all.

Most communities don't have a single entity that could do all this, but they can certainly partner to get the same things done. As you can see, Chattanooga's revitalization began with Lyndhurst's small investment in the MBTF. Rewealth begets rewealth. The momentum created by each successful revitalization activity helped inspire and justify the next.

Here's just one example of how a small donation at the right time, in the right place, can pay huge dividends. The annual RiverBend Festival began in 1981, sponsored by Lyndhurst. It was an outgrowth of a successful "Five Nights in Chattanooga" festival held on an empty downtown block, also sponsored by Lyndhurst. RiverBend now draws over 650,000 people. They are attracted not only by the over 100 performers, but also by the waterfront venue that becomes more beautiful every year, and by the virtually crime-free downtown.

The festival has become so successful that there's now a separate organization—the Chattanooga Downtown Partnership (CDP)—whose mission is to bring music (and thus people) downtown year-round. CDP creates over 150 days of programming annually, attracting almost a quarter of a million people to downtown shops and attractions. CDP (as their brochure outlines) also "infuses downtown spaces with fun, color, and animation" and works "to enhance the downtown pedestrian experience with lighting, banners, way finding, and inviting storefronts."

The Lyndhurst and Benwood foundations have played the role of champions. They sparked new initiatives, providing continuity of funding that allowed them to survive long enough to thrive. Creating renewal engines requires champions, but they can take any form: mayor, city council, university, neighborhood, redeveloper, business, or nonprofit (environmental, cultural, social, or economic).

Chattanooga's Renewal Momentum Has Slowed, but Certainly Not Stopped

The city is currently building a new football stadium . . . on a brownfield, of course. They are also partnering with the federal and state governments on the redevelopment of a huge industrial park called Enterprise South. It will eventually comprise about 3,000 redeveloped acres, and will boast an additional 2,800 acres of natural area as a buffer for both wildlife and the community. They are also making an effort to attract only clean industries to the site.

This brownfield was formerly a TNT factory and munitions plant, so the federal government is paying for the cleanup. It has an ideal location, adjacent to both the interstate highway and the railroad tracks. In fact, the state took the almost unheard-of step of building a dedicated freeway interchange for the site before the redevelopment was even underway. When a city develops a renewal culture that inspires confidence, this kind of proactive public-public partnering can result.

Harmonious public-public partnering also inspires confidence among investors and employers who are evaluating the community. When the private sector sees city, county, state, and/or federal governments at each other's throats, they tend to run in the opposite direction, for good reason. Chattanooga, on the other hand, has a long tradition of working in harmony with the county government, despite the fact that they've gone through five mayors since 1986.

For many communities, their greatest obstacle is the inability to address regional issues, and this is often due to the inability of city and county politicians to work together. Sometimes, the solution is for the city and county governments to become one, as they did in Louisville, Kentucky. I live in a combined city/county (Arlington, Virginia), and can attest to the efficiency of not having overlapping bureaucracies. Of course, this only works when a single city already dominates the economy and population of the county.

A Warning from Cleveland Arrives Too Late

Chattanooga and Cleveland share remarkably similar stories . . . In 1969 . . . the same year that oily slime on [Cleveland's] Cuyahoga River caught fire, Chattanooga was officially designated the dirtiest city in America. Both are fallen stalwarts of the industrial age. Both are waterfront towns that stumbled to remarkably similar bottoms two decades ago. Both became known for the civic partnerships they forged in their times of crisis and both have widely been viewed as comeback cities. But in

Cleveland, those public-private partnerships seem to have come undone. Meanwhile, little Chattanooga, Tenn., continues to chug steadily along on its storied road to recovery . . . The secret . . . has been an insistence on deep citizen involvement, across all social and economic strata, in deciding what the Chattanooga of the future ought to look like . . . this 'community visioning' process [was needed to] break through inevitable political barriers.

—Bob Paynter, "Chattanooga Back on Fast Track,"
Cleveland Plain Dealer, December 16, 2001

As the above excerpt regarding Cleveland attests, it takes more than public-private partnering to produce rapid, *resilient* renewal. It takes a renewal engine with a visioning process. Cleveland had neither a renewal engine nor city-county cooperation. Chattanooga was still enjoying the boom launched over a decade earlier by their renewal engine and cooperative approach.

The *Plain Dealer* article revealed how Cleveland lost their public engagement, while continuing what they called "public-private partnering": "Cleveland State University economist Ned Hill traces the unraveling of Cleveland's public-private partnerships to a subtle shift in the comeback strategy nearly a decade ago. The shift signaled a gradual return to what Hill described as a "less democratic, top-down community planning process that was driven almost exclusively by the city's business elite."

The article continued: ". . . The change began with Gateway, a project that gave us Jacobs Field and Gund Arena, but at a cost of about $470 million—roughly 70% of it in tax money. . . . The shift in development strategy continued . . . through the construction of the Rock and Roll Hall of Fame and Museum, the Great Lakes Science Center and Cleveland Browns Stadium. It was epitomized by the 1998 update of the city's downtown plan, "Civic Vision 2000 and Beyond," a waterfront-restoration and convention-center proposal commissioned by Mayor White and hatched largely by business leaders meeting in private . . . criticized . . . for being largely tourist-driven [and] produced by a closed and undemocratic process."

That article probably made Chattanoogans feel great, but it should have served as a warning. Chattanooga hasn't experienced Cleveland's level of abuse of public office, though there have been rumors of a conflict of interest regarding a homeless shelter project suggested by the mayor. Ironically, it was rumors of conflicts of interest at RiverCity Company that fueled the 2005 election heat.

Chattanooga needs to be more careful about such things these days, now that they have only half a renewal engine.

Reassembling a Dismantled Renewal Engine?

Cleveland's warning to Chattanooga was only a couple of years too late. My warning to them was a decade late. In 2007, Jack Murrah told me how—a decade earlier—he had pulled the plug on Venture, and let the visioning and culturing processes be disseminated through other agencies. I then explained the importance of keeping the three renewal processes—visioning, culturing, and partnering—under one roof, and how that probably contributed to the politicization of RiverCity Company in the election. His response, of course, was, "Where were you 10 years ago?"

Ten years ago, I was still writing *The Restoration Economy*, and was completely clueless about renewal engines. Maybe as an outsider I can offer a few suggestions for rebuilding Chattanooga's renewal engine, now that I'm marginally less clueless than a decade ago.

If any organization is considered a trusted "keeper of the vision," it's the Lyndhurst Foundation, though not by design or intention. In fact, the Lyndhurst Foundation has always tried to avoid such a role. They've preferred to play a supportive background position, rather than taking any overt leadership, and they've never really claimed the credit they're due.

As noted earlier, the Lyndhurst Foundation supported Chattanooga Venture's birth. Lyndhurst didn't really kill Venture, despite my earlier hyperbole: they merely stopped funding it. Venture had a million dollars worth of time to become viable, but failed. I'll bet that—when Chattanooga is ready to recreate their renewal engine—Lyndhurst will be there to help. In fact, they might already have taken the first step.

In 2007—his final year as executive director of the Lyndhurst Foundation—Jack Murrah helped create a parting gift to the city. He provided start-up funding to an innovative Web-based community engagement program called CreateHere. The founders of CreateHere—social entrepreneurs Helen Johnson and Josh McManus—also enjoy free office space in the Lyndhurst Foundation's headquarters; a large house Lyndhurst restored a dozen years ago to help revitalize a marginal neighborhood.

With no prompting from me, one of the first things Josh told me was that the idea for CreateHere came from their perception that the city had lost its ability to create and communicate a shared vision of their future . . . and they wanted it back.

Josh says, "It's harder to articulate a need for a shared vision when things are much better than they were, and there's no feeling of crisis." In other words, revitalization success can undermine continued revitalization success. This is why renewal engines should be created as permanent entities, rather than as a temporary response to a crisis. Without that continuity, we only get rapid renewal . . . not rapid, *resilient* renewal.

The CreateHere.org Website went live August 1, 2007, and the response from the community was almost overwhelming. It seems that Helen's and Josh's perception was accurate: Chattanooga citizens were missing their sense of control over their future. Ideas for renewing the city immediately started pouring in by the thousands.

Who knows? In the near future, the best way to create, evolve, and protect a community's shared vision might be over the Web; the same goes for the culturing function. In fact, new project partnerships could even be initiated via the Web. And thus, Chattanooga might be building the world's first electronic renewal engine. Well, a hybrid, anyway: it would have to work closely with RiverCity Company.

RiverCity's next big project is the 140-acre former U.S. Pipe site. It offers a great opportunity for the community to come back together, and perhaps rebuild their renewal engine. The appearance of CreateHere might thus be fortuitous, and this could be their trial by fire. U.S. Pipe is a great public visioning focus because they have to not only figure out how to best use the site, but also how to connect with the downtown waterfront, *and* contribute to revitalizing the neighborhoods in between.

Besides being a perfect opportunity to rebuild their renewal engine, the U.S. Pipe site also provides a place to try out new tools. For instance, Chattanooga has never used a property-tax-based TIF. In my first meeting with Jim Bowen at the RiverCity Company, the subject of the former U.S. Pipe site came up. It was being master planned at the time, but they weren't sure where all of the money was going to come from. I suggested that this large waterfront brownfield site might be their perfect first use of TIF. He agreed that it might be an excellent place to pioneer TIF in the city.

I specified "property tax-driven" because TIF can also be based on sales tax. Tucson has recently had tremendous success with a sales tax TIF that revitalized a dead part of town and paid back the redevelopment loan far faster than anyone expected. Chattanooga employed a sales tax TIF under former mayor Kinsey to finance the three recent Southside projects: the Development Resource Center, the Chattanoogan Hotel/Conferencing Center/Parking Garage, and the 200,000-square-foot expansion of the Chattanooga/Hamilton County Convention and Trade Center.

It's not surprising that Venture didn't last longer than it did. They had no renewal rules or processes to follow, no taxonomies to organize around, and no structure to model. Now, all of those things are known, so there's no reason Chattanooga can't recreate a next-generation renewal engine.

This is probably a good time to reemphasize a caution contained in Chapter 4. The simplicity and clarity of the renewal rules, processes, and model shouldn't fool one into thinking that revitalizing their community will be automatic or trouble free. In her last email to me before I finished this manuscript, Eleanor Cooper used a phrase that succinctly captures the essence of her community renewal experience.

She said, "I just wish we could have had the 'rule book' and your insights long ago. . . you really did a good job of making sense of a churning cauldron." "Renewal engine" implies a lot more predictability than you're likely to experience: Eleanor's "churning cauldron" is probably closer to the mark.

Chattanooga created their Vision in 1984 and their ReVision 2000 in 1993. Maybe the time has come for a "ReVision 21," or some such name, for the new century. Maybe it's time for those dozens of excellent local institutions created by Venture to come together and form a "real" renewal engine (again).

CreateHere might be able to help that happen. CreateHere has just launched an Emerging Leader program to further improve the city's capacity for fully engaged renewal leadership. I wish them well, and will be tracking their progress closely to see if the renewal engine model "goes electronic."

It's been a long time since Chattanoogans had to drive through their downtown with their headlights on in the middle of the day. Today, the clear air reveals a wonderfully revitalized waterfront on both sides of the gorgeous Tennessee River, connected by a pair of beautifully restored bridges. If I were in the market for real estate, I'd seriously consider buying one of their great old downtown buildings now, while they're still cheap. Not because they have a beautiful river; not because they are surrounded by beautifully forested hills; not even because they have a successful track record of revitalization.

Thousands of cities can make one or more of those claims, yet they don't inspire me with the confidence it takes to get my money. Many of their beautiful rivers and mountains will be severely degraded in coming years, thanks to sprawl and dewealth-based policies. I, like most investors, want to invest in a place that's getting better; not one in stasis, and certainly not one in decline. It's the trajectory that counts in investing, not the current condition.

In some cities, that revitalization was based on a visionary elected leader who might disappear, or on a senior member of congress who funneled federal funds into their trough. Others were strategically located to hitchhike on the growth of a major city or a region, making continued revitalization vulnerable to external circumstances. Still others found themselves at the center of an emerging industry, which might go into decline or move offshore. Chattanooga never leaned on such unstable supports.

If a long-discussed high-speed maglev train to Atlanta becomes a reality, Chattanooga might instantly become *the* residential choice for Georgian commuters who value quality of life. Why spend two or three useless, polluting hours a day in traffic when you can spend half as much time reading or working in comfort?

But even if Chattanooga doesn't boast the first rail line in America built to modern European and Japanese standards, I believe it's a great place to invest. As you've seen, they've already done a great job of revitalizing their waterfront at one end of the downtown. Now, the downtown just needs more residents, and that's already happening.

To get my money, a community needs to show that it has a renewal vision, a renewal culture, and a renewal engine that will keep functioning and keep adapting no matter what internal or external disruptions might occur. Chattanooga had all of that in the recent past, and my suspicion is that they won't let it slip away.

Chattanooga's high level of cooperation between city and county governments could once be chalked up as a cultural tradition, dating back to cleaning their air. More recently, credit for the high level of citizen involvement in city visioning and strategy could be laid at the doorstep of Chattanooga Venture. I believe the Chattanooga Way will be restored, and CreateHere is the first indication that it's already happening.

In November of 2007, it was announced that the City of Chattanooga had experienced an 8.4% population increase from the 2000 census. This addition of 13,103 residents brings the official population to 168,293, qualifying it as the fastest growing city in Tennessee. Referring to this announcement, Mayor Littlefield said, "The investment in transforming our community from the most polluted forty years ago to one of the most desirable cities in America today is paying off."

Bilbao: Birthplace of the Renewal Engine in Europe

An important part of Bilbao's success is that it mobilized resources and support from many quarters. . . . It actively committed itself to learning by organizing world-class events, as well as focused workshops for citizens. . . . While the physical transformations in the city are important, they are only a reflection of a deeper institutional and cultural change in the city life of Bilbao. Above all, the lesson from Bilbao is what can be accomplished when an entirely new element—the conscientious agency Metropoli–30, in the case of Bilbao—is added to the city and regional political structure. The key factor is that the political structure involved a cerebral function for the city, one concerned with self-reflection, planning, and long-term development. This collaborative instrument was significant and possibly indispensable to the city's effort to grow and thrive. Now, Bilbao 2010 carries this vision into the next decade.

> —**Tim Campbell, chairperson, Urban Age Institute, from
> his July 2006 article in** *Urban Land,* **a publication
> of the Urban Land Institute**

Founded in 1300, Bilbao currently has some 350,000 residents (about a million with the greater Bilbao metropolitan area) and is the largest city in northern Spain's Basque country. Two decades ago, if you had said "Bilbao" to someone who knew it, it would have evoked images of economic depression and environmental degradation. Today, the name evokes grand architecture, beautiful parks, and rapid revitalization.

It's interesting to note that the two greatest revitalization success stories in Spain—Bilbao and Barcelona (one of my favorite cities in the world)—are both essentially non–Spanish-speaking: Euskara (the language of the Basque people) in the case of Bilbao, and Catalonian in the case of Barcelona. Spain, as with many former empires, is an assemblage of previously sovereign nations, few of which were willingly assimilated. As with Quebec and Scotland, and a host of other examples, there's no shortage of citizens in these conquered territories (Quebec was conquered indirectly when England beat France in the Seven Years War) who would like to restore their culture and some degree of self-rule.

Bilbao has become almost synonymous in the public mind with its iconic Guggenheim Museum designed by Frank Gehry, which brought fame to both the architect and the city. But Bilbao's revitalization is much more far-reaching. Their success reveals an intuitive appreciation for the renewal rules and processes. It also reveals an unusual level of innovation, which led to the creation of what might have been the world's second renewal engine, after Chattanooga's.

The port city of Bilbao has been prosperous throughout most of its existence. But it bloomed especially during the Industrial Revolution—primarily in the nineteenth century—becoming a global center for steelmaking and shipbuilding. It was a center for many forms of technological development. For instance, in 1906, Leonardo Torres Quevedo demonstrated his "Telekino" device in the port of Bilbao. Before a huge crowd that included the king of Spain, he guided a boat from the shore. Thus, remote control was added to humanity's fast-growing list of new abilities.

Bilbao was the wealthiest city in Spain at the start of the twentieth century. But by the late 1980s, Bilbao was facing a bleak future. In fact, the conclusion they came to after much soul-searching was that—without drastic changes—they effectively had *no* future.

They had lost most of their steelmaking and shipbuilding industries, and some 70,000 residents had abandoned the city during the 1980s and early 1990s. When they looked around, what primarily met the eye was the ugly detritus and toxic legacy one would expect of a long-time leader of the global deconomy.

Bilbao's Renewal Engine Started with a Public-Public Partnership

In 1989, the Basque Government, the Province of Bizkaia, and the City of Bilbao— working as a public-public partnership (as did Louisville)—initiated a strategic plan, intended to restore the city's future. It was based primarily on addressing degradation and decay of their natural, built, and socioeconomic environments.

Their overall goals were to improve Bilbao's quality of life, boost the economy, raise the city's global visibility, and enhance the degree of social inclusion in the governance process. Assuming that there's no time like the present, that inclusion— what we're referring to as stakeholder engagement—started immediately. They invited over 300 leaders from government, business, academia, NGOs, and citizen groups to participate in the visioning and strategizing process. Like Chattanooga, they took a learning-intensive approach, sponsoring a series of lectures by world-class designers, thinkers, and planners that continues to this day.

Since public sector funding was extremely limited, one of the first realizations to come out of this effort was that they needed a public-private partnership to make things happen. Its purpose would be to design, fund, and implement projects that would fulfill the vision created by that group of 300.

Bilbao didn't make the common mistake of waiting until their strategy was complete before creating a public-private partnership to implement it. They immediately expanded their public-private partnership into a P3. Its first job was to create a strategic plan for the revitalization of metropolitan Bilbao by 2010.

Just a decade later, by the mid-1990s, public and private investments totaling some 16 billion Euros (over 22 billion of our deteriorating U.S. dollars) had been attracted by that strategy. This impressive number doesn't include large amounts of "in-kind" support of the revitalization effort provided by over 100 local institutions.

That P3's name is Metropoli-30. The "30" refers to the number of communities in the Bilbao metropolitan area (what the British call a conurbation) that were involved in the strategy. Initial members of Metropoli-30 included the public University of the Basque Country and the private University of Deusto; 51 small, medium, and large businesses; 29 local and regional authorities; plus 22 NGOs and other citizen-led not-for-profits. In other words, they engaged all five stakeholder groups.

They didn't "just" create a partnering forum to fund and implement their projects: they also created a public-private "think and action group" to *research* and *envision* it. What a concept: deep thought plus the ability to act. If this combination sounds familiar, that's exactly the approach Chattanooga Venture used. This group, in turn, came up with a long-term strategy focused primarily on three things: economic transformation, environmental improvement, and enhanced international prestige.

Metropoli—30 began forming in 1990 to envision and implement the overall revitalization of the city. The organization now has the endorsement of over 40 major local institutions. A permanent nonprofit P3, the 19 individuals at its helm were drawn from a broad diversity of trade unions, chambers of commerce, business associations, civic groups, and elected leaders. They held literally hundreds of public meetings to engage the many stakeholders. These meetings led to creating a formal network of academics, government agencies, businesses, and NGOs to serve as a vehicle for that engagement.

This network became the means by which the entire city awoke to the severity of their impending crisis, and developed both the will and the vision to do something about it. The process, similar to a SWOT analysis, led to the city's becoming aware of its renewal potential, and helped them start forming a renewal culture.

By the end of 1991 they had produced a revitalization plan, also called, Metropoli-30. As with Chattanooga, their renewal was unexpectedly rapid. Their goals were achieved so quickly that they had to update the plan, renaming it Bilbao 2010. Such adaptive management adds resilience to their renewal.

Courage and Honesty Make for a Great Start

Bilbao's recognition of their impending doom was partly the result of self-examination, and partly the result of an economic analysis performed for them by the newly formed European Union. While their late twentieth-century decline seems obvious enough in retrospect, they might not have come to grips with it soon enough, had it not been for this analysis.

Old self-images of prestige tend to loiter in the mental hallways of a city, long after they are no longer deserved. Worsening the danger is the fact that incremental decline tends not to trigger effective responses. Compounding the problem is that few elected leaders have the stomach to deliver bad news, fearing a shoot-the-messenger response from voters. The courage and honesty Bilbao showed in the late 1980s—telling their citizens "we have no future"—has been paying off enormously.

Bilbao made a formal break with their industrial past, rather than allowing it to linger in the hope of seeing it come back to life, as so many other cities have done. Communities that allow obsolete deconomies to loiter are usually hoping that their heritage in particular industries (such as steelmaking) will allow them to catch the next cycle of growth in those industries. We saw that Waukegan and Youngstown suffer no such illusions.

In fact, the next cycle of growth in dirty dewealth industries usually doesn't take place in the same city, in the same country, or even on the same continent. Pursuit of lower costs always drives dewealth industries toward countries with more primitive (or desperate) governments that are willing to sacrifice human health and natural resources—their future, in other words—for a quick buck.

Worse, failing to jettison those vestigial dewealth businesses usually impedes renewal. This is why Waukegan is trying to evict profitable employers from their waterfront. Since resilient renewal is based on enhancing quality of life, it's a pursuit that runs in the opposite direction of dewealth.

There's also a quality-of-citizen factor: when declining industrial cities cling to their past—inviting dirty old businesses to make a comeback—it sabotages the likelihood of their attracting or retaining the kinds of citizens their revitalization will depend on. Educated citizens and intelligent businesses are needed to grow service industries, creative arts, centers of learning, and tourism. Both run from environments that retard change. Both are repelled by places that are still on their way down. It's OK to be run-down: the critical factor (again) is your trajectory. A shared vision defines your trajectory, and a renewal engine propels you toward it. At least, that's what happened in Bilbao.

Bilbao was smart to recognize the futility of wishful thinking about resuscitating their old industies. They made their break from dewealth to rewealth as clean as they could, but didn't go so far as to shut down what remained of their heavy industrial sector. Bilbao had the vision and courage to purge any dreams of a shipbuilding or steelmaking renaissance. The only way they would ever be welcome again would be after those industries themselves made the de/re transition, such as ship renovation or steel recycling using clean technologies.

The future was plainly in rewealth, and they embraced it. That psychological break from the past was part of their *culturing* process, creating a renewal culture that would attract the kinds of activities that were in alignment with their vision.

Part of creating that renewal culture was the work Bilbao put into renovating their public policies and procedures for economic redevelopment. They modernized their public administrations to speed approval of renewal projects and established "formulas" for public-private cooperation that helped them form a consistent series of partnerships. They didn't forget the governance side of creating a renewal culture, as did Chattanooga. Furthermore, as with their visioning/strategizing and partnering, their culturing process continues to this day; almost two decades after it began.

> . . . the attitude of the population in Metropolitan Bilbao toward environment protection has changed dramatically since the implementation of the Strategic Plan. Instead of seeing environmental pollution as an unavoidable consequence of economic progress, respect toward the environment is now understood as a key issue in any economic activity. The environment is now considered as an opportunity, not a constraint, for sustainable job and welfare creation. The city has made good progress in the recovery of its river system, derelict industrial land is being recovered for new uses, private involvement in urban and industrial waste management is growing and the government is producing a new legal framework for these activities. . . . The quality of the urban environment is improving dramatically and the derelict industrial areas in the inner city are today 'opportunity hubs' for new urban developments . . .
>
> —*Notable Practice in Regeneration: Report by CAG Consultants for the Audit Commission in Wales* (2005)

The preceding quote should of create a feeling a déjà vu: Chattanooga's revival involved that same process of understanding the progression of enhancing environmental health, which enhances quality of life, and which in turn enhances the economy. The Welsh report went on to list some of the other elements of Bilbao's success. They included:

- availability of a range of good quality, affordable housing;
- a system of revitalised public spaces and urban infrastructure that provides an excellent urban habitat and a high quality of life;
- an integrated approach to planning and management that involves the different areas of the public sector and private initiatives in the process of urban regeneration, and that allows the fast implementation of plans being developed at different levels;
- the recovery of damaged urban infrastructure through the exploitation of obsolete or abandoned industrial spaces and the rehabilitation of the old town;
- an estuary that constitutes a 'spine' for Bilbao, acts as a physically integrating axis in the metropolis and is a distinctive factor in Metropolitan Bilbao's attractiveness.

The Strategic Plan

Bilbao's original strategic plan revolved around six elements: communication, transportation, environment, education, social aspects, and culture. The "change or die" dialog about Bilbao's future was always multifaceted, including the natural, built, and socioeconomic environments. Their transformation has included many of the "usual suspects" of revitalization plans: a new airport, regional transportation infrastructure, a new convention center, a new concert hall, and upgrades to the university system. But the magic of their success was in the quality of the *process*, not in the "stuff" itself. (See Chapter 15 for more on this last point.)

The strategy involved four approaches to improving their built and natural environments: (1) reducing air pollution; (2) renovating sewage infrastructure to restore the health of the rivers; (3) renovating solid waste infrastructure; and (4) renovating industrial waste infrastructure to avoid recontaminating the areas they were planning to clean up. This strategy was, in turn, based on these tactics:

- Investing in wastewater treatment facilities;
- Promoting public transit;

- Enhancing collaboration among universities and businesses;
- Performing environmental audits;
- Developing a database of environmental assets and challenges; and
- Creating policies, regulations, and tax incentives that would attract cleaner industries and more-sustainable businesses.

Their strategic plan, like all good plans, is an evolving document. The constant updating is done as a consensus-building process, one that began in 1989 and is intended to continue past its official 2010 target date. This community engagement strengthens the plan, and the planning process strengthens the community engagement in turn. This can form—if properly executed—a powerful, positive feedback loop of renewal.

The strategic planning had four phases. Phase I identified the critical issues the plan needed to address. Phase II was an analysis of the city's strengths and weaknesses. [Note: At Resolution Fund, one of the first things we recommend to our clients is that they perform a "*re*solution SWOT analysis." We provide an analysis template that ensures they address all kinds of restorable assets and all stakeholder groups.] Phase III identified the aims, objectives, and strategies for addressing the critical issues, while Phase IV focused on specific projects and actions.

Not surprisingly, the greatest weakness Bilbao uncovered in Phase II was the aftermath of their deconomy. The vast tracts of hideous contaminated sites were degrading human health, undermining quality of life, and impeding redevelopment. Making environmental regeneration and socioeconomic regeneration equal and integral underpinnings of Bilbao's strategy was key. A for-profit public-private company, called Bilbao Ría 2000, was formed to perform much of this crucial waterfront brownfield remediation and redevelopment.

Pablo Ubieta Otaola, director general of Bilbao Ría 2000, relentlessly included environmental, social, and cultural renewal in his work to help create an economic path forward. Bilbao Ría 2000 was launched in 1992, with 50-50 funding from the state and federal governments, plus support from the European Union.

While Metropoli-30 theoretically has no legal power to make anything happen, it has that power in reality. Why? The main reason is because its stakeholders have always included politicians who were committed to the plan. *They* possessed the authority to make things happen in their jurisdictions.

Riding this wave of success, the city is now launching an ambitious revitalization of the peninsula on the Rio Zorrozaurre. Other distressed former industrial cities—such as Buffalo, New York—are now looking to Bilbao for inspiration and guidance.

Bilbao's strategic plan openly recognizes that regenerating the urban and the natural environments after such intense degradation requires a strong focus on medium- and long-range objectives. It argues for clearly and constantly communicating the strategy to the community, in order to maintain public support over the long haul.

Keeping One's Balance: Public-Public Partnering Remains Essential

Too often, cities become so enamored of the resources tapped via effective partnering with the private sector that they start reducing public leadership. When the wrong private partners are recruited, they often devalue the public sector's importance behind the scenes: the weaker the public sector, the easier it is for them to get cozy deals that stifle both competition and innovation. The public good inevitably suffers, as do the politicians when the inevitable backlash hits.

Despite their heavy focus on public-private partnerships, Metropoli-30 hasn't lost its roots in public-public partnering. Bilbao used the partnering forum of their renewal engine to foster increased public-public collaboration among the dozens of communities in the greater metropolitan area. One of the most important and visible outcomes is better-coordinated *regional* transportation infrastructure renovation.

Since traffic congestion is rated Public Enemy Number One by citizens in many cities around the world, Bilbao addressed public transit early on. They built a new metro system (Metro Bilbao), which was later enhanced by a new tram line (EuskoTran) in 2002. The metro system critically linked the suburbs with downtown. It also served another vital—but more subtle—role as a "demonstration project," an early success that would build confidence and pride in the city's ability to renew itself. That's an example of how "rapid" and "resilient" can compliment each other.

These days, as hundreds of cities catch the renaissance bug, there's much competition to be the next rising star. Thus the proliferation of annual rankings of best places to live, work, and invest. Bilbao was smart enough to know that simply doing the right thing wouldn't be enough to put them on the global map. They determined to do the right thing in a breathtaking manner by engaging the best and brightest designers.

Bilbao's built environment is now a showcase of the architectural superstars. They hired César Pelli to design a landmark tower for the Iberdrola electric company. They hired Sir Norman Foster to design Metro Bilbao. They hired Santiago

Calatrava to design the sleek Euskalduna Palace (cultural center) and the graceful Zubizuri Bridge. The Guggenheim Bilbao Museum project, of course, retained Frank Gehry for the job.

The Guggenheim was actually the first public-private project to emerge from the Metropoli-30 renewal engine. The shockingly original exterior is now familiar to millions—probably billions—of people around the globe. While its design and materials are super-modern, it's evocative of a sailing ship; a salute to the city's heritage.

One of the keys to the museum's success is its location on a waterfront brownfield. City leaders, probably looking to the Sydney Opera House for inspiration, realized the value of location. If the museum hoped to be photographed as often as that Australian icon, it would have to be an integral part of the cityscape, and preferably on the water. Thus, they moved the old Port of Bilbao further downstream in the Bay of Biscay to make room for the Guggenheim. This had the fringe benefit of enabling them to modernize the port's design and infrastructure.

Moving the port also freed up a large tract of prime waterfront real estate in the city center. It then "only" required soil remediation to quickly transform it from the ugliest and least valuable real estate to among the most beautiful and valuable properties in the city.

The Guggenheim museum isn't just an expensive landmark. Though it cost $150 million, it drew 1.5 million visitors and took in $200 million in its first year (1997) alone, not including what those visitors spent elsewhere in the city. At least eight new hotels have opened in the city since 1997. Since 1994, hotel occupancy has doubled and airline passenger traffic has tripled. If you were quick, you might have noticed Bilbao at the beginning of the 1999 James Bond film *The World Is Not Enough*.

Bilbao is also home to the recently renovated Fine Arts Museum, recognized as one of Spain's best. Over on the banks of the river Nervion, you'll find the Maritime Museum, which hosted the RMS *Titanic* exhibition that is touring the world.

Connectivity is a key component of Bilbao's strategy. For instance, they created a promenade enabling waterfront strollers to enjoy the green space provided by the campus of the University of Deusto.

What Bilbao Might Have Done Better

Bilbao's Strategy 2010 was presented in April of 2001. It's an excellent plan, but let's superficially pick it apart and look for obvious ways in which your community might do even better. Strategy 2010 was founded on three principles: people, activities, and the appeal of the metropolis. Sounds great, but simplicity and terminology are important. Let's look at how basing it on the three renewal rules would make daily decision-making easier:

- "People" could be considered the equivalent of the "engagement" rule, of course. But "engage" is a much better principle for decision-making than "people," because "engage" is something you *do*. "People" is just a noun. The renewal rules are based on *action*: keep that in mind when you're formulating your own set of decision-making guidelines. If you were making a decision, which word would give you clearer guidance: "people" or "*engage*"? In Bilbao's case, the fuzzy "people" factor seems to have led them to focus primarily on training, at the cost of engagement.
- "Activities," as defined in Strategy 2010, seems to focus mostly on commerce and infrastructure (such as high-speed internet access). It thus combines the built and the socioeconomic environment. If you were making a decision, though, and someone said "activities," would that alter your decision in any significant way? I didn't think so. How about *integrate* instead?
- "The appeal of the metropolis" sounds the fuzziest of all, but this is probably the best of the Strategy 2010 principles. The intent was to focus renewal on the city center (infill, rather than sprawl), and to focus on enhancing quality of life. Quality of life is an integrative goal. Its pursuit forces us to renew the natural, built, and socioeconomic environments together. But if you're having a busy day and are trying to make a decision, is "appeal of the metropolis" simple enough to provide clarity? Probably not: how about *rewealth* instead? That one word means renewing what we have (rather than sprawling), and renewing our existing assets automatically raises our quality of life.

It's too early to assess the success of Strategy 2010, but indicators point to a decade of steady progress, although nowhere near as dramatic as that of the 1990s. The Guggenheim is a great success by any measure, drawing some five million tourists annually. It was a great example of bringing dead real estate back to life (rewealth). But the follow-through indicates weaknesses in the other two renewal rules: integration and engagement. The museum still sits in relative isolation, both physically and psychologically.

Despite the excellent new trolley line connecting the museum to the rest of the city, the area around the museum fails to draw the tourists. They tend to hop off the trolley, see the museum, and hop back on again. The neighborhood hasn't been effectively integrated into the museum strategy, so the natural ripple effects of renewal have been dampened.

The Guggenheim is seen by most citizens (other than the elite) as a tourist facility, not something that also serves them. A decade after its opening, most Bilbao residents have reportedly never set foot inside. Of course, that's a problem for most art museums: fine art has traditionally been the province of the upper classes. For some strange reason, the working class has seldom exhibited much passion for spending their precious few leisure hours viewing their bosses' trophies.

That universal art dynamic aside, there seems to have been significantly less citizen engagement in this second decade of Bilbao's revival. The same thing happened in Chattanooga, and is partly explained by the power of crisis to bring people together. After a decade of renewal, the crisis mentality passes, and the renewal is in danger of losing resilience.

Had Strategy 2010's three guiding principles been rewealth, integration, and engagement, maybe some of the decisions leading to these present challenges could have been avoided. All three of their principles—people, activities, and appeal of the metropolis—would still have been addressed, but probably more effectively.

Lessons from Bilnooga

Chattanooga and Bilbao were two of my best—though far from the only—sources of insight into the three renewal rules, the three renewal processes, and the renewal engine model. Together, I call them the *re*solution, but they could just as easily be called the "Bilnooga Principles": that's how central these two cities were to helping me detect them.

Once perceived, I started seeing them (or noticing their absence) everywhere I looked. The clarity provided by the rules and processes enabled retrospective analyses of the hundreds of renewal programs and projects I had been exposed to over the past decade. I discovered them in reverse order, though. Until arriving in Chattanooga, I had been telling everyone that Bilbao invented the first renewal engine.

The cities have many parallels:

- Both "hit the wall" in the mid-1980s: Chattanooga lost 18,000 manufacturing jobs between 1973 and 1983, the same time Bilbao—a much larger city—was also hemorrhaging jobs and residents.

- Both had a long history of heavy industry and air pollution: each reigned as a national "metro-grungemeister."
- Both had waterfronts in need of reconnection, remediation, and redevelopment.
- Both are leaders in "green" public transit: Chattanooga has the world's largest fleet of electric buses, most manufactured there. Bilbao's new tram system is "wind-powered," buying electricity from the bordering state of Navarro (Spain is the world's second largest producer of wind energy).
- Both are best-known internationally for their creation of an iconic public building on a riverfront brownfield.
- Both relied heavily on P3s: Between 1988 and 1998, Chattanooga spent $356 million revitalizing their waterfront, of which 82% was private money. Bilbao Ría 2000 was created with public capital of 300 million pesetas (a currency since replaced by the Euro). It never again tapped public funds, and today is coordinating renewal investments totaling some 200 times that amount.
- Both are sources of inspiration for postindustrial cities around the world: Bilbao's role as a model is well known, but much-smaller Chattanooga has been visited by city leaders from dozens of countries. Vietnam, for instance, has sent officials from both Ho Chi Minh City and Hanoi. In fact, a Japanese company that has nothing to do with redevelopment has long been sending its executives to Chattanooga, simply to catch the spirit of renewal.
- Both used (unknown to them at the time) the three renewal rules to form their strategy and guide their decisions, the three renewal processes to create their solutions, and the renewal engine model to organize their efforts.
- Both achieved rapid, resilient renewal.

Bilbao's renewal engine is still alive and fairly healthy. Chattanooga's was built first, but is now in pieces. However, the renewal rules and processes it championed live on in the many excellent organizations spun off by Venture. What's more, the rules (and processes) are better embedded in the hearts and minds of the general populace, whereas in Bilbao they seem more centralized in Metropoli-30.

My talks with government, nonprofit, and academic leaders in Bilbao lead me to believe that Bilbao might be moving in the same dangerous direction we saw in Chattanooga, a "gravitational pull" toward making public-private partnering and deal-making the prima donna that draws attention away from the co-stars: visioning and culturing.

The danger is that partnering tends to be less transparent—more behind the scenes—than the other two processes. Combined with the large amounts of money involved, it's a recipe for trouble. Confidential partnering conversations are essential, but must be balanced—in the same organization—by visioning and culturing functions that have heavy public engagement. If the projects are driven by that shared vision—and supported by the culture—it's a recipe for regenerative nirvana. Please excuse my repetiveness, but this is crucial.

Bilbao, along with all the other rewealth pioneers, has had no "guide to the creation and maintenance of renewal engines." So, they *seem* to be making the same mistake. (I stress "seem," because—whenever I asked leaders in Bilbao about the present-day process of public engagement—they clammed up. As a result, I've had to draw my own conclusions, which might be wrong. My Spanish is awful, so if I've misunderstood the situation, it's certainly a fault of my own.)

Hope on the Horizon

Both Bilbao and Chattanooga have excellent opportunities at hand to remedy the situation, to revive the level of public engagement in their visioning and culturing processes. Chattanooga has their huge U.S. Pipe project. Redeveloping that site and properly connecting it to their downtown is the best opportunity they will ever have to undo the damage done to the Chattanooga Way by the one-two punch of the past decade.

The first punch was by a mayor who accomplished incredible feats of rewealth, but did it in a strongman style that might have undermined public engagement. The second punch was an election that played on that separation of partnering and visioning, ripping apart much of the community's sense of togetherness in the process.

Bilbao also has a great opportunity to reengage the public, and they don't have to deal with the sort of trauma that Chattanooga has experienced. In 2010, their present strategic plan will "expire." Coming up with the next iteration is a perfect time to nip a potential problem in the bud, and restore some balance among the three processes of visioning, culturing, and partnering.

When renewal engines lose power over time, it often means that one or more of the renewal rules or processes are being ignored. Take the engagement rule, for instance. If nonprofits representing the needs of minority groups aren't engaged, you might not put enough attention on redeveloping affordable housing or renewing social services, and your employers might find themselves without employees. Nonprofit organizations tend to come and go, so if a renewal engine doesn't continuously recruit new partners, the loss of old ones could weaken the entire revitalization effort.

Chapter 12

Two Stories of For-Profit Companies on Rewealth's Leading Edge

In South America, two young friends build a $10 million beverage company that restores jaguar habitat, protects tribal lands, and revitalizes farms in three nations. In Madagascar, a mining company pioneers rewealth strategies in a dewealth industry.

My story choices for this chapter might take some readers by surprise: a small beverage company and a giant mining company. You probably expected architectural, engineering, construction (AEC) firms, planning firms, or ecological restoration firms.

But dirt-moving, bricklaying, community-designing companies are too obvious. Everyone knows they're making tons of money restoring our world. I wanted to surprise you with less-obvious examples. What could be a more surprising sources of global restoration than a consumer products company and a mining company?

The Guayakí Story

My 2002 book, *The Restoration Economy*, was written to such a great extent at Starbucks that I thanked the local baristas in the Acknowledgments. But the company's lack of serious commitment to organic, shade-grown, or fair-trade practices made me queasy about supporting them so heavily.

With this book, the source of my early-morning caffeine has changed to a large extent. Rather than irritating my kidneys and bowels with coffee, I switched (mostly) to yerba maté, like the gauchos of Argentina famously drink, as my first drink of the day. It's delicious, produces an excellent caffeine boost, doesn't produce those nasty coffee jitters, and even contains healthy nutrients.

The source of my yerba maté is a company called Guayaki, and they go far beyond "merely" using organic practices and choosing to be fairly traded. They are actually a *restorative* venture. The Atlantic rain forests of South America are being restored as a direct outcome of Guayaki's business model. So, I thank the restorative farmers of South America for keeping me awake and contributing to this book without knowing it. Here's their story.

Farmers Gladys and Alfonso Werle restore the world for a living. Well, they restore their 60-hectare part of it, anyway. But they are also contributing to the restoration of the Iquazú National Park that borders their farm in Argentina.

The park is on a thumb of land created to make sure Argentineans retain access to one of South America's most spectacular natural attractions: the waterfalls and rapids of Iquazú. The area of the falls is a meeting place of three countries: Argentina to the south, Paraguay to the west, and Brazil to the east and north. A determined tourist could see the falls and travel to three nations in a single day.

The park comprises 170,086 hectares (420,000 acres) on the Brazil side, and 55,000 hectares (136,000 acres) on the Argentina side, and is the largest forest reserve in southern Brazil. This subtropical rain forest houses about 1,100 bird species, many large and small mammals (such as jaguar, deer, otters, ocelots, and capybaras), and a wealth of other plant and animal species. The Atlantic rainforest biome is one of the most endangered in the world, and Iquazú National Park is one of the few places it's protected. But the park lacks a buffer area, which is often essential to maintaining the health of all but the largest of parks.

The park is surrounded primarily by agricultural lands, much of it monoculture crops of yerba maté. Yerba maté is not technically tea: it's a South American holly that's brewed as a tea. Maté is the national hot drink of all three of those nations, Brazil less so than the other two. Maté outsells coffee 7:1 in Argentina, and there are good reasons, in addition to its great taste. Health claims include stress reduction, appetite control, and easing of allergy symptoms, and it's loaded with antioxidants. A 2004 study conducted at the University of Illinois at Champaign-Urbana found that maté's high antioxidant content promotes cell survival better than red wine or green tea. Besides caffeine, it contains xanthine alkaloids (including a mood elevator and muscle relaxant also found in chocolate); and B vitamins. Like coffee and chocolate, yerba maté was so important at one point that it was used as a currency. Of the six commonly used stimulants in the world—yerba maté, coffee, tea, kola nut, cocoa, and guarana—yerba maté is considered the healthiest, delivering both energy and nutrition.

Yerba maté doesn't need to be in the direct sun to grow well. It's a native tree of the local Atlantic rainforest. It's now grown without any accompanying forest because, long ago, Christian settlers from Europe enslaved the local indigenous people and forced them to go out into the jungle to collect the precious leaf. Of course, being forest dwellers made it exceedingly easy for the slaves to just slip away and disappear. So, the Europeans cut down all the other trees and began planting the maté in monoculture plots so they could keep an eye on their captives.

That's the style of cultivation that survives to this day. But maté aficionados say that organic and forest-harvested maté tastes better and is more nutritious that maté grown on monoculture farms, where its growth is often chemically accelerated by artificial fertilizers.

This is where Gladys and Alfonso come into the story. Three years ago, their maté farm was like all the rest: barren of everything except maté. But they yearned to restore the natural forest. The area has a population of jaguars that find it increasingly difficult to roam their large natural range, given the tremendous and increasing fragmentation of habitat. Alfonso and Gladys wished their farm could become part of a wildlife corridor that would enhance the ecological value of the neighboring park. But they didn't know how they could afford to replant the native plants and trees that should be surrounding their maté trees.

Then they heard of a California-based company called Guayakí. It's named after the indigenous Ache Guayakí people of Paraguay, with whom the company was working to protect their native lands by buying wild-harvested maté from them at better than market prices. Alfonso and Gladys liked the idea of being paid more for their crop, so they contacted Guayakí, which needed more maté than the Paraguayan operation could provide (they exported about 200 tons in 2007).

They were disappointed, though. Guayakí told them that they only purchased maté harvested in a nondestructive way from rainforests, never from farms that were created by destroying rainforest. It was part of their promise to their customers, who liked the idea that drinking this delicious beverage would help preserve endangered wildlife habitat and support an endangered human culture.

But a unique partnership produced a solution: Guayakí offered them a chance to become a supplier. Restore the native forest on your farm and we will buy from you, they said. In fact, they went a step better: they promised to buy some of their maté as soon as the restoration began, enabling Alfonso and Gladys to afford the time and expense. (Note: Guayakí put their maté into storage and didn't add it to their products until the farm had been substantially restored, so they could maintain the environmentally sound integrity of the product's sourcing.)

Gladys and Alfonso have restored 14 native species of trees to their property over the past three years, and the farm—which also grows organic bananas, pineapples, and lemons—already looks very different from those of their neighbors. The goal is for it to become an extension of the park, or at least a buffer for it. In fact, the jaguars have already started using their farm to enter and exit the park, so that part of the dream has already come true. Guayakí is now working with two other nearby farms in their community of Andrecito, and they are starting to work with over 30 other "restoration farms" around Iquazú National Park.

Here's an excerpt from the March 2007 issue of *ODE* magazine (one of my three favorite magazines): "Alfonso, Gladys, and Guayakí hope this land . . . will become a showcase, proving that the Atlantic forest can be restored while providing farmers with a secure livelihood and providing the world with ample food. Alfonso suddenly strides into the centre of the field to examine one of the trees they planted. He looks at it intently and then turns back toward us with a smile. 'This is redesigning agriculture,' he shouts."

That *ODE* article was entitled "Beyond Organic," and was written by Jay Walljasper. It described how several companies represent "the next ecological and social revolution." Here's a line from *ODE*'s story on a new juice company: "Sambazon is part of a new wave of entrepreneurial companies seeking to promote ecological restoration and economic justice as (an) integral part of their business."

The *ODE* article said this about Guayakí: "Guayakí is pushing the frontiers of organic agriculture with one project that supports farmers planting native rainforest trees in the middle of their yerba fields. Rather than just avoiding unsustainable farming methods . . . the company is pioneering new practices to reverse environmental destruction."

David Karr cofounded Guayakí in 1996 with Alex Pryor, an Argentinean who runs the operation in South America, when they were both still students at California Polytechnic State University. Sales amounted to $5 million in 2006, $7.5 million in 2007, and they project $12 million for 2008.

Besides selling loose and tea-bagged maté, they've expanded into a line of tasty maté-based bottled beverages. Their creed is "market-based restoration."

Here's an excerpt from an email I received in February of 2007 from David: "We have 're' defined our business model from Market Driven Conservation to Market Driven Restoration. In fact, our business model is based on three principles:

"restoring health" (North American customers), "restoring community" (Ache Guayakí in Paraguay and Andrecito in Argentina), and "restoring forest" (Atlantic rainforest—one of the top five biodiversity hotspots in the world)."

In her brilliant 2001 book, *The Divine Right of Capital*, Marjorie Kelly quoted the founder-CEO of a progressive natural juice firm (after they went public) as lamenting, "I used to be in the business of making great juice. Now I'm in the business of making money." Despite the fact that all of Guayakí's products are derived from a tree, the founders say they are really in the business of creating a new restorative model for business. One of the great benefits of this profitable rewealth model is that it could solve the problem of how going public often strips ethically-based private companies of the principles that drove the passion that built the company.

Now that you've read the story of Guayakí, ask yourself whether "market-driven restoration" is a business model that would survive going public. The juice company founder's lament (quoted by Kelly above) derived its claim to being socially responsible primarily from donating a portion of its profits to charity, to treating its employees well, and from using higher-quality ingredients than the market "required."

Guayakí's restorative effect on the world, on the other hand, is directly linked to the way they earn their living. It's neither an add-on (like charity) nor a management style (like good employee benefits or high-quality sourcing), which could probably be changed without their customers' noticing. Their entire premise is based on providing customers with high-quality products that protect or restore rainforest, while protecting and revitalizing human communities.

If a publicly traded conglomerate were to buy the firm and was tempted to buy cheaper maté on the open market from brokers, it would undermine the entire model on which Guayakí has positioned and marketed their products, and would make no sense. And let's not forget that these restored forest/farms are sequestering a lot of carbon: as the market for climate change-related credits grows, that will likely turn into another productive fringe benefit.

His California-based company now has professional managers (including his brother), so David Karr lives on a 100-acre organic farm on historic Salt Spring Island in British Columbia with his lovely wife and new child. They've been busy undoing damage done to the land by earlier owners, and are building a beautiful new home using rammed-earth construction. As we walked the land, surrounded by stately, moss-covered Douglas fir trees, I was reminded once again of the bliss that can be derived from restoring our world for a living.

The QMM/Rio Tinto Story in Madagascar: Rewealth Mining?

> . . . a new reality in the world's mining sector. Like oil, most of the easy-to-reach deposits of basic materials like copper, nickel and gold have already been found and exploited. That has left lower-grade deposits in remote, politically volatile countries that will cost more to develop than the mother lodes of yesteryear. "They should close all the mines," proclaims Walter Maperi, a 34-year-old man who sells kava, an herbal drink, from a shack in a mangrove swamp . . . Mr. Maperi says he makes as much as $300 a day selling kava. "Nickel's not the only thing that allows you to live—before nickel, people managed," he says.
>
> —Patrick Barta, "With Easy Nickel Fading Fast, Miners Go
> After the Tough Stuff," *Wall Street Journal*, July 12, 2006

The above excerpt mentions one option for the future of mining: close them all. Is there another future possible . . . one that's compatible with the reconomy?

The phrase "rewealth mining" might be the ultimate oxymoron. But we all depend on mining for the products we use daily, so humanity won't have the option of stopping it anytime soon. As with most dewealth industries, efforts are being made in most countries to reduce the damage done to waterways and communities.

But in Madagascar, a company is trying to figure out how to actually leave the natural, built, and socioeconomic environments *better than they found them*. That's what I mean by "rewealth mining."

The mining industry probably competes only with the oil industry for the title of "prototypical dewealth activity." Although the petroleum industry does more direct, far-reaching damage to the planet—such as through global climate change—mining is more visible. Hard-rock mining (such as for metals) is usually done in open pits, and often close to human habitation, whereas oil pumps are more discrete, and are often offshore.

Picture the gigantic, toxic Berkeley Pit in Butte, Montana, and you've got the poster child of the deconomy. The destruction is on such a monumental scale that the pit is this pleasant, largely abandoned—but gradually reviving—town's premiere tourist attraction (along with its historic speakeasies). Migrating geese that spend the night on the pit's huge lake—easily visible from orbit—are usually dead by morning.

Remember the news articles you've heard about the use of public armies, gangs of local thugs, and hired mercenaries to put down protests against gold and copper mines that are poisoning the waterways in lesser-developed countries? Stories like those have made mining companies the epitome of dewealth: good for the economy in the short run, bad for the local environment and society, and bad for the economy in the long run.

Mining, like dewealth in general, isn't going to disappear. The laptop this is being written on is the product of mining and oil extraction. As reuse and recycling of metals and aggregates become more systemic around the world, we'll be able to reduce our dependence on raw materials . . . maybe even eliminate it someday. But don't hold your breath, especially if we keep breeding like cockroaches. (Just ask city managers in Los Angeles, where thieves posing as maintenance crews stole 370,000 feet of copper wire from streetlights over a four-month period in 2007, which they sell as scrap for $2–$3 per pound. This disabled some 700 lights and caused the city to spend about $1 million to repair them. There's is also a global plague of manhole-cover theft: scrap metal fetched $77 ton in 2001, $480 ton in 2008.)

Prior to the 1970s, the standard model of mining was this: (1) acquire land (usually by lease), (2) extract wealth while paying employees as little as possible and doing nothing to reduce environmental or human health hazards, (3) abandon the now-worse-than-worthless property and fire all the employees with no ongoing benefits, and (4) merge or bankrupt the company to avoid any liability for long-term damage to humans or wildlife by toxins leaching from the site. Many times, the original land was public, "purchased" from the federal or state government for next to nothing, thanks either to bribes or promises of economic development.

Beginning in the 1970s, a few mining companies have been trying to reduce the environmental damage their activities do. Others are trying to be more humane employers and better neighbors to local communities. This could be considered the first stage of mining reform, whereby they attempted to be less bad. Sometimes, these efforts resulted in meaningful reform. More often, they were little more than advertising campaigns. We might call such "greening," "social responsibility," or "sustainability" improvements the second phase of mining.

The third, reclamation phase of mining began in the 1980s and accelerated in the 1990s. The fast-growing sciences and companies of the emerging ecological restoration industry started to have an impact on public policy, as people realized that restoration was actually becoming possible. Legislation has since been enacted in many countries requiring companies to "reclaim" the land after they are done with it. The posting of restoration deposits and bonds is often required to ensure that the environmental restoration takes place, even if the company disappears after the mine runs out. Some companies do the absolute minimum reclamation necessary to meet the letter of the law. Others seem to make a wholehearted effort.

Let's return to Montana, where we find that the Rose Bud open pit coal mine has lain to waste over 15,000 acres of the state's beautiful landscape since operations began in 1968. Originally, little or no reclamation was done. Now, they restore some 200 acres annually, while removing about 12 million tons of coal in the same period. They make the extra effort to restore the original contours of the land, rather than just slapping a green bandage on the scar. They also take care to replace the topsoil on the surface, where it belongs, and they revegetate with a diversity of native grasses.

Thanks to these efforts, visitors to their former mine land can once again witness the mating dance of the endangered sharp-tailed grouse, not to mention antelope and wild turkey. In 2005, the Western Energy Company won a national award for "Excellence in Surface Coal Mining Reclamation" from the Department of the Interior's Office of Surface Mining for their restoration work at Rose Bud.

Mining for Bats

Wildlife is often willing and able to adapt to human activities, and is often quite adept at reusing our abandoned structures. Sometimes, nature doesn't even wait for us to abandon them, as with peregrine falcon nests on skyscrapers, and the colonization of offshore oil rigs by corals. Most mining companies are overtly hostile towards environmental groups (and vice-versa), but some have been willing to partner on worthwhile projects. In Illinois, we find a happy confluence of adaptive reuse by nature, and responsible partnering by a mining firm.

There, mining company Unimin Tamms Elco, the Wildlife Habitat Council, the Illinois Department of Natural Resources (Division of Natural Heritage), and Bat Conservation International have formed an unusual partnership. Unimin was reclaiming some of their old mines in Illinois, and asked the Wildlife Habitat Council for advice on how to do a better job of it. After restoring native plant cover, they decided to look for bats in their mines, and discovered the largest colony in the state. It housed over 10,000 individuals representing five species, including the largest-known colony anywhere of endangered Indiana bats.

The old mines were collapsing, so they shored up the mines as part of the reclamation, and installed a bat-friendly gate to keep people out. In other words, the abandoned mines had become wildlife habitat that was worth restoring. These are the sorts of partnerships the world needs far more of, since so much wildlife habitat is on private property.

*Re*solution: A Fourth Stage of Evolution in the Mining Industry?

The trend toward more and better restoration in the mining industry is exciting. But, for an operation to truly live up to a moniker like "rewealth mining," it must go further . . . much further. It would need to have a net-positive impact on the ecological, societal, and economic health of a region, before, during, and after the mining takes place.

I say "net-positive" because, while biodiversity will likely be decreased on the mining site itself, the strategy would have a regional focus that enabled that loss to be *more than offset* via conservation and restoration activities that would not have otherwise occurred. Not just mitigation, in other words: using the wealth-generating capacity of the mine to achieve ecological, social, and economic dreams that were previously unthinkable.

Given the largely negative industry heritage described above, and the purely dewealth nature of resource extraction, is there any place for the mining industry in the reconomy? Is there any way to actually apply the *re*solution to the practice of hard-rock mining? The answer is "yes." That third "reclamation" phase of mining was a start, but the emerging fourth stage is where the magic might happen.

Achieving such an ambitious program is beyond the means of even the largest company, by itself. It would require not just a focus on *rewealth*, but significant *integration, engagement*, and *partnering*. Apply those three renewal rules, plus the partnering process, and the impossible becomes doable. Apply the entire recipe for rapid, resilient renewal—the *re*solution—and the doable becomes likely.

You're about to discover a mining company that has assumed many of the visioning, partnering, and renewing responsibilities needed by a community that largely lacked such abilities. Better yet, their hope is to pass along some of this self-renewal capacity to the community—along with significantly enhanced infrastructure and a more sustainable economy—after the mine is closed and the company has moved on.

The QMM Public-Private Mining Partnership in Fort Dauphin, Madagascar

The fourth and latest stage of mining reform is being pioneered by Madagascar-based QMM (QIT Madagascar Minerals), a division of one of the global giants of mining, Rio Tinto. If this experiment is successful, Rio Tinto's size means there's a chance that this new phase, which might be called "rewealth mining," will set a new standard that could be widely adopted.

Even if other companies aren't interested in being more environmentally or socially responsible, QMM is setting an example that will raise the public's expectation of what's possible. Firms will eventually be expected to measure up to this level of performance, either via RFP specifications if they are on publicly owned land, or via legislation if on private land.

The Rio Tinto Group is the world's third-largest mining company. Its lineage goes back to an ancient Roman mine named Rio Tinto in southern Spain. NM Rothschild & Sons (London) and de Rothschild Frères (Paris) created an investment group in 1873 that bought the mine from the Spanish government, which was happy to get rid of the unprofitable operation. The new owners restored the firm's profitability, and it's grown steadily ever since, in large part via acquisition. In 1962, British-based Rio Tinto bought a majority ownership in the Australian firm, Consolidated Zinc. Today, it's often referred to as an Anglo-Australian firm, with a large portion of its stock owned by Australian citizens and companies.

In the latter part of the twentieth century, Rio Tinto's reputation among environmental and human rights activists could most charitably be called problematic . . . "reviled" might be more accurate. Any pronouncement they might make about becoming more environmentally or socially responsible was likely to be greeted by howls of laughter, and assumed to be nothing but PR "greenwash."

But since 2005, Rio Tinto has had a publicly stated goal of achieving a "net positive impact" on biodiversity in the places it mines. In Madagascar, QMM is taking that guidance even further, looking to achieve net positive social impact as well.

"Net positive impact" is another way of saying "enhance," and that—in turn—can be a way of saying "restore" or "revitalize." In other words, they aren't just saying they are going to reduce the damage they do: they are claiming to be striving toward leaving the world a better place than it was when they arrived.

Now, this might seem somewhat achievable if the site they choose has been previously subject to heavy abuse by unsustainable lumbering or farming activities, and so doesn't have much ecological or economic value. But how in the world could you hope to achieve net positive impact if you want to mine ilmenite (sand containing iron and titanium) in one of the world's greatest biodiversity hotspots?

That's the challenge, and the story, we're about to explore here. To tell it, we'll first have to learn about another mining company, QIT–Iron & Titanium of

Montreal, a $1 billion/year subsidiary that Rio Tinto acquired in 1989. Most of this story will refer to QMM, their Malagasy operation. Rio Tinto's net positive impact campaign encountered a real stroke of luck with the QIT acquisition, as they had a head start on this kind of thinking.

Rio Tinto's Richard's Bay Minerals operation in South Africa also helped them along the road to rewealth mining, owing to its significant environmental restoration program. But the leased property at Richard's Bay was almost entirely secondary scrub forest when Rio Tinto obtained access to it.

The Malagasy operation, in contrast, would be carried out on a variety of landscapes, including some primary habitat, thus greatly raising the stakes. It was here they decided to really push the leading edge. Fauna and flora (including seed storage at Kew Gardens near London) will be removed and transferred to protected areas or breeding operations as much as practically possible. QMM will also leave millions of tons of ilmenite in the ground in the conservation zones it has helped create via partnerships with highly respected conservation organizations. Just these two factors alone make this operation highly unusual, but QMM is going much further.

In fact, they've been studying and preparing for this operation since 1987, and have been testing restoration techniques for over a decade (mining won't begin until 2008). They brought in the Smithsonian Institution and the Missouri Botanical Garden in the late 1980s to begin studying the fauna and flora as the first step toward their environmental impact statement. They were surprised at the high level of endemic species, especially plants. Rather than running from or ignoring the biodiversity, they chose instead to deal with it as responsibly as possible.

QMM is pioneering the mining industry's rewealth frontier on many levels. They are using a process that "reprofiles" the mined land. It moves across the land like a giant caterpillar (actually floating on a temporary pond about 400 by 500 meters in size), displacing the living surface of the landscape, scooping out the ilmenite beneath, and excreting white sand—minus the mineral deposits—ready to have its topsoil replaced and replanted.

This technique, called dredge pond mining, was developed in Australia. It was used at the operation in Richard's Bay, South Africa. Since they only remove about 5% of the material, reshaping the land isn't as hard as it might sound. The higher levels of biodiversity in the targeted areas in Madagascar required some modifications to the dredge pond mining process, to insure the proper restoration of the ecosystems.

Simultaneously, QMM is inventing a revitalizing strategy for moving a mining operation into a community and leaving it better than it was when they arrived. In the past, mining was something that happened to an area, not unlike an invading army. Entirely new communities would be created, but they had no resilience once the mining ceased. The planet is now littered with toxic ghost towns as a result. These days, there are fewer uninhabited places on the planet, so new mining operations tend to impact existing communities, rather than building them from scratch. But the end result—ghost towns—often remains the same.

QMM envisions something different. When they moved into Fort Dauphin, it was a town with seemingly intractable environmental and socioeconomic challenges: joblessness, a variety of diseases, poor or missing infrastructure, dying fisheries, and devastated forests. When the mine runs out (in about 40 years), they hope to leave it with modern infrastructure, replenished natural resources, a diverse economy, better governance, and little visible evidence that mining ever took place.

What's more, they want the town to start enjoying these benefits before their ilmenite mining operations even begin. The community improvement process began in earnest in 2002, and is being conducted in a partnered manner, with strong community engagement. If it sounds wildly impractical, a utopian dream, it's not. It's not only real, it's already happening.

Fort Dauphin, (with a population of 55,000), is on the coast in the far southeastern corner of Madagascar. Fort Dauphin (also known as Tolagnaro) is sitting on an estimated 50 million tons of ilmenite (titanium ore sands) for which the world hungers. Let's see how QMM plans to feed that hunger, and achieve this seemingly impossible dream of leaving both the environment and the community in better condition than they found them.

> However the area is currently undergoing a massive transformation associated with the development of a new ilmenite mine by the Rio Tinto Group in the area. A new port as well as new roads are being built, these being the first investment in the region's infrastructure for many decades. The mine is controversial however due to the predicted social upheaval and adverse environmental impact it will have. In particular, health officials fear that HIV/Aids, which is almost unknown in Madagascar up to [sic] day, could spread to the island via Tôlanaro.
> **—excerpt from Wikipedia entry on Fort Dauphin**

Knowing they would need help in leapfrogging to the leading edge of restoration, QMM wisely partnered with the well-respected Missouri Botanical Garden (MBG), which is the North American center for the study of African plants. MBG helped establish community-based conservation programs starting in 1991, so they had expertise not just in biological matters, but in public engagement.

Better yet, MBG started investigating Madagascar in 1972, although they had to postpone those studies in 1976 because of political instability in the country. Madagascar was effectively closed to the world until the mid-1980s, when MBG renewed their plant inventory expeditions. They've had a continuous and expanding presence there ever since. During this time, environmental NGOs and the Malagasy government have become far more aware of the biodiversity treasure contained within the country

Traditionally focused primarily on research and education, MBG was a relative newcomer to operating conservation programs. Restoration programs were entirely new territory for them. Now, thanks to many years of MBG's research and preparation, QMM is exploring a wide range of restorative options, depending on the location and nature of the mined property. This is a far cry from the "paint it green" reclamation of many mining operations that just slap grass on the site and run.

In some cases, QMM will replant native species. In others, where land was already too degraded by previous abuse, they will plant commercial species that will help reduce extractive pressures on native forests (the new plantations will be harvestable in about 5 to 10 years). In wetter locations, they are investigating the possibility of turning the mine site into constructed wetlands that will provide new wildlife habitat, and help treat wastewater from Fort Dauphin before it reaches the fisheries.

Our old friend James Aronson (Chapter 8) has been tangentially involved since 2002, helping to inject leading-edge concepts related to the Restoring Natural Capital Alliance. "Given the embryonic state of ecological restoration practice in the country, and given the very limited funds of the government, I'm hoping that QMM's initiative will help usher in a new era of holistic, restorative environmental and social programs throughout Madagascar. A company like QMM—along with CBOs (community-based organizations), NGOs, and Madagascar's forward-thinking Ministry of the Environment, Water and Forests—have the potential to develop a suite of eco-restoration and Restoring Natural Capital strategies, tools, and models that are appropriate for Madagascar. They can also help with the urgent task of training young people as teachers, facilitators, engineers and scientists in the emerging fields of restoration."

As soon as the restoration ethic permeated QMM, they started looking for ways to restore Madagascar's many devastated forests and other wastelands to productive agricultural and forestry uses. This was partly to help the people, but also to reduce pressure on habitat, which was being lost at a truly alarming rate.

QMM knew from the outset that the intersection of the mining industry's reputation with one of the world's most treasured biodiversity hotspots was bound to be hugely controversial. Unlike many of the other places on the globe where mining takes place on a massive scale with the barest notice (such as Siberia), the eyes of the world were already on Madagascar. Not just any eyes, either: these were "eco" eyes. It was the last place they were likely to find a friendly or even open-minded reception, and for good reason.

"Remarkably responsible" is how Pete Lowry of the MBG first described QMM to me, much to my surprise. Pete has been consulting with QMM since 1989. This brings up a partnering risk that we haven't previously addressed in this book: the danger to a nonprofit or academic institution of damaging its credibility by partnering with a for-profit firm whose agenda might be opposed to their own.

MBG's ideal goal in Madagascar is, of course, to leave whatever pristine habitat remains as intact as possible. Given the economic realities, though, the country's future looks more like a "Haiti-in-the-making." So MBG's staff had to bite the bullet, and asked themselves the difficult questions of how they could be of greatest service to wildlife—and to the country—within the constraints imposed by the needs of its desperately poor populace. It would be hard to imagine a more dangerous bed partner for a biodiversity-oriented nonprofit than mining, but QMM made some unusual commitments that gave MGB the confidence to at least explore the possibilities. Pete's comment indicates the pleasant surprise that awaited them.

QMM's (Possible) Impact on the World

QMM's approach to their Fort Dauphin operation isn't just "remarkably responsible," it's an entirely new paradigm. Our world is rapidly making the de/re transition on many fronts, mostly in restoring the natural, built, and socioeconomic assets of communities. This is the pursuit of economic growth and enhanced quality of life—revitalization, to put it in a single word.

But what about manufacturing? The progress we've so far made toward the recycling and reuse of materials has mostly been retrofitted to a system that is still based on the extraction and processing of virgin resources. A few zero-waste production facilities have been created in forward-thinking countries like the Netherlands and Denmark, but they have mostly been small, at the proof-of-concept scale.

A few eco-industrial parks have been set up, as well. They recruit manufacturing operations with the goal of putting those who produce a certain kind of waste together with those who can use that waste as a raw material. Again, it's a great model for how the entire global manufacturing system should operate, but the current scale isn't likely to make any noticeable impacts.

When we think "manufacturing," most of us envision automobiles and toaster ovens. But building and infrastructure construction (and renovation) use vast amounts of mined resources like iron ore for steel, aggregates for concrete, silica for glass, and a wide variety of more valuable metals for wiring, control mechanisms, and coatings.

The bottom line, again, is that our need for raw materials from the earth isn't likely to slacken soon. Given that reality, where does mining fit into the de/re transition?

The basic paradigms of manufacturing will eventually switch to recycling and reuse, as Germany has been trying to pioneer (without much support from the rest of the world). Our assumption has been that all we can do is increase efficiency and reduce waste. These are noble goals, no doubt, but—once again—they only slow the world's degradation; they don't reverse it. Is there any way to mine in such a way as to leave the world in better condition than it was before, rather than minimizing the damage done? QMM seems determined to find out, and Fort Dauphin is becoming a window on a possible future.

Sand mining for valuable minerals like ilmenite is, in many ways, an ideal dewealth industry to start the process of integrating rewealth. Petroleum extraction and use, for instance, transfers immense quantities of carbon sequestered in the ground for millions of years directly into our atmosphere. On the other hand, metals like titanium often go into uses that "resequester" them into long-lasting products, many of which can be recycled at the end of their useful life. Iron, in fact, is the world's most thoroughly recycled material.

QMM's Impact on Madagascar

So, if the actual process of extracting and processing the ores can be done in a way that enhances nature and society in some ways, then their might be hope for integrating rewealth into this dewealth activity. Given the vast amounts of energy expended in that extracting and processing (not to mention product manufacturing), this restorative component would have to be on a fairly grand scale. Only then could it hope to significantly offset that energy expenditure, not to mention the physical disturbance to the wildlife habitat.

Until QMM came along, very little research into the restoration of Malagasy ecosystems had taken place. Almost none had been done on the sandy coastal areas, where most of the human population (and environmental impact) is. These areas are extremely challenging habitats for plants to get started. The decade-plus of restoration research and practice funded by QMM will thus be of use in restoring many other coastal areas around the country.

QMM has a five-pronged strategy for "net positive impact" in Fort Dauphin: (1) to ecologically restore the disturbed lands to the highest degree possible where appropriate; (2) to conserve the best blocks of healthy ecosystems both within and outside the mining site as offsets; (3) to reuse mined lands in a way that reduces pressure on threatened wildlife habitat elsewhere in the region; (4) to sponsor and facilitate environmental offsets to achieve net positive impact; (5) to dramatically improve both the standard of living (incomes) and the quality of life of the residents of Fort Dauphin and the surrounding area. In other words, the strategy is based on restoration, conservation, and community revitalization.

Let's examine how they intend to accomplish each of those goals.

Restoration of Mined Lands

The first step in restoring heavily disturbed lands is to conserve and reuse the valuable topsoil and reestablish ecosystems of native species, where possible. In the areas that were most degraded before the mining, QMM will put in wood-energy plantations of fast-growing introduced species. Locals will be able to sustainably harvest wood from these new plantations for the making of charcoal. Extensive study showed that no native species would work for this purpose, so this is a rare case of alien species contributing to the conservation of native species. QMM has already planted over 1,500 acres of these "firewood forests" on degraded lands, and are planting another 250 acres annually.

This new crop benefits the people's quality of life by giving them a nearby source of wood, since unsustainable wood harvesting has deforested much of the land, forcing them to spend more and more of their time traveling to the trees. It is also advantageous to the remaining old forests, especially those in a nearby park, by reducing pressure on them by wood harvesters.

QMM is thus restoring mined land while conserving undisturbed land. The general usage goals for these restored mining sites is thus to return lands to wildlife habitat where viable, and make them more productive for human benefit in other cases.

Conservation and Restoration of Threatened Wildlife Habitat

Eighty-five percent of Madagascar's wildlife habitat has already been destroyed, and the pace shows no sign of slowing. In fact, it suffers one of the world's fastest rates of species extinction. The future of the country's wildlife obviously lies in restoring these damaged lands. But the most urgent challenge is to protect what little viable habitat remains.

No matter how well the mined lands are restored or the conservation areas are managed, there's no question that there will be some harm to wildlife populations and habitat. So QMM has worked out a plan with the government and conservation NGOs to use some of their future mining profits to protect virgin habitat today. They will more than offset any damage the mining inflicts, and they are focusing on protecting areas of far greater biodiversity than the mostly-marginal lands of the mining site.

NGOs partnered with QMM in the Fort Dauphin area include Missouri Botanical Garden, World Wildlife Fund, World Conservation Society, Birdlife International, Fauna and Flora International, Earth Watch, and the Royal Botanic Gardens, Kew. All are participating in various aspects of developing the net positive impact approach, and all are represented on the Biodiversity Committee, of which Pete Lowry is the president. This is conservation that would not have happened without QMM, so you could consider it dewealth-funded conservation. Offsetting destruction by funding conservation is by no means a new concept, but it contributes to making QMM's "net positive impact" strategy exceptionally comprehensive.

Community Revitalization

QMM's mining operation requires greatly improved local infrastructure, as does the city of Fort Dauphin, so QMM is paying for a substantial portion of it. They are also using their influence to encourage development banks and external donors to add to these efforts.

For instance, QMM is investing $145 million into building a new port, and the Malagasy government (through the World Bank) is contributing $35 million. QMM has joint-ventured with the public sector in the port's operation. The mining operation will only use the port a few days a month, so the extra capacity will be available to build the local economy.

QMM has built one of the first modern sewage treatment plants in Madagascar, to help ensure that their construction camps don't pollute local waterways. Hopefully, its presence will act as a catalyst for the government to eventually install them in communities throughout the country, to help restore river, estuarine, and coastal ecosystem health.

QMM is greatly increasing the power-generating and drinking water capacity of the city, and will sell excess power to the local electric company at cost. They have also gone to the extra expense of installing multifuel generators that will be able to use biofuels when they become locally available. That single factor could have hugely positive long-term consequences. The region—and neighboring regions—could restore degraded land, control erosion, and rebuild topsoil via a multispecies biofuel strategy (such as the Oilforest Program). This could, in turn, help diversify agricultural incomes, and significantly lower the area's dependence on expensive, polluting foreign petroleum.

Unlike most mining operations, QMM's office buildings are built to last, so they will be of value to the community after they leave. What's more, all of QMM's worker housing will be reused by local citizens. QMM's health-care facilities serve both employees and local contractors (and the contractors' families). Some of the staff doctors do significant amounts of volunteer work in the community. Those health-care facilities will also revert to community use when the mine closes. Meanwhile, the firm is conducting a strong HIV/AIDS education and prevention program, as economic growth often increases STDs in isolated communities.

Speaking of contractors, locals are hired and trained whenever possible. This builds the community's skills and workforce capacity while enhancing its economy, since most of the payroll remains in the community. The project is expected to generate about 1,700 jobs during construction (which peaked in 2007), and about 600 ongoing jobs during Phase One, which will last until about 2012. A professional training center is currently being built to improve local skills.

The ways in which QMM is improving "their" home community of Fort Dauphin are too numerous to list here, but include resurfacing their potholed dirt streets and helping with social infrastructure like schools and hospitals. They've sponsored microcredit programs to support local entrepreneurs. QMM has even restored ecosystems for the primary purpose of renewing the supply of a fast-disappearing species of reed that's traditionally used in local basketmaking—a terrific example of integrating the renewal of ecology and culture.

Building a Fort Dauphin Regional Renewal Engine?

You'll no doubt remember that the three key functions of a renewal engine are to create a shared vision of the community's future (and a strategy based on that vision), to stimulate a renewal culture, and to provide a forum for creating the partnerships needed to achieve that vision. Fort Dauphin had virtually no capacity for convening such an entity, nor did they have the planning expertise to follow through.

QMM has helped plug that gap by facilitating Madagascar's first integrated regional environmental and economic plan for the Anosy region that encompasses Fort Dauphin. They have engaged foreign-based NGOs in its design, primarily Birdlife International, the Missouri Botanical Garden, and the Royal Botanic Gardens, Kew.

QMM strongly engaged local communities in the plan's implementation. Malagasy students were heavily involved in conducting the numerous studies on biodiversity. In fact, this regional planning committee has been so successful that other regions of Madagascar have already copied it.

QMM has extensively engaged Malagasy government agencies at every level during the course of designing the Fort Dauphin project. They've tapped World Bank resources through the bank-funded Integrated Growth Poles Project that focuses on local infrastructure development. A Global Development Alliance with the U.S. Agency for International Development (USAID) has produced a $6 million matching fund for enhancing health, education, and the environment of the region for a three-year period.

Involving multiple international NGOs is indicative of the unusual transparency in this operation. The normal modus operandi of resource extraction firms in lesser-developed countries is to offer significant funding to a single, locally based conservation or human rights group, gaining effective control over them in the process. Such control isn't possible when so many prestigious, well-established institutions are engaged.

Another indication of QMM's commitment to doing this right is the fact that they've invested millions into Fort Dauphin before mining even begins. That takes a certain level of confidence that the relationship isn't going to unravel before the profit is realized over the next 40 years. Remember Tom Darden's desire to channel his billion-dollar brownfield fund only into communities with renewal engines? That was driven by a desire to avoid "entitlement issues," whereby the community changed its mind on a project after he had already spent millions on remediation.

QMM has far more at stake, so helping the city create a functional renewal engine would not just serve the public good: it would help ensure the success of their project. They've already made a good start in that direction: now it's a matter of reducing the company's involvement and helping the community play an even larger role.

The integrated regional economic and environmental plan went a long way toward building local visioning and planning capacity. With a little guidance in the design and maintenance of renewal engines, and some facilitation in the transfer of responsibility, Fort Dauphin could take over this function. That renewal capacity might be the greatest gift of all, since—properly designed—it would lead to continuous enhancement of their natural, built, and socioeconomic assets.

The Malagasy government does not have a tradition of turning over responsibility to NGOs, so a successful renewal engine in Fort Dauphin would help them better tap such resources, possibly leading to improved governance nationwide. The government also has little experience with public-private partnerships that truly serve the public good. A positive experience with QMM could greatly enhance the reception received by other rewealth companies, making partnerships easier and more productive. In fact, the current government has recently adopted the use of P3s as an important part of public policy.

QMM could become an ideal model, since QMM itself is a public-private partnership: the government of Madagascar owns a 20% share in the firm, and the mining property is leased by QMM from the government. QMM's total investment in the project is expected to reach $585 million. If a significant portion of that money is spent in a way that leaves the place in better condition, it could have a large and positive impact . . . and none too soon.

Given that most of the inspiration for this leading-edge partnership came from QMM, this experience could inspire the nation to demand more from companies. Madagascar is a country that has been left poorer by many of the corporate enterprises it has attracted over the past century. If, as a result of this project, the renewal rules were to be embedded in national policies—and in their requirements of foreign and national companies—the net positive impact could be nationwide and long lasting.

Reality check: this is a huge mine, and this is a mining company. They are in one of the world's great treasure troves of unique species, and they are working with desperately poor people. If this project attracts some criticism over the next few decades, I won't be surprised. Nor will I be surprised if some of that criticism is deserved.

But the point of this story isn't to document perfection. It's documenting what seems to be the first serious attempt by a mining company to incorporate rewealth—both natural and community—into their strategy for a new mine. My hat is off to the QMM team that has been leading this impressive effort, and to Pete Lowry of the Missouri Botanical Garden, who has long supported it. Wouldn't it be ironic if it were a mining company that helped a nation shift from a deconomy to a reconomy?

Model or Aberration?

> [Interviewer] "Many countries are cashing in on the mineral bonanza. Did Costa Rica shelve mining altogether?" [Rodríguez] "There is mining in Costa Rica, but it is for construction materials. It was decided metals mining would not continue until certain conditions were met. First, as long as the country did not have the technical and human conditions to guarantee metals mining would not have [negative] social and economic impacts, it should not keep granting concessions. Second, mining law establishes very few benefits for the government and the country; and until the law is changed, the country would not grant concessions. Third, until there is a guarantee that the mining companies understand and have the ability to mine in fragile ecosystems, the country is not going to grant any more licenses."
> —*EcoAméricas*, February 2008, interview with Carlos Manuel Rodríguez, a lawyer who was Costa Rica's environment minister from 2002 to 2006

I don't know if Rio Tinto intends to replicate the QMM model, or if its corporate leaders simply consider it aberrant behavior. If the parent company does adopt it as a model, and if they implement it well, I believe it could become their most effective competitive advantage. In the 20th century, community leaders expected mining operations to destroy their landscape, and they expected the military or mercenaries to suppress any opposition to the mine.

As the *EcoAméricas* interview (above) indicates, 21st century expectations are changing fast, especially as public-private partnering becomes the norm, along with rewealth. The confluence of these two trends means communities no longer expect to be shot at, or have their ecology destroyed. Truth be told, they weren't really all that fond of it in the 20th century, either.

Again, QMM should be seen not as the ideal, but as the *minimum* a community or region should expect from the winning bidder of a mining concession. Could this rewealth model be applied to the petroleum industry? No: while global recycling of mined materials and local mine land restoration can greatly offset the effects of mining, petroleum is a one-time-use product that contributes to global warming. We need to be re-sequestering carbon, not de-sequestering it.

Note: As this manuscript was being finalized, the world's largest mining company, Australian firm BHP Billiton, made a $147.4 billion bid for Rio Tinto. This unsolicited offer was a move the *Wall Street Journal* (in a November 9, 2007 article announcing their initial bid of $99.2 billion) characterized as a trend toward "consolidating control of the earth's natural resources." Even at the current bid (which will almost certainly be sweetened), the merger, if successful, would be the second largest in history. Hitting $180 billion would make it the largest ever.

The offer was rejected by Rio Tinto, but if they eventually reach agreement, it could be either good, neutral, or bad news. If Rio Tinto's "net positive impact" goal—and QMM's "rewealth mining" strategy—is adopted by the entire BHP Billiton organization, this could be very good news. If BHP allows them the autonomy to go their own way, it's neutral news. But if BHP's culture discourages such practices, it could result in the untimely demise of a very positive trend. Another possibility is that Rio Tinto might succeed with a "Pac Man" defense, whereby they turn around and gobble up their pursuer. I, for one, am holding my breath . . .

As I watch QMM's bulldozers creating the new port, and the roads leading to it, the conservationist within me wants to scream. Then I remember the alternative; that an ordinary mining operation could have come here.

Similar roads and port would be constructed, but without the restoration, without the mitigation, without the conservation, and without the commitment to leaving the community of Fort Dauphin better than it was found.

Then, instead of screaming, I want to sing QMM's praises, as I've done here.

Chapter 13

Two Stories of National Governments on Rewealth's Leading Edge

A South African agency restores water and ecosystems, lifting tens of thousands from poverty while giving them rewealth skills. An English agency helps revitalize 21 cities.

South Africa's Working for Water Program

South Africa has a rich history in the restoration of natural capital, both culturally and academically. Creating a national agency to support such work would be leading edge all by itself. But their flagship rewealth program, Working-for-Water (WfW), takes things a major step further by adding restoration of social capital into the objectives. This 12-year old nationwide program is a public-public partnership, and—like a renewal engine—they are shifting into the mode of spinning off public-private partnerships.

WfW integrates restoration of watersheds, removal of invasive species, and reintroduction of native species. To do so, it engages the unemployed in this work, so that they gain jobs and useful eco-restoration skills that will serve them for a lifetime. This visionary program was an outgrowth of the enthusiasm and optimism that followed the overthrow of the National Party and its apartheid system. (Somewhat reminiscent of the way Chattanooga discovered its ability to work together for renewal—both politically and racially—during their response to the air pollution crisis of the 1970s.)

South Africa, though endowed with many natural resources, suffers from two serious shortages—wood and water. Worse, attempts to build up one resource have made the other scarcer still. The crisis arose because South Africa's only extensive natural woodland—the *afromontane* forests on the southeastern Cape coast, and coastal forests on the east coast—could not supply the lumber and firewood needs of a fast-growing economy.

So, in the mid-19th century, South Africa became a global pioneer in establishing plantations of exotic trees—like eucalyptus, pines, and Australian acacias—on both public and private land. These nonnative trees were especially efficient at absorbing moisture from the soil and lowering the water table below the reach of both native trees and planted crops. As early as 1943, natural resource managers realized that the plantations were a threat to their water supply.

What's more, thousands of tree seedlings escaped the plantations and invaded natural grasslands and river courses and were overtaking entire landscapes. Something had to be done. That "something" was the removal of these exotic trees by a virtual army consisting of many thousands of citizens who toiled industriously to fell trees and defeat these foreign invaders. More than a million acres of invasive alien plants have now been cleared by WfW.

Despite employing tens of thousands, WfW has only been scratching the surface of the invasive plant problem. In fact, despite progress, they are losing the battle. So they've decided to bring in the heavy artillery, harnessing the power of capitalism via public-private partnering. They are negotiating a P3 that will harvest invasive plants for commercial use, hopefully including biofuels.

Here's how it works: WfW will estimate the average volume of harvestable biomass (for instance: 50 tons per hectare) in an area. WfW agrees to pay a private firm a certain amount for clearing a hectare, let's say 2,500 rand ($312 U.S.). WfW then pays the private partner the difference between the cost of clearing and the value of biomass harvested from the clearing. It is expected that the value of the biomass will seldom exceed the cost of clearing, as not only harvestable material should be cleared but *all* invasive plants. But it will at least help the program pay its own way.

WfW is planning to start with two pilot areas (totalling 103,000 hectares, and about 10 million tons of biomass), before expanding nationwide. They are specifying that private partners use labor-intensive (rather than mechanized) methods of harvesting, to maintain WfW's goal of providing employment to the greatest number of citizens.

WfW's new public-private partnering phase is hoping to move them into the production of biofuels; a logical step for a project that harvests millions of pounds of biomass annually. This is a welcome sign of intelligence in the biofuels industry. In the United States, intense lobbying by giant agribusinesses forced the industry down the one biofuel path that makes no economic, environmental, or social sense whatsoever: turning edible crops into fuel. The only time we can justify turning corn or soybeans into biofuels is when they are grown in contaminated soil as a remediation technique. More on this in a moment.

Such a "mixed-use" approach to both agricultural lands and wildlife habitat will likely be one of the waves of the future. It makes just as much sense as the mixed-use trend does in urban redevelopment. Single-use zoning no longer makes sense in most urban situations, and it's making less sense every day in farms and forests (witness wind turbines on farms, agroforestry, etc.). The trick is to come up with a combination—like the fuel-producing phytoremediation technique just mentioned—that leaves the soil and/or ecology in better condition with each passing year.

Biodiesel: No war required.
**—placard seen at January 27, 2007 Washington,
DC, protest against the administration's
proposed escalation of the Iraq occupation**

The biodiesel and ethanol produced from edible corn and soybeans could be seen as "dewealth biofuels." They deplete the soil, deplete fossil fuels, destabilize rural economies in lesser-developed countries, and use huge amounts of increasingly scarce fresh water. "Rewealth biofuels," on the other hand, comprise ethanol and biodiesel produced from one or more of these three strategies:

1. Cellulose, such as from agricultural waste or from invasive plant removal during ecological restoration projects.
2. Plants grown in the style of the Oilforest Program, whereby oil, sugar, and/or starch-producing species are planted on land that has been degraded by unsustainable agriculture or forest usage. Properly chosen, the energy-producing plants can stabilize and rebuild the soil. They also provide shade and wind protection for native plants that are later interspersed with the fuel plants to help restore the ecology and the watershed.
3. Food crops grown on polluted soil. This is the one way in which turning virgin carbohydrates into biofuels can make sense. Planting them on brownfields produces crops that can't be eaten, so the energy industry isn't competing with hungry families for the sugar or grains. The plants take up the contamination, and the root communities of microorganisms break down complex molecules of toxins, thus remediating the brownfield in a way

that is not just "free" (compared to expensive, energy-intensive remediation technologies), but actually generates income.

a. This is a slower cleanup process, and so is not as useful in urban settings, where the constraint crisis (and interest on borrowed redevelopment money) demands quick reuse of real estate. But there are many rural brownfields that don't have that time pressure.

b. There are also many chemical-laden conventional farms wanting to restore their soils and switch to organic techniques. But they need half a decade of transitional crops to detoxify the soils before getting certified as organic. This "fuelfields" technique can be a perfect bridge to an organic future, and will help provide other farmers with biofuels that can be processed locally (or at least regionally).

Working for Water has been accused, even by friendly critics, of "trying to save the world on a single budget." It is certainly one of the most ambitious programs of its kind. Indeed, there is nothing in the world quite like it, and it is widely seen as a model for combining ecological, economic, and social goals elsewhere.
—**Paddy Woodworth, "Working for Water in South Africa,"**
World Policy Journal, **Summer 2006**

What could WfW be doing better? Many things, as is to be expected of a program that pioneered an entirely new, comprehensive approach to renewing their natural and socioeconomic environments. For one thing, they fell into the same trap that hurt CALFED's efforts to restore the San Francisco Bay Delta (described in Chapter 5): too much money too soon.

This is a common dilemma for public-public partnerships, as noted earlier; state and national agencies sometimes combine large budgets to achieve a common goal. Programs that take years to fully fund will often spend those years doing research, which is far less capital intensive than the actual restoration. Public-public partnerships, on the other hand, can find themselves fully funded at the stroke of a pen. The often-heavy involvement of politicians in public-public partnerships also produces pressure for results in time for the next election, leading to action that gets ahead of research. This can produce some rapid renewal, but often at the expense of resilient renewal.

WfW might be the ultimate public-public partnership. Its primary partners are the Department of Water Affairs and Forestry, the Department of Agriculture, and the Department of Environmental Affairs and Tourism. But it's supported by the Department of Arts and Culture, Department of Defence, Department of Education, Department of Health, Department of Justice and Constitutional Development, Department of Labour, Department of Land Affairs, Department of Public Works, Department of Science and Technology, Department of Trade and Industry, and the National Treasury. Also involved are provincial departments of agriculture, departments of conservation and the environment, along with various other provincial and local government agencies.

Even the Department of Defense is involved, helping veterans find training and employment through their Military Veterans Association Project VUSELELA. They are making sure invasives are removed from military bases and from the land surrounding them.

With a vast partnership network like that, it's not surprising that WfW moved quickly . . . maybe too quickly. For instance, record keeping was atrocious in the early years. Another early problem was management that mirrored the white male model of South Africa's bad old days. In 1995, WfW had a management committee comprising 21 people; 20 of them were white and 20 were men. As of 2003, the committee comprised 26 people, of whom 20 were black and 14 were women.

But scientific problems outweighed the bureaucratic weaknesses. Although it was widely assumed that the invasive plants were sucking up water at the expense of both native plants and agriculture, there was no real research behind the removal program. One result was that the program focused too heavily on renewal, and not enough on active restoration of native plants. As a result, many of the areas that were cleared became reinfested by exotics, sometimes to a worse degree than before.

In his excellent World Policy Journal article on WfW (quoted earlier), Paddy Woodworth recounts this conversation with a WfW field worker, and comments on it: "'Did you think that fighting in the liberation war would lead you to this kind of work?' I asked. 'We did not think we would live to do any kind of work at all,' one responded laconically. 'The work is not bad, it is better than staying at home,' said another. 'We have learned about these natural enemies, we can advise our neighbors not to plant them. But we need proper management, we need to get paid on time.' This is a chronic complaint among Working for Water workers, and remains a shortcoming in the program's operations."

Woodworth also quoted ecologist Patricia Holmes as saying, "It all started in such a rush that there was no strategic ecological plan. They had to spend money immediately, and this was ecologically disastrous. Instead of focusing on the areas worst-affected by aliens, and working systematically, they spread the program far too wide across the country for political reasons." Holmes acknowledges that the program today has been significantly improved.

Should they have delayed action, then? Some don't think so. Christo Marais was involved in WfW's creation, and says they had a very brief window of opportunity. If they had postponed for five years or so while the research was done, he says they would have lost both their budget and their political support. Woodworth quoted botanist Mike Powell as agreeing with Christo: "Kadar Asmal and Guy Preston had the vision to start it up in tough times; it would have been much easier for that government to build more houses, for example. For all its problems, we have to keep at it; it would be suicide to let it go now."

The good news is that WfW management is very open about the areas in which the program could be improved, so there's every likelihood it will continue to improve over time. Management challenges aside, WfW employed 32,000 people on a budget of $66 million in 2005. Their distinctive yellow-and-green trademark T-shirt can today be seen in most deprived townships.

Over its 12-year existence, this government-sponsored program has invested $450 million in renewing their country, employing and training many tens of thousands of impoverished people in the process. They've also set up childcare facilities, as well as education programs on both AIDS and avoiding unwanted pregnancies.

James Aronson says, "Working for Water is restoring social capital while restoring natural capital. The two are probably inseparable in a lesser-developed setting like South Africa. In fact, they should probably be inseparable everywhere." Not surprisingly, there's a link between the RNC Alliance and WfW. James Blignaut at Pretoria University, for instance, was an economic advisor on WfW's research advisory panel from 2002 to 2006, and maintains a close relationship.

What are the keys to their future success? Adoption of payments for ecosystem services is one key, but that's a need shared by conservation and restoration programs worldwide. Another key would be better policy support from the government. Simply embedding the renewal rules in decision making would help, but specific issues need to be addressed as well.

One of those is to establish a policy and legislative framework for the removal of invasive species. You would think that, after all these years, such policies would already be in place. But infighting among agricultural, water, and conservation agencies over the proper approach to invasives has prevented the implementation of pertinent policies or legislation.

Partnering for Progress

Christo Marais was a member of the partnership that came up with the WfW idea. He currently serves as their head of operations support. They now have partnerships with the World Wildlife Fund (South Africa), the South African Pet Traders Association, the South African Nursery Association, and with a company called Planet Wise that makes products out of invasive species.

> *What's nice about a partnership with a university is that—when we work with a student during their post-graduate studies—we can tell them about upcoming staff positions, and they will often get the post. Three of these former grad students are now working for us. This gives us staff that's ready to hit the ground running, and reinforces our academic partnerships.*
>
> **—Christo Marais, WfW (conversation with author)**

Academic/scientific partnerships have been formed with the University of Rhodes, University of Stellenbosch, University of Cape Town, Nelson Mandela Metropolitan University, Wits University, University of Pretoria, University of Western Cape, University of KwaZulu-Natal, and Fort Hare University.

Professor Kader Asmal, Minister Water Affairs and Forestry, was the primary political champion in the early days. Guy Preston is a prominent and highly respected scientist who was a cofounder of WfW. He's currently WfW's National Programme leader. Jay Naidoo was the minster responsible for the Reconstruction and Development Program in the cabinet of former president Nelson Mandela. He allocated the first 25 million rand from that program to the Department of Water Affairs and Forestry (DWAF) for WfW after being approached by his friend, the then-Minister of DWAF.

WfW has been so successful that it has several offshoots, such as Working for Wetlands, Working on Fire, and Working for Woodlands. Working on Fire is a public-private partnership with the Forest Fires Association. Its purpose is to enhance the sustainability and protection of life, livelihoods, ecosystem services, and natural processes through integrated fire management, in order to contribute to economic empowerment, skills development, social equity, and accelerated service delivery.

Together, these programs are providing thousands of jobs, are actively restoring desertified lands, are reversing loss of biodiversity, and are improving the socioeconomic well-being of the entire nation.

English Partnerships: A National Rewealth Model for the World?

You've already read how Chattanooga and Bilbao pioneered the renewal engine model. England is the first country to create a national agency that actually helps cities create something very similar to renewal engines. Rather than call this agency "English Regeneration"—which would be a perfectly good name—they chose to focus on the single most important process that makes regeneration happen at a rapid pace, and on a large scale: partnering. So the agency is called English Partnerships. (Note: English Partnerships shouldn't be confused with Partnerships UK. The latter is a separate organization created by the national treasury in 2000 to foster P3s for infrastructure renewal.)

As the birthplace of the industrial revolution, it shouldn't be surprising that the British are leading the world in government support of urban regeneration. (Note to U.S. readers: most of the English-speaking world outside of the Americas prefers "regeneration" to "revitalization" or "redevelopment.") After all, the United Kingdom has been creating restorable assets like brownfields and derelict industrial buildings longer than anyone.

> *England is small and densely populated. We need to use and reuse our limited land wisely. That's why the government should be proud of its achievement in increasing the proportion of new homes built on brownfield, or previously developed land from 56% when it came to power to 77% now. . . . Unfortunately, new national planning guidance . . . [is] likely to allocate more greenfield land for housing, leading to urban sprawl and increased road traffic. . . . there is far more brownfield land suitable for development than has previously been thought. . . . [the cities of] Plymouth and Gravesham, [used] brownfield development to revitalise urban areas while protecting surrounding countryside.*
>
> —Shawn Spiers, *The Guardian,* March 1, 2007

As the above excerpt from *The Guardian* illustrates, the British actually track the proportion of housing built on brownfields versus greenfields. In a world suffering rampant reblindness, that alone is enough to put the UK government on the leading edge: measuring and reporting is half the battle. But they have gone far beyond.

English Partnerships (EP) has a national brownfields program, as does the United States. The U.S. brownfields program is housed in the EPA, which is discouraged from becoming too involved in community renewal. A rigid Congress wants to keep them in the "public and environmental health" silo, no matter how logical the connection between community renewal and public health.

For instance, the U.S. EPA created a visionary land revitalization initiative to better integrate their numerous cleanup and reuse programs. But many proposed aspects of that program were slapped down by Congress. They were told that economic revitalization wasn't part of their charge, and to stay focused on human health.

The British, on the other hand, house their brownfields program in English Partnerships, an agency whose mission is a natural fit. EP's mission is community regeneration, which naturally encompasses all three renewal rules, and helps prevent silo thinking. English Partnerships is approaching the challenge at three scales: (1) helping to create *national* policies and legislation that support brownfields remediation and reuse, (2) helping to promote *regional* renewal strategies, such as through regional brownfield pilot programs, and (3) helping local leaders create grass-roots, *community*-led brownfields initiatives.

> *[the brownfield-first approach to planning] has acted as a catalyst, turning round the fortunes of run down areas and underpinning the revival of town and city centres.*
> —**Lord Richard Rogers, British planner and architect, in the foreword to *Untapped Potential*, a 2007 report by the Campaign to Protect Rural England**

English Partnerships services include:

- Forming joint ventures with private partners;
- Using their partnering expertise to broker agreements in communities that are doing their first P3s;
- Facilitating the master planning of projects in which public-public partnerships prepare a redevelopment site, and private companies (or public-private partnerships) do the subsequent redevelopment;
- Investing in projects that are important to the community (where market mechanisms have failed), and which might fail at critical points when short-term returns aren't sufficient to enable complete reliance on private financing. This is especially important when dealing with brownfield sites, affordable housing, and regional infrastructure issues;
- Providing technical, legal, planning, and financing advice, information, and best practices to communities that haven't developed sufficient internal expertise in those areas.

EP has many excellent services and initiatives, but the one I want to feature here is their Urban Regeneration Company (URC) program. EP has been evolving under a variety of names for almost a quarter of a century. Its current form was created in 1999, via a merger of the Urban Regeneration Agency and The Commission for the New Towns. It was also in 1999—as the global reconomic shift began in earnest—that they created the program that put them on the leading edge.

EP's URC program was created at the recommendation of a 1999 Urban Task Force Report chaired by Lord Richard Rogers. It didn't surprise me when I learned of Lord Roger's involvement: his presentation preceded mine at the European Property Italian Conference (EPIC) in October of 2003 in Rome. It perfectly set the stage for my talk, being loaded with "re" concepts, integrative designs, and engaged strategies.

Lord Rogers is one of the world's leading architects, so he was speaking from deep on-the-ground knowledge of what works. The conference organizers thus created a perfect convergence of practice and theory. (Note to meeting planners: it often works better to present theory before practice, so it might have been better for my talk to prepare the audience for Lord Rogers'. This was proved at the 2006 Gaining Ground conference in Victoria, British Columbia, when visionary redeveloper John Knott's presentation came after mine to great effect [he brought the crowd to its feet]).

> Uniting public- and private-sector partners, URCs are independent companies established by the relevant Local Authority and Regional Development Agency, working alongside English Partnerships and other local stakeholders including employers, amenity groups and community representatives. Their principal aim is to engage the private sector in a sustainable regeneration strategy, working within the context of a wider Strategic Regeneration Framework or masterplan which takes full account of the problems and opportunities for the whole area.
>
> **—from the English Partnerships website**

All three renewal rules—rewealth, integration, and engagement—are plainly obvious in even a cursory reading of the above URC definition. "Sustainable regeneration"—another way of saying "resilient"—can't help but take an integrative approach to renewing a community's natural, built, and socioeconomic assets.

What's more, all three renewal processes—visioning, culturing, and partnering—are encompassed by that definition. A visioning process can be assumed from the reference to strategies and master plans, since you can't strategize or plan effectively without a guiding vision. Culturing (the policy part, anyway) is implied by the fact that local, regional, and national agencies (EP) are among the partners. Creating a renewal culture is more than just public policy, but without rewealth-friendly governance, renewal is an uphill struggle.

The primary stated purpose for creating an Urban Regeneration Company is to form project partnerships. EP says "URCs have no statutory powers; they work through the powers of their funding partners to deliver the masterplan, champion key project priorities, and encourage private sector investment in their area."

EP has helped create 20 URCs so far, and more are in the works. EP is usually a permanent board member and funding partner. Funding is usually shared one-third each by EP, the relevant regional development authority, and the relevant local government agency. Current URCs can be found in Blackpool, Bradford, Camborne/Pool/Redruth, Great Yarmouth/Lowestoft, Derby, Gloucester, Hull, Leicester, Liverpool, East Manchester, North Northants, Peterborough, Salford, West Bromwich/Sandwell, Southend, Sunderland, Swindon, Tees Valley, Walsall, and West Cumbria/Furness. More seem to be on the way, such as in Wolverhampton.

Together, they are on track to attract over $40 billion in private rewealth investment, produce at least 150,000 jobs, and create some 66,000 housing units. Their combined domain is over 750,000 acres; no small area in a country the size of North Carolina.

But it's not just a matter of volume: the URC program is fostering a tremendous amount of creativity and learning, as well. One of the primary challenges any community renewal program has is assembling contiguous parcels of land in the right location to do redevelopment projects on an effective scale. This is one of the major roles played by English Partnerships. As a national government agency, they have the power of eminent domain—called compulsory purchase order (CPO) in Britain—but that's only used as a last resort.

As implied by their name, EP's goal is to partner with private interests, not alienate them. But almost every community has mothballed property held by absentee speculators. Almost every place has obstinate, greedy, and/or dyspeptic property owners who care not the least amount about the community as a whole. When such owners are encountered, and all attempts to work out a win-win solution are rebuffed, brute legal force is sometimes necessary to protect the public good.

In Leicester, for instance, they avoided excessive use of eminent domain (compulsory purchase) by using collaborative partnering similar to the "land readjustment" approach you read about in Chapter 5 (the British less pretentiously call it "swapping"). This greatly reduces the pain and alienation associated with the brute force techniques that are the norm in the United States.

So, what we have here is (almost) a national renewal engine manufacturing plant. EP itself is (sort of) a national renewal engine, fostering community renewal engines across the countryside. I say "sort of," because they don't actually create P3s that address national issues. And I said "almost" because URC's aren't really renewal engines, as we've defined them: Functionally, they are close, but there are critical differences.

For one thing, URCs are focused on the inner city, rather than the entire community. Their primarily focus is on physical issues—such as infrastructure and buildings—rather than on natural or socioeconomic issues. That's not to say they don't address the natural environment at all. For instance, they are helping to address watershed and flooding issues by promoting the use of green (planted) roofs and porous (permeable) paving. What's more, EP also helps the national government deliver other programs—such as the Sustainable Communities Plan—that can work with URCs to address regional scopes and environmental issues.

Another key difference from the ideal renewal engine model is that URCs aren't designed to be permanent: government guidelines suggest a 10- to 15-year lifespan. This is long enough to get things well underway, but resilient renewal demands that a permanent renewal engine be created when the URC expires. This will allow the community to periodically update its vision, and continue to create partnerships that are vetted according to that vision.

The good news is that the United Kingdom has not only recognized this need, but has already addressed it. In 2006, the national government, with EP's assistance, announced that they would start promoting the creation of City Development Companies (CDCs). This is another form of nonprofit public-private regeneration vehicle. It differs from the URC in that it encompasses the entire city, and even the region. It doesn't have a defined lifespan, and it addresses all of the issues needed to fully revitalize a community, including those of a social and environmental nature.

Here's an excerpt from the EP website that shows how well attuned they are to the need for permanence: "It may be appropriate that they [URCs] come to a natural end or [be] handed over to a successor organisation with different or wider remits. Sheffield One evolved into Creative Sheffield [www.creativesheffield.co.uk] on the 31st March 2007. Catalyst Corby merged with the Northamptonshire Growth Partnership last year to form North Northants Development Company.

Liverpool Vision also is considering a succession vehicle due to be launched in April 2008."

The newness of the CDC program places the United Kingdom in a position to move even further out on the leading edge of the reconomy. If they were to provide a template for CDCs that embraced all 12 sectors of restorable assets, all three renewal rules, and all three renewal processes, they would be tapping the experiences learned at the expense of much time, cost, and pain by renewal engine pioneers such as Chattanooga and Bilbao.

One cautionary note: when I say "permanent," I'm referring to the renewal engine function, not necessarily any particular entity. Human institutions—like humans themselves—can get tired, overweight, lazy, feeble, and corrupted over time. Just as infrastructure eventually needs to be replaced, rather than renewed, so too might your renewal engine need to be terminated and re-created.

A medical metaphor might help understand the difference between a URC and a CDC: a URC is like the surgery needed to save a mortally ill patient's life. It corrects the physical wounds—brownfields, WIHNARs, vacant buildings—needed to revive a city's heartbeat. A CDC can also perform surgery, but provides the ongoing rehabilitation—and lifestyle counseling—needed to restore and maintain the patient's long-term health. To put it more succinctly, the URC is primarily about rapid renewal, whereas the CDC is more about resilient renewal.

Who knows? Maybe the British have it right. When you've been run over by a truck, you need an emergency room. But when you want to live a long and healthy life, it's generally a good idea to stay as far away from hospitals, drugs, and surgery as possible. That's when you need to be working with someone—like a doctor of classical Chinese or Indian medicines—who focuses on helping the body heal itself via herbs, diet, lifestyle, exercise, and nontraumatic, nontoxic treatments (like acupuncture or massage). Enhancing the body's renewal capacity, one might say.

I would guess that the British URC model is the right one for cities that are in extremis, needing drastic and immediate alterations to their physical being. Those that are merely not feeling well—maybe in great pain, but not spraying blood all over the place—can probably create their permanent renewal engine (like a CDC) as their first step, without starting with a temporary URC-like entity.

". . . the U.K. is still be far and away the strongest [PPP market]" . . . "there are now good PPP opportunities in France" . . . "PPP's are spreading east and south across Europe" . . . "Germany is a real latecomer to PPP-type projects [but]

it has started to grow"... *"the U.S. PPP market is 'hindered by lack of knowledge and history."*

—quotes from the senior executives of five of the world's largest engineering firms, from the August 30, 2007 issue of *Engineering News Record*

Britain leads the world in public-private partnering by almost any measure of both quality and quantity. Why is the United Kingdom so far ahead of the world in partnering, especially when you consider the rocky start of P3s in England (mentioned in the next chapter)? Why are those partnerships doing such a great job of revitalizing so many of England's depressed former industrial cities? English Partnerships has to take much of the credit.

One of the strengths of the UK program is that each city can create the CDC they need: they aren't forced into a rigid program. Each is different, so some are working better than others. At the time the program was created, there were no rigorous criteria for renewal engines—as have been introduced in these pages—so, like everyone else, the British created their program from scratch. EP would be the first to admit there's room for improvement, but by all accounts, they've done a phenomenal job.

We aren't even treading water. We aren't even maintaining a deteriorating infrastructure. We are deteriorating toward third-world status while our competitors around the world are leaping ahead with major investments in transit and roads, bridges and highways, ports and waterways—while we fall behind.

—Rep. Peter DeFazio (D-Ore.), Chair of the House Highways Subcommittee, addressing the U.S. House of Representatives, March 12, 2008

If there's a glaring hole in the URC and CDC programs, it's that they seem to be geared toward fairly large communities. A more scalable program that could be applied by virtually any rural community seeking regeneration would be useful.

England has a stronger cultural connection with Canada than it does with the United States. This might explain why the quality (not the quantity) of partnering is more advanced in Ontario than in Texas, which is the hotbed of P3s in the United States. One reason it's not surprising to see the English ahead of the United States and Canada is that Europeans in general don't need the three renewal rules pounded into their heads as much as we do in the New World. They were restoring historic buildings, renewing infrastructure, and reusing infill properties centuries before any of the modern-day countries of the Americas existed. They are also stronger in engagement, never having fallen into the overly individualist mentality of the United States, where private property rights usually trump the public good.

The one renewal rule they *do* need to embrace more firmly is integration: renewing the natural, built, and socioeconomic environments in a more systemic manner. They could achieve so much more with current budgets if they were to tap the efficiencies and synergies inherent to integrative strategies. But that's a global governance deficiency, not a European one.

Thoughts on Establishing National Renewal Programs

China and India have been building and restoring cities far longer than Europe, so one might wonder why restoration isn't better entrenched in their policies. China is still recovering from the national trauma inflicted by Mao and his envy of the West. Most things traditionally Chinese were reviled, and this disrespect of their glorious past continues to this day, as fast-growing cities like Shanghai demolish their heritage at a horrific rate.

China is certainly not alone in confusing "standard of living" with "quality of life," but they will need to come to that understanding very soon if they are to avoid national catastrophe. Once again: pursuing an increase in either will boost one's economy in the short term (rapid renewal). However, strategies based on boosting standard of living tend to undermine long-term economic health, while strategies based on enhancing quality of life lay the foundation for resilient renewal.

India tends to have more respect for their heritage than does China, but that certainly hasn't stopped shortsighted or corrupt city officials from destroying it for a quick rupee. The city of Kolkata (formerly Calcutta) has an urban regeneration plan that seems remarkably comprehensive, but repeated calls and emails to the Kolkata Municipal Corporation (which developed the plan) went unanswered, so I've got no idea how "real" the initiative might be.

The United States certainly doesn't have anything even remotely like EP, although there have been literally hundreds of community and neighborhood revitalization programs created within the various federal agencies over the years. In fact, during some meetings at HUD a few years back, I uncovered five community revitalization initiatives within the same agency, but none of them seemed to be aware of the others.

In the United States, the president has a tool called an executive order, with which he can affect the behavior of federal agencies simply by telling them to do (or stop doing) something. An example is Preserve America, an executive order from George W. Bush (actually announced and championed by first lady Laura Bush), which required all federal agencies to restore and use their historic buildings in a way that contributed to the revitalization of the community in which they were located.

The dream would be to craft an executive order that requires all federal agencies to renew all of their built, natural, and socioeconomic assets in an integrated way that contributes to community or regional economic growth. The renewal rules (and checklists derived from them) are broad enough to allow any agency to figure out a way to comply. Ideally, renewal rule-based metrics would evolve, allowing White House staff to evaluate compliance.

Federal agencies are well versed in going through the motions. They know that most executive orders are for public consumption, and will soon be forgotten. Only if an administration rigorously measures compliance and puts some teeth into enforcement will agencies go beyond lip service. That lip service usually consists of having a workshop to discuss the new executive order, and assigning some flunky to write an action plan detailing how they intend to comply with it. It usually ends there. Restoring the United States, and the world, deserves better.

Can renewal engines work in nations that are even more politically repressed? If their economy is in the toilet and their populace is rebelling—and if they are convinced that a renewal engine will help remedy the situation—a dictator may make a sincere effort. It probably won't be anywhere near ideal, but once the renewal rules are embedded in the nation's thinking and decision making, it might set them on an evolutionary path to better governance. Stranger things have happened.

To advance the concept of national renewal engines, renewal engines should be applied to island nations as soon as possible. Islands function as windows on the planetary future, thanks to their geographic constraints. The world needs some national rewealth success stories. On island nations, rewealth strategies begun at the community level can scale up very quickly to the national level.

Rewealth is where the growth is, and where it will remain, so that's where public and private leaders desiring economic expansion should look. The important thing is tagging economic activities properly. Tagging helps us determine when "de" activities are *really* necessary. It helps us avoid doing dewealth by default, because of bureaucratic inertia or outdated policies and budgets.

As a global civilization, humanity is like a 40-year-old who hasn't yet been potty trained. We still foul ourselves and our homes (along with our water, air, and soil). Ten thousand years ago, if a storyteller had described a tribe that urinated and defecated in clean drinking water, as we do today, anyone listening would have called them ignorant savages. The sustainability movement is humanity's long-overdue toilet training. But rewealth is how we earn a living cleaning up the mess.

When rewealth policies and legislation take hold, great things can happen. Japan, for instance, has more dams, drained wetlands, and straightened rivers per capita than any other nation. In 2003, a national law was passed that requires many of the dams to be torn down, many of the rivers unstraightened, and many of the wetlands to be reflooded.

It will be interesting to observe the impacts on nature and the rural economies as Japan's hyperengineered landscape is "re"engineered to its earlier form in coming decades. As their physical landscape is restored, so might their economic landscape be. Not so long ago, Japan lead the world economy toward a greater appreciation of quality products and processes. Might it once again lead the world economy in a new direction? They are behind the rewealth curve now, but they've proven their ability to come from behind.

A Renewal Engine for Earth?

The only missing factor in that rosy scenario is that we'll need a planetary renewal engine. Just as EP creates renewal engines for communities, we need a UN-level renewal engine—"Earth Partnerships," or "Global Partnerships"—to help countries create their own "Russian Partnerships," "Chilean Partnerships," "Chinese Partnerships," and so on.

The planet needs a renewal engine to form renewal partnerships among nations. Every nation needs a renewal engine (like EP) to form regional partnerships. And almost every community needs a renewal engine to form local partnerships.

If every country had an EP equivalent, that $100 trillion global inventory of restorable assets would start shrinking at a breathtaking rate, and we'd be well on our way to rapid, resilient renewal on a planetary scale.

Granted, the partnering model will need to be adapted to differing cultures, legal frameworks, and political systems, but that's just a matter of tinkering. Also, despite the success EP has had, it would be better to have a re-word in the names to make their purpose clear, such as "Turkish Regeneration Partnerships," but we can wordsmith later.

Spawning national regeneration partnership programs wouldn't be the only function of such a global program though. More urgent is the need for a program that can address those renewal objectives that can't be addressed within national boundaries. Oceans and climate are the two most obvious.

A planetary program might emerge spontaneously from a program to build national renewal engines, which would—in turn—help build local renewal engines. Thus do we restore the earth, one community at a time.

Chapter 14

Two Stories of Leading-Edge Rewealth Organizations in Canada

A national rewealth magazine goes global. An international academic rewealth network grows in Toronto.

Canadian Rewealth Leadership

Before launching into the two main stories of this chapter, let me provide a few general insights into why I've chosen to feature Canada.

The province of Ontario, Canada (which is twice the size of Texas) is well on its way toward the leading edge of restorative development. They actually have a government agency with a "re" word in its name: the Ministry of Public Infrastructure Renewal (PIR).

A week after my November 2007 workshop at Nova Scotia Community College in Halifax, the province of Nova Scotia followed Ontario's lead and announced the creation of a Ministry of Transportation and Infrastructure Renewal.

One might find a few isolated instances of federal government programs or agencies that reflect the de/re shift in their names—such as the U.S. EPA's Land Revitalization Office—but it's exceedingly rare. Nonprofits arise more quickly than government agencies, so there's no shortage of rewealth-oriented organizations with names like, for example, the British Urban Regeneration Association.

The Ontario Ministry of Public Infrastructure Renewal recently published their Growth Plan for the Greater Golden Horseshoe. The Golden Horseshoe is a large zone around the western end of Lake Ontario that's a combination of farmland and heavy industry. The plan *mandates* at least 40% rewealth (not the term they use) for communities, and it will be part of the "Places to Grow Plan" being assembled for the entire province. PIR's Growth Plan for the Greater Golden Horseshoe was the first plan from outside the United States to win the American Planning Association's (APA) prestigious 2007 Daniel Burnham Award.

Now, a 40% minimum "re" focus might not sound like much, when you consider that most built-out older cities (such as Toronto) are already at 70% redevelopment or higher. But imbedding a 40% minimum into policy will double or triple the current rate of densification ("intensification" in Canada) of the more rural and/or younger communities.

Most towns and cities near Toronto are still about 80% based on dewealth (sprawl), so this will instantly reduce the sprawl rate by 25% (from 80% to 60%). Further from Toronto, the plan will make an even greater difference. Many formerly rural communities are now becoming bedroom communities, with the result that 90% or more of their growth is based on destroying farms and forests.

But the leading edge aspect of the PIR's plan isn't the numbers: it's the formal codification of the shift from dewealth to rewealth. Assigning numbers to "de" and "re" makes all the difference. It changes the plan from a fluffy "smart" or "sustainable" strategy that's open to interpretation, to a rewealth strategy that's enforceable.

Announcement of the Places to Grow plan has already spurred real estate speculators to purchase downtown properties, in anticipation of greatly increased demand for infill. The challenge, of course, is to prevent speculators from locking-up assets the communities need to renew. If speculators are holding onto many of the properties in anticipation of future revitalization, that revitalization might never happen.

PIR is in the process of establishing a line around currently developed areas, so communities will be able to ascertain exactly what's considered sprawl, and what's considered intensification/redevelopment. The greenbelt around Toronto, for instance, encompasses some 1.8 million acres (almost twice the size of Rhode Island), so there was nothing draconian about it.

The plan identifies 25 growth centers, which are the 25 largest urban areas in the Greater Golden Horseshoe. These are where new transit links and other public amenities will be established; sort of a grand version of Arlington County, Virginia's highly successful transit-oriented development (actually, redevelopment) strategy. Another integrative aspect of PIR's policies focuses on restoring key green space and restoring ecosystem linkages to provide wildlife corridors (although the plan itself presently focuses mostly on conservation).

The growth plan was the product of five years of public engagement. This approach paid off in the form of a very high level of instant buy-in from communities when it was rolled out. That engagement process included at least 24 "town hall meetings," plus many panels and stakeholder workshops (which usually put 75 stakeholders in room for a day with a facilitator). There were hundreds of "one-on-one" stakeholder meetings, such as with the leaders of environmental groups.

Canadian communities are more oriented toward growth planning by city officials. U.S. cities tend to be more dependent on downtown redevelopment corporations, community development corporations (CDCs), and the like. But the move toward greater use of private partnering is well underway in Canada. The United States is also moving toward more private partnering, but planning seems to be moving in the opposite direction, toward greater public-sector engagement. This is mostly a reaction against an excessive laissez-faire, developer-driven approach that has rendered so many U.S. cities, ugly, devitalized, and dysfunctional.

If the Greater Golden Horseshoe growth plan has a weakness, it's in implementation. PIR is expert in the use of P3s (what Canadians refer to as AFP: alternative finance and procurement) for infrastructure renewal, but there's nothing in the plan for passing along that expertise to the communities. And the communities need more than partnering expertise; they also need the capacity to incorporate this mandated shift toward rewealth into their culture. They need a shared vision of their future that is compatible with the regional growth plan. In other words, they need the *re*solution. If PIR were to train each of those 25 growth centers in the process of creating their own renewal engine, the chances of this plan's success would be greatly heightened.

Another weakness is that tax increment financing hasn't yet caught on in Canada. Rewealth champions there are trying mightily to increase awareness of the value of TIF, but government leaders seem to fear it. Some complain they are more conservative than their U.S. counterparts; less open to innovation. Others opine that it has to do with innate optimism. Borrowing against a revitalized future is an act of optimism. TIF could legitimately be seen as irresponsible gambling when used without reasonable expectation of success. But a well-designed TIF is the essence of responsible, forward-looking government leadership when a rigorous process for revitalization is in hand.

In November of 2005, the province announced the creation of the Ontario Infrastructure Projects Corporation (OIP), a government agency specifically formed to create public-private partnerships to manage their infrastructure renewal deficit, estimated to exceed $100,000,000,000. Ontario not only has a "re" agency, they've created "re" financing instruments. For instance, OIP is also charged with overseeing the Ontario Strategic Infrastructure Financing Authority (OSIFA). OSIFA offers long-term, low-interest loans to communities, universities, and public partners for infrastructure renewal. But OSIFA doesn't distribute tax-derived funding: the money it lends comes from selling Infrastructure Renewal Bonds (IRBs).

During a panel following my keynote at the 2006 Canadian Brownfields Conference, Tom Hodgins, Commissioner of Development Services for the city of Oshawa, Ontario, remarked: "My title is 'Commissioner of Development Services,' but it would not be unreasonable to refer to me as the 'Commissioner of Redevelopment Services', given that much of the Department's work is focused on redevelopment and restoration such as downtown redevelopment, brownfield restoration and redevelopment, harbour redevelopment, watercourse restoration, road restoration, etc." He indicated that the "re" work is where the growth is, making such a title change almost inevitable in the future.

Canada Sees the Future of Public-Private Partnerships

> *This project is part of a $33 billion investment Canada's government is making over a period of seven years, called Building Canada. The program stipulates that any major project, in the range of $25 million and more, must consider a partnership with the private sector. Minister of Transportation and Communities Lawrence Cannon said in the coming years, many more infrastructure projects will involve P3s. "Never has the winning combination of transportation and public-private partnerships been more promising than today"…A look at Quebec's newest projects suggests Canon is right. Coming a little late to the game, Quebec has embraced partnerships in recent years.*
>
> —Jason Magder, **"Making a Connection,"**
> January/February issue of *ReNew Canada*

Note the name of Minister Cannon's agency in the above quote: "Transportation and Communities." This is the sort of silo-breaking mentality that is fast putting Canada on the leading edge of the rewealth trend, not so much in quantity as in quality. They actually govern communities and their infrastructure together: what a concept. But, as that quote attests, they are also taking steps to boost the quantity, by requiring communities to at least consider doing a public-private partnership on larger projects (usually infrastructure renewal).

Jane Peatch, the executive director of the Canadian Council for Public-Private Partnerships (CCPPP) provided us a formal definition of P3 in Chapter 5. In that same email to me, she was careful to specify that the CCPPP does *not* consider privatization to be a form of P3. This stands in direct contrast to the United States, where P3 leaders still seem to be hanging on to the old model, and tend to clam-up when asked about privatization.

Peatch says: "What is clearly NOT used in a Canadian context is 'privatization', unless we clearly mean the sale of all assets to the private sector and only a regulatory relationship with government. The CCPPP Council is not a promoter of 'privatization' as such and normally our upper limit of separation from a government entity would be a concession arrangement which, at the end of the long term relationship, would be returned to the public sector."

Given the growing public outcry against privatization that has been building around the world in the past decade or two, Ms. Peatch has good reasons to be leery of having her group (CCPPP) associated with it. Entire NGOs have been formed and books written decrying the practice of selling public assets to private interests, such as mentioned in Chapter 6.

Ontario's term, AFP (the "new P3," as some pundits call it), came along much later than the United Kingdom's private finance initiative (PFI), so you might be wondering why Ontario chose to create yet another euphemism for P3, rather than just adopting the British one. The primary reason is that the PFI program got off to a very rocky start in the United Kingdom. In their case, it wasn't so much the privatization issue as it was a quality issue.

The British launched the PFI in the mid-1990s to investigate and test a variety of new procurement methods that engaged the private sector in designing, building, financing, and operating public buildings. It was first tried on a series of schools and hospitals, and the designs were so bad that public officials were reportedly embarrassed to stand in front of them for the ribbon-cutting ceremonies.

The Ontario Association of Architects (OAA) has been a leader in studying the potential impacts of P3s in Canada since 2002. They've published an excellent *P3 Primer* that's freely downloadable from their Web site. Regarding the initial UK PFI (P3) fiasco, OAA's Web site quotes one unnamed British architect as saying, "PFI has produced buildings that are a national disgrace!," and another as complaining "The first PFI schools were little better than agricultural sheds with windows."

This problem had been addressed by the time Britain's PFI program entered its second phase in 2001. Design quality had been added to the selection criteria (apparently, the original criteria were almost solely focused on cost), even for small projects like schools, and the quality problem was largely solved. The OAA article quoted an unnamed UK builder as saying, "To be successful at PFI, you better have a good architect! The Consortium won't even get short-listed if the design isn't exemplary."

But the damage had already been done. The UK public's trust in the private sector's desire and ability to serve the public good was undermined, and their shiny new euphemism was tarnished. Thus, Ontario felt it would be better to design a fresh new wrapper when they decided to formally take the P3 plunge. They were still using the P3 terminology when they first announced the use of P3s to renew

Ontario's infrastructure in 2002. They had shifted to "AFP" by the time they announced the $12 billion first phase of a 20-year public building (health care, education, justice) renewal initiative in 2005.

> *Public-private partnerships are quietly taking off, with billions of dollars already at work, and the limit is nowhere in sight. . . . it's important that the public and private sectors pool their resources and build on the advantages and skills that each can bring to the table. AFP [Alternative Financing and Procurement] does not mean privatization. . . . Benefits of AFP include accelerated investments in infrastructure; transferred risk of cost overruns and missed deadlines (to the partner); enhanced expertise, skills, and dependability; earlier construction start on more projects; more effective project management and monitoring; transparency and fairness in process; and on-time, on-budget project delivery.*
> —**Ken Sweeney, founding partner of Growth Equity Partners, "Private Money, Public Gains,"** *ReNew Canada,* **March/April 2006**

Ontario isn't saying it will use P3s for all public projects, just because it seems to be the better way to go. Apparently, Ontario has learned from the U.S., French, and Australian mistakes regarding misuse of privatization, and they've learned from Britain's mistakes regarding quality. The OAA also points to one of the key advantages of having the P3 tool in your back pocket: alternative financing vehicles free infrastructure and other large public projects—some of which can span many years—from a sword of Damocles that is always hanging over their neck.

That sword is the loss of funding midstream due to public budget woes, a downturn in the economy (which reduces tax revenues), changes of administration, and other factors beyond the control of project owners/managers. For instance, conservative politicians love to promise tax cuts while campaigning. Although they usually deliver the opposite, they do sometimes uphold their pledge, and that can pull the funding rug out from under projects that are already approved, and even some that are underway. There's no shortage of "highways to nowhere" and forlorn, half-built, state-funded housing or tourism projects on the planet.

The OAA also points out some of the potential downsides of the use of P3s. One is that there might be a tendency for school districts and other public agencies to bundle many small projects together to make them appealing to a private consortium. This could lead to homogenization of design, and could put many smaller firms out of business. Another potential threat is that these consortia often reach beyond the local area for partners, which means P3s could become a channel for new competition from outside the province or even the country. This, in turn, could lesson pressure on local governments to fund workforce development measures.

We are clearly at a turning point in the evolution of P3s. After a heady initial run in the absence of rules, public backlash has created what seem to be stop-gap measures, such as simply calling them something else. But look deeper, and you'll see that many of these renamed P3s really *are* different. They better protect the public's interests. They apply the renewal rules—especially engagement—to a much greater degree. And, they are developing replicable models.

Now, let's take a quick look at two organizations that are helping to advance the leading edge of rewealth. The rapid emergence of P3s focused on restorative development means that there's a wealth of positive and pioneering initiatives to cite, far more than can fit into this book. More journals and periodicals are thus needed to properly document and learn from these real-world efforts. That gap is starting to be filled. The best of the commercial publications in this arena is *ReNew Canada*, which is—as I write this—in the process of creating a global version of their publication in electronic format.

A number of colleges and universities are also stepping into the breach, creating curricula, degrees, diploma courses (for working professionals), research, and journals focused on rewealth in all its many forms. You'll learn about a few such efforts in this book, but I can only scratch the surface here. In this chapter, we'll focus on Toronto's polytechnical Seneca College.

The Story of *ReNew Canada*

The global reconomy has its own magazine and it's based in Toronto. It started life as a leading-edge national rewealth magazine for Canada in 2005, focused on metropolitan revitalization. Here's their story.

The idea of launching a national trade journal focused on urban renewal probably sounds daunting . . . and it should. But for two seasoned publishers in Canada, it has been an inspired and profitable success. Part of this success can be attributed to the growing global concern over strains on our environment and infrastructure in general.

But the more specific success factor—besides the high quality of their editorial content and graphics—is their timing. *ReNew Canada*, which bills itself as "The Infrastructure Renewal Magazine" caught the dewealth/rewealth shift perfectly. Now, after just two years, it's set to expand into the United States and around the world.

That's inspiring news, because it's already the best rewealth magazine on the planet. [Disclosure: I have a regular column in *ReNew Canada*, but I'm not paid for that writing, and I own no stock in the company. However, the Latham Group (a family trust, and a backer of *ReNew Canada*), is a partner in a new Washington, DC-based company, Resolution Fund, LLC, of which I am the CEO.] Anyone who can read English should be receiving *ReNew Canada*, no matter where they live. While the current focus is Canadian, most of the content has global relevance.

ReNew Canada was created by Todd Latham and Ray Blumenfeld. Their goal was to address the infrastructure information needs of those who want to revitalize communities across Canada. Their primary readership comprises decision makers in government agencies, corporations, and a broad cross section of rewealth professions.

Canadian infrastructure suffers from two crises (as is the case in most countries): the majority of it has reached the end of its life cycle, and most of the rest no longer has the capacity to meet current demands. Virtually all of it is in need of renovation or replacement. The Canadian infrastructure renewal deficit is large and growing fast.

ReNew Canada focuses on public-private partnerships for revitalization. Its mandate is to provide government and business leaders with access to the financing information, legal expertise, and specialized services of the many infrastructure supplier partners. They are brought together between the covers of the magazine so they can partner in the real world to help achieve sustainable urban economic growth.

A Conference Board of Canada report released in 2004 said Canada has lost its appeal as a destination for foreign investment. Over 80% of investors surveyed cited the poor state of Canada's infrastructure as being the primary reason. Substantial investment is needed to address these aging assets. [Note: this insight should be a caution to those communities, states, provinces, and nations who think reducing corporate taxes is the best way to stimulate economic growth. All the tax cuts in the world won't attract businesses into an area with dysfunctional infrastructure and a declining quality of life. Those tax dollars are better spent on renewal.]

Most private and public organizations put the financial requirement to rebuild Canada's infrastructure between $50 and $125 billion. The government alone cannot afford to pay the bill for this "infrastructure gap" and has no choice but to partner with private companies to enhance water, transportation, and other infrastructure components.

There are now three specific government agencies setting aside funds and negotiating with private companies to begin some of these contracts. But change is linked to knowledge. Without a forum to explore these new partnered approaches from an objective viewpoint, both government and industry have a hard time moving forward.

The landscape of infrastructure finance is also changing rapidly, with *ReNew Canada* playing the role of "cartographer" of the country's reconomy. Its 10,000-plus readers receive the print magazine six times a year, but news and events are updated and posted online on a daily basis. The overt focus is on infrastructure, but—as with communities—that's just the skeleton. Brownfields redevelopment, watershed restoration, historic neighborhood revitalization, and most other forms of rewealth are also addressed. Of course, none of that works without healthy infrastructure.

The idea for the magazine started in June 2004. Ray Blumenfeld was involved in the water industry through *Canadian Water Treatment* magazine. This prompted him to subscribe to newswire services providing daily industry information from across North America. One day, he received a press release about a multimillion-dollar public-private partnership that had been announced for a water treatment plant in the United States. Wondering what a public-private partnership was, he ended up on the CCPPP Website, and a light went on.

It became apparent to him that across North America, infrastructure is literally crumbling around us. This led him to pose two questions: (1) why isn't more information being disseminated about this crucial problem, and (2) how are local, regional, and federal agencies going to be able to pay for billions of dollars in investments and repairs? A search turned up nothing. No magazine existed anywhere that spoke to this crisis.

Ray came up with the name *ReNew Canada*, which accurately communicated the concept for this new magazine, and put together a media kit and editorial planner. He then called Jane Peatch, executive director of the CCPPP, and they met in Toronto in September 2004.

Jane thought the idea of an all-encompassing magazine covering current or proposed infrastructure projects was a good idea, and something CCPPP would like to be involved in. Industries responsible for infrastructure renewal include construction, cement, steel, water and wastewater, engineers, consultants, contractors, and more. The idea was to bring them all together. A number of these industries had their own magazines, of course. But there wasn't one for infrastructure in general, one that integrated the disciplines and brought the industries together. Nor was there one that focused on renewal.

Ray put together a business plan for the publication and We Communications, Inc, the company he worked for. In October 2004, he brought the plan to the attention of James Sbrolla of Environmental Business Consultants Inc.

James began a search for someone with a publishing background who could invest in the business and the new magazine. He called his friend Todd Latham, who was then working for Hollinger Inc., running a multimillion-dollar environmental business-to-business (B2B) operation. Todd was with Hollinger because they had bought Southam, Inc., which had bought Todd's first magazine venture (formed in 1989 and sold in 1999). After five years growing businesses for Hollinger, Todd was yearning to return to the entrepreneurial trenches.

After getting James and Todd to sign a nondisclosure agreement, Ray pitched the business plan to them over pizza. Todd loved the idea. He was so confident this was the right magazine at the right time that he acquired We Communications, Inc. just six months later. Working with Ray, they further developed the business plan, hired staff and freelance writers, began building a database, and called advertisers. They started connecting with associations, industry leaders, and governments to gather research, generate support, and form the editorial direction.

Within two short months of acquiring the company, Ray and Todd made the magazine launch announcement. The point of no return came on May 26, 2005, when the new company sponsored an industry breakfast. David Caplan, the Ontario Minister of Public Infrastructure Renewal, was the keynote speaker.

As fate would have it, on the day before this magazine launch announcement, Minister Caplan made another announcement: a massive $5 billion investment in restoring public infrastructure in the province through a program called ReNew Ontario. Kaboom! The planets had aligned—even the use of upper and lower case in "renew" was the same. The timing was impeccable, for both the magazine and the government program.

ReNew Canada had caught the rewealth tide. In October of 2005, the premier issue was distributed at a major brownfields industry conference in Ottawa. It was an instant hit and reached the desks of some very influential people. They immediately saw its value and bought both subscriptions and advertising for the next issue. The growth shows no signs of letting up.

ReNew Canada has become a fixture at infrastructure summits and seminars. It's a must read for a huge diversity of professionals. It's become a platform for political leaders like Federal Minister of Finance Jim Flaherty, Minister Lawrence Cannon, Green Party leader Elizabeth May, and New Democrat leader Jack Layton. Industry veterans like Glen Murray (former head of the National Round Table on the Environment and the Economy), Glenn Miller (Canadian Urban Institute), and environmental champion David Suzuki are contributors. *ReNew Canada*'s annual list of the Top 100 Canadian projects receives coverage in Canada's second-largest newspaper (the *Globe and Mail*), and in online resources like LexisNexis.

ReNew Canada forged much new territory with its oversized, high quality, recycled paper. But the real pioneering was done through its topical coverage of the infrastructure renovation gap, along with rewealth-oriented asset management, city building, and financing innovations.

As the Canadian infrastructure renewal industry evolves, *ReNew Canada* is the guide to understanding the changes, and to applying new solutions. Those solutions range from P3s—which are often misunderstood even by infrastructure professionals and government leaders—to brownfield remediation, green building, deconstruction, and much more.

ReNew Canada has been moving into the United States, which still lacks an infrastructure renewal magazine. The entire globe is now plagued with aging and obsolete infrastructure, and insufficient public funding for that crisis. *ReNew Canada* is thus well on its way to becoming an internationally recognized publication. Look online at www.renewcanada.net for their international electronic version.

Seneca College: Global Secretariat of the Revitalization Institute

As mentioned in the Preface, the nonprofit Revitalization Institute was born as a direct outgrowth of my first book. Readers emailed me, or came up to me after a keynote address at their conference, and told me the same thing, over and over: the biggest challenge they faced was integrating the renewal of the natural, built, and socioeconomic environments.

The brownfields remediation professionals needed to integrate better with the infrastructure renewal engineers and the historic building restoration owners. The ecosystem restoration scientists also needed to integrate better with infrastructure renewal (especially water and wastewater), as well as with redevelopers. And so on down the line: everyone understood their own rewealth discpline, but couldn't do their job properly in isolation from other rewealth professionals. They needed more-integrative tools and strategies.

But there was nowhere they could go: their professional associations had their turf to protect, and their software was either limited to certain types of assets, or to a certain portion of the assets' lifecycle, or both. Thus was born Revitalization Institute, the Academy for Community Revitalization and Natural Resource Restoration. I became its first executive director in 2004.

We experimented with many models to achieve the mission of helping to better integrate the many facets of the global restoration economy. We created a partner network of nonprofits, an affiliate network of businesses, and an academic network of colleges and universities. Of those three groups, it was the academics who responded most vigorously. They perceived the widening gap between the guesstimated (coming up with hard numbers would be a good academic research pursuit) $2 trillion worth of restorative development taking place annually, and the paucity of curricula serving that massive, rapidly growing industry.

Revitalization Institute spent most of its life as a U.S. 501 (c) (3) not-for-profit organization based in Alexandria, Virginia. It has recently been reborn as a global, Canadian-based nonprofit, based at Seneca College (Canada's largest college, with some 110,000 full- and part-time students). While still focused on helping the global reconomy expand and become better integrated, its work is now done almost exclusively through academic institutions.

Revitalization Institute's current mission is fourfold: (1) To advance curricula, degrees, and workforce-development programs related to rewealth; (2) To advance research related to rewealth; (3) To advance journals and other publications related to rewealth; and (4) To advance the ability of schools, colleges, and universities to contribute to the revitalization of their own communities.

During the four years it was based in the United States, Revitalization Institute built a network of some 60 NGOs, businesses, and academic organizations. All of the colleges, universities, and corporations were based in the United States, Canada, and Mexico. However, the NGO network included members outside of North America, such as in Poland and Ghana. While the scope has been narrowed to focus on the academic network, it is also being broadened to a fully global representation.

To make that transition effectively, two things were necessary: a new executive director from academia, and additional support staff and infrastructure.

Seneca College is a polytechnical institution with six campuses in the Toronto area. William Humber was director of Seneca's Center for the Built Environment at that point. He took over as interim executive director of Revitalization Institute, while the search for a full-time executive director began in early 2008.

I took on the title of distinguished visiting professor at Seneca, spending one week per quarter on campus to help strategize on research and curriculum development, teach classes, and consult with both staff and faculty. We're also working on strategies to help Seneca contribute more directly to the revitalization of the greater Toronto area. [Note: I'm considering taking on one or two similar positions elsewhere. Schools in Latin America, Asia, and the UK are particularly invited to contact me, but any location will be considered.]

Why was Seneca chosen? Well, it didn't hurt that since 2003, *The Restoration Economy* has been required reading in several of their engineering and environmental courses. But there were less selfish, and more important, motivations as well.

Seneca College has a quality that is sadly lacking in most academic institutions: the ability to do new things. Many schools have great difficulty accomplishing anything other than teaching and research, no matter how badly they want to do it. If an initiative doesn't fit the normal budgets, functions, and structures of the institution, the culture and bureaucracy tend to act like an immune system, rejecting the "foreign matter." Seneca College—thanks to William Humber's and (President) Dr. Rick Miner's leadership—seems to have a unique capacity for change and action. Bill has been at Seneca for over 30 years, so he knows how to get things done.

The other reason that Seneca came to my attention early on was because of their visionary curriculum. The presence of almost any "re" word in a course or degree program usually denotes leading edge, at least as far as rewealth is concerned. The leading edge of the leading edge would be "re" curriculum that focused on *integrated* approaches.

Seneca has a four-year diploma for engineering technologists called "Integrated Environmental Site Remediation." And, they created the course—under the inspired leadership of program coordinator Wendy Meininger-Dyk—before they were even aware of Revitalization Institute. The course is, of course, part of William Humber's Center for the Built Environment. They recently shortened the name of the course for practical reasons by removing "integrated," but the content remains as integrated as ever.

Seneca is currently putting together a broad range of rewealth-oriented online learning for working professionals. The first will be a diploma course in revitalization program management (about 50 hours). It will give public and private leaders—mayors, planners, designers, economic development officials, redevelopers, etc.—a working knowledge of all 12 sectors of restorable assets, as well as insights into how best to integrate their renewal.

Rewealth project management and revitalization program management will be focused on heavily at Seneca. Project and program managers are seen as the key discipline for moving the renewal of our communities—and the restoration of our planet—forward in a more integrated, efficient direction. This initiative is forming a partnership with the Project Management Institute, the leading global professional association for the project management profession. PMI will publish *Project Management Circa 2025* in October of 2008. It's edited by Dr. David I. Cleland, Professor Emeritus at the School of Engineering of the University of Pittsburgh. It provides multiple visions of the future for the project management profession, and I'm very happy to be writing one of the chapters.

It should be noted that Seneca's Revitalization Institute role is purely that of a coordinating body. Seneca is not a research university, nor do they offer graduate degrees. Any new research, curricula, and journals will be developed by the institutions within the network. Seneca will facilitate partnerships and activities, and is providing a physical home for the institute. Each country or region will have a lead university helping to coordinate activities at other educational institutions related to their language, culture, environmental needs, and socioeconomic challenges.

> [due to the surprising growth in infrastructure and environmental renewal resulting from the explosion of public-private partnerships] *. . . we are really facing a global shortage of civil engineers worldwide. [Design firms] are totally overbooked . . . I've never seen a situation like it.*
> **—Michel Cote, deputy chief executive at the global French engineering firm Bouygues, in the August 30, 2007 issue of** *Engineering News Record*

What Michel Cote's quote (above) doesn't mention is that schools are still pumping out construction professionals of all kinds whose curriculum is focused almost entirely on new development (dewealth). But some 80% of work in many countries is restorative development (rewealth). As a result, Revitalization Institute and Seneca College are focusing a lot of attention on the development of rewealth project management and revitalization program management software tools. Why? Let me offer an example from civil engineering by way of explanation.

The three rules/trends of rewealth, integration, and engagement are making things difficult for traditional civil engineers, while simultaneously opening wonderful new opportunities for the project/program management profession. For the past few centuries, civil engineering has largely been about the conquest of nature: constructing dams and levees, straightening rivers, and draining swamps. Now, the biggest trend in civil work is towards tearing down the dams, un-straightening the rivers, and refilling the swamps.

Environmental restoration, in other words. Almost half the U.S. Army Corps of Engineers' budget is now restoration—undoing their proud accomplishments of yesteryear—and it's the fastest-growing portion of the budget by far. There's a hitch, though.

Civil engineering alone cannot undo the effects of civil engineering. Pure civil engineering is all one needs to kill an ecosystem (such as by impeding or altering the flow of water). But civil engineering is only one of many disciplines needed to bring those ecosystems back to life: it's seldom just a matter of turning on the water again. An entire new science of restoration ecology has emerged (see Chapter 8). One of restoration ecologists' greatest challenges is working with civil engineers from the old school, where everything is mechanical and predictable, and where they demand complete control (which Mother Nature never grants).

Large-scale (such as regional) ecological restoration ups the ante further, introducing a plethora of "soft" agendas. The engineering work of previous centuries was usually driven by a single issue, such as draining wetlands for agriculture, or making rivers navigable so the products of that agriculture could get to market. That land is now inhabited (often densely) by people who can't be ignored or summarily displaced as easily as in the pioneering days past. Restoring those same wetlands now involves dealing with diverse social, economic, heritage, regulatory, and political issues.

Restoration often involves stopping or altering human activity on the land. That's a far trickier proposition than getting a permit to do the same dredging or lumbering that's been done on that land for over a century. As a result, project and (especially) program managers will increasingly be called upon to supply the expertise in integration, public engagement, rewealth financing tools, and public-private partnering. It's shocking how little of that is currently taught to architects, landscape architects, engineers, future policymakers, and even planners.

Speaking of rewealth financing tools, this is another area that needs more research and standards. As mentioned in Part II, some U.S. states are abusing TIF badly, which could spoil things for everyone. New Mexico probably has the worst TIF laws; they seem to have been designed specifically to encourage sprawl. This is like using massage to put knots in your muscles. Enlightened lawmakers in Albuquerque tried to add some local "re"strictions, but a dewealth-oriented mayor vetoed them. And, despite the leading-edge practices of Arlington County, Virginia (where I live), the state of Virginia also allows TIF to fund sprawl. Sigh.

Universities and colleges are now being recruited worldwide to expand Revitalization Institute's academic network, and to develop rewealth-oriented research, courses, degrees, and community outreach programs for every language and culture. Most of these relationships are formed at the departmental level, rather than at the institutional level. This is partly because institutional relationships often take years to formalize, and partly because Revitalization Institute wants to work directly with the faculty members who "get" the reconomy.

Soon, children around the globe will be able to graduate with degrees that are directly relevant to restoring our world for a living . . . and not a moment too soon.

From Dewealth Footprints to Rewealth Footprints

Let me end this Canadian chapter on a subject that had its genesis on the opposite side of Canada from Ontario's *ReNew Canada*, Seneca College, and PIR. In 1995, University of British Colombia professor Bill Rees' book, *Our Ecological Footprint*, was published.

It introduced the concept of "ecological footprint analysis," which selects a population, looks at its consumption patterns over a significant period of time, and calculates the size of the terrestrial and aquatic ecosystems that would be needed to yield the goods and services required by—and assimilate the wastes produced by—those people. That total area of land and water is our "ecological footprint," and the idea is to shrink it.

For instance, the resource footprint of the average U.S. citizen in 2002 was about 9.7 hectares (24.25 acres), while the footprint of the average resident of India was about .7 hectare (1.75 acres). Metrics are essential to understanding and addressing problems, so the footprint concept is a useful tool. For instance, the World Wildlife Funds's Living Planet Report referenced above relies on data compiled by the Global Footprint Network, as does the Zoological Society of London.

However, we can't hop off into a revitalized future on one foot. To address the extensive damage already done to the planet—and to address the revitalization needs of our communities—we also need a "restorative footprint" to complement that "depletion footprint." If Rees' current footprint tool represents our dewealth activities, then we also need a rewealth footprint. The goal would then be to shrink the dewealth footprint and enlarge the rewealth footprint. With both of these feet on the ground, we can stride off into a healthier, wealthier future, reducing our new damage while repairing our existing damage. This would be a great project for a *re*search university.

Along those same lines, a popular and positive current catch-phrase is "low-impact development," championed by smart growth advocates and conservationists. Under the dewealth model, it makes sense to reduce ecological damage and resource usage. But what we really need is *high*-impact *re*development, provided the impact is restorative. A low-impact goal is an admission by the developer that there's some aspect (maybe all aspects) of the project that will destroy or degrade something we value.

Pushing to minimize the damage is like saying, "please shoot me with a .22 bullet, rather than a .44." As a victim, that would be my choice of calibers too, but why be a victim of development at all? We need larger howitzers of rewealth, not smaller handguns of dewealth. Shoot me full of renewal. Please. People want to increase their positive impact on our world, not just decrease their negative impact. Some want to be a "bigfoot" of rewealth. Are you one of them?

Chapter 15

Closing Thoughts

Urban apocalypses, playing God, restoring women, smart growth, true urbanism, and other musings.

> *Be fruitful . . . and replenish the Earth.*
> —Bible, Genesis 1, verse 17

The missing middle part of the above biblical command was to multiply. Funny how humanity has had no problem obeying the part that requires sex, but we're only now getting around to replenishing, which requires work. The good news is that this "re" work usually pays well.

As long as we're quoting scripture, I'll mention that some folks accuse ecological restorationists of playing God when they recreate natural areas. Such critics are off-base on two counts. The first is that we've been playing God all along as we've destroyed nature and reshaped the planet. Why should we be restricted to only being destructive gods? Let's put the "re" in religion. The second counter to that accusation is that good restorationists—like good doctors—know that their role is to facilitate nature's own healing response. Nature does the heavy lifting: the restorationist/doctor is there to speed it, and remove ongoing stressors.

Without a more systematic way of addressing it, our vast global inventory of restorable assets could become what Pogo referred to as "an insurmountable opportunity." We must formally recognize this monumental shift as the new basis of wealth creation throughout our global civilization. Turning our dewealth lemons into rewealth lemonade will require systemically adopting the tools and practices pioneered by leaders such as those you met in these pages, and inventing many more.

There's an almost certain way to turn our devastated globe into a revitalized planet. We must adopt the three renewal rules to drive decisions regarding our policies, programs, plans, and projects. At the community level, we can do even better, and adopt the entire *re*solution, resulting in the creation of a renewal engine.

Imagine a world where every hectare of land or water is within the domain of a local or regional renewal engine. Imagine a world where those thousands of renewal engines can efficiently share knowledge and other resources. Imagine a global renewal engine, designed to restore those systems that can only be addressed at that level.

Regeneration isn't just a metropolitan phenomenon, nor are the renewal rules primarily a tool of government. Ranchers are using them to revitalize rural economies. Retirees are using them to create ideal lifestyles via restorative real estate investments in paradise. Entrepreneurs are using them to provide restorative products and services. Universities are using them to research restorative technologies, and to prepare students to carve out careers in this soon-to-be-dominant global reconomy. You've read some such stories here, and will discover more in *Rewealthy*, one of the upcoming sequels to this book.

Rewealth and Climate Change

We've spent much of this book learning about "universal" rules and processes. Let's take a superficial stab at applying them to universal (well, global) problems—climate change, for instance.

Climate change professionals—as with most others—are often stuck in silos. They do sometimes talk of integration, though. For instance, layering carbon credits on top of energy reduction credits to achieve better returns on greenhouse gas reduction investments. That's good, but still superficial.

One way to create an ideal strategy is to keep linking related restoration agendas until they reach a critical mass where they become self-funding, both initially and in the long term. For instance, if you restore degraded lands in a strategically chosen location, it allows you to plant carbon-sequestering native trees and shrubs that also achieve watershed restoration, brownfield cleanup, ecological restoration, fishery restoration, community revitalization, and more.

Besides the benefits to the local populace and wildlife, each of these agendas could have tradable credits or other financial incentives. Any one or two of those credits might not justify the initial investment, but when enough are combined, the project could become irresistible to a major corporation. If the land isn't contaminated, those carbon-sequestering trees could be fruit, nut, or oilseed trees. That would help feed people and wildlife while revitalizing a rural economy, triggering still more incentives.

Besides global climate change, we've got a global infrastructure renewal crisis, and the two share many obvious links. The entire shift from petroleum to sustainable energy is a form of renovating/replacing our power infrastructure. "Infrastructure" is a sleep-inducing word to most people, but renewing it encompasses a great number of exciting and critically important issues that are affecting you in an intimate and vital manner as you read this.

> As I wrote these words, a notice was hung on my front door from the Arlington County (Virginia) Department of Public Works. It said they are about to "*rejuvenate the aging* (water) *distribution pipes, which have been in service for more than 60 years*" on my residential street. Older cities in Europe and Asia would laugh at the idea of calling 60 years "old." Many of their systems are centuries old, which is why it's not uncommon for them to lose over half of their water to leakage. This was the first problem Britain tackled when they used P3s to renovate their water systems in 1989, and their mid-1990s droughts confirmed the wisdom of that rewealth investment.

Water is the critical issue for many places. Cities around the world are trying desperately to figure out how to get more water, but the best source of "new" water is right under their noses: reducing leakage by renovating water mains. The U.S. Geological Survey estimates that the amount of water lost to leaks in decrepit water distribution systems in the United States is enough to supply all 10 of our largest cities year-round. We lose some six billion gallons of clean, treated water annually; enough to supply every man, woman, and child in California.

Missing from the climate change debate has been an awareness of the significant amount of energy represented by each liter of fresh water; energy expended in pumping, bottling, filtering, and/or desalinating it. A climate change solution won't come from silos. The solution isn't greening power utilities, industry, automobiles, or agriculture, per se: it's about creating wealth in a way that restores air, water, and land. And, just as a national economy is primarily an aggregate of local economies, a global climate change solution will primarily derive from community-based solutions.

There is no reason that water, food, power, and contamination crises can't be solved simultaneously. In fact, solutions should be *required* to be integrated: we simply don't have time to waste in the "silo solutions" foisted on governments by lobbyists for private industry (mostly dewealth companies). True, there's big money to be made from symptomatic treatments—especially those mandated by government—but they will mostly stifle real progress, dulling citizens' sense of urgency by showing them "something" is being done.

Silo thinking isn't confined to business or government. Even foundations—which often have a fairly holistic view of the world—tend to fund projects and measure their success in silos.

Global climate change requires its own renewal engine, but the focus should probably be on the rapid, resilient renewal of the planet, not on climate change specifically. Only in this manner can we create the partnerships needed to leverage the resources needed to create integrated climate restoration projects on a grand scale. Only then will our climate change strategy be based on a vision that's shared by stakeholders worldwide. Only then will we effectively engage all available academic, governmental, business, NGO, and community resources, and tie them to an adaptive management approach that constantly improves the strategy.

Again, the global climate problem is based primarily on what happens in communities. If a renewal engine can renew a community, why not scale it up to the planetary level? Right now, a huge number of talented individuals and dedicated organizations are running around like Keystone Cops, for lack of an organizational model to address climate change. Now they have one.

Of course, much of that confusion also derives from climate change disinformation campaigns funded by the dewealth companies that contribute to the problem. It will help tremendously when people and governments learn to differentiate between dewealth and rewealth. If nothing else, it will be a guide to perceiving which companies and organizations are worth listening to, and which ones are merely trying to perpetuate the deconomy.

Recycling Communities to Recycle the Planet

Everywhere you find innovation today, a community is involved.
—Patricia Seybold, *Outside Innovation: How Your Customers Will Co-Design Your Company's Future* (Collins, October 2006)

Engineering, architectural, planning, and environmental science professionals all have rigorous processes for accomplishing their jobs, and degrees to prove they learned them. But community renewal tends to be sloppy and wasteful, often lacking any process at all. That's a scary situation for someone with a billion dollars on the line. Many billion-dollar redevelopment projects around the world are betting their company's future on the future of a community.

Large numbers of dedicated people are devoting huge amounts of time—and equally huge amounts of money—to reviving struggling cities. Most are talented, intelligent individuals. But their processes—if they have any—are often ineffectual. As a group, their expertise is transformed into a mishmash of opinions and best guesses. This often yields copycat strategies, as they fail to form an original, appropriate one of their own. These copycat strategies are often just tactics that focus on one important but narrow aspect of renewal, such as attracting a "creative class" of people, using sustainable building design, or being pedestrian-friendly.

Making the dewealth/rewealth shift means moving from recycling stuff (like soda cans) to recycling communities. That means we have to become as professional and as efficient at renewing "discarded" cities as businesses have become at renewing discarded aluminum. That's not a call for turning it into a hypercontrolled, engineered process that ignores human and natural complexities: it's simply a call for more research and rigor.

Three Final Lessons from Chattanooga and Bilbao

What do geniuses, bowels, beer, and crime have in common? Not much, but I'm going to cram them all together in this section anyway.

The Genius of the Place, or the Genius of the Individual?

You've read a lot about engagement of stakeholders and shared community visions in these pages. Now for a dose of balance: groups seldom produce great visions. They can contribute to great visions, but—as Ayn Rand might say—there's no such thing as a collective mind. Among ants, maybe, but not humans: the closest we come is mobs and mass hysteria on the negative side, and effective teams on the positive. But an effective team comprises a diversity of skills. Good team members are talented people with a shared goal who respect the genius of the individual. A team is not a committee.

It usually takes the genius of an individual to perceive the genius of the place, and John Knott's certainly not the only one who can do it. Chapter 11 mentioned architect Stroud Watson, and his long-term influence on the physical form of Chattanooga's revival. If you've got a talented designer or planner, by all means use them. If she or he is worth their salt, they'll want constant input from a broad diversity of other disciplines, cultures, and interests. If you know what's good for you as a community, you'll let their talent shine through, and not compromise it via "design by committee."

It can be a tricky balance. Trust won't come easily to those citizens who remember earlier destructive design and planning. Many of today's heritage preservation organizations and nature conservation groups arose to protect communities from their own insensitive, power-crazed planners, engineers, and architects. A new generation of designers and planners who value integrative, engaged, partnered approaches is arising, and the best of them are both brilliant and worthy of a community's trust.

But the old ways of turf protection, silo thinking, and *tabula rasa* planning aren't gone. That's why the *re*solution is so important: it's vital that a community's decisions be guided by all three renewal rules, that they create solutions using all three renewal processes, and that they have an organization—a renewal engine—to introduce, expand, and perpetuate such behaviors.

Irritable Bilbao Syndrome: Confusing Products with Process

Running a city is complicated, so leaders seek simplicity. This is one reason they latch onto prepackaged solutions that are easy to communicate. The problem is that you can't transfer visions, strategies, or plans from one community to another, but you can transfer rules and processes. Chattanooga and Bilbao applied all three renewal rules, and all three renewal processes.

But too often communities fixate on the physical manifestations of a revitalization process, and ignore the process itself. Many other cities decided that all they had to do was to build an iconic structure like Chattanooga's aquarium or Bilbao's Guggenheim Museum, and hey presto! . . . they'd get revitalized too. Fancy new museums quickly became a revitalization fad that Glen Murray—former mayor of Winnipeg and newly-ensconced head of the Canadian Urban Institute—wryly refers to as "irritable Bilbao syndrome."

The process is what's important to copy, not the specific projects that result from the process. Building a museum, or an aquarium, or a stadium, or a convention center just because it worked for another city is like seeing a happy person wearing a hat, and rushing out to buy the same hat, even if it looks terrible on you. Chances are, it's the way that person lives their life that makes them happy, not their hat.

But most folks would rather not change their lifestyle, and most cities will just go for the consumer approach to renewal: "Let's buy us a stadium!" (or a sports team, or a Calatrava tower, or a convention center . . .). Sometimes it works, but that's too often a matter of luck. As Alfred North Whitehead said: "Seek simplicity, and distrust it."

The Resolution to Crime, Racism, and Social Division?

It's worth emphasizing a point that was made in the Chapter 11 story of Chattanooga. Communities suffering from political, economic, or racial polarization sometimes do a better job of healing the situation by not tackling the problems head-on. The issues might be signs and symptoms of an insufficient sense of community. Working to clean and revitalize their city brought Chattanoogans together. Many social problems melted away during those years, without anyone's ever declaring war on them (which is usually a government's way of turning a problem into an industry).

The most reliable way to achieve a greater sense of community is by achieving worthwhile things together. Working together towards rapid, resilient renewal might be the surest way to heal such rifts, since it's as close as we're likely to get to a universal and achievable goal. The *re*solution already encompasses socioeconomic assets, but keep in mind that it might help rectify social behaviors, as well.

How to Brew Revitalization

Chapter 11 briefly mentioned the Big River microbrewery that helped advance Chattanooga's downtown's renewal. Microbreweries often crop up as renewal pioneers. I couldn't begin to list the number of times I've found them at the heart of an old industrial area's revitalization. Vancouver's Granville Island Brewery, for instance, is the oldest continuous resident of that magnificent regeneration zone.

Why the connection? The microbrewery trend is driven in large part by a quest for heritage and authenticity. This makes it natural for them to reuse (and thus honor) the buildings that helped launch the community a century or two ago. Of course, microbrew drinkers also desire more gusto and flavor, rejecting the weak, watery effluent that dominates the U.S. and Canadian markets. This trend is in direct opposition to the campaigns of the giants, which convince the masses to drink "light" beers that contain even fewer expensive ingredients, but cost just as much.

A final driver of the microbrewery trend is that most people enjoy supporting local entrepreneurs, rather than multinational brewers who spend billions on ads that make them look down-home and authentic (and who are now launching their own phony "microbrews"). The potent combination of history, community, and sensory pleasure helps explain the frequent confluence of microbreweries and neighborhood renewal.

Rewealth Versus Sustainable Development, Smart Growth, New Urbanism, Creative Classes, and Green Building

At various places throughout this book, I've made critical comments about two generally positive movements that have experienced strong growth in the United States over the past decade: smart growth and new urbanism. But I can also be irritating when the subjects of sustainable development, the "creative class," and green buildings arise. Here's proof.

Rewealth Versus Sustainable Development

I touched on some of these points in *The Restoration Economy*, but—with the future of the planet at stake—they bear reiteration. The business, nonprofit, government, and academic leaders of this de/re shift don't just have a good idea: they've already shown beyond any shadow of a doubt that rewealth comprises the only possible path to sustainable economic growth on a finite planet with a growing population . . . or even with a static population.

In fact, rewealth would be the only practical path forward *even if we had a shrinking population*. That's because of the gargantuan global inventory of damaged/depleted natural resources, and the prevalence of decrepit, demoralized communities with staggering local inventories of derelict buildings, crumbling infrastructure, dying (or fleeing) industries, lifeless streams, and poisoned properties.

As described near the beginning of this book, the primary problem with sustainable development (as currently practiced) is that it attempts to make sustainable *all three* modes of the development lifecycle: dewealth, prewealth, and rewealth. All three are in need of greening, no doubt, but only the latter two modes are inherently sustainable. No matter now much we "green" dewealth, it triggers the constraints—and exacerbates the crises—imposed by a growing population on a finite planet.

Unfortunately, dewealth is where most sustainability folks focus their attention. This is quite natural, since that's where the damage is being done. After all, why bother greening something that's inherently green, like rewealth? Logical as that might sound on the surface, this has been the undoing of sustainable development: allowing inherently destructive projects to fly the "sustainable" flag undercuts the credibility of the entire movement.

The "triple bottom line" mantras of ecology-economy-equity and people-planet-profit have a similar problem. These are six very nice nouns, but a verb would be helpful. Projects whose goal is to obliterate our ecology-economy-equity or damage our people-planet-profits can just as legitimately be said to be following the slogan's guidance as those whose goal is to sustain all three, or to restore all three.

We need to quickly embrace rewealth as the dominant mode of growth for the rest of humanity's time on this planet. It already accounts for over 90% of growth in many of our largest older cities. As cities go, so goes the world.

The deconomy/reconomy shift is fundamentally changing the nature of real estate investment and development. Black-hat developers are becoming white-hat redevelopers as they discover the nicely located billions of square feet of abandoned industrial and retail buildings that can often be had for a song. Instead of spending their time working backroom deals with crooked city and county politicians (and then spending more time in court fighting the ensuing public outcry), they find themselves celebrated as champions of community renewal.

I see the dichotomy where I live: Arlington, Virginia, officials have been working openly and collaboratively on restorative infill and transit-oriented redevelopment projects for over a decade. Meanwhile, in formerly bucolic, nearby Loudoun County—a hotbed of out-of-control sprawl where developers notoriously rule—the FBI is expanding its investigation of corruption and shady land deals. If for no other reason than to rid our communities of sprawl, and the nasty folks who often come with it, we must choose restorative development over sustainable development. The latter is the larger concept, but the former is where action should be focused.

Smart Growth: A Great Starting Point on the Path to a Reconomy

Smart growth might be exactly the tool that's needed in the United States right now; every country has its unique culture and must create solutions appropriate to that culture. But this book is largely about universal solutions, not the United States. More accurately, it's about universal elements—rules, processes, and model—that can be turned into custom-made public or private solutions for almost any place on earth. While smart growth is rightly respected in the U.S., the phrase often elicits smirks abroad, where folks are quite amused at our tendency to call everything we do—and everything we make, such as bombs—"smart."

Therefore, I encourage other nations to borrow freely of the wonderful tools that have been accumulated under the smart growth tent. But I also encourage you to apply these tools within the context of a rigorous program, based on measurable, understandable principles. Such a program would provide clear guidance for decision-making by anyone, at any time. It would enable communities to quickly determine if they have the processes in place that will create the solutions they need. And it will give them a shared model for organizing these efforts, so that communities will be better able to work together as regions.

Smart growth, new urbanism, and green building are all attempts to devise more intelligent approaches to land use planning, community design, and structures. All three can and do contain large amounts of dewealth (smart growth to a lesser degree). All three are transitional movements designed to improve the deconomy.

All three can positively impact your rewealth strategy, but are by no means alternatives to it. Rewealth is a fundamental shift—a reversal, in fact—in the nature of wealth creation, it's not just a land-use strategy. For instance, if you've already got a good smart growth organization locally, it might be an ideal seed for your renewal engine. Another example: one of the key tools in the smart growth kit is transit-oriented development (TOD). This should be linked to rewealth TIFs, because not all renewal projects are equal: areas with access to existing transit should generally be given preference over those that lack it.

It's not uncommon to find smart growth movements that don't attempt to integrate the renewal of the natural, built, and socioeconomic environments . . . or that don't properly engage all the stakeholders . . . or that lack a shared renewal vision . . . or that don't attempt to foster a renewal culture . . . or that don't make partnered projects the norm . . . or that lack an appropriate organization to perpetuate their efforts.

In other words, they are missing most of the components of the *re*solution. The one *re*solution component most of them will have is an emphasis on rewealth, but even that often isn't held to very firmly. The best smart growth initiatives have all of the *re*solution components.

New Urbanism and Rewealth: Are They Compatible?

In *The Restoration Economy*, I lauded all the "re" words in the "Charter of the New Urbanism." Unfortunately, those words seldom seem to make the transition into practice.

Let's revisit (one last time) how redeveloper John Knott likes to "consult the genius of the place" before attempting to revitalize it. To see what happens when redevelopers don't "consult the genius of the place," just look at the plague of sterile, chain-store-driven, overly commercial, pedestrian-oriented "new urbanist" redevelopments that are being championed over the last century's sterile, overly commercial, car-oriented sprawl developments.

To the degree that they are infill (many are sprawl), mixed use, and pedestrian friendly, these projects are a step forward. But, they often take the same *tabula rasa* approach that professional planners used to destroy our great cities over the past 60 years.

The primary problem I have with most new urbanist redevelopments is that everything's the same age, the same style, and hyper-commercialized with national retail chains. It's the tree farm, as opposed to the forest. They've obviously forgotten Jane Jacobs' prescription for urban vitality: high density, mixed land use, small blocks, and *buildings of diverse ages*.

People are likely to get burned-out on the present-day proliferation of these cookie-cutter "villages," and start yearning for true urbanism. But once the true urbanism is gone, it's gone for a long time. It will take decades for these new urbanist projects to attain the randomness, diversity, and surprises that comprise a true urban experience. I first ran across the term "true urbanism" (as an alternative to "new urbanism") in Suzanne H. Crowhurst Lennard's brilliant article "What Constitutes True Urbanism?" in the March 2006 issue of *Urban Land* magazine. She said, "The principles of true urbanism consist of essential, interconnected elements—all promoting each resident's social, mental, and physical well-being, along with the community's cultural, economic, and social well-being."

By destroying heritage, these prepackaged new urbanist redevelopments are destroying the city's opportunities for a "second chance," in case the current project doesn't work. As long as a city has its heritage, it has another chance at revitalization. Without heritage buildings that are worthy of restoration and reuse, a devitalized community becomes just another ugly basketcase begging for rescue, unless it has some other spectacular restorable asset, like a great waterfront.

New urbanism is a definite improvement over the design of most newly-developed housing. And that's the irony: it borrows from true urbanism to improve sprawl, but when new urbanism is applied to existing inner cities, that same approach injects the sterility of sprawl into truly urban places. Maybe we should take the name "new urbanism" literally: it's for new places, not old ones. Given its provenance in the iconic Seaside development of Florida, which destroyed 80 acres of wildlife habitat along the Florida coast, new urbanism's "sprawl improvement" orientation shouldn't be surprising.

Maybe the best application of new urbanism has been in the HOPE VI program of the U.S. Department of Housing and Urban Development (HUD). Created by Congress in 1992, its purpose was to revitalize the horrendous public housing projects of the mid-20th century, which seemed to use penitentiaries as their architectural model. In many cases, these public housing projects demolished poor-but-socially-vital neighborhoods of single-family homes and small apartments, replacing them with high-rises that destroyed all sense of community. The result was a massive rise in crime, prostitution, and drug use.

For much of the 20th century, development in built-up areas, particularly in older cities, faced multiple obstacles. The prevalence of large swaths of shabby and vacant buildings in city centers drove prospective investors to look elsewhere. At the same time, city administrations tended to hike building requirements, fees, and procedural hurdles, which lessened incentives for development. But in many cities, one of the most significant disincentives to attracting development was the looming presence of severely distressed public housing projects that generated seemingly intractable social turmoil for both residents and the general citizenry. . . . Although the outlook for public housing remains dim, the HOPE VI program has shown that the future can be brighter.

—Douglas R. Porter, president of the Growth Management
Institute in Chevy Chase, Maryland, "Designing HOPE,"
Urban Land magazine, February 2008

HOPE VI was designed to undo that damage by tearing down the high-rises, and replacing them with walkable neighborhoods, access to public transit, and safe communal greenspaces. HOPE VI has been one of the U.S. government's most enlightened and successful programs, as is evidenced by the City West project in Cincinnati, the Bedford Hill project in Pittsburgh, the Broadway Overlook project in Baltimore, and the Townhomes on Capitol Hill project in Washington, DC.

Unfortunately, the program has suffered severe budget cutbacks since the year 2000, and George W. Bush has called for its abolition. As with almost any federal program, it's far from perfect. (I say "almost," because—other than their insufficient funding—it's hard to find fault with some of the U.S. government's partner-oriented rewealth programs, such as the Environmental Protection Agency's (EPA) Brownfields Program, or the National Oceanic and Atmospheric Administration's (NOAA) Community-based Restoration Program.) HOPE VI has drawn justified criticism that the new urbanist redevelopments have lower capacity and concentrate on the upper income end of the poor, displacing the desperately poor.

But few will argue that the cities that have done HOPE VI projects aren't the better for them. The lesson is that new urbanism can be successfully applied in urban environments only when what was there before was completely and utterly wrong. New urbanism seems to be best suited for improving sprawl, not downtowns.

Should You Attract a Creative Class, or Recruit Restorative Residents?

"The [pursuit of the] creative class has become a cliché of contemporary urban regeneration," says Jamie Peck, a professor of geography and sociology at the University of Wisconsin-Madison. . . . In fact, the escalating race to attract a creative class has birthed a cottage industry of consultants charging six-figure sums to assess a city's potential. . . . Peck argues that this pursuit is tailor-made for cities on tight budgets that can afford only modest efforts at image building—and doomed to modest results, or worse. Indeed, there's scant evidence that [Richard] Florida-esque creativity strategies have moved the needle on traditional economic-development gauges such as job and income growth. . . . The bigger

problem with pursuing creativity strategies might be their potential to overshadow a city's more basic social, educational, and infrastructural needs.

—Andrew Park, "The View from Florida-Ville: What happens when every city in America craves the 'creative class?'" *Fast Company,* **March 2007**

The above article was too hard on Richard Florida: his "creative class" tactic is both useful and conceptually valid. The real problem is the rampant "me-tooism" among communities that makes them adopt the tactics of other communities, rather than taking the time to envision the right solutions for their own community. This herd instinct even leads them to imitate the plans of others before they've been proven to work. Fads aren't limited to consumers.

But Park's final comment about focusing on basic functionality was right on. The creative class is *just one* aspect of *just one* of the 12 sectors (culture) of restorable assets that impel community renewal. By all means, don't ignore cultural assets, but to think a cluster of bohemians is going to revitalize a city that's choking on smog, whose infrastructure is failing, or that's isolated from its water is unrealistic. (For all the negative publicity about how badly Boston's "Big Dig" was implemented, its goals were right on. Once the lawsuits and investigations have died away, the Big Dig will likely come to be seen as one of the world's most visionary and successful rewealth projects.)

The bedrock of the creative class tactic is Florida's "3Ts of Economic Development": technology, talent, and tolerance. A fine alliteration, but will remembering them change your decisions on a day-to-day basis? Is your community's default choice to avoid technology? Do you currently eschew talent? Do you work hard to repel open-minded citizens? I didn't think so. And even if they do alter your decisions, will this behavior result in rapid, resilient renewal?

On the other hand, you'll probably find (1) dewealth, (2) separated management of your natural/built/socioeconomic environments, and (3) top-down decision-making rather prevalent in your community. Adopting the three renewal rules of rewealth, integration, and engagement—plus the three renewal processes—would thus lead to measurable change and comprehensive solutions. If your decisions don't change, neither will your results.

The creative class dialog did us a great favor by focusing more attention on the power a community's culture has on its economic development. As someone once commented, "The best things in life are not things." It was also helpful to know that we can attract this creative class of people by making our communities more global, diverse, innovative, and so on.

All are laudable characteristics, but they are ultimately as difficult to implement as a self-help book that promises wealth and love if we can only think more positively, be more creative, set goals, envision being happy, etc. Ultimately, success—whether individual or community—comes down to what we do habitually, not what we do occasionally. Thus my constant (by now, no doubt obnoxious) harping on the three rules to guide our daily decisions.

Communities would do well to learn from the dismal record of attempts to change corporate cultures over recent decades. One managerial fad after another has promised corporate renewal if only the leaders and staff would become more _____(fill in the blank: innovative, diverse, global, sharing, appreciative, warlike, competitive, etc.), only to find that cultures are powerfully resistant to having change thrust upon them. This explains Andrew Park's contention that few—if any—of the communities that have invested so much in the creative class philosophy have anything measurable to show for it.

The creative class goals are admirable—as were so many of the goals of transforming corporate cultures—but the approach is too head-on. Cultures don't change as a result of efforts to make them change. They change as a result of achieving things together . . . things that appeal to all, such as rapid, resilient renewal.

Ray Bradbury said (in his preface to *Zen and the Art of Writing*): "So while our art cannot, as we wish it could, save us from wars, privation, envy, greed, old age, or death, it can revitalize us amidst it all." Both observations speak to the importance of renewing our socioeconomic assets while we're slinging the bricks and mortar. But without actual renewal of our natural and built assets, basing revitalization on attracting a creative class of people might be little more than expensive poetry.

Green Building Versus Green Rebuilding

As long as I'm alienating my fellow Americans, I might as well take a few pot-shots at our primary green building program: the U.S. Green Building Council's LEED (Leadership in Energy and Environmental Design).

> *In no more than five years—and maybe as little as 24 to 36 months—you will face a competitive disadvantage if your building is not green and operating efficiently.*
>
> —Brenna S. Walraven, the first woman chair of BOMA,
> the Building Owners and Managers Association,
> *Urban Land,* Nov/Dec. 2007

Brenna was talking about commercial buildings, but one only need extend her statement by a few years for it to apply to the residential market. LEED has made great inroads in recent years because it solved the two primary barriers to green building: it gave building owners the ability to specify green in two words—such as "LEED Gold"—and gave building designers/contractors the flexibility they needed to deliver a building that met the meaning of those two words.

> *Today, none of the leading companies will look at office space in New York unless it's green. They won't look at it. We "wasted" two decades trying to green the construction industry from the design and materials angle. But if the owners don't ask for green, few architects will risk losing a commission by arguing for it. Now, owners can simply say "LEED Silver" or "LEED Gold" and they think their job is done. I wish.*
>
> **—unnamed major real estate broker speaking to ULI President Richard M. Rosan, from "The Green Juggernaut," Charles Lockwood, *Urban Land*, Nov/Dec 2007**

LEED in the U.S., and BREEAM in the UK, catalyzed the green building trend by making it easier to specify and deliver "green," but LEED has serious deficiencies. In fact, it's largely brain-dead when it comes to the rewealth trend. LEED was created almost entirely by architects who—as is well-known in the trade—generally prefer leaving their own mark on the world, rather than working with the designs of other architects. In other words, many have an in-built prejudice against reuse, renovation, and restoration projects.

During my six years as Director, Strategic Initiatives at the Construction Specifications Institute (CSI), I was the staff liaison to the U.S. Green Building Council while LEED was being created. I wasn't directly involved in LEED, but I was writing *The Restoration Economy* at the time, so I was the one jumping up and down at the annual meetings asking why LEED didn't give any credits for brownfield cleanup, for reusing buildings, or for refill (infill redevelopment, which reduces energy expended commuting to suburban offices). LEED is only about buildings (the excessive influence of architects again): it purposely doesn't "discriminate against" buildings based on inappropriate locations or contexts.

Those "re" concerns have been addressed to a degree, but in a ludicrous manner. In "Well-Aged Infrastructure," an article by Kerry Freek in the January/February issue of *ReNew Canada*, Chris Borgal of Goldsmith, Borgal & Company Architects said: "With LEED, you get one point for saving a historical building. You also get one point for a bicycle rack."

As long as reusing a block-long, five-story historic factory building gives a designer no more points towards the owner's desired LEED rating than does a $100 bicycle rack, the LEED system is "re"tarded. As long as spending millions of dollars cleaning a brownfield site is worth no more than a bicycle rack, LEED is "re"gressive. In fact, as long as LEED lacks any form of weighting—as long as every green factor large and small is worth the same one point—LEED is brain-dead.

This system is what evolutionary ecologists refer to as a "frozen accident": the LEED team didn't have the time or resources to come up with a weighting system, so they published it in this simplistic form, intending to improve it later. Now, this "one point for everything" system has become deeply embedded in the construction process, and injecting some intelligence into it will be exceedingly difficult.

Until USGBC corrects such faults, it will continue to hold back one positive trend (rewealth) while advancing another positive trend (green design). That such a glaring discrepancy should remain in LEED a decade later speaks volumes about the residual dewealth orientation of the architectural profession.

Rigorous Revitalization

How many of your community renewal leaders have a diploma in Natural Resource Restoration Project Management, or a Masters in Brownfields Redevelopment, or a Ph.D. in Socioeconomic Revitalization? How many have degrees related to *renewal* of *anything* . . . historic buildings, infrastructure, waterways, farms, etc.? The answer is: virtually none. It's not their fault: few such degrees are offered by academic institutions, and those degrees and certificates that are have emerged did so only in the past few years. (See Chapter 14 for more on this subject.)

Thousands of distressed communities around the world have spent the last decade or two trying to reinvigorate themselves. They are often dreaming of a post-industrial, post-resource-extraction, or post-agricultural future. Each has a unique situation, but they all want the same thing: rapid, resilient renewal.

We're finally introducing a little rigor into an activity that accounts for some two trillion dollars annually. Best practices are great, but real disciplines have a basis in rules and processes, and they have a model for action. All of those now exist. Revitalization is (finally) on its way to becoming a real discipline, and the *re*solution might be its highest expression. Of course, rules, processes, and models don't automatically produce rigor, but they are the best possible foundation for the creation of an effective and accountable discipline.

The renewal engine is the key "technology" of rapid, resilient renewal. It's actually been emerging in various places around the world for two decades, but has never before been documented as such. One reason these prototypes went unnoticed is that reporters tend to focus on the projects, and not on the processes that produced them (which don't photograph as well). Another reason is that even the folks who invented them didn't realize what they had created. Their renewal engine was an ad hoc solution to their own local problems; they neither intended to create a universal tool, nor realized they had.

Thought yields doubt. Ignorance yields certainty. I don't for a moment think I've gleaned all the lessons that could be learned from the communities that pioneered the renewal engine model. My hope is that this book will enable communities to build renewal engines more rapidly, while structuring and managing them in a way that makes them more resilient. But my hope is also that—as more communities consciously create renewal engines—this will enable them to be more rigorously studied and improved.

The rough guidelines in this book should thus become more sophisticated over time. Given the current rarity of fully formed renewal engines, having even an imperfect one gives a community a major advantage over those completely lacking one. That said, remember the magic that comes from playing the "restorative chord," when the rules, processes, and model of the *re*solution sing together. Do you have a water quality/quantity crisis or a transportation crisis? Form a *regional* renewal engine. Do you have a dying downtown? Are you surrounded by brownfields? Are your historic buildings in need of massive investment? Form a *community* renewal engine.

There are probably few crises that the *re*solution can't fix. It's worth repeating that the *re*solution—the rules, processes, and model presented here—don't comprise a strategy or a plan for revitalizing your community. For that, you need planning and design professionals. The *re*solution is about increasing your community's renewal *capacity* . . . its ability to attract and support the right kind of regeneration. My advice has been high level and general because it's meant to be universally applicable. That said, building a renewal engine will help keep those design and planning professionals from falling back into old dewealth habits.

At the risk of wandering away from rigor and into the metaphysical, we might better appreciate each citizen's contribution to a revitalization initiative by viewing them in the following way: an individual's consciousness is a point in time when their hopes for the future meet their memories of the past, yielding a desire and opportunity to change the world of now. The word "individual" can be replaced by "community," with no loss of meaning.

Urban Apocalypses on the Horizon?

> *Deprivation . . . can cause us to act foolishly. First, it can cause panic, delirium, and illness, all of which can impair our perception, intuition, and reason. Second, it can bias our perception and intuition, e.g., a person suffering from severe thirst will tend to perceive opportunities for relieving thirst and not perceive other opportunities. . . . Third, it can retard learning, and the resulting ignorance can cause us to act foolishly. . . . Because we need practical wisdom to avoid deprivation, and deprivation can interfere with practical wisdom in a variety of ways, we face a variety of potential vicious circles involving imprudence and deprivation. Collectively, these form the cycle of poverty.*
>
> —Scott Harris, *Wealth in the Information Age*
> (working manuscript dated 1997)

Converging trends will likely lead to at least one—and possibly a series of— "urban apocalypses." They'll most likely hit between 2010 and 2020, when the de/re shift will be most intense, and the damage of the dying deconomy will be at its height.

By "urban apocalypse," I'm talking about a civil war-like socioeconomic implosion at the metropolitan scale, not just urban riots. Global urbanization is spawning increasing numbers of megacities; cities whose population and economy is larger than that of many countries. Burgeoning crises in infrastructure, food, water, energy, and contamination will widen the income disparities that are sweeping the world. The rich-poor gap will become the living-dying gap.

For instance, Lagos, Nigeria is expected to grow at an annual rate of 4.5%, thus doubling its population every 15 years. India is one of the most rural countries in the world, but their urban population already exceeds the combined urban populations of the United States, the United Kingdom, and France. Urban dwellers are expected to account for 550 million out of an estimated total of 1,350 million Indians by 2021, and their governing mechanisms at every level are both antiquated and already overwhelmed.

Such numbers will likely make for some interesting new global socioeconomic dynamics . . . on top of the impact of three global crises. There's only so much suffering and hopelessness people will endure before violence erupts. This is especially ominous when you consider that 43% of the world's urban population already lives in sprawling, unplanned, squatter-based, shantytown slums mostly lacking public infrastructure and social services. The slum population of Kolkata, the seventh largest city in the world but only the second largest in India (after Mumbai), has a slum population larger than the entire population of San Francisco.

Mass violence shouldn't be surprising, considering that the world population of billionaires jumped 66% between 2003 and 2006, and the number of obese people in the world (about 1.2 billion) has grown to approximately equal the number of starving people. The UN projects 2 billion people living in slums by 2030. Some researchers see these megaslums as "epidemiological pumps" harboring pathogens that have disappeared elsewhere. Crowded slums give viruses and bacteria an ideal environment for mutation, and might then release them back into the world. Empathy aside, what happens in slums affects us all.

Combine all of these factors in a megacity that has inadequate infrastructure and other significant weaknesses in their natural, built, and/or socioeconomic environments, and a tipping point of dysfunction could be reached. The city's apocalypse might flash and die, flash and linger, or flash and spread.

One of the greatest urban revitalization challenges is that of informal development, whereby slums are created from scratch on "unused" public or private land, often by rural "refugees" looking for opportunity in the big city. In some cases, the squatters have some legal backing for their appropriation of others' property; such laws are based on the pernicious deconomic notion that land is being wasted if it's not developed.

"Squatter sprawl" is a global phenomenon, comprising the majority of sprawl in cities like Mumbai and Lagos. In Latin America, such spontaneous neighborhoods go by names such as *favelas, barrios, villas miseria, coventillos,* and *barriadas.* Some are highly dysfunctional, but most show surprising levels of entrepreneurial self-organization, such as for the provision of power, security, transportation, and water.

While some governments deal with the challenge simply by bringing in the bulldozers and police whenever a "real" developer wants to use the property (which was sometimes legally theirs to begin with), others are looking for—and finding—ways to incorporate these inadvertent, haphazard neighborhoods into their renewal. Besides obvious legal challenges regarding title and land tenure, a major challenge is that few—if any—taxes are collected from these areas, leaving cities not only with fewer funds to spend, but with little power to influence development via tax incentives.

You've seen in these pages how the presence of the renewal rules fosters rapid, resilient renewal. You've seen how their absence stymies recovery. What will happen when all of these trends converge on a city that largely lacks those renewal rules in their policies and culture? Without the ability to respond in an integrated, engaged, partnered manner, the resulting crises will likely trigger a feedback loop of destructive behavior, rather than an escape path of renewal.

We all know how quickly things can turn ugly when dense crowds of people become scared. Picture it happening in the dark, after the power infrastructure fails. Add desperation, hunger, thirst, injustice, and anger to such a situation. Imagine it on a scale of millions of people (not just the tens of thousands that might panic at a protest or sports event). You've now got the recipe for an urban apocalypse.

> *If you don't have food, so many things can come into the brain.*
> —**Anderson Mbewe, a former poacher, in Joseph J. Schatz,**
> **"A Cheaper Plan to Stop Poachers: Give Them Real Jobs,"**
> ***Christian Science Monitor,* October 23, 2007**

Given that we are globally moving closer to the old city-state model, we could see more than a few megacities erupt into a type of civil conflict previously seen only on a national scale, such as Rwanda or post-U.S.-invasion Iraq. We'll likely see at least one such urban apocalypse by 2020. It might well be triggered by a "natural" disaster, caused or exacerbated by climate change.

I'm not just talking about lesser-developed nations, either. I could name a city or two here in the United States that could become vulnerable to an apocalyptic scenario if their populations continue to increase, and if they don't make the dewealth/rewealth transition. They probably aren't the cities you'd expect, but it would likely result in more harm than good if I were to name them. Reducing confidence in a community's future can hamstring them for a long time. They can easily identify themselves via a *re*solution SWOT analysis, or at least use the 12 sectors of restorable assets as a checklist.

We can avoid urban apocalypses. Preventive measures exist that should be obvious by now to anyone who didn't skip from the front cover to this page. Create a renewal engine for the city or region. Now. Create a shared vision of your future. Imbed the renewal rules into your public policies. Form an ongoing series of partnerships to renew your natural, built, and socioeconomic assets in an integrated manner. That's as reliable a formula as you're likely to find for preventing both ordinary urban decline, or a full-blown urban meltdown.

As with individuals, some communities are motivated to take action mostly by fear of loss, while others are primarily motivated by promise of gain. So, even if decline or apocalypse are unlikely scenarios for your area, form a renewal engine anyway: no one is likely to complain that it created an unnecessary increase in the quality of life.

There could to be some "corporate apocalypses" as well, as dewealth-based companies that fail to make the transition to rewealth either find themselves too large for a shrinking market, or find their feed stocks priced beyond any chance of turning a profit in a world that increasingly demands "re" materials over raw materials. Such firms will mostly be either extraction-based industries (like oil), or raw land-based industries (like publicly traded development firms). They will likely hit a tipping point in the de/re shift where their business model very suddenly becomes nonviable, and possibly even illegal. I can think of a few huge, household-name corporations that are unlikely to exist in 2015.

Those that operate with a castle-on-the-hill mentality—unable to effectively integrate, engage, or partner—are the ones most likely to find themselves with no choice but to close. If this behavior describes an entire industry, then they will likely take a large number of related professions, associations, academic disciplines, entrepreneurs, and government agencies down with them—as well as any communities that depend on them.

The good news is that the *re*solution offers a way to build community resilience to such a socioeconomic catastrophe, and lessen the chance of the natural disaster trigger-event as well. Again, it's best to avoid using the soporific word "integration." Simply focus on an integrative scale—such as a community, region, estuary, or river basin—to help the necessary disciplines/agendas come together for your apocalypse-prevention program.

A War for Rewealth?

Chindia (China and India taken together as a growing economic component of the world economy, whether or not they ever choose to work together) is the 800-pound gorilla sitting on European and American conference tables. But it's a gorilla whose future we prefer not to fully acknowledge. We prefer to think of them only as potential markets for the (few) goods we sell, as sources of cheap labor for the goods we buy, and as the recipient of our dirtiest industries. Americans write-off talk of Asia's becoming the global center of business and finance for a number of reasons.

One of those reasons is that English is the international language of business, which we think gives us an advantage. We forget that India has the world's largest English-speaking population, at 350 million. We forget that the Philippines, basically a Spanish-speaking nation, has more English speakers than Australia. We don't even want to think about the fact that China has over four times as many English-speaking citizens as does the United Kingdom. So let's not imagine that we have an insurmountable edge in the language department. Here in the U.S., we're in last place among all industrialized countries when it comes to multilingualism. The language factor works against us, not for us.

The other reason we think China and/or India will never surpass us is more germane to this book. We look at the way we've been cleaning up our environment, and the way China and India are polluting theirs, and we say "that's not sustainable . . . it's all going to come crashing down." On the surface, that makes sense: we've seen over and over in this book that economic growth that undercuts quality of life leads to economic stagnation, and eventually desperation. There are two problems with that view.

The most obvious is that we haven't so much been cleaning up our environment as exporting dirty industries. That gave us the illusion of being more ecologically responsible, but global climate change is now reminding us that there is no "other place" for our waste: we all breathe the same air, there's only one ocean (despite our many names for it), and we all live in the same weather system.

The other problem with believing that either China or India will self-destruct is that readers of this book have seen what can happen when desperation—such as that of Chattanooga and Bilbao—leads to a long-term, well-organized effort to revitalize. Europe and the U.S. are currently locked in battle to be the global economic leader. Judged solely by the relative value of the dollar and the Euro, the U.S. has been getting its butt kicked since the turn of the millennium. Of course, the dollar has, to a degree, been purposely devalued to keep exports high, which helps mask the severe damage that's been done to our economy as a whole this century.

If China and India were to do what Chattanooga and Bilbao did when they got desperate, the U.S. and Europe might find ourselves running #3 and 4, rather than #1 and 2. In fact, if China were to imbed renewal engines in their communities on a systematic basis, even a combined European and U.S. economy might soon rank #2.

What if Europe were to integrate with Africa? What if all the Americas (North, Central, South, and the Caribbean) were to integrate to a significant degree—to revitalize their economies and restore their natural resources? Might a world war for rewealth break out, with the competition based on the speed of renewal? (This would be as opposed to "the war for wealth" described by *Der Spiegel* correspondent Gabor Steingart in his excellent 2008 book of the same name.) The war machine in that case would be the renewal engine, a weapon of mass restoration. Whoever built the best and most renewal engines—and whoever did the best job of integrating them at the regional and national levels—would likely win. Hey, I can dream, can't I?

The problem with that scenario is that China and India have been very busy wooing both African and South/Central American countries. Those nations have suffered centuries of colonial and neo-colonial abuse by Europeans and by the United States. They haven't forgotten how—in the 19th and 20th centuries—one democratically-elected leader after another was assassinated or overthrown—and replaced by bloody, right-wing puppet dictators—by foreign powers desiring cheap access to their natural resources. The southern hemisphere has no such history with China or India, so our former colonies might be forgiven if they are more open to Chindian partnerships than we might prefer.

Is the Leading Edge of Rewealth Female?

My choice of individual story profiles in this book might give the impression that rewealth is a man's world. Tom Darden, James Aronson, and John Knott (and myself) are all the same gender, all American (despite James' best efforts), all Caucasian, and all nearly the same age. I apologize for that shameful lack of diversity, but I hope you'll agree their stories were worth telling nonetheless.

The global reconomy is mostly run by men, but that's an artifact of the overall dominance of men in today's world. Generalizations are always dangerous, but I'll state this bluntly: my on-the-ground experience tells me that the leadership that most communities *need* to achieve rapid, resilient renewal is often best provided by women.

The fields of engineering, planning, architecture, science, politics, and economics are all dominated by men. But the most critical challenge common to all those disciplines is a shift toward *renewal*, a shift toward *integrating* the natural, built, and socioeconomic environments, and a shift toward *engaging* other disciplines. All three of those trends are rooted in qualities and behaviors that seem to come more naturally to women than to men. Practitioners will continue to be primarily men for some time to come, but their professional associations and colleges should immediately seek increased feminine leadership if they wish their discipline to remain relevant in the face of those three irresistible trends.

The practice of bringing places back to life should—and I predict will—eventually be dominated by women. The component design and construction disciplines might still be male-dominated, but who's going to aggregate and focus all that expertise on the goal of rapid, resilient renewal? I'm convinced that the management of regeneration projects and programs—and their implementation—should be increasingly female, all other things being roughly equal when individual hiring decisions are being made.

Many of the most innovative and effective community revitalization programs I've encountered were led primarily by women. When stakeholder engagement is key, a woman is usually the man for the job. The same is true for integration: even if restoration-related engineering and sciences continue to be dominated by men, you'll often need a woman to effectively meld their efforts, fusing the renewal of the natural, built, and socioeconomic environments into revitalization.

Women are restoring our world everywhere I look. Check out Roseanne Haggerty, in New York City. In 2001, Roseanne received the MacArthur Foundation's $500,000 no-strings attached "genius" grant for her work on the problem of homelessness in the United States. She also won the 1998 Peter F. Drucker Award for Nonprofit Innovation. Her "genius" strategy is pure rewealth: renovating defunct old hotels into low-cost, publicly subsidized housing for the homeless.

Roseanne doesn't just help the homeless; she partners with them to provide solutions. They do most of the renovation work. In the process, they earn income and gain valuable rewealth job skills. The kicker is that they end up with a place to live that really feels like home, because they *personally* made it habitable. Better yet, they are creating living units, not just men's dorms. Contrary to popular belief, homelessness isn't just about men or women: many families are homeless. In New York City in March of 2007, for instance, 7,246 single adults used the city's shelter system, but 7,863 families were also sheltered.

Haggerty's nonprofit organization, Common Ground, was founded in 1990 and has been expanding its services internationally. It has annual revenues of about $15 million. Common Ground's integrative, engaged slogan: "*We are solving homelessness through innovative programs that transform people, buildings, and communities.*"

Their "re" strategy also saves communities money, as pointed out in their 2006 annual report: "A Common Ground housing unit costs about $40 per night, compared with $55 for a City shelter, $74 for a state prison cell, $164 for a City jail cell, $467 for a psychiatric hospital bed, and $1,185 for a City hospital bed."

Her first project was the formerly impressive Times Square Hotel, which had long since fallen into the state of decrepitude that had afflicted the entire area. It now offers 652 units of supported housing, complete with on-site social services. The entire Times Square area has been cleaned up and revitalized, making this an especially smart choice of location. Haggerty has tapped into the greatest socioeconomic/environmental trend of our time (rewealth), and has hitched her charitable work to it, to great effect.

James Aronson, John Knott, and Tom Darden have never won a MacArthur "genius" award, nor a Drucker award. Nor have they ever won a Nobel Peace Prize.

That honor goes to Wangari Maathai of Kenya. Her Green Belt Movement refor-estation project restored ecology and watersheds while revitalizing rural villages and renewing quality of life. It, too, was done on a grand scale. But Wangari's story has been much told: Tom, John, and James were probably unknown to you, which is why they grace these pages instead.

There are innumerable other stories of women restoring the world and revitaliz-ing our communities. Another example is Marjora Carter, whose Sustainable South Bronx initiative includes removing a Robert Moses highway, reconnecting people to their waterfront, ecological restoration training, reconnecting people to a park, etc. She also rails against the lack of integration in the planning for the South Bronx. Still another example is Florence Reed, whose Sustainable Harvest International integra-tively restores farms, forests, and communities in Central America.

The present and (especially) future role of women in the restoration of nature, and the revitalization of communities, deserves its own book, so that's one of two sequels I'm working on. I've already begun to compile material for that book, and invite readers to share stories and contacts for that effort. In fact, that's another reason for the male-dominated content of this book: I purposely excised some stories involving women, saving them for that sequel.

A Word about the New Orleans Tragedy:
The Levee Failure Was Only the First Catastrophe, and Probably Not the Worst

> *There are two things I wanted to do. I wanted to show the things that had to be corrected; I wanted to show the things that had to be appreciated.*
> —photographer Lewis W. Hines (1874–1940), who was hired by the Tennessee Valley Authority (TVA) in 1933 to document the construction of the Norris Dam. TVA appreciated his photography, but was less thrilled by his documentation of the dam's destructive-ness: it flooded out vast numbers of families who had farmed the land for generations, many of whom received no compensation

Given that I'm based in the United States, international readers are probably expecting me to say something about the recovery efforts in New Orleans. Here goes . . . I was invited to speak (pro bono, or for token payments) and help in New Orleans four times (a week at a time) during the first 18 months after the levee fail-ures, and I'm still involved to a degree. I'll keep this short, because it's a painful subject.

The monumentally inept response to this disaster has done more long-term damage to this great city than did the levee failures. People expected the city to receive appropriate aid, and for it to quickly recover, as have all other major U.S. cities after a catastrophe. As long as people believe that will happen, private resources will flow. As soon as that recovery is in doubt, private resources—other than charitable—stop flowing.

But leadership at all levels—city, state, and federal—seemed absent. A small example: the American Institute of Architects-New Orleans sponsored my talk at the city council chambers about a year after the tragedy. The crowd almost filled the large meeting room, and included not just architects but community leaders of most kinds, but not a single city council member nor elected leader of any kind.

But it was my failure as well. Never has post-disaster New Orleans ever had a shared vision of their future. Never have they had an effort to enhance their renewal culture. Never have they had a neutral, corruption-free forum for the creation of project partnerships driven by such a vision. In other words, while they are rich in restorable assets and in talented people who are dedicated to their community, the city possessed very little internal capacity for renewal. They desperately needed a renewal engine, but it wasn't until about a year after Katrina—while researching this book—that I encountered the first examples of renewal engines, and it took me a while to realize the model's crucial importance. When New Orleans needed a renewal engine the most, I didn't have it to offer.

Not only does New Orleans lack a renewal engine, but the three renewal rules are almost totally absent from their policies and their political culture. The overall culture *is* oriented toward the first rule: rewealth. The city is a treasure trove of culture, both built and social, and New Orleans was the birthplace of the historic building restoration movement in the United States.

When predatory developers swooped in post-Katrina and started proposing massive demolition projects, the citizens—indeed the entire country—were quick with their outrage. New Orleans' largest industry has long been tourism, and that tourism is grounded in the restoration and reuse of their gorgeous old buildings and streetscapes.

But the other two rules are a different story entirely. Integrated approaches to restoring the natural, built, and socioeconomic environments were (and still are) almost totally lacking. Even obvious integration factors were overlooked: initial efforts to bring back citizens focused almost exclusively on housing, completely ignoring schools. Then they wondered why couples with children weren't returning . . .

Effective engagement of all stakeholders has been intermittent, at best. As a result, their partnering process is incredibly weak. The paucity of partnering is partly due to its not being an established norm in local governance, and partly due to low trust levels. Louisiana has a reputation for being a hotbed of corruption, where insiders are adept at fleecing outsiders. This has scared away more than a few private sector players who wanted to win recovery-related contracts. The public sector, on the other hand, is leery of a new wave of carpetbaggers and "reconstructionists." This is a distrust extending back to the aftermath of the U.S. Civil War, when the city was invaded by scam artists and speculators from the North.

The city's rewealth orientation has thus enabled them to repel some of the most destructive proposals. But, the near absence of the other two renewal rules has hamstrung restorative activity. Add in political perfidy at the federal level, and a momentary infrastructure failure has been transformed into a long-term community failure.

The only sustained efforts I've witnessed have been at the neighborhood level. They include local heroes like Ray Nichols, who came out of retirement to create the Priestly School of Architecture and Construction. This wonderful charter school was conceived as a way to harness the Warsaw Effect, a strategy taught in my catastrophe recovery workshops. The Warsaw Effect is a strategy for training and employing citizens to rebuild their own community after disaster, in a way that also produces a skilled rewealth workforce that can restore natural, built, and socioeconomic assets—and revitalize communities—anywhere in the world. Ray and I were talking about it just two days after the levee failure, and Ray followed through on the idea like a bulldog.

Priestly began operating in 2006, and their next step is to raise funds to restore an abandoned historic school building, which will help revitalize a poverty-stricken neighborhood. As an example of the government's lack of engagement, the city recently put that building on its demolition schedule, even though it had known about—and supported—the Priestly plan for almost two years. While the Priestly School was getting underway, Ray was also helping to form the Carrollton-Audubon Renaissance, a neighborhood revitalization organization that has been quite effective.

Think what folks like Ray Nichols would have accomplished if they could have framed their neighborhood work within a larger citywide or regional vision. Think what they would have accomplished if they had had access to a partnering forum that connected their efforts with potential public and private partners. Think of what New Orleans' 73 (official) neighborhoods could have accomplished if they had been able to build confidence in the city's future via a renewal engine.

The most important product of renewal engines is renewal partnerships. New Orleans needs renewal partnerships in large quantities, and the quality of those partnerships will be crucial. Good public-private partnerships can rescue a community from the most desperate conditions. Bad ones can stop progress toward renewal in its tracks, piling catastrophe upon catastrophe.

Redefining Wealth Requires New Words

A change of language is needed. We talk of sustainable development and sustainable economies, but it is time to move on to restorative development and restorative economies. We need clearly enunciated principles which form the content of public education and which we can share and promote—new commandments, if one likes.
—Richard Chartres, Bishop of London, debate on the
UK's Climate Change Bill, Nov. 27, 2007

If the Bishop of London can call for rewealth-based commandments, I guess I can at least call for adherence to renewal rules. But he started off the above quote by acknowledging the power of language.

It's vitally important to remember that "dewealth," "prewealth," and "rewealth" don't just refer to making money. Natural resources are wealth. Health is wealth. Knowledge is wealth. Leisure time is wealth. Beautiful surroundings are wealth. Honest government is wealth. A loving family is wealth. Wealth also takes various forms depending on whether we're talking about individuals, organizations, or nations. A reconomy renews *all* forms of natural, built, social, and economic wealth.

It is dewealth that is being replaced by rewealth, not prewealth. Prewealth will always be with us, since both new and restored assets need maintenance or conservation. What we'll be doing a lot less of is destroying irreplaceable resources (petroleum, old growth forests, fossil aquifers), and replacing perpetual assets (watersheds, fisheries, ecosystems) with transitory assets (shopping centers, homes, factories). From now on, our future is based on making everything better . . . not on trading something we've treasured forever for something we need in the moment.

When one country invests in another's currency, the decision isn't based solely on how much money that country has. It's based on their faith in the future of that country. That, in turn, is based in large part on the trajectory of their quality of life, and the trajectory of their natural resources. This is one reason the U.S. dollar's value has been plummeting, and why nations that used to invest almost exclusively in the U.S. dollar are now diversifying their portfolios.

The fascinating 2004 feature film *The Machinist* seemed to be an American production, but was actually financed and shot in Spain with an American writer, an

American director, and American actors. In the "making of" featurette, star Christian Bale makes a telling comment. He asked what it says about America that, in order to fool viewers into thinking they were looking at a U.S. city, they had to shoot in all the worst parts of Barcelona.

One last point about language. We need to get away from the sprawl-versus-density dialog. Far better (though not as succinct) is "economic growth that enhances quality of life" versus "economic growth that diminishes quality of life." 5,000 years ago, we could enhance our quality of life through dewealth. These days, thanks to the constraint crisis, dewealth almost always reduces it, and only rewealth increases it. Some might say that such a shift is spiritual in nature.

Redefining Revitalization

Everyone wants revitalization (or "regeneration," for most English-speaking Europeans), and we're spending trillions of dollars to achieve it. But do we really have concordance on what we're trying to achieve?

"Revitalization" is a much-abused word. It's often used to describe (and to justify) virtually any activity that generates jobs or business activity. In other words, generic economic growth. As we've discovered so painfully over the past couple of centuries, not all forms of commercial activity are in a community's best interests.

Renewing the life of a community is about more than putting more money in the citizens' pockets. The root of "revitalization" is "vital," meaning life. The *Oxford English Dictionary* offers the rather circular definition "to restore to vitality." An activity as crucially important as renewing our communities and our planet deserves a more specific and measurable definition that's equally concise.

Renewal that's both rapid and resilient requires an increase in quality of life, as well as an increase in income. As you now know, this is best achieved by economic growth that's based primarily on renewal of *existing* assets, rather than unthinkingly creating more and more of what most of us no longer want more of.

My candidate is "rapid, resilient renewal." I doubt that the general public will ever get into the habit of saying "rapid, resilient renewal," so why not make that our definition of revitalization/regeneration? A formal, expanded definition could be "the process of enhancing a populace's quality of life via economic growth that's based primarily on the renewal of their region's natural, built, and socioeconomic assets."

I've purposely specified "region," rather than community. As stated earlier, while most renewal engines will be initiated at the community level, they will only achieve their full potential when expanded into a regional renewal engine, or when linked with other community renewal engines to create regional revitalization. The unstated goal (here stated) is rapid, resilient *global* renewal. My first book, *The Restoration Economy*, was mostly about restoration. *reWealth!* is mostly about revitalization. My recommendation is that restoration project managers make that same transition, from repairing parts of a system to renewing the system itself, so that it becomes better able to maintain and repair itself in the future. No matter how good a project manager you might be, your restoration project will never achieve its full potential unless it's part of a revitalization program.

A Simple Policy Directive for Revitalizing States, Provinces, Regions, and Nations

Revitalization is a complex and often-complicated (*not* synonymous) process. So let me simplify it for policymakers at the higher levels of government. If you wish to revitalize your state, province, region, or nation, there's one factor you can address in policy that will produce rapid, resilient results far in excess of anything else: assist your communities in the creation of their own renewal engines. That should be obvious by now, if you've read the preceding chapters.

Creating a renewal engine is the least capital-intensive part of the revitalization process. It's also the single most valuable part of the process. Communities are the economic engines of your domain. Your policy objective should be simple: to increase their capacity for renewal. With a properly designed and implemented renewal engine, each community can find the path to renewal that's right for them.

The mistake made by most policymakers is to focus on a particular solution—heritage districts, job training, iconic buildings, convention centers, stadiums, airports, etc.—and to encourage all communities in that one direction. The predictable end result is communities competing with each other in your district or country, rather than with those in other districts or countries. Comprehensive renewal of a community's natural, built, and socioeconomic restorable assets has a nice safety net: their quality of life is dramatically increased, no matter where they finish in the race for economic growth.

Policies that encourage the enhancement of your community's renewal capacity are the ultimate in scalability. Appropriate renewal engines can be created for almost any size community, from a rural agricultural village to an industrial megatropolis. Back up your policy with legislation that provides a modicum of incentives and educational assistance in creating those renewal engines, and you will be well on your way to creating rapid, resilient renewal for your entire area.

In short, your job is to stimulate their capacity for renewal, not to dictate the nature or form of that renewal. Give them the ability to design, fund, and implement their own solutions: don't specify solutions for them. The former approach is as fool-proof as a strategy can be: the latter extremely risky. Yet the latter is the approach taken by policymakers since time immemorial; little wonder that high-level economic renewal policies have such a dismal record.

> *Economic growth relies on the extraction of renewable and non-renewable resources . . .*
> *Economic growth also promotes the conversion of ecosystems to roads, urban areas, agri-*
> *culture and wasteland . . . Large scale ecological restoration ultimately requires an end*
> *to economic growth.*
>
> —Joshua Farley and Herman Daly, commentary
> in *Ecological Engineering*, November 2006

Farley and Daly's comment (above) only holds true if "economic growth" is based on dewealth. If it's based on rewealth, the conflict disappears, and their claim is false.

Besides restoring what we already have, we need to build new stuff in a way that allows our grandchildren to have their own reconomy. I call this designing for "restorability." Too many of the residential and commercial buildings (and even some public buildings) we're building now will be little more than piles of construction waste in 50 years; demolished because they weren't worth renovating and reusing. Some of them looked substantial when first built, but were actually flimsy junk hiding behind a thin veneer of brick or stone. So prevalent are such veneers that one wag referred to this architectural plague as "veneerial disease."

We've talked a lot about the rules and processes and models that help produce rapid, resilient renewal in a community or region. Combined as a system, I called them the *re*solution. Let me simply the message here in these closing passages. A single paragraph should suffice.

The two key factors that will attract rewealth investors to your community are these: 1) quality of life, and 2) the perception that your quality of life and your economy are (or will soon be) on an upward trajectory. But attracting the reinvestors' and redevelopers' interest isn't enough. The single most crucial factor in getting them to actually part with their money is *confidence*. They must feel confident that the community knows what it wants, so projects won't be delayed or cancelled at the last minute. They must feel confident that projects won't have to swim upstream against archaic dewealth-based policies, codes, and regulations. They must feel confident that the community knows how to be a good partner. In other words, the community needs to implement the *re*solution . . . to create a renewal vision, a renewal culture, and a renewal engine.

Rewealth completes the economic life cycle. In the long run, we must earn our living from *re*plenishing resources, rather than *de*pleting them. We should be enhancing our investment portfolios by *re*novating and *re*using our useful or historic old structures, not from *de*molishing them. We should build companies around *re*mediating contaminated lands, not from *de*spoiling virgin properties. We should grow crops in a way that *re*builds topsoil, *re*moves old agricultural chemicals, and *re*stores surrounding wildlife habitat (including native pollinators), not in a way that *de*grades the soil and *de*creases the quantity or quality of wild lands. We should be relying on *re*development as the default, and *de*velopment as the exception.

> *Forests precede civilizations and deserts follow them.*
> **—François-René de Chateaubriand (1768–1848)**

Reconomies revolve, whereas deconomies devolve. What dewealth creates usually has a far shorter functional life than that which was destroyed in its creation. Dewealth eventually destroys the civilizations it creates, if the transition to rewealth is delayed too long. The deconomy was civilization's birth and growth process . . . childhood, in other words. It's long since time to grow up.

To borrow the slogan of the M.I.T. Energy Club: rewealth makes us "the people we have been waiting for." It's not a change in human nature that will save us (though that would be lovely, too), but rather a change in the nature of how we create wealth.

Everyone can earn rewealth. To paraphrase Pogo once again, "We have met the solution and he is us." Rewealth enriches today and tomorrow together. Rewealth leaves everything better for everyone.

Winston Churchill said, "We shape our buildings and afterwards, our buildings shape us." One might paraphrase that for the reconomy: we renew our world, and it renews us.

Appendix 1

Links to Organizations Mentioned in *re*Wealth!

21st Century School Fund: www.21CSF.org
Canadian Council for Public-Private Partnerships: www.PPPcouncil.ca
Cherokee Investment Partners: www.CherokeeFund.com
Construction Specifications Institute: www.CSInet.org
CreateHere (Chattanooga): www.CreateHere.org
English Partnerships: www.EnglishPartnerships.co.uk
Guayakí (yerba maté company): www.Guayaki.com
Louisville Waterfront Park: www.LouisvilleWaterfront.com
Metropoli-30 (Bilbao): www.BM30.es
National Council for Public-Private Partnerships (United States): www.NCPPP.org
Noisette Company: www.NoisetteSC.com
Ontario Ministry of Public Infrastructure Renewal : www.PIR.gov.on.ca
Project Management Institute (PMI): www.PMI.org
QMM (QIT Madagascar Minerals): www.RioTintoMadagascar.com
Renew Canada: www.RenewCanada.net
Resolution Fund, LLC: www.ResolutionFund.com
Restoring Natural Capital Alliance: www.RNCalliance.org
Revitalization Institute: www.Revitalization.org
Ría 2000 (Bilbao): www.BilbaoRia2000.org
RiverCity Company (Chattanooga): www.RiverCitycompany.com
Seneca College (Canada): www.Senecac.on.ca
Working for Water Programme (South Africa): www.dwaf.gov.za/wfw

Appendix 2

An Invitation to Participate in Two Sequels to *re*Wealth!

Rewealthy

The first sequel to this book will probably appear in 2010, and the working title is *Rewealthy*. It will be focused a bit more on corporations, entrepreneurs, investors, and career opportunity seekers, whereas this one focused heavily on communities. It will feature even more stories than did this book, since real-world examples often provide the best lessons.

I invite you to contact me if you have a story you think should be in this first sequel. I've identified some potential places and stories of interest that I'll list here, in case you can help me research them: the Beijing-Hangzhou Grand Canal restoration in China; Pacific Gas & Electric Company (PG&E) of California; the Gaviotas II/Marandúa project of Colombia; Buffalo, New York; Kolkata, India; Guayaquil, Ecuador; the Grand Avenue public-private partnership in downtown Los Angeles; the $4 billion redevelopment of the Anacostia Waterfront in Washington, D.C.; the Dockside Green brownfields redevelopment project in Victoria, British Colombia; the Wadi Hanifah restoration project in Riyadh, Saudi Arabia; Seoul's $560,000,000 Cheong Gye Cheon stream restoration/urban revitalization project; the restoration programs of the Aga Khan Foundation; and the waterfront regenerations of Dublin and Belfast.

Top priority, of course, will go to communities that have renewal engines, or that have policies based on the renewal rules. A few of the above stories (such as in China, India, and South Korea) might have been in this book, but I was unable to contact officials in time to meet this deadline. Still others were delayed because I lacked the time to visit them: I prefer to write stories from the standpoint of personal experience whenever possible.

Rewealthy Women

As mentioned in Chapter 15, the second sequel to this book is about women and rewealth, and it will probably appear in 2012. Its working title is **Rewealthy Women**. The focus will be on the role of women as present and future leaders of the global reconomy, whether as entrepreneurs, investors, social entrepreneurs, elected leaders, NGO/foundation executives, or whatever.

At this point, I'm not sure if I'll write it all myself, or merely serve as editor for chapters written by others, thus providing a forum for the protagonists to tell their own stories. The latter approach might allow the book to appear sooner than 2012.

If you, your company, your organization, your agency, or your community belongs in either of these sequels, please e-mail me at storm@resolutionfund.com.

Appendix 3

Resolution Fund, LLC

A new U.S./Canadian firm provides communities worldwide with resources for rapid, resilient renewal.

A s you read this, thousands of communities around the world are trying to form some kind of community organization that will revitalize them. Most will waste a lot of time and effort reinventing the wheel. These communities are trying to create renewal engines, but don't know it.

The closest they come to having a model or template is when they try to duplicate a successful program created by another community. But few of those successful communities properly documented their revitalization process: it was usually created on-the-fly.

Some communities already have at least the beginnings of a renewal engine, but lack sufficient local redevelopers, investors, or other private partners to fund their renewal projects. They desperately need to be connected to resources from outside of their community, or even outside of their country. A new firm has been created to serve both these needs: (1) helping them create a renewal engine, and (2) helping them connect to funding sources that prefer the safety and efficiency of investing in communities that have renewal engines.

Resolution Fund, LLC, was created in the summer of 2007 by three U.S. partners (this author is one of them) and one Canadian partner. Its primary mission is to deliver the *"resolution"* that you learned in Chapter 4.

As of this writing, Resolution Fund's *Renewal Capacity Program* teaches—and helps communities implement—this recipe for rapid, resilient renewal, resulting in the creation of an effective renewal engine. The current program comprises three phases: (1) a series of four educational workshops to prepare the community, (2) a series of three action workshops to create or advance the renewal vision, renewal culture, and renewal engine, and (3) ongoing "matchmaking" support by phone, e-mail, and local events that help connect the right investors and private partners to the right community on the right project at the right time. The program's goal is to enhance the community's capacity for rapid, resilient renewal.

The workshops of Phase 1 are procured individually, with no commitment to complete the program. They can be scheduled as close together or as far apart as necessary. This modular approach allows communities to proceed at the pace their citizens desire, and that their budget allows. It also helps avoid disrupting initiatives that are already underway.

Resolution Fund is currently seeking partners for several additional projects and services:

1. Managed fund: Besides connecting communities to a network of funding sources, Resolution Fund will also help create a managed fund. This would allow individual and institutional investors to focus their portfolios on restoring natural resources and revitalizing communities. An established SRI fund would be an ideal partner: Resolution Fund would provide the rewealth "filter," as well as early alerts to rewealth investment opportunities (both real estate and corporate). The partner would actually own and manage the fund.

2. Online database: Resolution Fund is seeking a technology partner to help provide a publicly accessible online database of a wide range of rewealth resources: investors, for-sale properties needing restoration, properties under restoration needing professional services, restored properties for sale, rewealth services (technical, financial, legal), organizations seeking partnerships (academic, NGO, neighborhood), communities seeking private partners, private firms seeking opportunities for community partnerships, and so on. This data would be input by registered users, and the searches would also be performed by registered users.

3. Other software: Resolution Fund is working with several for-profit and non-profit partners on software tools that will help communities and regions inventory and organize their restorable assets efficiently and effectively, and help them manage their revitalization programs and project partnerships in an integrated, engaged manner. This involves GIS, project management, asset management, and other applications. Additional partners are invited.

Resolution Fund, LLC, is headquartered in Washington, DC, three blocks from the White House. One-day *Rewealth Seminars* for public and private executives, entrepreneurs, investors, and professionals are held at this location. See www.ResolutionFund.com for more information, or e-mail Storm Cunningham at storm@ResolutionFund.com.

Glossary

Three global crises (referred to in *reWealth!*, but introduced in *The Restoration Economy*):

- **Contamination** (of our natural and built environments)
- **Corrosion** (of our buildings and infrastructure)
- **Constraint** (whereby population pressures and poor land use forces us to sprawl, destroying sometimes irreplaceable natural and cultural treasures).

Deconomy: an economy based primarily on dewealth (see reconomy).

Reconomy: an economy based primarily on rewealth. Also known as a "restoration economy" (see deconomy).

Renewal partnership: a public-public, public-private, or private-private partnership focused on community revitalization or on the restoration of natural, built, or socioeconomic assets.

Restorable assets: aspects of our natural, built, and socioeconomic environments that are in need of restoration, renovation, reuse, or replacement, and that contribute to community revitalization when renewed. The 12 sectors of restorable assets are:

Natural assets	Built assets	Socioeconomic assets
Ecosystems	Brownfields	Community services (security, aid, etc.)
Watersheds	Infrastructure	Education
Fisheries	Heritage	Culture
Agricultural lands	Catastrophes	Commerce

Stakeholder: any public or private individual/institution who can affect—or who will be affected by—your efforts to renew an area. The five basic stakeholder categories are businesses, government agencies, academia, NGO/nonprofit organizations, and citizens. The news media is sometimes a stakeholder, as well.

Trimodal development perspective: (introduced in 2002's *The Restoration Economy*): Posits three modes of economic development to enable budgeting, planning, and reporting systems to clearly differentiate what portion of its lifecycle an asset is in. This allows us to more effectively retard sprawl, fund maintenance, and accelerate renewal. The three modes (updated to this book's terminology) are:

- Dewealth: wealth-creation based on developing, depleting, and/or degrading our natural, built, and/or socioeconomic environments. It is the natural beginning of a community's or civilization's lifecycle. Also known as "new development," "destructive development," "extraction," "pioneering," or "sprawl."

- Prewealth: wealth-creation based on maintaining our built and socioeconomic assets, and on conserving our natural assets. This is the relatively stable, continuous "middle" of the lifecycle. Also known as "maintenance/conservation."

- Rewealth: wealth-creation based on redeveloping, replenishing, and/or restoring our natural, built, and/or socioeconomic environments. This is the end of one lifecycle, but the beginning of another, since restored assets also require maintenance and conservation. Thus, a cycle of maintenance/conservation and periodic restoration/reuse/replacement can continue virtually forever, as it does in nature. Also known as "restorative development."

"Universal" concepts introduced in this book:

- Rapid, resilient renewal: the basic goal of most communities and regions.
- Renewal rules (to guide decisions): (1) Rewealth (renewal of assets), (2) integration (of natural, built, and socioeconomic environments), (3) engagement (of all stakeholders).
- Renewal processes (to produce solutions): (1) visioning, (2) culturing, (3) partnering. All three are performed in accordance with the three renewal rules.
- Renewal engine (to turn decisions and solutions into actions and projects): a permanent, nonprofit, public-private organization that houses the three renewal processes, and that has the goal of rapid, resilient renewal.
- *Re*solution: a "universal" system for rapid, resilient renewal of communities or regions; it comprises the three renewal rules, the three renewal processes, and the renewal engine model.

Index

About the Author

Storm Cunningham is the CEO of Resolution Fund, LLC, in Washington, DC. Resolution Fund helps communities, counties, tribes, regions, and nations renew their economy, their natural resources, and their quality of life. It does this via workshops that increase their renewal capacity, and by connecting them to appropriate partners, investors, and redevelopers.

He is also the founder of Revitalization Institute, the global nonprofit academy for community renewal and natural resource restoration, now based in Toronto. He is also a Distinguished Visiting Professor at Seneca College (Canada's largest college).

Cunningham is the author of 2002's *The Restoration Economy*, which has been hailed by government and business leaders around the world as "Extraordinary," "Remarkable," "A modern classic," "A landmark work," "Required reading," and "The most important and valuable business book I have read in many years."

Storm Cunningham was—from 1996 to 2002—Director, Strategic Initiatives at the Construction Specifications Institute, a 50+year-old association of 17,000 architects, engineers, contractors, and manufacturers.

A former Green Beret SCUBA medic, he is an avid SCUBA diver, motorcyclist, and amateur herpetologist. He lives in Arlington, Virginia.